Which Witch Do[

– or –

"Professionals" behaving badly

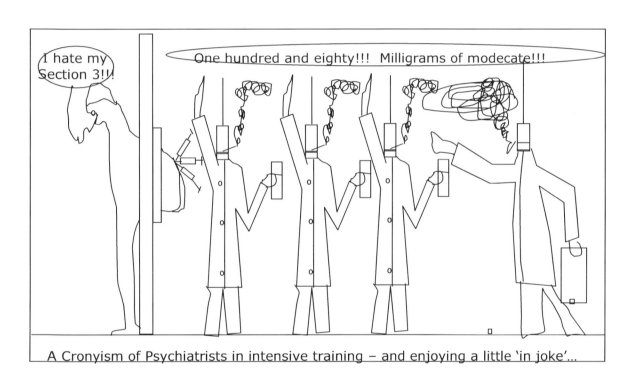

The first part of his autobiography,
covering 1957 to 2001, on the theme,
"with doctors like these, who needs enemies?"

Simon Richard Lee BA, MA (Cantab.) CEng MIEE MInstMC
Zen Buddha

Which Witch Doctor?

– or –

"Professionals" behaving badly

A True Story – a Spiritual Thriller pulled from the Gothic Annals of Psychiatry!

My memoirs of my share of the 20th Century. How from all of September 1978 to January 2001 (half my life so far – over 22 of my 44 years) I suffered great loss and trauma under the wrong diagnosis and so incorrect treatment – for mythical 'schizophrenia'. A myth kept up by a long string of 'Doctors' who plainly "did not know their schizophrenia from their manic depression"! ("arses from elbows...") In parallel, perhaps bizarrely, **I had twenty-one powerful Spiritual Experiences,** 'Powerful Petrifying Premonitions' – which nearly **all came true** in those 22 years...

Genuine Religious Experiences GRAUNCH
with the purely Materialist 'Black Arts' of the
Average Local Arrogant Atheist Psychiatrist!

Simon Richard Lee

The moral rights of the author have been asserted.

All rights reserved. No part of this publication may be reproduced, stored in a retrieval system, or transmitted in any form or by any means, electronic, mechanical, photocopy, recording or otherwise, without prior permission of the copyright owner.

This book was twenty-five – or should it read *forty-five?* – long years in the making, with many 'hiccups' along the way!

As a result the copyright notice below for this book
is issued with some feeling, if not passion

Copyright © Simon Richard Lee, 2003-2018

ISBN 9781723727344

All typesetting and illustrations are by the author.

First Edition – 16th March 2000

Revised and abridged – July 2000

Revised - February 2001

Completed August 2003

This book is dedicated to my lovely daughter Jeni

"I will pour out my spirit on all flesh;
 your sons and daughters shall prophesy,
 your old men shall dream dreams,
 and your young men shall see Visions."
                                        Joel 2:28

I would also like to remind all those who took it upon themselves to judge me, and even to try to destroy me, from 1993-1999 (Whore, Harlot and the Tart of Tarts, as in this book, were the main culprits) of the Biblical saying of Jesus: -

"Judge not, lest thou be judged!"

Any 'return judgements' herein are strictly THE TRUTH – hence not libel!

INTRODUCTION – February 2001

Disabled by the outcome predicted by Spiritual Experiences!

Twenty-one Spiritual Experiences, which have nearly all 'come true' mostly years later, since I saw them sporadically between November 1977 and August 2000.

This book gives a description of each of twenty-one uncanny and mostly ominous 'Spiritual Experiences', or 'powerful petrifying premonitions', that I saw infrequently between November 1977 and August 2000, a twenty-three year interval. Infrequently since, often many years later, they have been sporadically 'coming true'! The second half of my share of the 20th Century, then, saw quite a few such 'Spiritual Experiences'…

As I suffer from a serious mental illness called 'bipolar (I) affective disorder', you will not be surprised to learn that I saw most – *but not all* – of these when I was 'high'. Equally, as I have of course 'let slip' when ill and 'high' that I see such things, to Psychiatrists, it is perhaps not surprising that they have mostly claimed that there is a – strong? – element of *schizophrenia* to my illness.

As a result of their claiming that what I have seen *must* be hallucinations, they have for 22 whole terribly worrying years, claimed that I suffer from either 'schizophrenia' or a 'schizo-affective disorder' – the latter being a *mixture* of manic depression *and* schizophrenia.

My latest team, my psychiatric social worker, my Doctor, and my Community Psychiatric Nurse, have all independently come to agree that all their predecessors, over all that half my lifetime to date, were completely wrong. Without of course, in the interests of 'psychiatric cronyism', ever saying as much!

In despair, on reading their own manuals some years ago, especially the 'Diagnostic Systems Manual' (DSM–IV and now DSM-V) I could see no such schizophrenic symptoms in myself. Nor could my family. So we are all hugely relieved that my current team has at last overturned that dreadfully wrong 'label'.

A major theme of this book is to give as full an account as possible of these twenty-one 'Spiritual Experiences'. Then at the appropriate point in the autobiography needed to 'set the scene' – to give some kind of interpretation after later events of my life 'fulfilled each Spiritual Experience' – usually visions. Often as you will see this only happened after many worried attempts by me to 'guess the meaning' of these experiences or visions. Nearly all took the form of static images, just like still colour photographs. My aim, whether or not this book is ever published, is to give a sufficient account of them to prove – to myself at least, others will be hard to convince (they weren't there to see them) – two things. Firstly, that they have all come true – they are in the past – henceforth I am free of the confusion and utter torment I often used to feel just thinking about them!

Secondly, that these no less than twenty-one 'visionary experiences' over twenty-one years (two were simply an emphatic confirmatory repeat of an earlier 'message', saying 'that is now all over!' making them even more emphatic…) have indeed led me to interpret other similar 'spiritual visionary prophetic insights' in the Bible. These are discussed at length in my other book 'Spiritual Energy'.

Hence this account of my 'Spiritual Experiences' or 'hallucinations' – until I have, to my own mind, completely 'proven my case' that they were in fact the former, I leave the issue open! – is intended to achieve three things: -

1. Now that this series of twenty-one complex, bewildering, mystical, enticing, spiritual visionary images has finished its 'cycle' after all of a massive twenty-two years – just over half my lifetime to date! – I can at long last, in 2001, finish this definitive, final account of them all – started in 1998. I have *never* known what they meant until each had come true in real life, often years later. In the meantime, I just knew that most of them portended evil things in my life. So, especially when 'hypomanic' with my 'bipolar (I) affective disorder', I have often tried in the past to 'explain these omens', without waiting endlessly patiently for the true meaning to emerge. This has always, without exception, been blindingly obvious to me when the time for the true meaning to emerge has

2

come along – *only ever, after* the very largely horrible, often sinister, events predicted by these Spiritual Experiences! So, in conclusion, only now they have all 'come true' in real life am I able to finish this account of them all.   An account which I *know* is the full true version at last of my '21 Spiritual Experiences in the 20th century' – after so many humiliating guesses by me!

2. As a result of this '100% reliability of pure hindsight', I will in writing all this down, be able to kiss goodbye to these 'Spiritual Experiences' forever.   If any other Atheist Psychiatrist, or even worse, my own family and most friends, who have often distanced themselves and even poured scorn and even mockery on me because of them, tries to accuse me of being 'schizophrenic' because I used to see them, I will have the perfect riposte.   "Here, read this, it tells you all about them, and incidentally PROVES they predicted the future. They were therefore not 'hallucinations' like you have always claimed. I am NOT a schizophrenic – I used to get *inspired* and saw prophetic glimpses about the world and my own life. Get stuffed with your 'hallucinations'!"

The rest of this book describes all twenty-one of my Spiritual Experiences, then, with a potted autobiography in parallel. This autobiography, which gets increasingly detailed as time goes by, shows how they have all definitely 'come true' in my own life.

CHAPTER ONE

Spiritual Experience Two – shared in Cambridge with over a thousand other onlookers...!

Spiritual Experience Two. 30th January 1978. Four 'bright nightly lights' over Cambridge town centre – others present immediately told me that there were in fact a total of FIVE of these eery lights in the night sky!

I was a second-year undergraduate at King's College, Cambridge, in 1978. I left the college about seven o'clock on the night of 30th January 1978 for a tutorial in the town. I was studying physics and maths and I recall it was a physics tutorial I was supposed to be going to. I was in a hurry as I was a bit late leaving.

However, as I left the College and came onto King's Parade, the high street in Cambridge town centre, I was astonished to see about four or five hundred passers-by, who clearly had just been taking the evening air, standing stock-still on the West side of King's Parade. They were all staring into the cloudy winter night sky, looking above the shops and the skyline on the eastern side of that street.

Of course I looked up that way too, and saw a strange eery light drifting northwards, right to left as I looked, about 400 feet up, and well below the low cloud. As it disappeared over Caius College on the left, another light appeared – they seemed to be golden-yellow – on exactly the same path, and the same speed, from where the first had appeared. Then it followed the same eery, yet majestic, dead straight path slowly over the skyline of shops and St. Mary's Church, and again disappeared over precisely the same point over Gonville and Caius College.

I saw a total of four such meticulously spaced 'dead line astern apparitions'. However, as I headed off for my tutorial – now very late – I heard others who had seen them – as I said, three or four hundred people – talking excitedly about 'five lights' or even 'five UFOs'! So I knew, with so many people as witnesses, that I must have turned up just in time to miss the first of FIVE 'unearthly lights'.

As I write I am very glad that hundreds of people shared this strange experience with me. It has always helped reassure me over the years, that the fact I had since had so many other 'Visionary' Experiences – by myself – did not necessarily mean I was totally mad! I remember my impression that the excited discussion afterwards – there had been little talk, mostly awe, as they appeared – was of "UFO's", then as now very topical.

My own reaction, characteristically of this and the twenty similar other Experiences I was to have between 1977 and 2000, was rather different. I had never been at all 'religious' in my life, despite a solid Christian education at both junior and secondary school. However, I remember thinking that same night – "*five* bright lights – that means either 'the Hand of God' or 'five years'".

CHAPTER TWO

LA ('middle class', and relatively speaking) DOLCE VITA?

My autobiography 1957-1978 – the 'easy' first twenty-one years of my life so far!

I said that seeing this set of lights in the night sky over Cambridge marked a 'sea-change' in my life. We will be talking a lot in the course of this book about this part of my life 1978 onwards, after my 'bipolar affective disorder' struck shortly after this second Spiritual Experience followed Spiritual Experience One, then the third Spiritual Experience appeared, in yet a third distinct fashion.

Before looking at what may have caused my 'bipolar affective disorder' we will look at that early happier half of my life to date.

I was born in Welwyn Garden City, Hertfordshire, on March 30th 1957. Peartree Maternity Hospital is now a YMCA nursery school. I am the eldest of three – my parents had come from Gloucestershire and lived in Hatfield. I had the distinction of being born on my Aunt Pat's Wedding Day – so apologies for enforced absence by my parents were of course accepted – and congratulations flowed freely each way that day!

My very first memory of life is at age four, and might sound rather like a nightmare! It is of an anaesthetic mask coming down over my face, in the children's ward in a huge, grim, London Hospital. This terrifying memory is from when I had an operation to have my adenoids and tonsils removed. I've had a runny nose and carried a handkerchief ever since.

I was very withdrawn as a child, and vividly remember clinging to my Mother, and crying, all the way to my first day at infants' school! However, once there I shone at schoolwork – although not at games – and had a very happy time.

My parents moved house twice in Hatfield, to end up where they now live, quite near what is now the University, then a technical college, in 1963. I changed to Newtown Junior school then, and soon found myself the brightest academically – although neighbours and friends easily outpaced me at sports. I particularly enjoyed Maths and Arts and Crafts, although my artistic side was only to resurface at College in sudden 'love poetry' as in my book 'A Many Threaded Tapestry'. My secondary school was to prove rather neglectful of that side of my character – so I made up rather late for that by writing verse as an undergraduate.

Apart from just one term, where I slipped slightly, I was consistently assessed as the 'brightest in the year' according to my school reports. In the meantime, I swam in the swimming club at the very modern local pool at Hatfield, played football and cards and many other games including snooker, billiards, table-tennis and tennis with a peer group of boys – and some girls – of a similar age. I also had various hobbies, especially building and laboriously painting plastic 'Airfix' kits – especially of military aircraft. I must have carefully cut out and glued together and painted literally hundreds of these at Primary School and in my early teens. At one time my bedroom ceiling had dozens of aircraft suspended by fishing line! However, it was always academically rather than at games and 'practical things' that I was to shine at school and University...

In 1968 I took the scholarship examinations to the local 'Direct Grant' or "Bright boys'" school in St Albans. To my parents' delight I won a free place – half the places in each year were sponsored by the County Council, so they had no fees to pay – and the five-mile bus journey each way was even provided free as well! Years later I learned that the famous Professor Stephen Hawking, now heavily disabled, had been there as well about ten years earlier – and we had many of the same teachers for most subjects! As my own other 'Spiritual Energy' book addresses very directly many of the great cosmological issues raised in his book, 'a brief history of time', there is a certain unofficial 'school cosmological tradition' and link or even bond between us.

Both of us are disabled, in very different ways, after all...

I started at this quite well-known school in September 1968, and soon found there were plenty of challenges – and that, by the nature of the place, lessons, fellow pupils and the teachers were all both demanding and intelligent!

At the end of the first term I was 'catching up' on missing two years of elementary French, that most other boys in my 'form' had studied before at their junior school or 'prep. school'. After an early confession to the French teacher, nearly in tears, that I felt lost because I was at a total disadvantage, he could already see my potential and kindly reassured me there was nothing to worry about, I would soon catch up! He was right. By the end of the first year I was in the top three in French in my class, and in the second year was ranked first in the last two terms!   The maths teacher spotted that I was quite introverted. He wrote in my end of first term report, 'he is coping very well – but is so serious about it all! I'll soon make him smile!'   Indeed, this fondly-remembered maths teacher, JOW Webb or 'Joey', affectionately known to thousands of pupils over a lifetime there till his tragic death in a fire, epitomised a very notable attribute of that school – a terrific tradition of having a sardonic, dry, often satirical sense of humour.

Most of the teachers shared this, and early satire shows like 'Monty Python' and 'That was the week that was', and the satirical magazine 'Private Eye' were followed fanatically by those boys whose parents approved of them having access to such advanced and 'dangerous' humour. Naturally these lucky fortunates generously relayed the best of the humour to those of us who were not allowed to stay up till such 'risque' shows came on TV late at night!

So it was that when I and my peer group from St. Alban's School were all at Cambridge, many people there commented on what a rich vein of humorous and witty remarks we all readily produced – and seemed to share equally!

I was to shine academically at this school as much as at my primary school. At the end of the first year, I received a prize for being the third-best performer in my class or form, and was to repeat this 'Form Prize' performance for being in the top three in each form until the fourth year. Other prizes, for Chemistry and French, were to come my way in due course too. There were also two school trips in that first year too – to the school's farmhouse in the Brecon Beacons, which was memorable for lots of walks in breathtaking mountain scenery – and in July 1969, to St. Malo in France. I remember regretting I had missed watching the first lunar landing by Apollo 11 on television, but managed to follow it by buying English newspapers. I also remember good food and drink, and many interesting trips out to places like Mont St. Michel and the Ranche Barrage with its hydro-electric tidal power station. Most of all I remember being distinctly homesick towards the end – a feeling I was not to experience again until the traumatic events of 1995.

Break times were notable for the frenetic playing of cards, chess and board games – especially the war game, 'Risk'. We also swam, played tennis, rugby, and hockey – and football and other games in the 'Orchard', a large field set aside for games at the bottom end of the school.

The second year was much like the first. We studied a wide variety of subjects very intensely, and also as I just said played hard too. At the end of the year I had to choose some subjects to drop, and others to take up, as we were to be 'streamed' into ability-based 'sets' for the third and fourth forms – and the looming of our taking our first public examinations, then called 'O levels'. To my lasting regret I took the advice of the teachers and dropped both woodwork and Art, in particular, to take Latin and German. As a result, I got onto an increasing track of taking ever more academic and theoretical, dry subjects, which was to continue into Cambridge and even into my career.

Years later, when I was in my final term at the school, my old Art Teacher passed me in the street and we got talking. He said he had always regretted my dropping my Art as I had been 'very good – and the best by far at calligraphy (artistic italic handwriting)!' He gave me an open invitation to come up to the Art Room at any time and pick up where I had left off. I was by then however so 'locked in' to my academic scholarship track of winning a Scholarship to Cambridge that I never took up his offer! I have always regretted this.

The second year was as happy and successful as the first – I really found my feet academically, and in developing a strong sense of humour, and slowly becoming less introverted. I continued to both work hard and play hard, and was very glad, just like everybody else, that the archaic school tradition of 'Saturday morning school' had now finally been dropped. As I said, I won a prize for coming third in form again, as well as a French prize that year. Quite a comeback from my near-tears in French at the very outset, the previous year!

There were two memorable holidays as well. That New Year of the Winter of 1970, a group of us went on a skiing trip to Austria. The introduction to skiing – in lace-up gear, archaic by today's standards – was memorable, as were the evenings in the bar, where us 13-year olds tried the drinks without restriction, especially along with the fireworks on New Year's Eve. The school's Divinity teacher acted rather 'out of profession'. He never skied, but was to be found propping up the hotel bar all day, often with a pretty girl from the English girl's school sharing the hotel with us, on his knee!

It was a very cold trip. One day the temperature on the slope was -18°C, so most of us were forced to shelter in a nearby hotel basement until the end of the session, when the coach took us, still frozen, down the valley to Woergl, the town where the hotel was. However, I got up to a good 'Stem Christie' level of skiing quite quickly, and thoroughly enjoyed it, enabling me to enjoy many ski trips years later with my family, throughout Europe.

Again, in the following Summer of 1971, my good friend and academic arch-rival Nigel persuaded me to join him for a month in France – to stay in a commune or 'Village Europe' with about twenty other English pupils from all over Britain, and twenty French pupils of the same age. The aim was to soak up the French language, culture, and food and drink – and to learn lots of arts and crafts and sports. It sounded fascinating, so that August I went to Victoria station for the fifteen-hour train and boat journey to Cognac in south-west France. Nigel ended up in a grammar school or lycee in Cognac itself, whereas I joined a second group in an old chateau about five miles away.

In the next month, in the company of about forty French school-pupils and teachers and helpers, mostly from Paris, I was to learn a lot of French – especially the 'forbidden' rude words and phrases! I also acquired a near-perfect Parisian accent that has often been commented on since by French people on the odd occasion when I have re-visited France. We also played a lot of different sports, went cycling and camping, did a lot of 'arts and crafts', and explored the brandy distilleries in Cognac itself. We met up with the 'other lot' twice, on return visits to each others' quarters. The end of the trip came all too soon, and I left with lasting memories of French food and drink, especially French snacks like 'rillettes' of Duck or Goose, and pureed fruit – all delicious on a fresh baguette! So, back to school, with top French and fond memories!

Studying now got intense as we started the full 'O level examination' syllabuses in our different chosen subjects. At the end of the third year, the Summer of 1972, we all took exams in, by default, Maths, English language and French, and I delighted myself and everybody by being just one of three students out of 100 to get top grade '1' in all three! I also remember that year for a memorable English teacher who took us to see Roman Polanski's film of 'Macbeth' – which was extremely disturbing and gory, and apart from years later, finding 'The Exorcist' equally off-putting, I have not watched a horror film since!

My friend Nigel had prided himself on his English – yet, like me he was to study science at Cambridge. I vividly remember him saying when he heard my achievements in all three 'O' Levels: - "I should have got your grade 1 in English and you should have got my grade 2"!

The following year, 1973, got very intensive indeed in terms of studying – yet when I took my seven subjects that year, I again did very well. The only slip was in my then favourite subject, geography, where I 'only' got a grade 2! Mind you, there were only three 'grade 1' passes in that subject in the school that year, so I did not do badly. Otherwise it was a clean sweep of '1' passes for me again...

By this stage I was becoming aware of a major lack of distractions in my studying compared to other 'boys'. Unlike most, at 15 I had yet to pass puberty – so as yet had no interest in the opposite sex. In fact I was not to do so until I was all of 17, just about the last in the year to do so, in the Lower Sixth. Suddenly the cruel 'little boy' remarks from certain of my less kind fellow pupils had to stop, as I soon passed six foot – and my feet now filled size 12 shoes, and I weighed 12 stone!

However, I still believe this 'delayed-action growing up' was to become a major factor in my becoming prone to mental illness – and developing 'bipolar affective disorder' at Cambridge. We will consider several other major factors in due course, when we discuss Spiritual Experiences One and Three in a while.

At the time being the 'latest developer' in the year gave me acute hang-ups for about two years from when I was 15 until when I was 17. I even started to wonder whether I would ever in fact 'grow up'. It eventually took a lady neighbour, then dying of MS and confined to a wheelchair, to point out that I had very large feet and would 'definitely be over six foot'. Six months later I indeed started shooting up, and grew from 5'4" to my present 6'1½" inside a year!

My 'O' level years had their intense studying interrupted by lots of holidays in my parents' succession of ever larger caravans. We went to the Lake District a couple of times, to the West Country, to the North Norfolk coast – all with many very memorable walks with the family dog in beautiful countryside. My brother Jem and sister Libby were then both at the local Grammar School in Hatfield, so we all welcomed the 'rest and relaxation' of these very fondly remembered family holidays. The climax was a trip to Switzerland and Italy with the caravan, climbing many spectacular mountain passes, to return home via the Black Forest and the Rhine in Germany. The Black Forest welcomed us with the most intense thunderstorm I have ever experienced – about 9" of rain in one hour!

My father was at that time a successful businessman, running a local engineering company he had started with two ex-colleagues from the giant GEC, and supplying mostly paper machine control systems. These used very innovative software, and as a result were sold across Europe and North America, based on an early minicomputer – about equivalent in speed to a small Personal Computer of the early 1990's. On paper, by 1971 his shares were worth over £1,000,000 on paper – an absolute fortune by today's standards.

However to get started he had had to recruit a parent company, and once 'Digimatics ltd' got too successful, this parent company ruthlessly exploited the fact that the legal agreement both sides had originally started out with, was very much in their favour. In fact it was 'full of holes', letting them take over the fledgeling 'winner' and buy out my father's shares for about £7,000 – a tiny fraction of the million or more they were truly worth!

After that traumatic loss my father's career never really recovered. He held down a variety of jobs, mostly consulting, then in 1980 started his own company yet again, in which I was to be heavily involved up to 1988 when it folded. After over a year or so of redundancy, he spent his early sixties till retiring in 1996, working rather too hard for his liking for a major process control company, fifty miles and a difficult journey on the M25 from home, at Bracknell in Berkshire...

Back to my schooling, the fifth form was intended to be largely a break between 'O' and 'A' levels – in the looming Sixth Form. However, partly to get back at least some of my drawing and artistic talents, I did take technical drawing 'O' level that year – getting another top '1' grade – and made sure I was actually in an Arts-based set out of the four. Most people who like me wanted to 'do science' in the Sixth Form, instead chose the "biology 'O' level" set.

Then the Lower Sixth, with options firmly chosen for a science degree afterwards, for me, of mathematics, physics and chemistry. I think if I had my time again, I would have kept up my Art, and then chosen mathematics, Art and chemistry. That is just wishful thinking now, in the face of severe pressure to choose all scientific subjects from just about everybody influencing me then.

We Sixth Formers had our own Sixth Form Centre and were starting to become treated a bit more like adults rather than 'boys'. We did academic work for four and a half days a week, then on Friday afternoons did either the Duke of Edinburgh's Award Scheme (DEAS), or trained in the school's CCF or Cadet Force, or did voluntary work. My name 'came out of the hat' to do the preferred option for most of us, of the DEAS. I spent much of the next two years on gruelling cycling expeditions, cycling over very steep hills for 150 miles in four days carrying camping equipment and all the necessary 'rations'.

I got very fit indeed as a result of this and the need to pass a physical proficiency test for both Silver and Gold Awards. In addition I had computing as an interest throughout, and went on various group residential trips to discuss various themes or topics, chosen for us in informal surroundings, led by prominent people including Ariana Stasinopoulos. I passed the Silver Award easily, and did all the work for the Gold Award – but crucially, lost interest at the point of producing my 'log' for the final cycling expedition in the Peak District – so never went to Buckingham Palace to meet 'the Duke'!

As for work, I was once more to flourish, particularly at mathematics and chemistry – winning my last prize, in chemistry, in the Lower Sixth. However, I did well in physics too, and got a clean sweep of top 'A' grades at the end of my time. In a national test sat by the whole school in mathematics when I was in my last year, I came second in the whole school!

We were also allowed by the school to try a 'special paper' or 'S level' in two of our three subjects – I remember wondering 'why not all three?' – and I attained a distinction or grade '1' in both mathematics and physics. All of us who attained such a 'clean sweep' of grades or anything approaching it, were strongly advised to take the 'Oxbridge' Entrance Examinations. These were taken either at the start of the Upper Sixth if projected grades were adequate, or in a special 'Seventh term of the Sixth Form' – then such 'seventh term-ers', like me, took eight months or 'a year off' before starting University.

The school prided itself on getting about twenty out of 100 pupils into 'Oxbridge' out of each year, so there was a lot of competitive pressure to 'get in there', from the school. I have often wondered since whether in the Sixth Form I was already over-stretching myself academically. Certainly the plethora of pressures – both academic and social – at Cambridge was to prove a major factor in my 'problems' in my second two years there, as we shall see in due course. However, hindsight is a wonderful thing – there is no saying what might have happened had I chosen to go to one of the other Universities that offered me places, Bristol or Imperial College, London...

I passed puberty very late, I said earlier. Indeed, it was only in the Lower Sixth, when 17, that 'it' happened – and I suddenly at long last found a new interest properly, and the distraction that I unlike other pupils had missed out on so far – girls! Some male friends in the same year one day brought a pretty, petite, blonde creature from Hatfield Girls' Grammar School to my house to play bridge, as I recall, and so it was I met my first girlfriend, one Helen.

As I was to marry another Helen, also from north-west England, this first Helen I will refer to throughout as 'Helen Mark I'. There must be something fatalistic about girls called 'Helen' who come from the north-west, for me – both relationships were to end in complete disaster! 'Helen Mark I' and I had a 'kissing and cuddling only' relationship for about nine months – then she suddenly 'chucked me' for someone else. It was to turn out later (I made the fatal mistake of dating her again at Cambridge) that she was quite promiscuous. I was initially very upset over losing my first ever girlfriend. However, I realised it was all over when I visited her on her holiday in Denmark, and she was very cold to me, while I was travelling with five friends round most European capital cities, and seemingly endless 'sights' – and art galleries. This 10,000-mile trip round Europe in one month in 1974 was on an 'Inter Rail' ticket costing just £48 each to us school students!

At a disco in the Upper Sixth I met and went out for a while with Liz, a girl from St. Alban's Girls' Grammar School – until I suddenly 'dropped her', which she said she could not understand at all. I just felt it 'was not quite right' – and again, this was just a 'kiss and cuddle relationship'.

Then, in December 1974 I went to a disco at Liz's school, and found myself very much admiring, then talking to one of the organisers afterwards at length while she swept up. This was Ginette, who had the build and attractive looks of a top model – six foot tall, with classic features, and bobbed dark hair.

She turned out to have just as attractive a personality, and when I walked her to her bus-stop to go home to neighbouring Harpenden, I combined a passionate kiss with an irresistible urge to 'grope' her stunning breast. So started a relationship that lasted about nine months, and got very, very steamy – yet never 'went all the way' – we both felt too young, I think.

I often took my 80 cc motorbike over to her house for talk and 'snogging and extended groping' – however we never 'went all the way'. I got to know her parents very well, and they both thought we were wonderfully matched, as did my parents, who still keep in touch now she lives in the USA. She once told me she was falling rapidly in love with me in a letter, and I had always been madly in love with her. Her mother even once told my parents she would love it if we eventually got married. Then a double tragedy struck.

First her father, a lovely genial Senior Inspector of Schools, had a heart attack and died. I went to the funeral – my first ever – and Ginette and her mother both said my support was 'very mature and strong'. Inwardly, I felt gutted... Then, within six months of this, her mother, clearly overwhelmed by the loss of her extraordinarily close and loving husband, developed motor neurone disease, was confined to a wheelchair and rapidly lost the power of speech and most muscle control. Just six months later she died of this, following her husband.

Meanwhile Ginette and I had very sadly drifted apart – with me finding I just could not cope with looking after her following her father's death! I think my 'bipolar affective disorder' may have been starting its nasty influence on my life even then...   Meanwhile, late in 1975, she had gone up to London University to study architecture, and I think still blames her lower than expected 'A' level results on the break-up of our relationship. (However, she was to make a major recovery from her tragedies, and shone at University College, London, and ended up 'top of year' in her finals!)

I went to her Mother's funeral, but could not stomach accompanying Ginette to the cremation afterwards – and 'chickened out'. Her new boyfriend and 'flame' from London was not there either – so who can say what might have happened between us if I had braved the trauma of the cremation instead of 'chickening out' like I did. I would certainly cope now, after all I have been through – as the rest of this book shows quite clearly!

I was desperately sad to 'lose' Ginette. So much so, that for the whole of nearly the next two years I found no such 'spark' with any other woman, and so had no girlfriend – after just three in two years. So I remained a virgin until I was twenty, when, really desperate to change that 'simple fact', and really for no other good reason that I can recall, I started dating 'Helen Mark I' again. She was now also at Cambridge, but a year ahead of me on her medicine course – not having taken a year out. That rather feeble reason for going out with her again, was to finally invoke my 'bipolar disorder'.

In the meantime, while 'celibate' between Summer 1975 (end of affair with Ginette) and the Spring of 1977 (start of affair resumed with 'Helen mark I') a lot happened. I started my 'seventh term' only to feel a sharp pain in my lower right chest and have it diagnosed as a rupture of the lung wall or 'pleurisy'.

Luckily the antibiotics worked quickly, so I only missed a few studies towards the scholarship exams for my chosen college – the most academically fierce in Cambridge, and so then the hardest to get into – King's, with then all of seven applicants per place! The school had advised me that I was being rather ambitious, and with the eruption of pleurisy, got very concerned. However, I put up with the pain for a month or so, and duly took the Scholarship exam in November. When the fateful letter arrived just before Christmas 1975 from King's, and I opened it and remember just saying the word 'Scholarship!' everybody was naturally very relieved – and delighted!

Meanwhile, as an aside, I had started with two friends, Pete and Andy, the school 'Conservation group' whilst in the Lower Sixth. At Cambridge, until events intervened, I was intending to take a very demanding 'General' pair of final year options – environmental biology and nuclear physics.

My time from January 1976 to October that year, and Cambridge, my 'year off' was spent without girlfriends – but working very hard. After two months at my father's still thriving Digimatics ltd in Welwyn garden City I got fed up with being regarded as just "the boss's bright son" so got a job at ICI, just up the road, through the husband, who worked there, of a Lady Manager at Digimatics.

I spent four very happy months there being ferried frequently to Dumfries in South Scotland – by limousine and first class train to my hotel! Quite a luxury for a student! After

I finished I was given a glowing reference by my boss – I had gone far further in the time available, than he had expected from anybody, he said. I had completely disassembled from binary code, and successfully re-written and tested, the control programme for a chemical plant! Not surprisingly, as I was then only 19, they were only too happy to keep asking me back throughout all my vacations, and for a year afterwards, as a 'contract software engineer', which really helped with finances, as they paid very well...

That Summer before College was spent in Israel, a month on a kibbutz followed by two weeks being a tourist along with Peter, a fellow Cambridge 'fresher' and 'kibbutznik' – at another kibbutz. I had happened to sit next to him on the El Al 747 Jumbo on my way to Israel.

I remember the kibbutz well for lots of things. Picking millions of olives in hot sun near Tiberias on the Sea of Galilee. A truly cosmopolitan mix of both residents – some clearly still bearing the tattoos and scars of Nazi concentration camps – and volunteers from around the world. Vegetarian living yet delicious fresh food – especially olives (again!), yoghurt, bananas and avocados. 'Shabbat' (Jewish Sabbath) on Friday night – with the only meat of the week – always kibbutz-reared chicken with rice!

The illicit smoking of cannabis by some people (not I, at that stage of my life!) Occasional parties with Israeli beer, and odd trips to the bars of Tiberias with Omri, my olive-picking team leader, driving us volunteers by minibus. Swimming in the Jordan by an old dam, and travelling through minefields to this spot on the border with Jordan itself, with armed guards. Overall, lots of guns and Phantom jets in this war-torn country...

Then afterwards, the sights and sounds of hectic, cosmopolitan Jerusalem, based at the youth hostel for all of three days. Bartering with Arabs, astonished at our persistence – due to 'student poverty'! To Bethlehem and Nazareth, to find tourism had taken over, by bus full of soldiers – both men and women. The Dead Sea and climbing the Rock of Massada at 4 am. Eilat on the Red Sea, for three days' relatively tranquil rest and snorkelling on the Coral Reef. With temperatures of 120°F, thank God they had primitive air conditioning in the Youth

Hostel! So back to Tel Aviv, leaving my companion Peter to continue his travels onto the Suez Canal, and the jet home.

Then studying hard for two weeks, then the first trip to Cambridge for "freshers' week", frantically making first new friends, and doing the rounds of introductions to Tutors and inevitably taking up old – and new – interests.

As at school, I took up hockey, squash and tennis, and for a year joined the University Industrial Society. I was coerced to play only one game of Rugby for the college – but St. John's beat us 66-0, so I vowed 'never again will I play against such superior opposition!' Hockey was more my game anyway, and our team was often mixed, so it was great fun. In my second year I was made *de facto* secretary of the Hockey Club – they could not find anybody else to volunteer! – so that continued all the way through.

I also took up rowing for two years, a new interest for me, and soon found myself stroking the Third College VIII – until the last term when I swapped with the 'Number 6'. I also soon found new friends and old – with a large and quite loose group of 'lads – and some lasses' in the College Bar – of course including Keith, ex head-boy at my old school. Steve and Mike became fast fellow science student friends – but I managed to mortally offend Steve with some remark that as a devout Atheist he found particularly distasteful – when I was severely ill in my second year. As a result he hardly spoke to me in our final year, and we were then on different courses anyway, as I changed to computer science after the second year. We haven't spoken since, even though I wrote and profusely apologised later! Then there was Duncan, still a firm friend, Paul and Anne-Marie, and of course Pete, who also drifted away like Steve, after my illness fully 'took hold' in 1978 – all now happily married with a family. I hardly ever hear from any of them...

However, nobody in the College gave me the 'spark' that Ginette had – nobody ever has, not even my ex-wife, I must confess. So in the middle of the year I started to revisit old friends from school, like Liz, my ex-girlfriend, studying Engineering at Newnham, and Andy, also an engineer, at Queen's College, next door to my own college. Then of course,

Nigel and Rick at Clare on the other side of King's (Nigel then doing Natural Sciences like me, Rick is now a child Psychiatrist).

I think it was loneliness, some jealousy that most people in the college in my large 'circle' seemed to be in couples, and above all a foolish desire to 'lose my virginity', which drove me to seek out my old flame, 'Helen Mark I'. Despite the cold and callous way she had previously treated me in 1974...

She seemed to be 'available', so pretty soon I duly 'lost it' with her – and we had a sexual relationship for about three months that Summer – though she turned to be very frigid – with 'about as much passion as a wet haddock'. Certainly she never seemed to derive any sexual pleasure from my love-making, which in turn was a real let-down for me.

Anyway, in the July of 1977, our studies were over – yes, I admit it, I did have to study very hard in the course of all this! - and Helen and I were staying with teacher friends at a school in London, when we got her final medical results – a very good II:1 – and mine – a very high First in Chemistry, leading to an overall 'scrape' of a First, as my other results, in maths and biology of cells were a II:1 each – and in my 'main' subject, physics, only a II:2!

I was surprised after that rather erratic set of results to get a First, but characteristically 'Helen Mark I' just smiled rather smugly, and said, 'I told you, you would get a First!' About a week later we returned to Cambridge, and she simply disappeared for a couple of days. When she re-surfaced I asked her where she had been and she told me that she been staying with a mutual friend from her old school. For some reason, my naïve suspicions were aroused, and when I checked this story with this friend, she said it was untrue. Previous rather strange and provocative remarks by Helen about 'promiscuity' came to mind, and in a cold sweat I challenged her about her alibi. Straightaway she confessed that she had been sexually two-timing me all this time – and had a second boyfriend at another college nearer Newnham.

Of course I immediately 'chucked' her – and was immediately plunged into a deep depression, chronic anxiety and overall, regret that I had been so utterly foolish as to 'go out with her' – mostly just to lose my virginity – a second time around. The first experience should have taught me better...

This I can trace back, as can the Doctors, to being the first incidence of my 'bipolar affective disorder'. This stress, on top of a hectic first year at college, as well, perhaps, as 'dabbling with cannabis' (but never anything stronger, and 20 times weaker then than today's version, I understand!) for the last two terms of that first year, made me 'lose it'. As I mentioned way back, I was treated for this chronic anxiety with the drug 'stelazine', which took until the third week of my second year at College, in October 1977, to have its full effect and get me better. As a result, I went through the nightmare experience of attending my first two weeks of lectures and not being able to understand a word. Meanwhile I had to spend a holiday with friends in the Dordogne, without Helen as planned, and totally devastated by her cruelty.

I wrote to her a year later and told her I had been very ill because of her promiscuous two-timing, and yet had 'seen three Spiritual Experiences' in that very year of 1978. Her reply was typically callous and dismissive, and scorned any responsibility for what was to turn out to be a lifetime of problems for me so far. 'Didn't you know. Ill people see things' was about her only real comment.

So I struggled on, and about the middle of the first term of 1977-78 got back to studying physics and maths, my chosen two options for the second year, as though very little had happened. However, various factors were to conspire, the following term, after I saw Spiritual Experience Two as we have already discussed, to make me turn not depressive but the opposite – 'hypomanic' or 'high'. This depression in 1977 has been followed by just one bout of further depression, for several years on and off now, in all of twenty-one years. However about once a year ever since I have felt either slightly, or occasionally more severely, 'euphoric' in the same way.

There were several factors in my 'rebounding' from chronic anxiety and depression to a feeling of euphoria throughout the summer of 1978. One of course was Spiritual Experience Two, which initially totally perplexed and fascinated me – particularly with its large fellow audience! Then at about the same time I finally 'found a spark' with a beautiful girl, from my own college. However she had been severely and suicidally depressed the year before, and later denied my claims that she had initially shown some reciprocal interest – until she realised that I too had psychological problems. This soon turned into an infatuation in the Easter term, and I found myself acting like a complete fool over her. In the circumstances I tried to keep it subtle, and wrote her poetry – for the first time in my life since primary school I was suddenly writing quite good poetry. The poems I wrote about her – right up to 1984, shortly before the infatuation ended when I met my ex-wife – appear in the Appendix. This one-way love affair or infatuation yielded nothing but that poetry, and a lot of pain and suffering for both of us. We only ever touched once, and that was when she gave me some change for a beer in the 'Cellar Bar' at the college! I can see now, that her look at me then was one of sheer pity... I only ever got to talk to her once! Later in a letter, somewhat primly and tersely she told me that had amounted to an 'invasion of her room'!

In the meantime, my Grandfather died in March, which was also around my 21st birthday – to the party for which I tried to invite the object of my infatuation, obviously with no success – to some embarrassment for me with close College friends. The party went very well otherwise, with many, many good friends present. Granddad's death was 'the massive log that broke the Camel's back' – I had been very close to him, and got quite ill at that point, especially at the very sad funeral. He had never got over the death some years earlier of Gran, his wife, and had been lonely and living alone in a cottage in Gloucestershire.

I even felt, now 'hypomanic' for the first time and so with no insight into the increasingly terrifying feelings I experienced, that I not my grandfather's local Vicar should have conducted the funeral service – with no qualifications or experience!

So that brings us up to the start of 1978, where we started. I saw Spiritual Experience One in early November 1977, as illustrated and discussed overleaf.

The net effect of two such dramatic Experiences – the first may have been for me alone, but was very profoundly effective – suddenly pushed me into investigating 'religion' generally, as I could see it was saying something very profound about 'trinities – and the Holy Trinity in general, of Christianity'. Little did I know what this fervent activity, which replaced my official studies, especially in maths which I stopped almost completely, would lead to.

CHAPTER THREE

Spiritual Experience One. Early November 1977. 'Three identical Trees (-in-One!?)'. A Spiritual Experience in my mind's eye, and highly compelling!

Seeing this Spiritual Experience in my mind's eye was to have a compelling effect on me immediately. This Spiritual Experience One was to inspire me to divert from the course of my 'official studies' for the rest of that academic year.

Its initial impact was twofold, and very dreamlike and ecstatic. Firstly, it was clearly 'Three Trees in One' – a Trinity, which immediately gave me the strong impression I was 'being given' a firm notion of Trinities to follow up, by whoever – God? – had 'sent the Spiritual Experience'! Secondly I saw in it a strong notion, equally, of a pair of 'opposing' trees *yielding* One Tree - this notion of 'Trinity-ness'. As this notion developed over the years, I took 'Twoness and Threeness' from this Spiritual Experience as, quite simply, the main themes of what has since become my book 'Spiritual Energy'.

I said this Spiritual Experience caused me to neglect my studies. For the whole of the Summer term, I virtually dropped my maths, but kept up my physics, and studied a wide variety of 'alternative subjects'. These were : - Eastern religion; philosophy in general, even touching the 'occult' briefly out of interest; the Bible – mostly the gospels and the final book of

Revelation; Robert M Pirsig's then best-seller 'Zen and the Art of Motorcycle Maintenance'; and Fritjof Capra's 'the Tao of Physics'. I wrote to Bob Pirsig, and he wrote back several times. Back in 1980 I sent him a copy of the 'yellow' and 'orange' papers in my 'Spiritual Energy' book, that were inspired by this Spiritual Experience. He commented "I have received many treatises about my book, but yours shows by far the most understanding of what I was talking about!"

Fritjof Capra gave an informal talk in Cambridge that very term, so I met him and talked physics and religion with him, and a number of eminent Cambridge academics. All of this was leading me to seek meeting points, rather than the traditional conflicts, between science and religion – which is precisely why I ended up writing my 'Spiritual Energy' book on the subject!

I mentioned an early fascination with the Book of Revelation, which can have an unhealthy influence with all its symbolism and emphasis on mystical numbers. However, it also provided my early investigations of 'Twoness and Threeness' with absolutely loads of ammunition – as evidence that these are 'fundamental building blocks of the Spirit'!

So, the groundwork for at least the 'yellow' and 'orange', and some of the 'red' papers in the accompanying 'Spiritual Energy' book were laid as I got increasingly excited. Simultaneously I got highly inspired, yet at times confused and frightened by what I had let myself in for that Summer. There were strong tears and crying myself to sleep, as well as euphoria, in my ecstatic mood. As a result of all this deep philosophical thinking I tried to interest my would-be girlfriend I mentioned, but wisely she avoided any involvement with me or my solo 'quest for the truth'. In the end, however, it was to be my obsession with this lovely creature that was to end my 'quest' abruptly.

In the exams, I got an astonishing II:1 and even just missed a First, having only got a Third in my much neglected maths, because my physics had drastically improved since the previous year. This was partly due to excellent tuition along with two of the brightest physicists in the whole University (Martin had come first in the first year exams!)

However, I had neglected my physics for the sake of religion and the philosophy of science – to find that at that exam level, that same philosophy of physics, and science in general, helped me write very good answers at an abstract level to teasing Tripos exam questions! Swings and roundabouts…

So it is fair to say that although I was acutely mentally ill and euphoric with 'hypomania', as yet untreated at the time I took my exams, I only just missed getting another top grade or First! As I entered the Summer's physics practical sessions under no less a tutor than Anthony Hewish, the Nobel prize-winner, it was soon evident however that my massive 'unrequited love' was getting unbearable. Something had to give. I remember I managed to offend her by sending a note to her instructing her to stop spending so much time – however innocently – with one particular mature student. I was getting quite jealous, and even possessive, of her. (She was in college during the Summer as well, at the same time, preparing for her own second year course).

Soon I was asked to see the Senior Tutor, and as I recall, very kindly and discreetly informed that this young lady had told her that she had no interest in me and would prefer to be left alone – to which I of course agreed. So the incident that happened a few days later was most unfortunate – and as it turned out, tragic. I had now given up my practical sessions as I felt distinctly disjointed, euphoric and generally psychologically unwell.

That weekend, I was walking out of my own staircase when I looked across and saw the 'object of my desire' coming out of the punting area (I lived in a room by the river in my final year). Behind her emerged the very friend of hers I had recently warned her about. She was carrying a punting paddle, and clearly was going punting with this character. Her reaction was immediate, as was mine. I froze. She kicked the punt paddle hard, and ran to the riverbank and burst into tears. "This is all my fault!", I thought to myself. "I never meant to do this to her!" Totally confused, I walked past her up to the college's bridge, and for some peculiar reason best known to my 'hypomania', now in full flow, decided to give her and anybody else who 'cared' – a 'cry for help'.

This was in totally non-suicidal fashion – it was broad daylight and I was immediately to swim to the bank. However,

"I simply cannot take any more of these tormenting feelings!" I remember thinking to myself. "This has gone on far too long – it has been six months of agony! Help!" So – I took off my shoes and jumped 20 feet off the bridge into the cold dirty water below, full of punts and boats... I remember hitting the bottom and cutting my right heel on something sharp down there in the depths of the Cam – either a stone or a piece of glass. There was blood on the bridge as I retrieved my socks and shoes from where I had placed them after removing them – for safety in the water...

Suddenly the college authorities were alerted at last, after six months, that I was in some psychological difficulty. My Director of Studies, Richard Lambert, arrived at my room and asked "What on Earth is going on, Simon?" I could not give a simple answer just like that, to something very complex that had been brewing up for months. He went off, and well-oiled college wheels, familiar indeed with such undergraduate 'crises', ground into motion.

I was told I was being taken to hospital – naively, I thought, to have my foot treated. It was a Friday evening, and when we arrived at Fulbourn Mental Hospital, just outside Cambridge, I thought to myself, "there must be some mistake!" Once inside, I soon found myself getting very agitated by the feeling of being 'watched over', and my first night's sleep was quite disturbed. The chap in the next bed was having severe delusions and he said, as in hindsight I was to agree entirely, that he suffered from schizophrenia. His name was Peter and he was a milkman. He was quite pleased to have met a student from the University in that very pleasant Open Ward, as I still recall it from then, and we chatted, at length but not easily, as we had both been through traumatic problems.

Then, the following morning after breakfast, we set off to the local village, as I recall, to buy some cigarettes for us both, and a paper for me. I still had no medication inside me as I was still being 'assessed' – and all the Consultants were off for the weekend. We were chatting on the way back, then puffed and walked in silence, when, suddenly, I looked up and suddenly realised that my third uncanny 'Spiritual Experience' of three in one year – was starting up overhead.

The first had been purely a strong yet dream-like image in my mind's eye. The second had been 'lights – in the company of hundreds of other bystanders'. This one was completely and utterly different again. There in the cloud-scudded sky above, was one cloud that was different – and directly ahead as we walked. It was in the perfect, unmistakable shape of a dragon's head, breathing fire and smoke! In the course of the next five minutes, this cloud changed shape, in totally supernatural fashion, to three other images.

At the end, I remained overwhelmed and silent – confused by why I was being given all these images this year – by somebody 'clearly supernatural' – that I did not fully understand. Indeed, it was to take all of eighteen years for me to finally deduce the meaning of this Spiritual Experience, which I vaguely thought at the time was some kind of 'rebuke from God' for my behaviour towards 'that' beautiful girl, now totally out of reach. Or was it in fact some reference to the strange Spiritual Experience in Revelation chapter 12, that had so perplexed me that year? No, the winged horse in this Spiritual Experience, simply did not fit such an interpretation! Peter, however, reacted very dramatically. Despite being heavily sedated, he started dancing on the spot and singing the Negro Spiritual song, 'Jump up, turn around, pick a bale of cotton!'

Then he said simply "The Lord has come down to Earth today! Well DONE, Simon!" I did not know what to think!

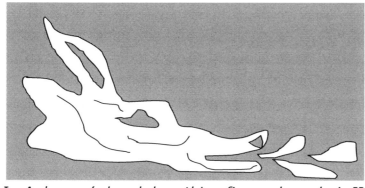 

I. A dragon's head, breathing fire and smoke! II. The dragon 'gives birth'!

III. Pegasus, the Winged Horse of Greek Myths and Legends *IV. Long-haired Woman*

Spiritual Experience Three.   August 1978, Cambridge.   Four images 'drawn' – by a cloud!

I come to the definitive interpretation of this vital Spiritual Experience in chapter nineteen, after I have described the coming about in the then future of the events it prophesied. In the meantime it totally baffled me...

My initial reaction to this Spiritual Experience was then one of confusion. I felt, why is – clearly, God – giving me all these 'Spiritual Experiences'? They have only made me feel most peculiar! I was in a good place to feel that way. However, later that day, as I drew lots of very quick pictures in the Art Therapy room in the Ward, on various unrelated subjects, an 'inspired thought' occurred to me. "I have got to get this information about these three Spiritual Experiences this year, and all my resulting thinking, to the newspapers!" So it was the following day that I got a bus to the station without telling anybody where I was going. Then onto the train for King's Cross in London, and onto the offices of 'the Times', only to find that on a Sunday afternoon that eminent newspaper was all closed down...

At least, I got in through an open side door and wandered around the empty corridors for a while – until a security guard found me and kindly yet firmly escorted me off the premises. I was at a loss what to do, and in the end walked about three miles to Camden, where my old friend Ginette still has a house, rented out now as she lives in the USA. Luckily she was in, and surprised to see me, but seemed to know how to handle the situation very well, with no previous experience of 'escapee mental patients'. She rang the hospital, and after the police called later, just grinned and said, 'You will get me quite a reputation!'

The hospital were very relaxed about me staying in her spare room overnight, and I returned the following morning – Monday – again by train, having had long, over-stressed and somewhat strange 'chats' with Ginette into the small hours. Then for the first time I was seen by a Doctor, a Consultant this time – apart from the Registrar, who I later found out, had fiercely formed and documented her own opinions that my behaviour was 'definitely schizophrenic' – over the weekend. At least, I have of course since seen her highly coloured and inaccurate 'report' to that effect, written after just two days of observation of me.

[Aside: That 'report' meant I was to be prescribed totally the wrong drug, chlorpromazine, for the next three years, until after I changed to a Doctor much more astute – and local to my native Hatfield – in 1980! It only made me feel terrible for all three of those years, and it was only in 1983 that I was to get 'correct' treatment. Despite that, I finished my degree and worked full-time throughout that time! Only in 1980 did I start getting full relief from my actual illness of 'bipolar affective disorder' by being prescribed lithium carbonate. This helped greatly with my symptoms, for the first time since 1978, and Dr Gander who prescribed this as soon as he saw me, knew that it had very few side effects. The only one I noticed was water retention and so developing a large stomach – although I have long since adapted to that effect, and today am extremely slim once more! It does on the other hand make one very de-energised.]

The saga of 'leaving the hospital' continued after I saw the Consultant, and they were preparing my first 'depot injection' of modecate, or chlorpromazine. That Monday afternoon I got very bored and fed up, and got the bus to town, with the intention of going back to King's and persuading Steve, my friend who had the keys to my Mother's car that I had been borrowing, to let me have them.   There was no need of persuasion. The door to his room was wide open, and the keys just lying on his desk. Soon I found myself driving away from what I still see today as the 'terrible confinement of a mental hospital' – towards 'home and freedom'.

Fate was to intervene. My parents had been on holiday, and had been alerted on their return, to my confinement at Fulbourn, and were in fact driving in the opposite direction on the same road, in equal haste. Luckily we both recognised the other car going past, and stopped in conveniently placed lay-bys on that country road. They drove me back to Fulbourn, and were soon satisfied that I could no longer tolerate the confinement there.

After some discussion with the staff, they were allowed to take me home, after my first ever – small – injection of modecate.   This was on condition I started seeing the Consultant at his clinic, had counselling for my 'problems' with a psychological counsellor attached to the University, and agreed to regular injections. After some obvious reluctance over the last condition, I was therefore allowed home after just three days in hospital – clearly not judged a serious case.

Exhausted by my ordeal, the same two friends who had introduced me to 'Helen Mark I' took me to Southern Scotland for a week's holiday in a farmhouse, with a group of acquaintances. I vaguely remember it – writing some of my early poetry, which was much admired by my acquaintances; not really joining in much, and generally feeling utterly exhausted, and totally isolated from the occasion. The Consultant Psychiatrist had warned me my concentration would be affected by my recent experiences – and indeed this was, then and later, the main sign there had been any problem!

Having not completed my practicals under Professor Hewish in the 'Long Vacation term' that Summer, I decided that as I had been so ill, I would neither continue with physics nor try to take my originally – over-ambitiously – planned Final Year options of Environmental Biology combined with Nuclear Physics! Instead, with all my vacations so far spent at ICI doing 'computing', that I had studied at school as well, I scanned the final year prospectus to find that there was indeed a computer science course available. I checked, found I could change, and did so, while ill. A poorly made decision that was taken when I was ill, that was to affect my whole life up until now! I duly took a 'two week crash induction course' – I had missed the chance of doing the full induction course by not changing subject earlier. As for the previous year, when I had been ill over being two-timed miserably, I found I could hardly concentrate on this – nor for the first few weeks of lectures.

Also in 1978, three things had happened, that have a bearing on the rest of this story. You may have noticed that I have been carefully counting 'sexually-oriented relationships with women' so far. I had three girlfriends at school – but my 'would-be obsession-girlfriend of 1978' at Cambridge was, if I count her, number five. Meanwhile, the previous Winter of 1977, I had had a 'two-night stand' with a girl from Girton, a womens' college. When I 'performed' three times with her in my room one night – then could not repeat anything at all, not surprisingly, the following night in her own room, she just said 'good-bye'. It turned out she was a bit of a nymphomaniac, then doing the rounds of men in mine and other colleges... So my obsession was number five!

Also in the Easter holiday of 1978, when I was just getting ill, my family and I went on a skiing holiday to Formigal, in the Spanish Pyrrenees. This was the first of many such family skiing holidays. I had started my habit of heavy smoking, about then, with the onset of my 'hypomania'. The family still have a photograph of me, first thing in the morning, smoking on a balcony in our flat, in my dressing-gown and snow-boots...!

The third feature of that year of 1978 came while I was recovering from my 'hospitalisation' of the Summer. This was the wedding of my cousin Jeremy, to a pretty girl from the same village in the West Midlands. He was to precede me in my family by some years, by being divorced tragically over his medical condition. In his case this was diabetes. Tragically, he was to die some years later as a direct result of this...

CHAPTER FOUR

My traumas after all this terrible experience, from 1979-80

My final year at Cambridge 1978-79. Aftermath of 'illness – and Three Spiritual Experiences'

As for the second year, the start of my third year, in a new subject, computer science, was depressing and frightening. Once more, for the first half term, I was to find myself unable to concentrate on lectures and practicals, due to my recent illness. The fact is that my tiny dose of modecate injections every fortnight was a distinct hindrance rather than any help – as it was totally the wrong drug for a faulty yet emphatic diagnosis! The new counselling sessions with a lady counsellor, however, helped overcome my acute feelings of loneliness that were to last all year. My computer tutor, Arthur, was also very kind, helpful and understanding – hand-picked for me with my 'problems'!

My college friends had nearly all abandoned me, it seemed, because of fear and stigma, and I found the computer scientists were a rather unsociable bunch, preferring their 'man-machine interface' to 'normal', sociable human interaction. I usually have found that true of computer people!

So it was that I only made one friend that year on that course, an Indian post-graduate from Aston, called Jagdish, who was taking the course as a diploma. He was convinced throughout I would get a First in my finals, and was surprised and disappointed for me when I only ended up with a II:2. As he never got the distinction he wanted either, that was a letdown too.

There were a few obvious factors in my not attaining a high grade as in previous years. Firstly I found the course very abstract and theoretical. Secondly the library had extremely restrictive rules and very few books, which one could only take out for 24 hours at a time. Finally, for a University with as eminent a reputation in computers – after all a Kingsman, Alan

Turing, had invented them! – there were very few actual computers... There were terminals on the IBM 370, running the University 'bureau' system, which I found far inferior to the commercially supplied system in use at ICI, where I worked still in all vacations. Sixty students worked around the clock in one-hour 'shifts' on the single 'Nova' minicomputer, the same as I had used to use at my father's company Digimatics ltd. (as a result, I was picked out to demonstrate basic operations, on the first day we used this machine). The modern luxury of 'Personal Computers' simply did not exist then...

The final and dominant factor affecting my work and attitude to studies, were of course my recent traumas – with illness and no less than three women. Although the object of my 'obsession', I must say, behaved impeccably throughout, if she was, for understandable reasons, her own problems that is, rather off-hand and cold. As a result I only took the bare minimum of courses, even though my Subject Tutor at King's, Ken, had pushed me hard to do more than that. As a result of not taking more than the minimum, in my Finals I was presented with a set of papers that I found strange, and difficult. I could not answer enough questions, or often, complete the ones I started.

Meanwhile, with virtually no social life I was incredibly isolated and lonely. I stopped rowing, and did not always play hockey. Also, having been let down by three relationships inside one year, I was not in a mood to seek more 'girlfriend – or especially, would-be girlfriend' problems. As a result, only sometimes 'looking', I was to remain celibate from Winter 1977 to Spring 1982 – over four years. That, compounded by being on totally the wrong diagnosis – and hence treatment – was to compound my isolation and misery, and feelings of regret I had 'fallen into the psychiatric lobster pot' of mental illness. No way back – and no way out – for me, or so it has always seemed. Barring a miracle, I had been told that my 'illness' would last a lifetime.

There were two highlights to that last dismal year – both family holidays. In Easter 1979 we went skiing to les Arcs in France, taking Katie, a school friend of my sister. This modern resort linked into a large system of slopes, so we scoured the mountains for different slopes to try. We tried the night-life –

both organised by our travel company and by ourselves. One memorable restaurant where Katie, Libby and I went only seemed to serve dishes containing veal – no other meat! Soon I resurrected the old 'Monty Python' sketch about a similarly bizarre restaurant that served only 'rook'. Soon we were all rolling about with laughter, reciting the menu and parodying it: - 'Rook escalopes, rook steaks, rook fricassee, and yes, rook pie, rook pie!' Having had a decent meal of this 'rook'/'veal' we returned to our flats, still in stitches.

The second highlight was after my Finals, and I was working back at ICI. This was another family holiday, this time taking the latest caravan to a lovely campsite by the beach in Spain. I was soon brought out of my depressed reveries, which often – as at the time of writing this – involved sleeping in till midday, full of black thoughts. For Libby and I – my brother Jem was not there – soon made friends with a charming French pair of students, Dominique and Jacky, and then soon afterwards with Peter and Irmgard, a German couple. We went out together to the local town a lot, and had long chats into the night. All this socialising really helped to cheer me up! We lost touch with the Germans, but the next year Libby and I were invited to Paris for a very memorable wedding of Dominique to Jacky. It turned out Dominique was pregnant, had Celine later, then found out Jacky was unfaithful and she was left to bring up Celine alone. We hear from her sometimes, and the last time we heard anything, she had found a much more reliable boyfriend.

A year at ICI – then onto 'pastures new' with my Father's new business venture

Towards the end of my time at college at Cambridge, I had careers advice along with everybody else, and applied for and was offered two jobs close at home, both at £4,000 a year. Then ICI made me an offer I could not refuse, of £6,000 a year as a contract software engineer. Clearly their prior experience amounting to a total of about eighteen months, outweighed any reservations about 'nervous breakdowns' etc. I duly found myself working alongside Janet, a housewife contracting part-time, on a microcomputer based graphical accounting system. This was under David, who was to come to Lee Micromatics ltd, my father's new venture, in 1984, after my second great trauma late in 1983 – to help out, as he knew me well. I worked very hard, and wrote over a megabyte of bug free 'RTL/2' code that year. Lack of energy still bothered me – and my only problem that year was occasionally being reprimanded for finding it difficult to wake up and so get to work on time. I have always since had the same problem – I am usually very depressed first thing in the morning, especially when waking.

That Christmas 1979 the family had another skiing holiday – this time at Courmayeur at the foot of Mont Blanc (Monte Bianco), in Italy. We went by coach, which was exhausting, and skied the first day having just arrived overnight with very little sleep! Then, in early 1980 my father, who had been saving money from his one-man consultancy since 1977, Lee Micromatics ltd, started persuading me to come over and join him in this from ICI. He had exciting ideas of using microcomputers, just arriving in the market, to emulate his success of the 1970's at his previous venture Digimatics ltd!

I duly left ICI with a glowing reference in July 1980, and we took Libby and my Mother to America, for them to have a holiday. He and I were to have a training course on the Z80 computers and software of our supplier-to-be, Xycom Inc, who were based in Michigan near the Great Lakes. There were already cracks appearing with the engineers at our industrial partner in this venture, who refused to join us – saying they already knew all the material!

First we visited my Godfather and his Chinese wife near New York for three days – then saw all the sights and sounds of that great and frightening, super-fast metropolis. Then onto Detroit for the course, and Libby and Mum came up and joined us at the middle weekend of the two weeks of course-work, also taken by the two agents for Xycom in the UK, and we travelled overnight 400 miles to Niagara Falls. I still fondly remember the reaction of the female Canadian Border Passport Officer at 6am, to seeing my passport photo. This was taken when I was 14; I was now 23! She said, 'Holy crow! Is that you?' Everybody laughed, and I *was* let into Canada, I hasten to add!

After the two-weeks were up – memorable for ordering a 'bucket of seafood' for two of us in Ann Arbor – and trying to eat – literally – a full bucketful – I returned to New York for a few days. The rest of the family then spent two weeks in the Bahamas, which my Father afterwards regretted as it took a huge chunk of valuable funds out of the company.

At about that time, keen to break the loneliness barrier and get some social life, I had talked to a local neighbour – a Quaker elder called Margaret, who is still an occasional friend. She turned out to run the local 'Gateway club' for people with learning difficulties (which was called 'mental handicap' in those days). I soon started driving a minibus every Friday night, ferrying a busful of people to and from St Albans to the club in Hatfield.

Down to work along with our 'industrial partners', there were a lot of problems of 'professional pride'. They were far more lavishly equipped than us – with the latest high-speed Hewlett-Packard, all-singing, all-dancing emulators. These could develop code – either assembler, or the Pascal Dad and I had trained in – on a wide variety of microprocessors, not just the Z80 processor used by Xycom. They were much, much faster, and vastly superior to the equally-priced yet tinny by comparison, floppy-based Xycom machines we were using.

Also, as the Pascal supplied by Xycom was slow and interpreted – and as our system was also interpreted – we decided we could not use Pascal as planned, in which to develop the new system. Writing 'an interpretive language using an interpretive language' was one slow layer too many!

Stress soon mounted on both sides, and I started feeling symptoms of my 'hypomania' starting to re-emerge. Soon I had to 'confess' this problem to them – which surprisingly, actually helped! This was because their team leader in turn came out and explained why he was always very stroppy and dogmatic – he too had a problem, with his thyroid gland. By Christmas very little work had been achieved, and we were all very much behind our incredibly tight schedule. In hindsight, had the team as a whole been able to buy one of these £30,000 HP machines, the project could have been saved. However, my Father, in his 'infinite wisdom', had already bought a Xycom development system, and could not afford to change now... When he asked our partner to buy one for us, they just laughed!

So by Christmas 1980 the project was jeopardised... Meanwhile my health was at last starting to get some better attention. I transferred at last from my Consultant at Cambridge, still treating me with the chlorpromazine that has always given me a bad reaction. My new Consultant, Dr Gander, at the Queen Elizabeth II Hospital at Welwyn Garden City (QEII), was a close friend and colleague of my Mother, who had been put in charge of the medical centre at the UH (University of Hertfordshire) – or Hatfield Polytechnic, as it then was.

He took one look at me, said I clearly did not suffer from straight 'schizophrenia' after all, but that my illness was in fact manic-depressive. His diagnosis was 'schizo-affective disorder' ("And I don't mind at all that you object to it being called that – it is debatable. Yes, call it just 'affective disorder' if you wish, Simon"). He put me on lithium carbonate tablets immediately, and lowered the dose of chlorpromazine, which had been rising steadily. Apart from complaining bitterly about having a bloated stomach, which faded after a year's acclimatisation, this extra drug made me feel much less volatile in mood. I still take it today.

In 1979 I had written down an essay that tried to pick the 'wheat from the chaff' of my thoughts while I had been getting ill the previous year. I was careful to preserve this, and now it appears in my 'Spiritual Energy' Book as the Yellow Paper or 'Complementary Opposites'. Again, in 1980, I finished the second of a 'trilogy of papers' with its successor, called 'Where Opposites Meet' – now the Orange Paper in that book. The third is now the Red Paper there.

Around that time I wrote to the best-selling author Robert M Pirsig, of 'Zen and the Art of Motorcycle Maintenance' fame, with these two essays. He actually replied, 'I have received many such pieces of writing about my book, but yours shows the most understanding by far, of what I was talking about'. That encouraged me to continue – and as he advised, get 'less intellectual, although that is appropriate at first'!

CHAPTER FIVE

January 1981 – and my longest Spiritual Experience of all

Spiritual Experience Four. 15th January 1981. My parents' house in Hatfield. Much more prophetic information about the future. The longest Spiritual Experience I ever saw, in terms of number of crystal clear images in a very compelling series.

By now under a lot of stress, only slightly alleviated by the new drug lithium, that I was taking now, I guess I was a little bit hypomanic that new year.

I had seen a very clear image in my mind's eye in Spiritual Experience Two, five lights in the night sky in Spiritual Experience Two, then a cloud adopting compelling and highly defined and unmistakable shapes in Spiritual Experience Three. I was not at all prepared to see an entirely new form of Spiritual Experience in early 1981. This appeared when I was lying in bed at the family home in Hatfield, suddenly, as I was preparing to sleep but was wide-awake in anxiety. The first of all of ten whole sets of bright lights appeared in the air above me (I saw the last one outside the bedroom window!)

Their shapes were as crystal clear and unmistakable as all their predecessors. Indeed all my remaining Spiritual Experiences were to take one of these four forms, as follows: - bright night-sky lights; mind's eye; cloud shapes; lights seen when trying to drop off to sleep. We will see this is true of the remaining seventeen Spiritual Experiences of the whole series of twenty-one, as we come to them in due course in this book.

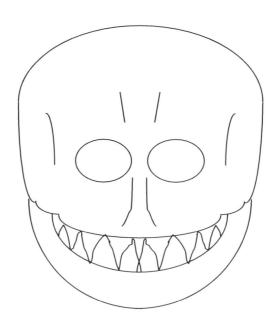

Spiritual Experience Four – Image One.   A powerful image of 'Evil' or 'Death'

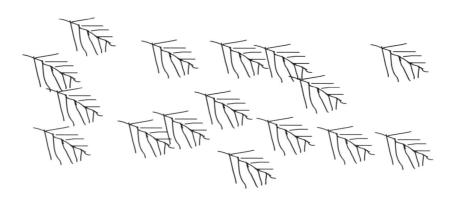

Spiritual Experience Four – Image Two.   Feathers of angelic wings, falling on me

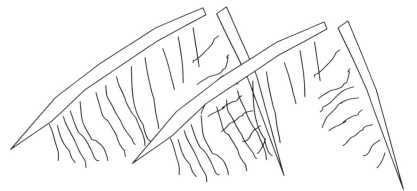

Spiritual Experience Four – Image Three. Bones of angelic wings, falling on me

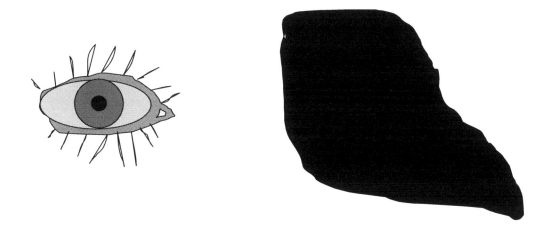

Spiritual Experience Four – Image Four. The eye and ear of a black labrador dog

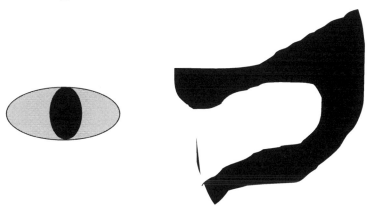

Spiritual Experience Four – Image Five. The eye and ear of a Black Persian cat

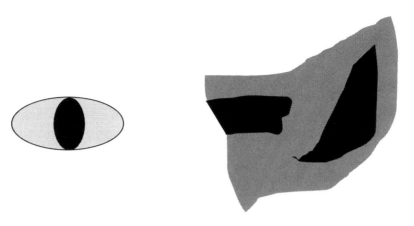

Spiritual Experience Four – Image Six. The eye and ear of a Grey Tabby cat

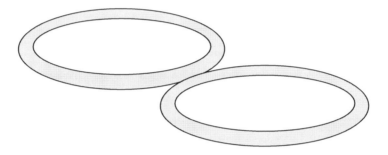

Spiritual Experience Four – Image Seven. A pair of linked gold wedding rings.

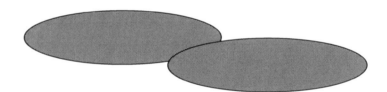

Spiritual Experience Four – Image Eight. A pair of Ancient Egyptian Wedding Seals OR Funeral Seals, as one can see in the Louvre Museum in Paris.

Spiritual Experience Four – Image Nine. Six ghostly heads and shoulders of people, that appeared one after the other – at the time I recognised none of them

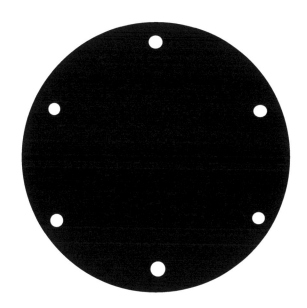

Spiritual Experience Four – Image Ten. A black disk with six lights.

We can only give a full interpretation of this Spiritual Experience Four in Chapter Nine, once the events it predicted had definitely 'come true'.

In the meantime, as for all its predecessors, apart from the vaguest hints of a possible future marriage (I then had no girlfriend, and no prospect of one), with the rings and seals, this Spiritual Experience Four completely baffled, even frightened me…

CHAPTER SIX

Between 1981-1982 – VERY hard at work...

So, back to 1981, and the major recession for the world economy that struck that year. As I have said, our 'difficult' industrial partners at Lee Micromatics ltd in my father's venture were paper makers, and once the recession hit that Spring of 1981, they started retrenching very hard. You had better ask an economist friend why paper companies feel the pinch of recessions more than most – I don't know the answer!

Anyway, by that Autumn they had pulled out of the agreement with us, as their research and development centre was threatened with closure! Meanwhile I had plugged on with hardly any help from them and their 'whizz-bang' equipment, with much encouragement from my Father, and by late 1981, working at least eight 24-hour days, had most of a viable product up and running. Meanwhile, we had been joined by Mike, a hardware expert and ex-colleague of my Father's at Digimatics ltd, his previous solo venture.

I remember that meanwhile I had been actively involved with my 'Mencap' work for the local Gateway club, and in the Spring of 1981, went on a trip as a helper with a group of 'mentally handicapped', as they were then known, to Hatfield's twin town of Zierikzee in Holland. Unfortunately I embarrassed myself by becoming severely ill on the trip – due solely to the 'pressure at work' at the time. I drank myself silly, and smoked loads of lovely small Dutch cigars... I was worried sick about it all...

After the departure of our industrial partner, and very worried about how finances had become without them and the contingent Government Grant, on which we had depended, that Winter the family decamped skiing to Meribel in the French Alps. I remember a thoroughly enjoyable time of rest was had by all... Finally, the only other memory of note I retain about 1981 was joining a local social club, that I was to remain a member of for some eight years.

1982 – a year of 'mixed blessings'.

By the Spring of 1982 our 'Microfast' product had emerged – despite virtually no finance apart from my father once more going out consulting, now we had lost our essential industrial partner and so vital Government 'Mapcon scheme' money. He got several industrial companies interested in the product, which offered the novel feature of 'software without programming – just draw the *flowchart* of what you want and the system will *instantly* run it. If you find any problem with any of your programmes – just change them, even while they are still running, with the same pictorial interface!' In the end, to our delight and relief, we got an order – from FBC (Fisons-Boots Consortium) for their hydrazine or rocket-fuel plant at Widnes (forever 'sunny Widnes' to us!) Today hydrazine is used as a very powerful cleaning agent for power stations, I should point out! This system was installed in the next four months till Autumn 1982, with a lot of work for Bill, Mike and I. Some of the early bugs in my software, in this complex system, using two computers in one chassis, and lots of intelligent instruments, were really quite amusing to all of us…!

However, they were soon all removed, and within two months of commissioning this system, which turned out to be the only 'Microfast I' machine of its type that we were to sell, it was deemed to be a 100% success – by both us and the delighted FBC, our customers!

So that Spring, with our family again skiing in Val d'Isere in France, near Meribel from last year, we had reason for optimism. If we could sell some more systems, we could still turn Lee Micromatics around… Sadly, despite the rather bombastic efforts of a local marketing company on our behalf at a 'Control and Instrumentation' exhibition that year, we made no further sales that year or into 1983, even. Finances got very dire, and Bill had to make the very loyal Mike redundant…

The great saving grace of most of 1982 for me, was early that year, meeting my first girlfriend in a five-year 'famine of celibacy'. This was the very sexy Glenda, who first attracted me when I met her at the Gateway club, where she started working as well. On our very first date, when I cheekily asked to 'inspect the new wallpaper in her bedroom' as an excuse to then proceed to make passionate love to her – after all of five years' 'famine', like I said – her reaction was inspiring, after she readily climaxed with me. "You are one of the world's great lovers!" were her exact words. She was twenty-eight, I was twenty-six, and she was vastly more experienced than me – as twice-divorced, and living alone on benefit with her young daughter Davina to support. It seems a pity that if I am indeed 'that', I have had so little practice since knowing Glenda, in the art of love-making. My love-life seems to encounter vast empty interludes...

My hot, steamy, and very intimate relationship with Glenda lasted nine months, until I took her on holiday to Crete. I was exhausted and wanted a quiet time – whereas she missed 'the bright lights' – and it was her first ever trip abroad. Hence our two weeks there, in a remote coastal spot, were a complete disaster. I 'chucked' her as a result of that holiday, shortly afterwards. There were however, no regrets on either side when I bumped into her in Hatfield twice recently. We only remembered the good times – my job providing her with the good times – lots of drinks and meals out, but never the brand-new clothes a woman on benefit craves, rather than being a 'second-hand rose'.

The final important thing about 1982 for me, was that I bought my first place of my own – a flat in Stevenage, that I got on a '100% mortgage' late that year, just after ending with Glenda.

CHAPTER SEVEN

1983, and three more Spiritual Experiences follow the three of November 1977 and January and August 1978

I was to have three Spiritual Experiences that year of 1983 – the first, Spiritual Experience Five, while fully well, Spiritual Experience Six while getting very ill indeed, and Spiritual Experience Seven while recovering during my first real taste of Mental Hospitals... We move straight to Spiritual Experience Five as it came in mid-Winter, very soon after the New Year.

Spiritual Experience Five. Small hours, 1am, of Sunday 30th January 1983. Once more, as for Spiritual Experience Four, I saw lights in the darkness over my bed – this time at my flat in Stevenage.

Spiritual Experience Five – Image One. Eight lights or Stars, in a highly symmetrical pattern.

Spiritual Experience Five – Image Two. Astonishingly perhaps, a pair of sunglasses!

Spiritual Experience Five – Image Three. A Communion Chalice – symbolising The Holy Spirit? Or is it just a wine glass, symbolising alcohol?

We shall see that at first I thought this Spiritual Experience had only two Outcomes, which both came true, in very negative fashion, in 1996 – see Chapter Nineteen. However, earlier in this year of 2000, three *positive* Outcomes – the first of all my eighteen Spiritual Experiences to have positive Outcomes – came out. I can only hope there is another sixth positive Outcome, and even possibly two more, the seventh and eighth – yet to transpire as I write in April 2000! So in all this most complex and last Spiritual Experience to fully 'come true' will have done so by turning out to have all of *EIGHT* Outcomes! The story unfolds from Chapter Nineteen on...!

Dramatic events overtook the family in 1983! Despite massive efforts by the whole team, the family firm, Lee Micromatics, had had no sales for a year and nearly went bankrupt. On 1st July 1983 – my mother's birthday – we were formally 'taken over' by Fisons Scientific Equipment Division. Our one successful system sale, to a company in 'sunny Widnes' owned by Fisons and Boots, had come to the attention of one Michael, new head of that Division, and when he heard we were in trouble he could see some potential, and put together a take-over bid. This saved the family home, and the otherwise inevitable impending redundancies of my Father and myself.

I was to take no less than three very memorable holidays, one with the Gateway Club to Aldeburgh, in May that year, and another in July 1983, to Lyme Regis with my parents, significantly the location for the filming of John Fowles' – of 'The Magus' fame – "The French Lieutenant's Woman". I say significant – when I saw the film I strongly identified with the suffering of the main character, played by Meryl Streep, that won her an Oscar. In October 1983 I went by myself to the North Yorkshire Dales, to Leyburn, and spent a very lonely time in a cottage owned by Beryl, the widowed friend of Margaret, the Quaker friend I mentioned earlier. I took some very lonely, isolated photographs, certainly...

Meanwhile, that June, fed up with the side-effects of the drug 'chlorpromazine' I was taking, I had stopped all my medication as well as abruptly giving up smoking. The stress did not let up after the take-over – one member of the Fison's management team was really jealous that we had been rescued in this way, and kept making very raw, sly digs in private to my father and I, that we had 'conned' them into this deal! In the end they made him redundant, but not before all this 'dirty pressure', in the absence of both my normal medication and the 'comfort' of smoking, led to a complete nervous breakdown on 11th November 1983 – Remembrance Day.

The night before this, having already seen Spiritual Experience Five earlier in 1983, I was to have what much later in my life, I realised had been a 'Visitation' – from Jesus Himself! I described this eery journey, with a star approaching me fast from the North-West, then leading me on a journey South, then East from Stevenage to Ware – and much help from some very concerned business acquaintances there – in my poem 'Ship of the Night', reproduced overleaf.

This 'Star from the East' was at the same height and speed, and had the same colour, as the four out of five 'bright nightly lights' I saw with hundreds of others in 1978 in Spiritual Experience Two. He reappeared for all of six hours in 1983 over the Hertfordshire countryside, and the eery path led past all three of my three homes of my own since then – at Dane End, Hertford and Ware! Spooky yet reassuring as I write now! Not surprisingly, after you read the account in the poem overleaf, I was admitted to hospital at midnight on 11th November 1983 – Remembrance Day, the day after this...

As soon as I was in hospital I was desperate to escape from that confinement, as in my totally ill, medication-free state, I then saw the Acute Ward I was placed in. In those days it was a very free and easy place, far better run than now, and most patients were far lower grade 'sufferers' than today, which also greatly helped make it a pleasant place. At first I could not see that at all, and kept escaping – once in my pyjamas and dressing gown, on a freezing November night! However, I was immediately put back on lithium carbonate, which started working within a week – and as a result of being so confined, also started smoking again – which also had a calming effect.

The crucial factor in the fact that I was only there six weeks – I was allowed to discharge myself in time for Christmas shopping, the day before Christmas Eve 1983 – was that two new drugs appeared then. At the time these were hailed as 'wonder drugs', although they are now regarded as 'old-fashioned', with too many side-effects. These are called 'haloperidol' and 'depixol'. My consultant, Dr Gander, had been aware they were to be launched about then, and had patiently waited to try them on me – and patients with an 'affective disorder' or 'schizo-affective disorder' like mine. Indeed, they both turned out once launched to be a major advance on the 'ancient and venerable' chlorpromazine, that I had so loathed – and still do – because of its side-effects.

He first tried haloperidol with the lithium for two weeks, then depixol for two weeks, then settled on haloperidol. I have been taken off for terrible months, only to then be put back onto this combination of drugs and get well, in five of seven awful, excessively lengthy hospitalisations since 1983, between 1995-2003!

Spiritual Experience Six. 10th November 1983. 'Manifestation' of Jesus Himself – as 'the Star from the East' or 'the Morning Star'!

I reproduce below a poem from the Appendix that describes Spiritual Experience Six of seeing the latest Light in the Sky, and immediately recognising it was the same as the five lights in 1978 in Spiritual Experience Two. Then following this 'Star from the East', wondering what it meant, for fifteen miles in the middle of the night, from Stevenage to Ware, where I live now.

SHIP OF THE NIGHT

15th February 1984

(This all took place between 1am and 8am on 10th November 1983)

I left the flat, the door closed, I'd left my keys inside.
In despair I turned and fled, and wondered where I'd hide.
Into the dank November night, I sniffed the midnight air,
walked on down the darkened streets, the mist wet on my hair.

The glow of street lights was so eery, the mist came down in patches.
I pondered all the hard times, the locks and snares and catches.
Wondered as I marched, the stars came out, Orion over West,
"Where now, what for, and how, and what is for the best?"

Southbound through Orion, a stranger star appears,
travelling up above me, removing foolish fears.
A guardian of the night up high, over my right shoulder.
I'd seen some long ago like this, when I had tried to hold her.

That love is dead now, but memories have not died,
now I'd a weirder companion, to take me for a ride.
I nearly turned but swiftly now, the friendly light led on.
The ship of the night came lower, newly leading from beyond.

As I walked out through old Hook's Cross, I'd never felt so gloomy.
Thoughts came crashing through of *her*,
a longing shuddered through me.
The empty road, all traffic gone, the night so still and calm.
I turned for Ware at Watton-at-Stone, never seeing past the farms.

As I walked on South-East, the star turned in its tracks –
came closer down towards me now, I thought of all the facts.
To glass-less eyes He seemed as a compass needle,

pointing up and down
and seemed to say "all right so far - don't ruin this and frown".

I took the Wadesmill turning, the star turned further East.
As dawn emerged to warm the air, I didn't feel so pleased
to lose my friendly eye up there, I now know Who He was!
I kept on, ten miles travelled, to remedy old loss.

As dawn broke bright, He rose up, and flew into the sunrise
where He'd come from, the Morning Star, I lost Him from my eyes.
I grieved a little, passed on South and passed another cross.
Wadesmill, A10, traffic, day, another sane time lost.

Spiritual Experience Seven. 10th December 1983.

For most of November and December 1983, I was in the mental hospital at Welwyn Garden City, being put onto the 'right' medication for my actual condition, not some other, that at last, after all of five years, was to 'set me straight' for the next ten years.

Spiritual Experience Seven prompted me to *beg* the sender of all seven Spiritual Experiences so far to *stop* sending them. My prayer was answered, until five years later in 1988, I started to finally understand some of the earlier Spiritual Experiences. Then I prayed to see another one, and this prayer that the Spiritual Experiences actually resume was indeed answered, as we shall see.

For back in 1983 these six Spiritual Experiences to date – soon to be followed in hospital by Spiritual Experience Seven, as we now see, only confused and tormented me with their 'hidden cryptic future meaning or meanings'. Also, just as important, and very demeaning, they led the medical staff, and worse, my immediate family and friends, who usually 'turned away' as a result, to believe that I was schizophrenic *as well as or instead of just* 'hypomanic'!

In early December 1983, I was judged by the Doctors and nursing staff to be nearly fully well and without any symptoms under my new medication regime. As a result I was allowed to start having lots of leave from the Ward, and went mostly to my parents' house, and sometimes my own flat. Also I started doing 'occupational therapy', including Art Therapy, and also was taken on 'trips out' to do some voluntary 'social work' by minibus. The second of these trips was to decorate the house of a disabled lady near the Viaduct in Welwyn Garden City.

I was outside, having a smoke and a break from this decorating, when suddenly I looked up and realised I was seeing yet another 'cloud Spiritual Experience'. In fact, it was a cold, overcast day. However, there was a break in the clouds in the *perfect shape of the continent of Europe!* Right in the middle of the position of the World War I battlefields in Northern France, was the *upside-down shape of a large explosion!* Was this a 'peace bomb in the Somme', I thought to myself? Indeed it was, as we eventually see in the sequel to this book!

CHAPTER EIGHT

Interlude of four years, prayed for, of 'no Spiritual Experiences'

A prayed-for and well-needed – and deserved – 'Interlude from these Prophetic Spiritual Experiences' for four years, between January 1984 and February 1988.

I said just now that I prayed for these tormenting Spiritual Experiences to stop after seeing Spiritual Experience Seven – and that this prayer was answered until 1988 – until I actually prayed to see more!

I also said that I had two compelling reasons for not liking them at all. Firstly, just because I have a bipolar disorder, everybody jumped to the conclusion that they were in fact 'hallucinations' – which they have always claimed was in fact due to me also having 'schizophrenia'!

When I tried to explain that they were from God, and so counteracted my illness, by inspiring me to believe I was 'in touch with Jesus' and receiving help from Him by seeing them, all the Atheist Psychiatrists – and even all my equally Spirit-less family – just smiled knowingly amongst themselves.

As a result, after 1983 I generally followed the advice of the rock singer Stevie Nicks of the band Fleetwood Mac in their song 'Dreams': – "I've seen my crystal visions. I keep my visions to myself!" With the all-powerful 'profession' of Psychiatry having such power and influence over me, I had to protect myself from what these Materialist Atheist Infidels could do to me if I even *mentioned* such 'Visions or Spiritual Experiences'…!

Compounded with this was the fact that until 1988 I did not come to understand any of my prophetic Spiritual Experiences. Then at last I learned the basic and most fundamental 'fact of life' or even 'law' about such prophetic Spiritual Experiences – as for the many similar Spiritual Experiences to mine that are described in the Bible: -

"You only learn the meaning of a symbolic prophetic Spiritual Experience after what it predicts *has eventually happened; only with the benefit of hindsight.*

If you try to speculate about the meaning of a set of prophetic symbols before their meaning has actually reached the time when it has definitely come true in real life, you will only confuse or even torment yourself – possibly even get ill! NEVER try to interpret a symbolic prophetic Spiritual Experience in advance. The best advice is to keep it to yourself. If you see many such Spiritual Experiences, as I have, wait until the inevitable point when they have 'all happened' and only then write about them or describe them as I am doing. This, as in my case, may need a lot of patience!"

1984 and all that – when George Orwell turned out to be a few years premature

One major source of stress in the latter half of 1983, following our company's take-over by Fison's, had been the fact that our 'enemy' board member had tried to follow through his envy and hatred of us. He intended to totally discredit our product, by having a firm of consultants he knew, prepare a report on Lee Micromatics and the 'Microfast'.

So for three months in late 1983 I had put up with what I regarded as an intrusive interrogation by these consultants. Meanwhile Michael had made me a director of the company and boosted my salary by 50% when Fison's took us over. This compensated for this 'investigation' somewhat, as I was paying off a £1,200 loan from my bank which had helped equip my new flat at the start of that year – when I had gone a 'bit overboard' with my purchases! Repaying this loan now became very easy and comfortable, and after I was in hospital, that episode saved me so much money that I fully paid it off in January 1984.

So, 1984 came around with our 'Microfast' product fully approved of, in fact, by these consultants, who however recommended we redevelop it to make it a much more powerful system. In hindsight, however, their report was very flawed. They could easily at the same time have recommended we re-write it in the high-level language 'C', then rapidly gaining popularity. Also, they could have recommended we 'port' the software onto the then emerging personal computers. If we had been strongly recommended to do either or both, the company, I am sure, could have been saved from closure years later in 1988...

Also after my illness in late 1983, my ex-boss David at ICI, from 1980, joined the company – which was to turn out in the end to be disastrous. He could not adapt to life in a small company on a tight budget, and constantly wanted too many 'perks' without any justification. In the end he caused so much trouble, especially turning another employee against us, out of sheer pique, that my father had to make him redundant, and we have not spoken a word to each other since then (1987).

61

1984 was memorable not for Orwellian government, then, but for Board Meetings with Fison's members who were also on the main board of that huge company! Also I started a lot of hard work in redeveloping the system as suggested by their consultants' report – adding many more Z80 computer boards into the design, and putting a lot of the 'front-end' functionality into a separate PC.

We were at last able to recruit some staff – so I had help with the software from first Philip and Ballitch, and later Nitin, in 1985, and also supervised Peter on the hardware side. Meanwhile, apart from keeping the bank at bay, it was clear that Fison's were to be very cautious and conservative about their investment in us. They never spent a penny more on us than they had to!

In June 1984 I was feeling fully recovered at last from my crisis of 1983. I was still very much involved in my social club, and through it that month met a pretty little thing I will call Louise, who clearly 'fancied' me too. So there was a second 'two-night stand' of my life. This was ruined when she revealed that she was engaged to somebody else. As a result, I suffered the usual effect on my 'performance' that people get when they feel nervous or guilty about making love! She immediately 'dropped' me – to my great relief – and went off to do the decent thing and return to her fiance, to whom, I learned later, she eventually got married. So this, after my nine-month affair with 'Glenda Gland' in 1982, was 'relationship number seven' of nine so far in my life...

After this brief flirtation I wrote my poem "Midsummer's day Dream", portending that I was desperate to meet somebody much more substantial in her affections and longer term than Louise. Indeed, this was to happen a year later in 1985, when I met Helen, my wife-to-be, then at 25, attractive yet still a virgin, in a definite case of mutual 'love at first sight'...

1984 was also memorable for two superb holidays. The first was that May, when the Gateway Club took a mixed group of both people with learning difficulties and some physically disabled people from Manchester, to Sicily.

There, disability of any sort was and as far as I know, still is, very much stigmatised and 'hidden away'. The food – and lavish supplies of wine with mineral water – were superb, and we lived like royalty with the superb hospitality of our hosts, the 'Instituto dei Spastici' in Caltagirone, in the centre of that large Mafia-ridden island.   There were many outings in the week, and we even got the wheelchair-bound party down steep steps in one town to explore some extensive caves!

The most dramatic moment was when we stopped at one of the main centres of Sicily's 'mafiosi', and when the wheelchairs were offloaded from the minibus in the very central main square, the whole town literally stopped and turned round to stare at this unprecedented 'sight'!   Italians, above all the Mafia, detest and hide away any mental or especially physical 'flaw'!

There was also the delight of horse-riding on lively genuine Arab steeds at the adjoining stables – and the sheer joy of watching the expression on the face of a paraplegic boy from Holland as he was led around on top of a lovely horse!

Then in September I went on holiday with two female friends and a male acquaintance from my social club, to another Mediterranean Island, Crete. We enjoyed lots of Greek food and wine, eating out very cheaply most of the time. We hired a car and toured the island. Two of these friends, Dave and Marion, started dating after this holiday, and long since got married, with a daughter a bit older than my daughter Jenny.

My destiny unfolds in 1985 – meeting my then future Veterinary Surgeon wife.

By mid 1985 we were nearly finished with the redevelopment of the company's 'Microfast' computer system into its successor the 'Microfast 2'. In the meantime Michael had fallen out with his board and been head-hunted by another company – again to become a young, high-flying Director. After that most of his acquisitions while in charge of that Division of Fison's came under question, and among others we began to be pressurised by Fison's to perform better – as we still had no sales nor a finished product. Just before they 'pulled out' my Father indeed secured a sale for the now finished system – from a zinc smelting company based at Avonmouth, near Bristol. Celebrations were intensive – this had saved the company once more from closure. This sale was to be successful, and we were to sell three more such systems to this smelting operation by 1987.

This success was followed by another – the industry journal 'Control and Instrumentation' took an interest, and in November 1985 we had a full cover story about the system – the very month of their biannual exhibition! This exhibition, at Harrogate in Yorkshire, led to another sale to a maker of non-woven textiles based near Halifax, the following year, 1986.

In the meantime, the first meeting with my wife to be, Helen, was very amusing to both of us, and set us up for a lengthy courtship then our marriage in March 1987 – based as we both agreed on 'love at first sight' for both of us.

I said we met under amusing circumstances – again this was through the social club I had joined years before. She turned out to have moved into her Veterinary Surgery's flat in the next block in the very same group of flats as me, and we met at a 'cake party' that July, given by another member of the same club, where everybody was supposed to bake and bring a cake. However, my first line to her was "I've 'cake-crashed' this party! I guessed there would be far too many cakes, so I did not bring one!" This was after I looked up and saw her standing watching highly amused, while I 'spoofed' about five other people there, that I could with their help, 'levitate' someone with just one little finger from each of us! This of course ended in total failure – and gales of laughter from all concerned – and the onlookers!

Soon I called round to her flat, that led to a date, and after that I was totally determined to end her self-confessed virginity as soon as possible… This took about two weeks of seduction, but then we immediately realised we were totally sexually compatible, so the relationship blossomed completely. I had some reservations when I discovered that she was then 25, but I was her first ever boyfriend, which was why she had been a virgin till I met her.

Perhaps if I had paid more attention to those reservations I would never have got her to accept my marriage proposals just three months later. I made three in a month, as in my poem at the time 'Proposal Ode', the last of which she accepted. My parents were delighted we had got engaged so

64

quickly – hers were furious. They never fully accepted me into the family, yet were to pay for a truly lavish 'top hat and tails' wedding the following year, on 28th March 1987. I insisted that it was no later – two days later was my 30th birthday, and I had a stubborn wish to be married while still in my twenties!

We took a memorable 'bed and breakfast' holiday in the Lake District that Summer, with a lot of memorable meals, and absolutely gorgeous scenery around the various lakes, with long walks taking lots of photographs, in the memorable company of Helen's black Labrador dog, Gemma. I still have pictures of her swimming for sticks I taught her to retrieve, in various lakes including Derwent Water...

Finally that year came a working holiday for my parents and Helen and I. A I said just now, the family firm was the front-page story at the C+I exhibition at Harrogate, so Helen and my Mother enjoyed being 'salesladies' for a change. We explored the delights of Harrogate, especially the famous tea-rooms, for a week.

1986 – a year of happily 'being engaged' and an easier life at work.

Life at work saw orders that year, so pressure from Fison's eased off, but they still decided to pull out of the two year old partnership – very cleanly, I must say, due to their desire to 'contract back' to more traditional ventures than computer systems business like us. With the system finished apart from needing minor enhancements for each of our several orders that year, the pressure on myself in particular eased right off. There were many trips to Bristol, and Yorkshire, to sort out 'teething problems' with new systems.

So I settled down for a year or so of 'being happily engaged' prior to the planned wedding, the following March 1987. Helen had my illness fully explained to her in a meeting between her, my then Psychiatrist, Dr Gander, and myself. He was to keep us basically happy with my health for years...

Helen and I took another holiday together with my family that Spring, that helped our then happy 'bonding together'. This was with the local Polytechnic's ski club to Courmayeur in

Italy, where we went by coach – skiing started immediately after a sixteen-hour overnight coach journey. I remember Helen and I and some of the other less experienced skiers 'pootled around' on the lower slopes, while the more experienced skiers – and the rest of my family – took to the 'black runs'. A memorable 'budget' holiday was had by us all, in the company of many enthusiastic young students, and some of us 'older ones'.

Also that Spring came a 'blip' in my illness, that interfered with Helen attending the BSAVA Conference, or small animal Vets' conference. She was to complain several years later that every time this conference came around in the Spring – I became slightly ill, which interfered with her 'ongoing professional education'! This just reveals that most 'bipolar I affective disorders' have a seasonal effect – peaking with the 'joys of Spring'. However, we were both quite annoyed with this seasonal effect of my illness on her career, and its development, over the years.

That Summer we took a two-week holiday in Skiathos in the Greek Islands – where my sister was working as part of her multi-faceted career, in a hotel. This holiday was extremely lazy – and a 'beach holiday' – mostly eating out rather than cooking, as well as occasionally visiting Libby in her work. One memorable thing about the whole time was arriving at the airport – which was extremely small, and the aircraft had to approach steeply between high mountains – into turbulent air, guaranteeing a bumpy landing!

Finally, ending a year of holidays, we went to the Lake District that Autumn, for a memorable week of stick-throwing with Helen's dog Gemma, and many walks either in pouring rain or glorious Autumn sunshine. We had found a bed and breakfast place near Keswick that took dogs, so found a central spot from which to tour around and see most of the lakes – and 'sights'.

1987 – the year of my marriage – a new beginning – mixed with the 'beginning of the end' for the family firm – so a real roller-coaster year overall

The first three months of 1987 were taken up with two main activities. I had bought a marital home, a three-bedroom semi-detached house in Knebworth, a village on the outskirts of Stevenage, famous for its annual rock concerts at the local 'stately home'. We had only moved about two miles from the block of flats where we had both lived, and now spent the next three months decorating and equipping this new house. My flat funded this – Helen had no capital to put into this new joint house.

The second main activity was of course preparation for our wedding, set for the 28th March. This mainly involved a lot of travelling to her parents' home county of Cheshire for Helen – but I also went up in February to meet the vicar and have a quick rehearsal. In the event the actual wedding, in contrast to many Royal Weddings that also were taking place around that time, went perfectly – without one slip of the tongue by anybody. Then, the pressure on us was rather less than for such grandiose events – even though our own wedding was grand enough, with full 'top hat and tails' dress for the main party, over 100 guests with good food and wine in abundance – all funded by Helen's wealthy parents.

The day before, when we arrived, happened to be the day of the first of two days of hurricanes that year – the second was in October. I remember that as we drove up together in my car, we counted over 12 overturned lorries on the motorway! There were the traditional pranks with kippers in the car as we left, mostly 'planted', I remember, by my two very drunk cousins on my mother's side!

I had saved hard for the honeymoon, and had revealed to Helen just before the wedding that we were going to have an exotic time – with two weeks on a tour of the Far East – Thailand, Malaysia and Singapore, through the famous Kuoni World Tours company. First our honeymoon night itself was spent in a hotel in Dovedale in Derbyshire, about fifty miles from the church – which I kept secret until we got there. The following morning we had a sunny, breezy walk in that Dale, then drove home to our new home – now man and wife. There we packed ready for the trip to Kuala Lumpur the next day, which was to be a twelve-hour flight, with one refuelling stop in Dubai in the Gulf!

We arrived drained by the flight and slept much of the next day 'catching up on our sleep' at our decent, but cramped, hotel in the city centre. That evening we had some cocktails in the hotel bar – and Helen unwittingly asked for a 'rainbow' – which turned out to be a mixture of no less than *seven* spirits, in multi-coloured layers, topped with a coffee bean, then set alight on top! She got very drunk and slept in the following morning...

That afternoon we went on a trip to a Buddhist shrine on the outskirts, passing great poverty in the shanty-town round the edge of Kuala Lumpur, which contrasted vividly with the luxury of the centre. Finally, onto the stench and sheer cruelty of – wait for it – a scorpion farm, breeding scorpions to export to satisfy the requirements of macho animal trophy-hunters worldwide. A very 'masculine' exhibit for one's office desk...?

The following day, after two nights in 'K.L.', we flew north to Thailand – and a week in Bangkok. This was again memorable for its rich/poor divide, and as seemingly very rich tourists we never could ignore the poor beggars – especially women with children. There were many trips out to see Buddhist temples, very exotic gilded palaces, a floating market in the river delta a hundred miles west, where we bought lots of silk – and luxury shopping malls, in the midst of slums. In the nearest of these I bought Helen a lovely necklace made of all sorts of – flawed – Far Eastern stones, costing £200 or so.

The low point of the cruelty and 'low life' inflicted by Bangkok on its poor, came with a trip to one of the Red Light districts – and the famous 'Pink Panther' club. The way that young women were being degraded there appalled us, so we left after one expensive drink... Back at the hotel, by total contrast, we also bought two tailor-made but very cheap suits for me, likewise some tailor-made shirts, and various tailor-made 'outfits' for Helen... A lasting memory of Bangkok just has to be the incredible volume and noise of surging traffic, with little three-wheel taxis or 'tuk-tuks' weaving suicidally about. We only tried one once – once was enough!

Then another aeroplane flight, to the holiday island of Penang in Malaysia. Here we had a lovely time in a hotel overlooking a gorgeous white sandy beach. On the first night we met another honeymoon couple on a similar holiday with the same travel company, so we teamed up with them to swim, go boating, and drive round the area to try the incredibly cheap Singapore noodles and other local delicacies. Helen also tried lager beer – the local Malaysian 'Tiger' – for the first – and last – time ever, as there was no wine. She was decidedly ill on these five or six bottles, but very amusing just before this!

The final five days of our fifteen out there were spent in Singapore, where we flew after three days on Penang, soaking up the equatorial sunshine. We found a shop in a local shopping mall, selling camera lenses and hi-fi at very cheap Far Eastern prices – and bought a CD player, a video recorder and some lenses. We went on the bus to a bird park, and then sipped cocktails in the bar of the famous Raffles hotel. We visited very inexpensive food emporiums, similar to those, I understand, also to be found in Australian cities.

However, we both agreed that five days in that rather prim, litter-free, somewhat artificial and sterile city was more than enough, compared to not enough time in Thailand. So we were both glad to return home on the plane at the end of the holiday, even in fact having in the end found Singapore rather boring, and an anti-climax compared with the earlier part of the honeymoon.

Then we learned to our horror on the plane, talking to other passengers, that the duty-free limit per person was just £25, not £250 as we had honestly thought, and budgeted for. Hence we were very relieved to arrive in the small hours at Heathrow airport, to find no customs guards on duty then at all! So we returned laden with clothes, hi-fi equipment, jewellery, and so forth, without having to pay any import duty!

We returned from the honeymoon to problems at work for both of us. Just the week before the honeymoon, at my strong suggestion, Helen had got a far better paid job in Hertford, in a practice where she was supposed to handle both horses and small animals – pets. However, someone she kissed at the wedding must have given her glandular fever, for our GP confirmed that this was why she suddenly felt totally drained and exhausted on our return.

I will always remember her stubbornness and bravery in continuing to work despite this crippling virus, desperate to hang onto a brand-new and seemingly excellent job, with far better pay and conditions. Although she was forced to agree to work on 'commission only' as a result of this problem, and only to work on small animals, not horses, both were to work massively to her advantage in the end. A few months later she was over the glandular fever, after sleeping a lot, and had doubled her salary, which has only gone on increasing ever since, with ever better working conditions. Finally there was never any heavy work with horses – which she dreaded, even though at 5'10" she is very tall, well built and strong.

My work in turn was to start getting much harder suddenly. At the end of the previous year we had taken on two new staff, both aimed at boosting sales. However, Phil, who had come from the UK supplier of our Xycom Z80 computer equipment, found it was becoming far too expensive in comparison to the ever more popular personal computers. He soon left, having hardly made any sales, except to existing customers. Dave was brought in to market the mainstream 'Microfast' systems – but we only sold two that year. One was our precious demonstration system, sold in desperation to the smelting operation in Bristol for next to nothing over cost price. The other I remember well working on, and thoroughly enjoying the experience, that Autumn. This was an agro-chemicals system that I took on, after Peter, among other members of staff who had read the writing on the wall over low sales, left the company that year. (I was in fact to end up in the same management consulting company he went to in Stevenage, PA Consulting Group, two years later in 1989). In the end I wrote all the software for this system, even extending some systems software a great deal, then personally commissioned it at site – in just two weeks! That was the closest I ever got to completely installing a whole computer system for a complete plant – single-handed!

However, that was our last sale. Meanwhile the system that – unusually for a process control company – my father had skilfully sold into the Tate Art Gallery in London, failed to provide the 'kudos' and prestige we had hoped over its year of use since 1986. So the rest of 1987, into early 1988, was to see all remaining staff leave the company, while my Father and I scrabbled around to raise cash and fruitlessly tried once more to find a backer. The problem in hindsight was something I have mentioned before – we had not changed software to a portable language and were still writing most 'code' in low-level 'assembler language'. Meanwhile Personal Computers were readily available now at prices around a tenth of our obsolete Z80-based Xycom equipment.

Nobody wanted to buy from, or take over, a company using such over-priced and now obsolete equipment. Furthermore we totally lacked the massive resources and time needed to rewrite the code to run on a Personal Computer, as my Father had totally committed us (me!) to assembler language back in 1980. By the end of 1987 it was clear that Lee Micromatics ltd was doomed...

Helen and I had a break from both our sets of troubles at work that August, when we again took a well-needed holiday in Anglesey with Gemma, after visiting Helen's parents in Cheshire. The break finally got Helen over her problems, but my family firm's, and in particular as a result, my Father's problems were just beginning...

Then that Autumn, we decided that as Gemma was in her 'prime' now, it was a good time for her to have puppies. As a result, I drove her twice while 'on heat' to a butcher in Bicester in Oxfordshire, who bred such pedigree 'working' labradors (as used as retrievers in hunting). However, she did not 'take' to the husband we chose for her, a young and equally 'untried' dog who was years later to end up in the English first four team of labrador retrievers.

He was black like Gemma – so there was only a one in eight chance, genetically, that they could produce a yellow female puppy. So when I decided for us, half joking, that 'if she has a yellow bitch puppy – we will definitely keep her!' – how fateful that was to be for Josie, when she was born. For after my third trip down the following Spring, Gemma was kept there this time, and finally got pregnant by the same dog. Then on 5th May 1988 she produced six black – and just one yellow female – puppies. Josie's subsequent health problems needed all of Helen's skill in order to save her life...!

I have no record, nor any other way of recalling, where each of our various Christmas holidays were spent in these early years of courtship and marriage. However, they were all spent alternating between, or visiting both, family gatherings with my parents' or Helen's, along with Jem and Jane, his permanent fiancee, and sometimes her Mother, and of course my sister Libby.

CHAPTER NINE

A year of some turmoil – and the Authors of Spiritual Experiences revealed

1988 – a year to unravel earlier baffling Spiritual Experiences and then have my request granted to see more and know for sure who was sending them. Redundancy for my father and I – and his near-fatal accident as a direct result.. A 'slobber of labradors' – how we coped with and then sold most of Gemma's 'litter'!

It was the fact of Gemma's pregnancy, and the arrival of two kittens – Purdey then Steed, the previous year – that was to get me once more 'thinking about Spiritual Experiences' that year – after being free of their disturbing effects so far, while clearly not 'fulfilled yet', since 1983. Once more, after four years of peace from stress on the whole, work again got through to me, with the struggle to keep Lee Micromatics alive! So did my old – and two new – Spiritual Experiences!

I have already made it clear when discussing the Seven Spiritual Experiences mentioned earlier, that I only arrived at their 'true meanings' years later. In fact it was only in the Winter, into the early Spring of 1988 – ten years after seeing the first one back in January 1988 – that it 'started dawning on me' what at least some of the meaning of these baffling things had been.

I had drawn them all years before, which always allowed me to 'discharge myself of their power' and withdraw immediately from dwelling on them. Now, after four years of not being bothered by them, in January 1988 I once more studied these drawings, and began to discern clear evidence that some had come true, and in fact that Spiritual Experience Four had been 'completely fulfilled' by our marriage the previous year of 1987! This 'process of realising in hindsight' that Spiritual Experience Four had indeed 'come true', came when I noticed that my drawings of the 'eyes and ears' of animals in fact corresponded exactly to those of the three pets we had in 1987! The dog and two kittens even appeared in the order in which they had come into our lives! So it was this very homely and personal touch by Jesus in this Spiritual Experience that led me to 'perceive' the rest of the interpretation!

Definitive Interpretation of Spiritual Experience Four – see Chapter Five

Spiritual Experience Four – Image One. A skull warns of impending Evil, totally in the end destroying our doomed marriage.

Spiritual Experience Four – Images Two and Three. The fact that I saw "Angel's wings" approaching me from the dark above my bed in this Spiritual Experience, portended that in 1985 I would meet one 'female medic' or 'Angel' very important – my future wife, Helen – who as I have said is actually a Vet! This interpretation is fully confirmed by the fact that the remaining images in this Spiritual Experience seen back in 1981, quite impossibly if you are without any kind of religious faith, predicted events in 1987 when we were married.

Spiritual Experience Four – Images Four, Five and Six. I met Gemma, Helen's black labrador dog, in 1985; Purdey, our black cat joined us in 1986, and we got Steed, our grey tabby in 1987. It was only after our marriage that year that it ever occurred to me these three pets featured in a Spiritual Experience! Indeed, not one of them was even born when I saw this Spiritual Experience in 1981, so this is an incredible piece of homely prophetic imagery!

Spiritual Experience Four – Image Seven. Wedding Rings, linked. This was the clearest visionary image I ever saw in all twenty-one Spiritual Experiences! Helen and I were married on 28th March 1987, just two days before my thirtieth birthday – I was determined to still be in my twenties when I married!

Spiritual Experience Four – Image Eight. This image showed that our marriage was doomed! It is ambiguous whether these two black seals, just like ones I have seen at the Louvre and other famous museums since, portended marriage or death. Did they portend the death of our marriage, from 1993, some six years after it started?

75

Spiritual Experience Four – Image Nine. These six ghostly faces appeared one after another in this Spiritual Experience. They turned out to symbolise – in cartoon form, which as yet I had no way to recognise – my future in-laws from 1987 onwards! I have only spoken to any of them once – Helen's father – since Christmas 1994.

Spiritual Experience Four – Image Ten. As for several of my Spiritual Experiences – including Spiritual Experience Two – the six lights of Image Ten indicate a number, in this case obviously six, of years. Indeed it was six years from seeing this Spiritual Experience in 1981, to 1987, when we were married. It was then a further six years till 1993, the 'beginning of the end' for that marriage, as Helen could not cope with my 'mid-life crisis' then – such was its cruelty!

In 1988 also, lots of stressful things were happening to my family and I at once! In January my Father Bill finally persuaded Fisons that indeed, along with his fatefully awful choice of computer hardware to work with, the existence of a £230,000 or so debt to them 'on our books' was a massive impediment to being 'rescued' from liquidation once again. At last, but too late, they kindly agreed to write it off. Too late, because with no income, from that January Bill and I as the only remaining employees drew no salary, and in February he indeed applied to the liquidator to wind up the company...

As a break from all this, as I said earlier I took Gemma to "Henry's honeymoon hotel" for the third and last time – and this time indeed she got pregnant! We prepared to have the company liquidated around April, and face our remaining creditors (only about five small ones and one big one – Xycom – by then) in a daunting "creditors' meeting". Meanwhile Bill and my mother were also feeling the strain, and planned to go skiing yet again for a week in France that month just before the meeting, to escape from all the pressure.

Meanwhile, back to my Spiritual Experiences. For a long while I had been worried by my 'bright lights in the night sky' – Spiritual Experiences Two and Six had clearly 'come from the "Morning Star" – but they were, in view of my subsequent chronic illness each time, to say the least ambiguous! Had I indeed been 'visited by Jesus' on two occasions in 1978 and then as predicted then, again in 1983? Or were these eery lights rather more sinister – was this the 'enemy Morning Star', the Devil, making me ill? In some disquiet I prayed the following 'arrow prayer' generally 'upwards': - "Lord, please confirm just Who sent all my Spiritual Experiences so far - and please prove it to me!"

Indeed, a few days later from that prayer of 16th March 1988, I saw another Spiritual Experience, and in prayer was told to wait another 21 days or three weeks – for more. So it was that exactly three weeks after seeing the Spiritual Experience of 21st March 1988, to my vast relief, I finally had it confirmed that all my Spiritual Experiences come from no less than the Holy Spirit - and Jesus Himself!

Spiritual Experience Eight. 21st March 1988 - the Spring Equinox. I was in bed with my then wife. I told her I could see lights above the bed, as years before! She could see nothing, and said "Go to sleep!" Clearly, as so often, this Spiritual Experience was just for me!

Spiritual Experience Eight - Image One. The sun, with two orbits around it. Instantly I recognised this was saying 'two years hence'!

Spiritual Experience Eight - Image Two. One after the other appeared a total of eight 'military' crosses, the last one much fainter than the others.

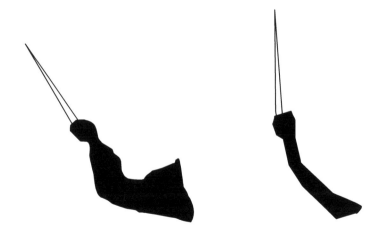

Spiritual Experience Eight – Image Three. Two glimpses of a sword being drawn then raised.

A lot happened that April, immediately after seeing this Spiritual Experience Eight. My parents, stressed out by all that had happened to Lee Micromatics ltd, went skiing – and my father was obviously very distracted, for he had a life-threatening ski accident – on his very first 'run'! He crashed into a chair-lift pylon – and cracked no less than eight ribs! He was taken by helicopter to the local ski clinic, and was in intensive care for several days. I remember after that I spoke to him for the first time by telephone at his hospital bed, and tried to lighten the situation with some rather black humour. I said to him, "What was the big joke then, Dad?" Bill replied, "What joke?" I replied very deadpan, "Well, a joke so good you fell down and cracked all your ribs".

There was no way that he would be fit to handle the creditors at the forthcoming liquidation meeting that month of April, so I took it in the end – and was very daunted beforehand – only to find that the only two creditors who turned up seemed to fully accept their losses.   In the meantime, I had a short nightmare series of thoughts, where I temporarily forgot my initial reaction as in the caption of the first image of Spiritual Experience Eight, that it referred to a time two years ahead! I speculated for several days, before fully taking that fact in, that the 'eight crosses' corresponded somehow to my dad's eight ribs, and so that the 'two swords' portended something even more terrible for my parents.

This feeling only fully lifted when they finally flew home by air ambulance, some two weeks later. Naturally I was very relieved to see them.   I was not to perceive the true interpretation of this Spiritual Experience Eight, as ever, as for all my other Spiritual Experiences, until the predicted two years had elapsed, and the event ominously portended had unmistakably happened. This turned out to be an important and dramatic world event, rather than in my personal life. The only one of my Spiritual Experiences to predict such a world event – and totally accurately!

Definitive interpretation of Spiritual Experience Eight – on 2nd August 1990

As usual in those days, I wrestled with the meaning of Spiritual Experience Eight, quite fruitlessly in 1990, once I had waited patiently for what I knew it definitely said about waiting two whole years for it to come true. Patience is not my strong point – so I prayed to Jesus that any more Spiritual Experiences sent by the Holy Spirit and Him, should be much more short-term. Indeed, in 1994, all of six years later, after another lengthy 'Spiritual Experience gap' like 1984-1988, I responded to seeing two Spiritual Experiences in one day by praying beforehand to see more while on holiday with Helen and Jenny. This prayer was duly responded to with three more Spiritual Experiences on that holiday, all omens of the following year, 1995!

All five turned out to be fulfilled, or clearly starting to be so, within a year or less, so my prayer was definitely answered! It turned out to be very important for Spiritual Experience Eight to come dramatically true as it did – in order to validate the meaning of Spiritual Experience Nine, as below, which told me in turn who was sending me these worrying things. This it did with a vengeance, in August 1990! I remember watching the start of the Gulf War on television, and like many millions of others worrying about what that August's events might lead on and escalate to. Suddenly and very dramatically I realised that Spiritual Experience Eight, which I had seen two years previously, had totally accurately predicted the precise date – to the very day, two years later – when Iraq would invade Kuwait and so start the Gulf War!

The two 'orbits round the sun' I had always known meant 'in two years time from 1988' when I saw Spiritual Experience Eight. Now it suddenly became clear that the eight militaristic crosses (rather than Christian crosses) symbolised eight months – with the last one faint, indicating the start of *August*. The two swords, then, showed the Gulf War starting with this invasion on the *second* of August 1990 – which was a totally precise prediction! Only God could do this, and I had this confirmed three weeks exactly after Spiritual Experience Eight back in 1988, i.e. who was sending me these Spiritual

Experiences, in a further Spiritual Experience Nine.   Not surprisingly I had realised that anybody – especially Satan – could *claim to be* Jesus and the Holy Spirit as in Spiritual Experience Nine – but Spiritual Experience Eight, closely linked, completely *proves it!*

Spiritual Experience Nine. 11th April 1998. Under the car at our house at Knebworth, changing the battery! As requested in prayer beforehand by me, the senders of my Spiritual Experiences identify who they are – and proved it with Spiritual Experience Eight. A Spiritual Experience formed by two clouds, similar to Spiritual Experiences Three and Seven.

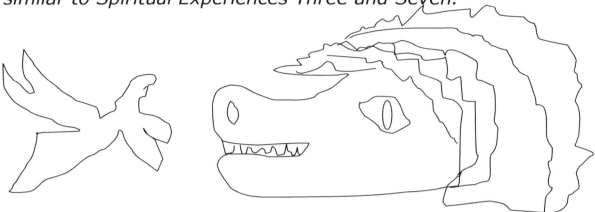

This Spiritual Experience Nine clearly shows a female Angel in conference with a friendly-looking lion. Angels are creatures of the Holy Spirit – so the Angel here clearly symbolises that my Spiritual Experiences came from the Holy Spirit. In addition, as soon as I saw the lion I thought of 'the Lion of Judah' – a biblical synonym or title for Jesus himself, or Jehoshuah as he was truly called in the native Aramaic he would have been brought up to speak. My Spiritual Experiences, then, were also from Jesus Himself!

Hence, after ten whole years, I finally had it confirmed, to my vast relief, that my 'hallucinations' were not that, like everybody including most hurtfully my own family maintain, but definitely *Spiritual Experiences*. Furthermore they clearly came from Jesus and the Holy Spirit Themselves!

The latter half of 1988 – Gemma's 'slobber' of puppies, redundancy, holidays and new beginnings after eight whole years at the family firm

Bill and I were made redundant late in April, shortly after I was greatly reassured as above by Spiritual Experience Nine – and forewarned that two years later something dramatic would happen, by Spiritual Experience Eight, which as I said, I had seen 21 days earlier. We both immediately started looking in earnest for new jobs – while preoccupied with the demise of the family firm this had only been half-hearted. I was to 'hit lucky' and get a local job as a Software Manager in Hertford, inside two months. He was to face eighteen months or so of redundancy, very solitary and depressing, before getting a job a long way from home (55 miles or so) in 1990!

Meanwhile Gemma was due to have her litter – her 'slobber of labrador puppies' was what I elected just had to be the collective term! – early in May. So while Helen worked I was on the telephone a lot to job agencies, and awaited eagerly the day when Gemma gave birth. This turned out to be 5th May 1988, and Gemma went into labour – and started to panic – while I was at home one morning, while Helen was at work at the Veterinary practice. As soon as the labour started, and Gemma started to get very excited and anxious, I phoned Helen and she advised talking to Gemma and stroking her, to calm her down. Helen would get back as soon as possible to give Gemma a calming injection. She had the first puppy, and did not know what to do! So I got her to lick off the afterbirth, and got the puppy in position to suckle. I went out of the kitchen where all this was happening to announce the first birth to the wife on the phone – and on my return – found Gemma had run upstairs, abandoning the first puppy on the kitchen floor!

I chased after her, and found her in the bedroom, shaking. Luckily I checked under the bed, and spotted a bag containing a second black puppy. Helen arrived at that moment, luckily, with the instant instruction to 'get the bag off so the pup does not suffocate!' This puppy, the biggest male in the eventual litter of seven, was to become the dog of Helen's parents. Helen calmed Gemma down with an injection for what she described as a 'milk fever', I got her suckling both puppies, then I was left with the job of supervising the arrival of the rest of the slobber, while Helen went back to finish her surgery. Eventually a *yellow female puppy* came – fifth in turn as I recall – so I again phoned to say 'my' dog had arrived! As I said before, we had decided to keep any yellow female puppy!

By about four o'clock Helen was back home, and announced that 'that was it' – a total of seven fine puppies – six black, one yellow. They were only to stay with us until the weekend, for Helen's father had agreed to build a heated pen for them at his much bigger house. We loaded up my car with a basket, one mother and seven puppies, and drove that weekend to Cheshire, and installed the puppies in their new home. They were to stay there until all but two – our Josie, and Helen's parents 'Flash' as I named him – were sold to new owners.

After installing the puppies in their luxury pen, Helen and I set off to Anglesey for a much-needed holiday at her parents' caravan. This lasted about ten days, then it was back to Cheshire to 'check' the new dogs were OK. It turned out that Gemma was getting a bit fed up already, but she had to put up with it! We made several trips up to see them all from Knebworth, in the next twelve weeks. Meanwhile I got my new job as a Software Manager – brought in to an instrumentation company to start their move into microprocessor-based instruments. This started that July, and we picked up Gemma, her new companion and yellow daughter Josie, and a large cheque from Helen's father for the sale of five labrador puppies – that went to buy a large Welsh Dresser!

The new job soon proved rather isolated, to say the least – I had been promised a department of four or five programmers, but the managing director was always reluctant to spare the time to recruit them. In the end, by the following July I had worked alone on designing and testing fully the prototype of a hand-held data logger with built in printer, that was highly accurate – and quick. I left on principle that July 1989, after instead of me being given a department to run, a 'technical manager' was brought in above me. This was not my idea of promotion or progress, or even support... The logger was sold by the thousand to supermarkets after I left, after new legislation required the logging of the temperature of freezer compartments. Having already left, I never got any reward from this massive level of high-value sales!

Back to 1988, and after about three months after being installed with both dogs at the house at Knebworth, as well as the two cats, we had both been installed in seemingly secure jobs. I was on a good salary, and Helen's salary was rapidly rising, and already far surpassed that of most of her contemporaries from her University at Bristol, whom we often met for various weddings and parties at that time. Then disaster struck once when Purdey, our black cat, got 'out with the Toms' and developed feline AIDS and died… Disaster nearly struck again that Summer when Josie, about three months old, developed a severe kidney problem. It took all of Helen's skill over a month to get her over this – but she nearly died very young. After that she never looked back, until she had a stroke and died earlier this year of 2001, I understand from my daughter Jenny.

So it was a very looked forward to time, after quite a year so far, when we went to Brittany and stayed in a 'gite' that September for two weeks with Dave and Marion, our married friends from the social club where we had all met, on a much-needed holiday. We ate out a lot, saw many sights and did lots of walking.

So – back to work for all of us for the autumn, and I still remember my father suffering over being out of work that year and the whole of the next year. However, we still managed to all enjoy a good Christmas. As I recall Helen and I spent a 'Labrador time' with her parents and their Labrador puppy Flash, from the litter, as well as our Gemma and Josie – as well as time with my family as well, 'down South' in Hertfordshire.

CHAPTER TEN

My prayer that my Spiritual Experiences stop again is answered 1989-93

1989 to 1993 – five completely Spiritual Experience-free years to be followed by five Spiritual Experiences in one traumatic year in 1994!

After seeing Spiritual Experiences eight and nine in 1988, amidst all the varied traumas of that significant year in my life, I prayed the following prayer: - "Thank you both very much for identifying yourselves to me as the senders of my 'Spiritual Experiences', Holy Spirit and Jesus! In future please only send them when absolutely necessary, or when I actually pray to you and request more such disturbing 'Manifestations' of Your Presence!" I got the immediate feeling that this prayer was fully agreed with, and was indeed not to see any more Spiritual Experiences over the next five years.

The five years 1989 to 1993 were completely Spiritual Experience-free, and it was all of six years after the last one, a long time from April 1988, in July 1994, that I saw any more. These two in one day – 9th July 1994 – were again unbidden, but in hindsight were clearly indeed 'absolutely essential warnings'.

So, the narrative is now Spiritual Experience-free for a further six years until mid-1994, just as we have just gone through another long gap – of nearly five years, between December 1983 and March-April 1988.

1989-1990 – I get a new job, Bill eventually gets a new job after nearly two years' redundancy, we move house from Knebworth to Dane End, and otherwise everything is calm and 'middle-class married bliss'... Helen gets pregnant!

As I said before, I always felt under-used and under-resourced, never being given a true 'Software Manager' role, throughout my time at my job in Hertford 1988-1989. Around

March 1989, as a result, I started looking for a new job. After several interviews I scored nearly maximum marks in the tests at an interview in nearby Stevenage, for a job as a management consultant with PA Consulting Group, where my old colleague at Lee Micromatics, Peter, had gone to work. I arranged to start work there in July 1989.

In the meantime Helen had been complaining that her journey to work, often on night duty as a Vet, was too far. One day a 'flyer' came through the post from an estate agent, advertising a four-bedroom house in the village of Dane End at an apparently very good price. We went to look at it and immediately put in an offer. We quickly moved in that May.

Also in that March we took a skiing holiday with our friends Dave and Marion, to Hinterglemm in Austria. We took lessons, and I deliberately dropped several classes to be in the same class as Helen, who had only skied about twice before. That way I kept her company, and ended up getting a 'complete refresher course' in skiing – even doing parallels properly for the first time! On many other holidays earlier in the 1980's with my family, we had not taken lessons, so I never progressed as much as on this Austrian holiday... The hotel food was excellent, and I also remember we all had our first ever massage with the hotel's resident professional masseuse!

I started my new job in July, and remember feeling dismally "I have jumped out of the frying pan into the fire!" For shortly after I joined, the new section I joined, to do similar process control work as I had done before, started being closed down! As a result, for the whole first six months I was put in a small room and given the irksome task of writing up other peoples' work. Hardly the 'frontiers of development work and high technology' I had been led to expect! I waited, frustrated, until at last the following January 1990, I was finally put 'on fees' – on a proper management consulting assignment in London, that was to last eighteen months. This again was a let-down – there were long periods of sitting in the clients' office with absolutely nothing to do, interspersed with intensive, but too short periods of high activity. So work for me in both 1989 and 1990 was full of frustration and a feeling, after Lee Micromatics and all that responsibility – of being 'under-used'.

My Father, Bill, of course, meanwhile felt totally under-used – until he got a new job far from home in Berkshire, involving a 55 mile drive each way to work, in early 1990! In the meantime he was supported by my mother, in her job as the head of the medical centre at the University (then Polytechnic) just down the road from their house in Hatfield.

I let Helen down in a strong way, meanwhile, for both her BSAVA Conferences – by having 'a turn' and being 'high' slightly on both occasions, in April 1989 (at Birmingham, as I recall) and in April 1990 (in Harrogate – again – as I recall).

In the meantime, in the early Spring of 1990, having been installed at Dane End for over six months, Helen and I at last decided to try to start a family – so she 'came off the pill'. Three months later, in May, she came into the bedroom one morning very excited – carrying a pregnancy testing kit definitely showing 'positive'! Soon it was time for regular visits to the Doctor, and eventually scans, and the baby was worked out to be due around my sister Libby's 30th birthday – 22nd February 1991. There was great excitement in both families – Helen and I already had her sister's boy as a nephew – but this was to be my parents' first grandchild! Then a couple of months later my brother's partner Jane also announced she too was pregnant – so the excitement for my mother in particular was redoubled!

Helen and I went on a holiday to Lynmouth in Devon with both dogs that August, and stayed in a hotel that allowed for people like us with dogs. We had a great time, Helen taking it easy with the baby inside her, and did a lot of walking and exploring Lynton and Lynmouth, and the North Devon beaches.

Back at work, she braced herself for not being given any maternity pay, under the revised terms of her contract after she had glandular fever when she started – and so to be off work for only as short a time as possible. Although there was a major global recession starting to bite hard around the end of 1990, my job was secure and sufficiently well-paid for us to be able to live for those few weeks around the birth, without suffering at all. So I continued to commute to the National Grid Headquarters in Southwark in London, Helen got ever bigger and prepared to work up to the last six weeks before the baby was due. Meanwhile my father and mother were much happier now he was working, and now had not one but two grandchildren on the way. Everyone enjoyed that Christmas – the best for a long time!

1991-1992 – Jenny's birth and first year of life, and signs of pressure in my work

Helen duly stopped work in January 1991, six weeks before her 'due date', and her final scan showed that all was well. We both got more and more excited about the forthcoming arrival, as well as Jane's new baby. Then, on Libby's birthday, exactly as my mother and I had in fact predicted, 22nd February 1991, I got the vital phone call at work in London at 12 o'clock, that the great moment had arrived and Helen had gone into hospital. I immediately got to King's Cross Station and caught the train home – and arrived at the bedside clutching a portable hi-fi to help calm her down – just at the very instant she went into labour!

The labour lasted until 8:54pm exactly – according to the clock in the bay – so only took about seven hours – with Helen not in too much pain as she had as much gas as she wanted. I played soothing music, talked to her, and popped out for the occasional anxious cigarette. I remember Jenny emerging in a final sudden rush after only several hard 'pushes' by Helen, guided by the midwives – as well as the perfect blue and white umbilical cord, that both midwives commented was totally healthy – one of the most perfect they had seen! They said, "Well you may smoke, but your wife clearly doesn't – you should see some of the umbilical cords of women who smoke – they are grey!"

I brought in a Chinese takeaway and some candles for us to celebrate our baby having a perfect delivery, and then my parents arrived and were very keen to pick Jenny up and cuddle her. We had decided on the name for her if she was a girl, beforehand. I can't remember what the choice would have been for a boy. Her full name is 'Jennifer Margaret Elisabeth Lee' – her father a bit of a poet is he! We called her Margaret after Helen's mother, and Elisabeth – with an 's' – after Libby, her Aunt Elisabeth, whose birthday she shares. Also, 'royalty'!

When Karina, Jenny's cousin and life-long bosom pal, was born a few months later, also with a perfect delivery, my mother suddenly had two granddaughters – and poured presents, mostly toys and clothes on them both – as Helen's parents did too for Jenny.

So – no holidays that year, instead a lot of disturbed sleep, even though generally, as babies go, Jenny slept very well. We turned one of the bedrooms into a nursery for her, and bought a cot that was later to turn into her bed – it was adaptable. The cats and dogs took to her easily, although we had to be careful not to leave her alone with the cats – for fear they might suffocate her. By now we had another female cat – a stray called 'Misha', a very pretty Persian, to replace the demised Purdey, as well as still having our grey tabby Steed.

Almost immediately, as Helen went back to work a few weeks after the birth and I was also working of course, Jenny started a childhood with babysitters, and then childminders when she started walking. My ex- now employs an au pair to look after her while she is working...

About then I ruffled a few feathers by bypassing the project manager at the National Grid Company and faxing the supplier of their software. I sent off a less than tactful fax about the abysmal lack of quality of one round of software updates they sent us, without showing him the rather undiplomatic fax first. As a result, my time at NGC was soon up! It was back to Stevenage in July 1991 at last for me, once more to languish with little or no work to do, until September 1991. I managed to get on a training course or two, and then picked up a few bits and pieces of work, but not enough. So the new manager at Stevenage warned me in March 1992 that if my level of being assigned to sufficiently lucrative work did not improve, I would be made redundant! Again, after redundancy four years earlier!

Meanwhile Jenny continued to thrive, a very healthy baby, and a big one – a thumping 9 lb. 6½ oz at birth – as in the poem I wrote that year! She met her new cousin, Jane's Karina, as well as Thomas, Helen's sister Anne's boy. We took her everywhere by pram, and about the time when I was being threatened with redundancy, she started to walk and became a proper 'toddler'. My ex- has at least let me have some photographs of her very happy first year…!

Meanwhile my father got 'stuck into' his new job, but failed to convince his new management that that huge company needed to develop something like the 'Microfast' product we had at Lee Micromatics. So, he continued to thrive for the next four years until he retired, as a marketing consultant, while my career was about to take a second nose-dive, this time far worse as by 1992 the world was in the grip of a major recession.

The final memorable thing about Jenny's first two years was that I got interested in bringing together all the Spiritual Experiences that I had seen to date, all my philosophical writings over the years, and my poetry. I called the resulting collection 'A sort of scrapbook'. The Spiritual Experiences, with more added as they have happened over the years since, are at last adequately described and interpreted in this book. All those poems appear in my companion book 'A Many-Threaded Tapestry'. (See the end of the present book for these).

However, this present book is mostly intended as a personal record, quite private in the first instance. Hence it is in 'Spiritual Energy', the public successor to that 'scrapbook', that all my philosophical writings have ended up, and gone on to be rewritten several times.

So, following my redundancy on 1st September 1992, I set up my new PC in our lounge, and set about the task of 'Househusband cum babyminder cum software engineer cum dog-walker' while Helen continued to work. I must have written to dozens of job agencies and replied to dozens of adverts – all to no avail, as the recession was so deep, and my skills were then not broad nor current enough for most employers. My three years at PA had really 'thrown me off track' as far as skills and work in industry were concerned!

To my disgust, my ex- now claims that 'I never played any part in looking after Jennifer, or her upbringing'. A complete lie – between September 1992 and October 1993, when I was to last only two weeks in a contract job miles from home that made me very ill, I was unemployed and seemingly unemployable, had zero income, was totally dependent on my then wife, but working flat out on: -

- Looking after Jenny full-time while Helen worked
- Looking after the house
- Working on my computer, training myself by redeveloping the 'Microfast' as a better product, in the C++ language
- All perfectly satisfactorily – and all at once, making me get highly stressed but never 'ill'!

CHAPTER ELEVEN

The real biting start of "Eighteen Years' Bad Luck (6+6+6!)" 1992-2010

1993 – and the real biting-in of a 'mid-life crisis' of a huge "eighteen years' bad luck"

As I just said, I spent most of 1993 at home, totally solitary and isolated in a small village, unemployed and struggling to do all the above major tasks simultaneously, while Helen was out working! This was probably the most bleak and lonely year of my life – I knew hardly anybody in our small village, and while I was off work we couldn't afford holidays. So it was only at the end of this ghastly year of mind-bending near-'solitary confinement' that I finally 'went out' in desperation for social life and started to get involved with the Church in the village, which was quite active. This was as well as occasional forays to the only pub in the village, just once to play in the pub quiz team.

In the meantime, back in 1990 my Consultant Psychiatrist, Dr Gander had retired, and after seeing him privately while working at PA, in 1992 I had seen Dr Jack Dominian in Harley Street twice – but nobody else in the meantime.

My family got concerned that I needed to be seen by some Psychiatrist at least right now, and the 'catchment area' for Dane End was run by the hospital at Harlow. That is normally where anybody else in my position and geographical location would 'naturally' have gone to be seen.

However, fatefully, my Mother knew Dr Gander's replacement well, in her role as manager of the health centre at the University of Hertfordshire, and indeed she was instrumental in having him appointed as resident Psychiatrist there, that year of 1993. She was insistent that I should see this 'Dr Whore' instead of the Consultant at Harlow, who by all accounts would been very conservative, unlike this Whore. So after a lot of discussion with my GP, mostly about money and the 'funding' by his surgery of me going to Welwyn Garden City

(QEII) Hospital not Harlow, I finally met this 'Dr Whore' as I have since come to call him after his appalling treatment of me.

Initially Dr Whore left me alone, saying I showed signs of both 'bipolar affective disorder, and slight schizophrenia'. However, within three months he had made the first of three very categorical and dogmatic changes of diagnosis, and hence gave me completely new treatments. Over the next eighteen months he was to completely change both my diagnosis and treatment no less than three times, making me far more ill, not better, each time!

First of all he declared that my diagnosis of 'affective disorder' did not feature in the theoretical model he adhered to, the DSM IV model from the USA. Years later, when my family and I actually read this book, we found that was a complete and strangely sinister lie! DSM IV fully documents both schizo-affective disorders, which most Psychiatrists had up to now said I suffered from, and the closely related bipolar (I) affective disorder, which I and my family always felt much more appropriate. This has since been fully vindicated by my entire new medical team!

His attitude to my then, by and large, highly successful treatment with haloperidol and lithium of the last ten years, that had enabled me to work in industry all that time, was even more bizarre. He dismissed it to us as a 'fudge', and first reduced, then altogether stopped my haloperidol depot injections, then doubled the lithium level – to fit a treatment now for a new diagnosis of 'bipolar affective disorder'! Having not been hospitalised for ten years, I was not wary enough of his 'bribe' to achieving this drastic change, of stopping depot injections. Also at that early stage I was taken in by his reputation, as relayed through my own mother – that he was 'brilliant'! – which turned out to be far from the truth, at least as far as his appalling two years of treatment of me was concerned!

Meanwhile, by October I was starting to get approached to do work, based on what I could now put down on my CV about work I had done that year – albeit at home, but of course that did not feature – on both C++ and the X-windows graphical windowing system. So it was that in October, having been unemployed for over a year, I was interviewed for such work at a company in Bicester, 60 miles from home. Gemma's mate Henry came from there, you will recall. I was so pleased to be offered a job that I took on travelling 120 miles each day cross-country, far too lightly.

When the stress of that, and getting to work by 8.30 am each day, started getting to me, on top of now having no haloperidol in my system as before, I rapidly got so 'high' that I had to stop working inside two weeks. Rather my employer terminated my contract on the grounds that I was clearly ill, and behaving erratically! We had bought an expensive Peugeot 505 estate car on the strength of this contract job, and now had to pay the instalments on this out of just Helen's salary, as legally I could claim no benefits as I was technically working for my own company. I had started a job at Milton Keynes, nearly as difficult and time-consuming to get to, back in March, but left it after three days – not through stress but because the working conditions and travelling were so utterly bleak.

This contract job in October 1993, however, had a much worse and totally devastating effect on my health. Indeed, looking back, I was sick from then, under Dr Whore's 'tutelage' and alleged 'care', from October 1993 to October 1995 – two whole continual years of illness! No wonder my recovery since is going in huge fits and starts!

So a very tough year for our immediate family ended with an unhappy Christmas – with me now made very ill by Whore changing me off vital medication through a very arrogant, first totally wrong decision, of all of three. As soon as I had returned to the stress of a job far from home, this appalling change of treatment and lack of judgement made me extremely ill back in 1993!

In the meantime we had no holiday that year, so had no let-up from the tight confinement of a lonely existence in a small parochial village. Helen got more contact with other villagers than myself, as Jenny's mother. It was through these contacts, even though we were funding this through her salary alone, that we found a child-minder for Jenny, now nearly two years old, for the several months that Winter that I was too incapacitated to resume looking after her as for most of 1993. I remember we all felt very desperate about my illness – and yet nobody thought to ask Whore to restore my haloperidol.

Indeed, he was now starting to mutter blackly that I might not in fact be manic-depressive but schizophrenic. 1994 and 1995 were to see that change of view destroy me!

CHAPTER TWELVE

A year of a Crucifixion experience – 1994

1994 - Another misguided and desperate attempt to return to work ends in disaster – and hospital again after 'ten years out'! The first of four 'Crucifixion experiences' there, over the next five years, totalling two whole years in mental hospitals. A flurry of all of five Spiritual Experiences, the most ever in one year. As I indeed requested Jesus back in 1988, these were all 'short term predictive omens'. Baptism of the Holy Spirit, the Gift of Tongues, help from my Church.

1994 started where 1993 left off – with me again out of work, and looking after Jenny, and working downstairs on my computer, with us now very impoverished, only being on one income. It was not until April that year that I claimed Invalidity Benefit, as it then was, and not until November that I realised that I could claim back to the start of November 1993 – when I got a couple of large 'windfalls' that lasted some months, from the Benefit people!

Desperately lonely, and with the family, especially Helen, pressurising me to go out to work while off the haloperidol I needed, and so really quite ill, I decided to get involved with local social activity. Helen encouraged me, and for the first time in my life, despite having written 'spiritual' writing off my own bat, I got involved with the active local Church, as well as, whenever I could afford it, going to the village pub for a drink. This way, I got involved quickly in going to neighbours' houses once a week, for 'Bible study', and virtually the first topic was 'the fruits of the Spirit'. After reflection on the booklet we used, I indeed totally revised my 'Tree of Life Diagram' as illustrated my other book 'Spiritual Energy', to very nearly its current form.

I went to many such 'House Groups' as well as the very different, far more conventional Church Services in the first few months of 1994. It turned out that there was a lot of resentment in the local Church-going populace about the very 'Victorian', 'old-fashioned' style of services. Indeed, since I was forcibly made never to return to that village, in 1995, they have replaced Bert, the very caring but 'old-fashioned' Vicar, with a woman Vicar – and no doubt have replaced the pews with soft seats, and hymns with modern 'spiritual songs'. The latter had already started the last ever time I went there, late in 1994.

At about the same time, down to 'lack of hard cash' rather than any 'spiritual zeal', I gave up smoking – for the second time since 1983, when everything also went wrong as a result, directly afterwards. Helen and my Nursing Sister mother of course really approved of this major move! I had no benefit money to pay for my 'habit', and Helen simply could not afford to subsidise it any longer...

At the same time, early Spring 1994, as I said the whole family put pressure on me, now slowly 'getting better' after November 1993 and my fateful change and drastic reduction in medication just before that – to 'get a job'! The recession was still very fierce – but after several offers, I eventually took such a 'contract job' in early March 1994. In hindsight this was very foolish – a full 110 miles away in the 'Black Country' in Loughborough, a full three hours drive each way in our (still with us, and still very expensive) Peugeot 505 Estate car!

Crazily, I had no savings to start such a job – but took it, desperate for cash, even though on the wrong medication as prescribed by Dr 'Whore', this was doomed to failure. I was recommended a very cheap 'bed-sit' bed and breakfast place on the 'wrong' – industrial – side of town near the factory where I was working. Apprehensive of losing this job like the last, through illness, I took this advice from the people who interviewed me, rather than get a hotel room in the much more obviously pleasant residential side of town. Until I got my first pay cheque as a 'contract employee, or contractor' I felt terrified of risking using my credit card for such a hotel room.

Not a good way to start on a new job so far from home! Looking back I was clearly still ill, and had been pushed into this position of working while made ill by Dr Whore, by a close family desperate that I should in fact work, whatever my state of health! I was to last a little longer than before, then plunge into another, this time very serious illness for which I was hospitalised – which was drastically exacerbated by another complete change of diagnosis and thence treatment by 'Doctor'

Whore! So started the first of five 'trips to Hell and back' in seven years, between 1994 and 2000.

Suffice it to say – this contract job, so very far from home, was 'Hell – in the Black Country' as immortalised by D. H. Lawrence for me in my youth.

The entire department that I joined, turned out to have left the company, in despair at the conditions, some months before, in the middle of developing software for an important contract! So I was the only one there, assisted by a long-haired, somewhat 'hippy' youth from an adjacent department.

I was loosely informed that 'some programmer who had now left' had written a lot of C++ code that nobody else in the company understood. Could I decide whether the company could use this set of programs? Asked whatever I needed by Merek, the Polish section manager, I was so alarmed by the prospect of this desperately under-resourced and isolated 'job' that all I could think of to ask for, was some replacement chairs for the section! The old existing ones had jagged edges of metal showing in the arms… In the end, some mercifully few weeks later, this apparently simple request backfired on me and ended the job!

Of course, this C++ code was entirely undocumented, so I spent the first week printing out the code, a two-foot-high pile of listings, and staring at it. The lack of technical information about it was stunning – the person who took me on was rarely available, yet was the only one in the company with anything (very little in fact) to say about it. As with my previous job in Bicester in 1993, this feeling of 'working in a complete vacuum', combined with living out of a very bleak bed-sit, far from home, and above all being on totally the wrong medication, with no neuroleptic tranquilliser, i.e. haloperidol, soon made me very ill. About three weeks into this job, I 'flipped' in despair, and complained to my astonished 'hippy colleague', with the obviously outrageous statement 'I HATE computers!' No doubt, some weeks later, when the entire department threatened to have a 'mass meeting' about me, this was one major reason!

At about the same time, I was living in the crummy bed-sit, with only a – very broken – TV for entertainment. Its screen was distorted and red! Even though the next week I got my radio/cassette/CD player from home, it only slightly relieved the tedium. In increasing despair at the 'vacuum' at work, and becoming increasingly close to 'high', finally, on 16th March 1994, I took to reading some Christian magazines and books I had been lent by Charles, the retired rather than active Vicar of the two in Dane End at the time.

I read in one book about the 'Baptism of the Holy Spirit' and how wonderful it was – and how anybody who really needed it, would be granted it if they prayed honestly and sincerely for it. By now I felt totally lost, and pressurised to work in a weird job, far from home, from a totally isolated bed-sit, getting more and more ill and so 'weird' and depressed feeling.

I immediately knelt and prayed desperately for this lovely 'Baptism' – and immediately Received It – with a powerful feeling of 'being accompanied and helped' that was not to leave me for the next few crucial months, and indeed till today. I found myself saying a few very lovely words, haltingly, in a strange language, and knew I had been given the beginnings of the 'Gift of Tongues'.

This was only to be made fluent in me later that year, but was to be a real help and Healing Force in the years between then and now. I have since developed *two* such fluent Gifts of Tongues...

I kept ringing Helen to say I could not cope, many times from the phone box on the street corner. In the end after about three weeks she said 'transfer to a hotel'. By now my first weekly pay cheque had come through, so I felt able to make this step. I moved first to a local hotel, still in the 'industrial area' of Loughborough. I was only to manage a few days there, as it was very rough, and on my third night in the very rough bar, some local hoodlum stood behind me.

In the bar mirror I could clearly see him shaking with rage at something or somebody – me? I remember that the line came clearly to my mind from a favourite Bob Dylan song, 'there are eyes staring clear at the back of your head as you drink!' I panicked, and very full of fear at this 'threat', checked out of that hotel at midnight that very night, and checked into one in the residential, far less rough part of town, the same night. Helen was furious at this waste of money – and obvious illness – yet on the phone insisted I kept working! In hindsight

– how non-understanding, unsympathetic and cruel can one get?

The following week I broke down completely, missing a vital part of my 'medication' thanks to 'Doctor' Whore. I had been hearing and reading a lot about 'black holes' especially as described by my fellow Old Albanian Stephen Hawking, and had been getting – in view of my then highly recent 'Baptism of the Holy Spirit' –very 'ethical' about them. While I continued to try to 'overcome impossible odds' at work and made no progress at all, the Church's 'Jim' (Jesus in me) campaign was also launched that Spring, and I got involved in it in a local Church in Loughborough.

So – Black Holes, and the possibility of 'black hole machines' – chronic emerging illness – Heavy Spirituality – all combined to make me very ill. Soon I was imagining there was even a 'black hole' in the black spherical car compass in my car! In the end, I got totally paranoid about this, and drove the car by a wild route about twenty miles outside Loughborough, in the middle of the night, trying to 'confuse the black hole' as I saw it in my confused state. I remember dumping the car compass – black hole? – on a heap of gravel on a remote road!

I drove back to Loughborough at dawn in a very deluded state, convinced vaguely of having achieved some 'major victory'! To celebrate, I decided to take the next day off with '"flu" – and immediately resumed smoking – a cigar to celebrate my 'victory' – at 7a.m.!

Helen had finally appreciated too late the previous weekend that I could not cope, and brought our three-year old daughter Jenny up to see me. Even though I was clearly getting very ill, and was very agitated while we walked around a local moorland park, she refused to let me yet again 'back out of a job – through acute illness'! Yet again she showed how cruel and un-fellow-feeling she is! Yet the job was soon doomed to end anyhow!

I took increasing time off work with 'flu the following week – totally untrue, but I could think of nothing better. I was now extremely ill, and desperate to go home and forget this terrible job – and town, as I saw it! In the end I saw the long-promised new chairs arrive, but disappear because surrounding sections were envious that I had ordered new chairs... I later reliably heard that their trivial anger over this 'favouritism' was the major reason why they asked for a 'mass meeting' about my 'arrogant behaviour' – mostly over daring to ask for chairs that were at least safe, not dangerous!

However, I signed off that week, very ill now, and headed South, totally unsure about my future. Immediately I was seen by 'Doctor Whore', who in particular probed about my thoughts about 'black holes equating to evil spirits' – now featured, most of my thoughts anyhow, in my other book! Pretty soon after this I learned that he had completely changed my diagnosis and treatment – just on the casual basis of a five-minute interview! He handed me a prescription for the anti-schizophrenic drug 'rispiridone', and said: - "I am changing your diagnosis from 'bipolar affective disorder' to 'mild schizophrenic'! Take this drug INSTEAD of lithium – IT WILL MAKE YOU WELL inside six weeks!" Typically over-confident, over the top, melodramatic, and arrogant!

Indeed, exactly six weeks later I was suffering terribly, confined on his Welwyn (Acute) Ward, getting rapidly worse under his 'care'...

After two weeks at home, I finally agreed to go in for a 'couple of weeks' to Mymms Ward, the Open Ward at the QEII (the Queen Elizabeth II Hospital at Welwyn Garden City, Hertfordshire). Instead of getting better like Whore had promised – I was getting steadily worse! This was agreed with Helen, my parents and I to be on a 'care share' basis – they would have me home as much as possible, while I stayed every day – and most nights – in hospital.

However, I found Mymms Ward terribly restrictive and indeed BORING – and soon started walking out for long 'treks' around the local area – as far as Mill Green, about two miles ago, and the town centre, three miles away. This 'long walking' went on – day or evening, for two weeks – while I only found a few interesting people 'on the Ward' to talk to. As a result my feet eventually got terribly bloody and cut up, and I got very ill...

At the end of two weeks of strong tranquillisers, and rispiridone, replacing now ten years of lithium and haloperidol treatment, I was getting very confused and indeed very ill under these conditions, and 'Doctor' Whore's treatment – and such abuse…!

In the end, very concerned about my feet, I went to the casualty department, as Mymms Ward showed no care, nor concern over them. I made the mistake of stating boldly which Ward of the hospital I came from. Instantly there was a 'conference of Doctors' – and I was sent away with no treatment at all! This happened once more. On the third time, a very full 'conference of Doctors' was called – and they opted to get a laughing, mocking Nurse to bandage my entire legs – utterly cynically and cruelly ignoring the real problem, my agonised FEET!

At the end of two weeks, I was totally bored, frustrated and very ill – yet a very lovely female patient complimented me on my personality – and often playing nice music on the radio/cassette I had brought in – by saying "You are like Jesus! You *are* Jesus, aren't you, Simon!" In view of my recent 'Baptism of the Holy Spirit', I had to deny this – but it turned out to be a great help when I was transferred upstairs to the infamous 'Welwyn Ward' a couple of days later, to have such a compliment. Despite my current traumas, I wasn't such a bad bloke after all, according to this view of me, honestly expressed…!

In the midst of all this time on Mymms Ward and eventually the Acute Ward, Welwyn Ward, at the QEII Hospital, I was to spend quite a lot of time either at home or my parents' home, at least in the first three weeks. I thought back to my time on Welwyn Ward in 1983, and went 'upstairs' there eventually effectively 'kicking and screaming'. Shortly after I went there, I went home overnight, as part of the 'care/share' arrangement with Helen and my parents, and as a direct result of this trip there was a disastrous incident. Off my normal drugs I was now taking, under 'Doctor' Whore's cruel insistence, a whole raft of other tranquillisers. These were diazepam (valium), lorazepam, the new rispiridone (which had patently failed to produce the promised 'miracle cure in six weeks'!), haloperidol, and a drug that totally destroyed me, thiorodazine or 'melleril' (its trade name). It has always made my head swirl – very drastically!

That fateful night in May 1994 at home, and very relieved to be so, from Welwyn Ward, but very confused – by all these drugs – I took the full dose and fell asleep. When I woke up I simply forgot I had taken this massive 'cocktail of tranquillisers' – and took a second dose of the whole lot. These drugs are all known – like all anti-psychotic drugs – to make your throat very dry. Taking such an accidental 'overdose' made me feel very close to death – I could not breathe, my voice croaked, and on top I felt very extremely ill indeed!

In the middle of the night I got up, leaving Helen and Jenny in bed, and wandered aimlessly around the house for half the night, feeling close to death, very much suffering from this accidental overdose, and unable to breathe properly.

Helen appeared with Jenny in her arms on the landing about 6 a.m. I immediately raised my hands in the air and, unable to speak by now, made a sound like 'this is the kill!' to try to indicate how I felt – I knew it was the drugs causing these acute problems – I felt they were killing me!

Helen fully accepted this true version of mine at the time, and wrote it down in her diary, which my parents still have. She only later turned it fatefully, into an 'attack by me on her' – totally lying – to get me evicted then divorced in 1995…

Obviously she was frightened, as I had been all that night, by my behaviour on this 'overdose of a cocktail of strong – and wrong – drugs'. She called the police in panic, and when they arrived, along with my parents, I took my chance and locked them all out of the house, with just me and the pets and Jenny inside. I was soon talked out of this 'siege' by the police, and was soon taken back to the Ward – by my parents. Significantly, the police, my parents and Helen at that time all dismissed the incident as down to the overdose of totally wrong mind-bending drugs, which I eventually recovered from enough to explain to them all!

I got some support from the Church in my village throughout my 'stay'. Throughout my total of two weeks on Mymms Ward and my succeeding six weeks on Welwyn Ward, Charles, the retired vicar from Dane End, was to visit about once a week, with a couple of visits by Bert, the 'real' Vicar, as well in that time. Just once one of the 'lay folk', Chris, who turned out to be a really pious bigot, turned out to see me – on Mymms Ward.

However, when I tried to get him to relax and fool around with a boomerang I had been given by my sister-in-law, he just looked very uneasy and indeed embarrassed. As if it was not 'manly or Christian' to throw a boomerang in a playing field! He could not wait to get home! Some people, like him, have such stiff, proud, arched, 'adult' necks, that they just don't ever relax them!

The final aspect worth discussing on the subject of my stay in the Open, Mymms Ward, was that I was allowed to do Art Therapy – and found myself translating my ideas about 'black holes equating to evil spirits'. I saw these appearing and disappearing invisibly in and out of their void – and had read that they could spontaneously appear 'out of nothing' then disappear – so strengthening my equation! I went on to start to evolve and draw my 'pyramid beast' diagram, discussed in my other book 'Spiritual Energy', in Art Therapy sessions 'downstairs' at the QEII from Mymms Ward. I saw evil spirits – or black holes – being drawn to, and being at their most powerful in the middle of, disputes over faith and religion!

So, in late April 1994, I 'went upstairs' from Mymms Ward to the Acute Ward, Welwyn Ward. So followed an even more disjointed and traumatic, and now nearly totally confined, six weeks. I choose now to gloss over it. There were to be some extremely disturbed people to meet – labelled like meat 'schizophrenic' like me – in my case, it turns out totally falsely – or 'having a bipolar disorder' or 'depressive'. I had my own room, most of the time, and found it had totally changed since 1983 – and was far more strict and oppressive! My fears had been justified, when on Mymms Ward! Indeed although 'Dr' Whore soon relented on my treatment and restored my lithium – so soon returning my speech to normal, from an incoherent stammer due to 'pressure of speech' due to not taking it for weeks – I got much worse. I gloss over the rest...

In the end Whore could not resist the temptation, and single-handedly (or was it along with Satan?) imposed a 28-day Mental Health Act 'Section 2' on me – totally illegally – as he got the necessary social worker needed to sign this to 'rubber-stamp it' – I had never met her! My GP only arrived two days later, but the 'Section' had already (illegally) been in force for two days. He tried to say that I was not in need of such legalistic medicating, but in the end gave way to Whore's 'fait accompli' – the section had been in force illegally for two days already, so who was he as a mere GP, to argue with a 'Consultant' like Whore?

There were various other cock-up's, some more sinister than others, at that time. Then I settled down to being on a 'Section', handed to me coldly by 'Nurse Bracket', and immediately inquired about my rights of appeal against this career-threatening legal measure. I put in for both methods, an Appeal to the Hospital Managers, and a Mental Health Tribunal, then sat back with the others in the smoking-room, with the portable hi-fi that I had brought along, and waited indefinitely for a reply. Unusually, very unusually, I was to receive the reply from the Mental Health Tribunal very quickly, within three weeks. On the other hand that seemed like an aeon in that awful place, in 'Drug Hell' as I was.

Indeed, while I waited very patiently but in agonies to be released from this prison, where I was confined to stay on the hospital grounds, I received the first of two great compliments from Glaswegians that I have received in such places. Jim said to me while in great physical and mental pain himself, "You're a really nice guy, Simon – you are a real Heelander!" I have since learned that calling someone a 'Highlander' in this way is the highest compliment a Glaswegian can pay – and to a Sassenach like me – is a rare honour!

As I said just now – I choose to gloss over the next four weeks of 'Drug Hell' on Welwyn Ward. I heard in 1998 that Jim, my Glaswegian friend, died on Welwyn Ward of a 'heart attack'. What a horrible way – and place – to die!

There were certainly many other very interesting characters there. Indeed 'Diamond' who features heavily later in this book, stayed from halfway through my stay in 1994, although there was no spark of any friendship then!

I doubt she even remembers me from then. Indeed I remember her as reminding me of being – literally – 'just some diminutive, long black-haired, physically attractive yet weird witch' who quite definitely stooped over me once in the smoking room – and waved her hand over my stomach in some bizarre, eery motion – like performing a spell!

My other lasting memories of that time are of endless chats in the smoking-room through a thick cloud of cigarette smoke, along with my 'music machine'… and the endless 'queues for "medication" and teas or coffees'. Indeed the cry 'medication' has since often sent a chill down my spine, for good reason, there as in a couple of other places since…!

So, after five weeks on that dreadful Ward, I heard that I had been awarded a 'Mental Health Tribunal' against Whore's treatment – although nobody from my family had yet dared suggest that his 'treatment' was totally incorrect – as turned out to be the case. I saw him as usual the following Thursday 8th July 1994 and – astonishingly, to his beautiful female Registrar's horror – in that Ward Round, he offered to discharge me! Looking back, he was clearly afraid of the Tribunal next week; having 'bribed me' with the offer of 'no depots' the previous year, he now 'bribed me – with the prospect of discharge – while still very ill!' Of course, he knew that I was bored stiff and eager to go home, so I readily accepted this bribe of coming 'off my section' and returning home – even though I still felt very ill!

CHAPTER THIRTEEN

Spiritual Experiences Ten and Eleven were very important!

Spiritual Experience Ten. 4a.m. 9th July 1994. A powerful impression of the phrase 'The Nine of Diamonds'

Jesus Himself was obviously moved by my recent 'Crucifixion experience', and saluted me as I finished this first taste of 'mental hospital' in ten years, still very ill thanks to 'Doctor' Whore being afraid to face a legal Tribunal about my treatment. This was with not one but two further visionary omens…

I remember my first night at home – my parents' house, at least – after all the traumas of Welwyn Ward, was quite disturbed! I found being in a home environment in a comfortable quiet bed, after ten weeks disturbed sleep in a hard hospital bed, in a noisy, hostile and extremely strange environment, was itself such a luxurious change it disturbed my sleep! I tossed and turned half the night, and then about 4 a.m., was wide-awake, when I had my only ever Spiritual Experience of *words* from God forming in my *mind* overwhelmingly.

A strange and as ever very cryptic Spiritual Experience it seemed too – from then until recently. It was the phrase 'the nine of diamonds' repeated several times! As soon as I 'got this' I received the prayer message from Jesus, "you will see another Spiritual Experience tomorrow!" I was very excited about both this strange apparition and the prospect of another Spiritual Experience coming the next day, and managed only a little sleep that early morning of 9th July 1994, until Helen arrived the following day without Jenny, for a meal with our family in the evening. Jenny was discreetly left with the new child-minder Helen had had to employ while I was hospitalised.

Everybody that day, like me, was very traumatised by recent events, and as astonished as I was by the fact that I had actually been discharged very irresponsibly – without the promised 'cure' with rispiridone of some twelve weeks earlier, as had been dogmatically and completely assured by 'Whore'.

We all felt, especially then, but not the following year, Helen, all our hopes had been completely and falsely raised, only then soon to be dashed, by him!

We chatted angrily about 'Whore' and 'the QEII' and their poor level of care of their patients, especially on Welwyn Ward. After supper, it was mid-Summer, so I went outside about a quarter to nine, to have a smoke. I stood on the patio or terrace looking north-west, and got a strong feeling of warmth – spiritual warmth – as I could see that there was a huge cloud starting in the West, amongst other clouds, trailing Northwards to end up over Western Welwyn Garden City. As for other previous and later times, this was a Spiritual Experience in the shape of a cloud making up a highly detailed 'picture in the sky'!

Spiritual Experience Eleven. 8.45 p.m. 9th July 1994. What I called soon afterwards 'the Solitary Sombre Seraph' – although that now seems misguided!

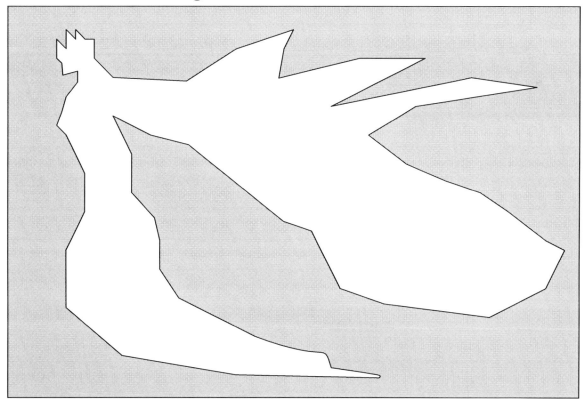

Immediately after seeing these two Spiritual Experiences, as ever with all my Spiritual Experiences, I drew them out – this time on my new computer. I had not seen a Spiritual Experience in five whole years, so knew these were very important to Jesus – and me. Of course, when I excitedly showed these sketches to Helen, and Bert, the Vicar, to see if they meant anything to them, there was a baffled and awkward silence from both of them! It only served to make them even more certain that I was completely crazy! These Spiritual Experiences were clearly only for ME!

CHAPTER FOURTEEN

Spiritual Experiences on a Summer holiday – 1994

Enter the Holy Spirit in Power!

As I said in the last chapter, I was to leave the QEII Hospital still very ill. I found that Jenny was now out of my care, and entrusted to a child-minder. Furthermore, 'Doctor' Whore had 'told' Helen to split me off from the main bank account, what with her working and me on Invalidity Benefit – which she obediently and dutifully did. Two major reasons for feeling very isolated that Summer... I found that, still ill, I could only sit around the house, smoke, and vegetate – further reasons for feeling like a vegetable! Looking back, Whore had totally disabled me with his 'miracle cure' of April!

The next few months saw little change. I was assigned an assistant Social Worker – who initially chatted prissily and in ignorance of my feelings. It was she, in fact, who warned that as the next stage of Whore's 'programme' for me, that 'they', in their 'infinite wisdom' had decided that calling me first a 'sufferer from bipolar disorder', then switching wildly to 'mild schizophrenic' was not enough.   Now Whore wanted to try me on 'clozapine' for 'acute schizophrenia' – and she terrified me by describing the side-effects of this poison. Nausea, vomiting, black-outs and in 1/50th of cases – blood poisoning – the white blood cells were destroyed by this drug, banned for years previously as a result!

She also got me a 'Government Friend' to visit me in my village – and he was about as appropriate and relevant to my background as a slug! Towards the end of that year, first he stopped coming. Then, in very sinister fashion, she stopped seeing me – and started having long private chats instead with Helen, about this 'wonder-poison', clozapine – not involving poor me at all!

Eventually I felt at least some inclination to rise above my feelings of 'mental desolation – and mental rape' of that Spring.

I got involved in the Church again in the village – and pretty soon, Charles, my friend the retired Vicar was visiting me, obviously very concerned. He was instrumental in getting me a great deal of help with spiritual healing, later that year, that was to prove highly significant, that year of 1994 and the next fateful year...

The months rolled on to September, and we at last managed to take Jenny on our first real family holiday – which at three, she thoroughly enjoyed and can still partly remember. This was to my brother Jem's second home at Christchurch, near Poole in Dorset. I remember very vividly, that Spiritual Experiences Ten and Eleven must have had a very profound effect on me.

I was very ill still, despite Whore's glib assurances that I was in fact 'very well' – to protect himself? Yet I prayed, and asked others to pray – that I should see other Spiritual Experiences (plural) on this holiday! I learned later that there had been some cruel mockery and abuse – not least among some so-called 'Christians' in the village – at this seemingly 'Joan of Arc complex' I then had.

Nevertheless, as we will see, I did see three Spiritual Experiences whilst on holiday at Christchurch! Their meanings were to turn out to be distinctly ominous.

Christchurch, and its famous Priory, on holiday, September 1994. Occasion for no less than three more Spiritual Experiences in 1994, to add to the two of 9th July 1994!

We arrived in Christchurch for our long-needed holiday on the afternoon of Monday 19th September 1994. We had been told I could not smoke in the house – so very 'wired-up', I was to spend most of our time at the house downstairs, while Helen looked after Jenny upstairs. In the end, of course, this was to produce lots of complaints from Helen! However, my main business on that holiday was to 'see Spiritual Experiences, as prayed for' – and see them I did!

Three weeks previously, full of the Holy Spirit despite all the ordeals I had been through, I had prayed to see a Spiritual Experience 'exactly on 21st September 1994'.

Indeed, a terrifyingly ominous reply was to come at dusk of the day before – in Jewish terms, the very start of that day!

Spiritual Experience Twelve, then, provided a lot of 'food for thought' – but strangely not much fear – as if the Spiritual Experience gave the feeling that 'however dreadful these predictions are, you have little to fear – I am with you!' At the time I saw it, we had been there just one day and Helen was already complaining that I was not spending enough time with them, but seemed very distant and very solitary. Not surprising really, having just prayed 'in stepping out in faith' to see Spiritual Experiences!

Spiritual Experience Twelve. 20th September 1994 at 7:50 pm – sunset.. A Trio of three Dragons, or 'Legalists', seen in Christchurch, Dorset. Portended I was to be under attack from the Devil in Person – imminently…!

After the opening horror of this, I was of course prepared for more Spiritual Experiences – but tried to enjoy the holiday as much as possible while still quite ill. We soon discovered the lovely harbour and marina at Christchurch, and as my sister-in-law Jane had advised, went over by ferry to the local beach on a spit outside the harbour – down the river from Jem's and Jane's house.

There we swam, built sandcastles, watched the swans, cormorants and gulls – and went on the children's train round a local park. Then we walked back through a long walk through reed beds. Jenny had her face painted at some stage that day, as I remember from looking at photographs from the time – like a tiger!

We visited various sights around Christchurch, in particular, and memorably, a local bird park. Jenny loved the Penguins, and doves – and recently recounted to me how we stood in a cage full of budgerigars – and they pecked at her ice cream, which looked a bit like a budgie!

On the Sunday I went to Church at the local Priory, a non-denominational, totally independent Church, which survives upon donations.

The service was very impressive and dramatic! On the following Wednesday I went to Evensong there, and as promised at the very end was given, in my mind's eye, two Spiritual Experiences – the second and third of the holiday!

Spiritual Experience Thirteen. 6 p.m. Wednesday 28th September 1994. Three Crosses – symbolising three similar meanings-in-one

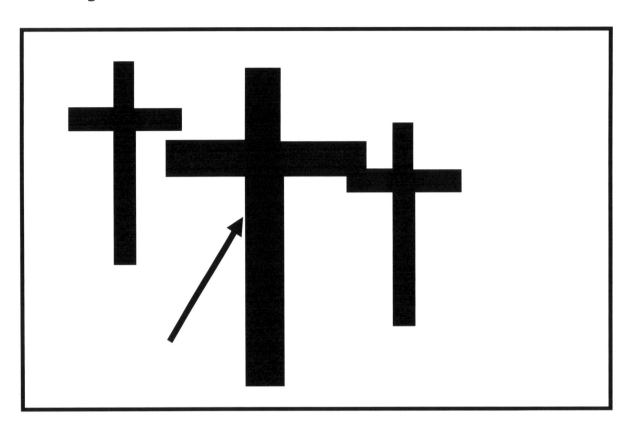

Spiritual Experience Fourteen. 6 p.m. on Wednesday 28th September 1994 – immediately after Spiritual Experience Thirteen, in prayer in Christchurch Priory, Dorset, at Evensong.

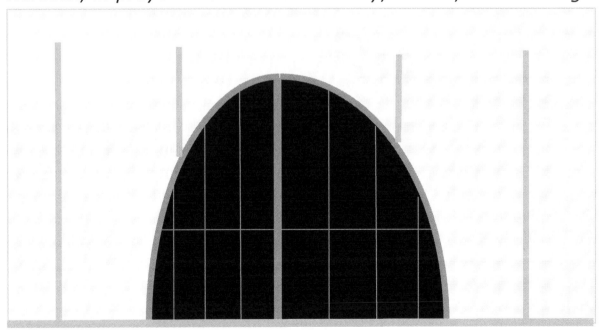

CHAPTER FIFTEEN

Spiritual Healing at the 'Harley Street of the Anglican Church'

The Autumn of 1994. Enter the full Wisdom and Graceful Power of my Goddess, the Holy Spirit of Truth Herself! Healing in Power at the one-time London Healing Mission. The Gifts of Healing and Tongues added to my Gift of Prophecy (as in 'seeing twenty-one Spiritual Experiences'). A fateful letter to the Government.

When we returned from our holiday in Dorset, I soon learned that my much-publicised 'prayers to see Spiritual Experiences' on that holiday had been the subject of some derision and mockery of me in the village – even among some people who claimed to be 'Christians'. By mocking someone who saw Spiritual Experiences they betrayed a total disbelief in the Bible – in which many people see Spiritual Experiences! Still awed by what I had seen, and how my prayers had been completely and immaculately answered by Jesus, I kept silent and 'above such imbeciles'.

I was still very ill, despite Whore maintaining at my now monthly out-patient appointments with him that I was 'doing very well on his new wonder-drug'! I was now in fact at the centre of two whole years of being abused by him and his allegedly 'brilliant' but quack diagnoses and treatments! At last the local Church finally woke up to that fact, and Charles and Chris offered me the chance to go to a very strong, but controversial, Church for Christian Healing. This was the then still very active – but since regrettably closed down since the retirement of its Vicars, Andy and Audrey Arbuthnot in 1995 – 'London Healing Mission' – often called the 'Harley Street of the Anglican Church' in Britain!

Charles and I went down there taking two hours, by several slow trains, one Thursday evening, and we met Chris in Notting Hill Gate where it was based. He had driven there after work, and was to drive us back. On subsequent trips by myself – about twelve in all – I drove myself down, and always drove back far clearer headed – until I reached a point where that feeling of health lasted all week. Then something told me that enough good had been drawn from that place – and I stopped going before Christmas. I needed to go again recently, but when I rang up I learned that it has been shut since 1997.

At that first service Chris knew what he was doing. He took me up to see Andy, who was taking bookings for individual healing sessions – one-on-one – with members of the team. I was booked in – but could only be seen six weeks later, they were inundated with requests! Indeed had I turned up with Chris and Charles some three weeks later it would have been entirely too late – for then the 'books were full' and were closed. I believe it is called "God's timing"!

The service lasted about an hour and a half, was very plain and simple, and I soon found myself being swept along with the surge from the first truly 'charismatic' service I had ever been to. The Holy Spirit was 'invited in' by Andy – and swept through like a warm, powerful breeze. The team held a half-hour healing session after Andy's "chat" rather than sermon – which was the first of many such memorable and very inspiring chats I heard him give over ensuing months. These were all available carefully recorded on tape at each Service.

In this healing session there was full healing by laying on of hands, of which I received a great deal at first, together with being 'anointed with the Holy Spirit' at least three times – I had already been baptised in the Holy Spirit that March 16th, you will recall. I received a great deal of healing effect from that very first session, and as I went again, was to receive more help, until the last few times there, the healers were no longer 'moved' to lay hands on me. Shortly after that I stopped making the long 35-mile trip there and back every Thursday, judging that in God's eyes I had received maximum help! Often people in the service would fall down, 'under the Holy Spirit' – but I never did. Such was the charismatic feeling of the 'Presence of the Holy Spirit in Power' in that plain, simple little basement chapel.

On my second or third trip there, I had a truly wonderful – and it turned out, essential, even life-saving – experience. There was the first Communion Service I went to there, and after that I had found it so effective I made sure I always got to the monthly Communion for the next couple of months. Afterwards, having discussed the 'Gifts of the Spirit', Andy asked anyone who wanted to come up to the front and be given the 'Gift of Tongues'. As I already had it in small measure, but felt it had been frustrated by the Satanic influences of earlier that year – especially in June – I was uncertain whether to dare go up.

In the end, sensibly enough in a chapel, I prayed a quick prayer and got the answer "Go for it! You need it reviving and strengthening!" Andy was clearly highly spiritually perceptive, for when my turn came and I went up to him where he sat, he said "But you've 'got it' already, haven't you?" I explained a little of the background, and that my definitely granted Gift needed freeing from the prison of the last year's events in my life. Immediately he started speaking in Tongues himself, I found myself joining in, and he said "There you are! There all the time! Just keep practising!" He got me to say a few words about what had just been revived in me to the whole congregation, then I sat down and practised by myself.

In a few weeks this suppressed Gift was nearly fluent through some practice. Tragically and sickeningly, however, when my so-called 'Christian' wife overheard me talking in my (Angelic, I hear after praying about it) Tongue, she immediately told Whore I was definitely 'hearing voices'! A two-fold betrayal – not being a real Christian and so not knowing what this lovely language was like – and telling my 'Doctor' it was really me 'hearing voices'!

Along with my Gift of Tongues I must also have acquired the Gift of Healing, just from being Healed myself, that Autumn of 1994. Because of my problems since however, it was not to 'surface' till the Spring of 1998, only fully in 1999. After six weeks I turned up for my 'one-on-one' session with Raymond, one of the healing team. He was quite an inoffensive-seeming chap, who however turned out to be equipped with a huge spiritual insight – and a similar 'arsenal' of Spiritual 'Gifts'! Virtually his first words to me, for instance, were 'You are full of the Holy Spirit!' So I told him about my 'Baptism of the Spirit' on 16th March 1994, and some of the awful circumstances of that year. I also described vividly my 'Gifts of Tongues and Healing' gained at the Mission.

We briefly discussed how the team worked. I was particularly struck, I remember, that they were all trained to go through the – physical – motions every morning, of 'putting on the girdle of truth, the breastplate of righteousness... Taking up the shield of faith, the sword of the Holy Spirit, the helmet of salvation – and putting on the shoes of the gospel of peace'!

We discussed my problems, notably that I deeply resented the diagnosis of 'schizophrenia' and that I felt I instead suffered from pure bipolar affective disorder. He said to me, 'Well, I am no Doctor, but you are not a schizophrenic! No schizophrenic could drive 40 miles and reliably get here by themself – through London and its streets and traffic!' This 'word of God' made a lasting, almost life-saving impression on me, especially during my abuse by Whore in 1995...

He went on to give me a two-minute 'saying' in Tongues. We both laughed when he said this strange Tongue sounded like Eskimo language! Then, remarkably, in a way that I admit envying at the time, he added to his Gift of Tongues – by interpreting what he had just himself said. Normally, 99.9% of the time, one person speaks in Tongues, and another interprets. Clearly, here was another like Andy Arbuthnot, with deep spiritual insight – and great spiritual powers! I do not now, after all that has happened since, remember that entire 'message' by any means. However, all of it was very true of me – even though he had only just met me – and so it clearly came from God.

Just three things from that message stuck clearly in my mind. The message said that I tended to 'get big ideas' – no harm in that, as long as the ideas are true! Then he said, 'you have a division in your mind!' When Helen later heard this, she hurt me by mocking, 'yes, that is your schizophrenia, like Dr Whore says!' When I tried to reason with her she just mocked me more! This 'message from the Holy Spirit' ended 'you will do great things for God!' – and that was it!

This trip to see 'Raymond' saw another trip arranged – for both my wife and myself to see him again, two weeks later. Instead, however, one 'Julia' was to stand in, and give us a Ceremony to 'exorcise our family trees'. We were asked to 'confess all sins, remembered or forgotten'. I confessed a 'possible' family sin of witchcraft in the dim distant past, and kept silent, and was appalled, when Helen neglected to 'confess' the Freemasonry in her Mother's immediate recent family. For her mother's immediate family are all Scottish 'Brethren' who emigrated years ago to Northern Ireland to farm...

Around November, I got up enough strength to do two important things. With more energy than for many months, firstly, I decorated our lounge – and painted the entire room very quickly. Then, fatefully, and inviting trouble, I wrote to Virginia Bottomley, the then Health Minister – with a bitter complaint about Whore and his illegal and very dangerous games with 'Sections and such'!

No wonder he was extremely vindictive, and totally abused his viciously-imposed legal powers over me, the following year of 1995! Yet should some young 'Doctor' like him have sunk so low as to abuse the power that the Law gave him over me in my weak position as his 'patient' – and thence entitled to care, not such abuse, even taken immediately to a life-threatening degree? I am convinced that the abuse rather than care that he doled out to me that following year, and got many of his nastier staff to dish out to me too, was due to sheer hatred and spite over this. Just one – totally justifiable – letter of complaint to the very highest possible level!

That Christmas, as I recall, was spent quietly with my parents – and of course Jenny. The brief calm before the full storm ... for the next year, 1995, was to be the 'annus horribilis' – the very worst year of my life, in which I was to lose everything! It still stinks of having seen a loose conspiracy against me among the medical staff at Welwyn Ward, in particular of course Whore. When they invited my dumb Vet then wife to join in – she relished inflicting such cowardly cruelty – on her own helpless legally-confined husband!

CHAPTER SIXTEEN

First third of 1995. Crucifixion Experience One - of three in a year!

1995, first 'annus horribilis'. Most acute 'mental crucifixion' of all. Eight whole months in mental hospital, forcibly confined! At the end of it, eviction and homelessness ruthlessly enforced by Helen – followed by divorce!

When 1995 started, I felt better than since 1993 – despite Whore's unwelcome intrusions and so-called 'care' – destruction in disguise! I had been receiving benefit since April 1994 – backdated since to November 1993 with Whore's sanction – so qualified to take a course on various computing techniques, at the University of Hertfordshire in Hatfield, starting that January.

With all my time at the LHM, I felt much stronger, so took this 'last-ditch' attempt to recover my tarnished career in computing. It was only to last under a week, before the 'conspiracy of incompetence – or was it something worse?' of that year took hold, and I was to find myself back in the QEII, on the Acute Welwyn Ward, under most confusing and painful circumstances!

This time I was immediately subjected to the maximum extent of the Law, short of a full 'Home Office Order' – a six-month, no less, confinement in hospital – with no rights to refuse to take my drugs for the whole first three months! This is called a 'Section 3 of the Mental Health Act' – just like a jail sentence, where you could not leave the hospital grounds. Today one cannot leave the very ward! I was judged guilty without a trial – or even evidence.

Now for the third and most obviously totally absurd 'diagnosis' he luxuriantly indulged himself with, about my case – 'amongst the most acute cases of schizophrenia'!! For young 'Doctor' Whore started giving me, as threatened for months, the poisonous drug 'clozapine' or 'clozaril'. I immediately resisted, despite the legal threats, because it had the most terrible effects on me, in that place terrifying, even in tiny doses! Above all, I just knew I was no 'schizophrenic'. I had God's word on that the previous year of 1994, at the LHM!

It is worth discussing the way in which I came to be there – and how I came to be 'put away' that early morning of Sunday 5th February 1995. I had been out for a drink at the bar at the University to celebrate ending the first week of the course. As everyone on it was on low income in the form of benefit, we were all a bit appalled at the venue – the Fielder Centre at the UH, previously built by British Aerospace and used to lavishly entertain rich Arab magnates while they decided how many warplanes to buy! It was still used by the UH to provide lavish, expensive entertainment for conferences, so while we ate our lunch of home-made sandwiches, and bought their very expensive coffee, the 'guests' were being treated to a lavish banquet each lunchtime!

Helen added to much torture of me, as soon as I was back on Welwyn Ward later that month, by claiming the course organiser had said I had been 'aggressive' during that first week. Why then, did absolutely everyone involved bear me no grudges and kindly buy and sign a 'Get Well Soon' card? She acted so weirdly from about March that year, that any amount of abuse and mental cruelty was carried out against me by her in that year of imprisonment then divorce! She has carried on relentlessly, over contact with my daughter Jenny.

What a 'Tart of Tarts'!

That fateful Saturday evening I drove to Hatfield from Dane End, had a couple of drinks and soaked in the atmosphere – then realised I felt unfit to drive. About 10pm I set out to find a taxi to get home, sensibly leaving the car behind in my Mother's slot – as I have said before she was in charge of the Health Centre there. That meant walking past my parents' house – I knew they would be asleep – and about two miles more, to the Railway Station in the Old Town. As I walked I rapidly sobered up, and as I approached the station and its taxi rank, smoking my pipe, noticed three obviously drunken youths walking along on the opposite side of the street, in the opposite direction. They called out something incoherent about 'pipes', which of course, alert to the danger, I ignored, and walked on.

The next thing I knew, there were running footsteps behind me, and I spun around. Before I knew it, my pipe was wrenched from my mouth, and a strong hand shoved me backwards in the chest!

I must have been knocked out as my head hit the floor. I remember coming round groggily to find myself lying in the dark in a subway there, looking up at a tall dark figure in the mouth of the subway, looking sinisterly back at me.

Then, just as I feared further attack, there was mocking laughter and he and his mates ran off. Furious, and with my only pipe taken and no doubt destroyed, I caught the taxi to Dane End, paid up the huge fare, and found that there were two measures of whisky left in one of our decanters. I drank those to steady my nerves and calm my feelings of frustrated rage.

Helen came downstairs from being asleep, and later totally falsely accused me of drinking the whole decanter – in a divorce petition, no less! I must have passed out, for the next thing I knew, she must have panicked – or was it all part of Whore's plan to force me to take a poisonous drug, clozapine? I came to groggily, and found myself, with no shoes, in an ambulance going to the QEII Hospital, about 7.30am on Sunday 5th February 1995.

I was interviewed by a young house-Doctor, but not by a Social Worker or my GP, and told I could 'either go in voluntarily – or under a Section'! There were no other choices, so convinced while concussed, that this was all a total set-up, on principle I asked for the Section! However, I was expecting just a 28-day 'Section 2' not the full weight of the six-month 'Section 3' that was now imposed. However, at the time I had no shoes, and could not argue when two burly policemen appeared, to escort me up to Welwyn Ward, on the third floor of the Psychiatric Unit. (I have always thought it is a crazy place to locate an Acute Ward, with many suicidal patients itching to get onto the roof!)

However, as immediately I was taken off lithium and put on high doses of tranquillisers of various sorts, as the previous year, and above all put on the drug clozaril, with all its dire, obnoxious effects ('side effects' they call them!) I knew I was in serious trouble – and a major battle with Whore.

I immediately applied for both a Hospital Managers' Appeal, and a full Mental Health Tribunal, my only access to appeal against this 'six-month prison sentence' as I saw it. However both authorities were to fail me totally in my genuine hope then, that they would soon see me, like the three weeks of the previous year's confinement. However, the Managers' Appeal was only to be heard two months later – and then sinisterly, I was given absolutely no formal notice of it. As a result, on principle, I refused to let this sham 'show trial' go ahead. Only my prissy then 'Social Worker' and my traitorous wife were there and knew about it, and my family and I were not warned at all!

The Tribunal only came a deeply insulting full five months later. By then I was at Fairfield Secure Unit, nearly at the end of the appointed six months of legally imposed confinement! Needless to say, although being shown some human decency and respect at that Tribunal, for the first time in five months, was most gratifying, my argument that if they released me from the Section I was perfectly willing to remain there voluntarily, was turned down.

For the first three days back in that dreadful place, Helen adamantly refused to bring in any shoes, and was very stingy. Having 'put me away' so excessively and cruelly, she now started compounding that with increasingly cruel actions, with no concern for my feelings, and not consulting me beforehand, for the rest of that year. Her father, it later turned out, had heard about my alleged and false diagnosis of 'mild schizophrenia' of the previous year – and looked up 'schizophrenia' in his local library! His comment was 'it must not be allowed to happen again – or else!' So Helen must have been under a lot of totally misguided and misled – by Whore – pressure from her very austere and old-fashioned parents, to do all the terrible things she did to me from then onwards.

When I asked her for my cheque book and bank card – she refused! Another insulting act – behind my back she had taken 'Power of Attorney' over my income from benefit – and was to 'eke out' pocket money, like I was some child, until I recovered from all this abuse, and so illness, in August! She clearly adored and relished this humiliating degree of power and control over me!

She also started to regularly go to see Whore in his office, meanwhile leaving me to languish on the Ward and not bothering to visit me. She must have fed him a nice line of breathtaking lies, that I saw hallucinations and 'heard voices', was paranoid, and had bizarre delusions. For there was no evidence of these ever in my stay, as there has never been any sign of any of these symptoms of 'schizophrenia' in my life. For all these things, along with totally false and baseless allegations that I am aggressive and even 'violent' appeared, as I later discovered, in Whore's report for the Managers' Appeal that never happened!

Catch-22! I am first alleged to be schizophrenic, so my 'dutiful, ever-loving, ever-loyal "wife"' feeds the 'Doctor' concerned with loads of fairy stories and lies – to back up that viciously and totally incorrectly applied diagnosis.

Once again, did my letter to the Secretary of Health of the previous year have a lot to do with this 'conspiracy of incompetence – and vicious "care"'? I cannot think of anything else I know of – but that by itself was surely not enough to justify such appalling mal-diagnosis (deliberate?) and equally disgusting treatment – until I 'escaped' from it on 11th May, three months later!

The 'care plan' went badly wrong from the start. My own appointed Nursing Team of three Nurses, again very strangely and weirdly, totally ignored me for most of that three months – and certainly broke all the rules, by not even introducing themselves as indeed being my 'shift'. The only way I found out that I was in fact supposed to have a 'care team' was about a month in, when I happened to read the staff notice board!

The 'medication plan' was soon off the rails too. For a start, particularly after my assurance from Raymond (and thence, God!) that I am not a schizophrenic, of the previous November at the LHM, I was fiercely defiant that the diagnosis and treatment was all a terrible mistake! No wonder I worried about conspiracies, with my own then wife and the staff mostly behaving very strangely and fiercely, not at all caringly. Particularly when one of the patients, Don, kept on and on about Freemasons, and that he was the head of world freemasonry, as well, believe it or not, as being God the Father, Jesus, and the Holy Spirit, in one person! Clearly he was a severe manic-depressive. After three months of incessant chatter from him about freemasonry, with me getting increasingly ill and feeling more and more abused by the staff, especially 'Doctor' Whore, I actually started to believe him!

The plan was to raise the clozapine level slowly up to the optimum therapeutic dose of 800 mg, starting at just 75 mg. However, I strongly objected – just 75 mg a day was enough to make me feel constantly nauseous, often inclined to vomit, and above all in that bleak place – to pass out, for two hours at a time, within twenty minutes of each dose! On top of that, although Sister Cathy and Charge Nurse David repeatedly and fruitlessly protested to him about that on my behalf, for reasons only known to him and Satan, Whore stopped my lithium and instead proceeded to 'bomb' me with a bizarre series of experiments with other tranquillisers.

I quickly stopped taking, on principle, any more than 75 mg twice a day, of clozapine, and settled into an entrenched battle with both Whore, and hence his staff, and worst of all, incredibly, totally on their side, my wicked ex-. A 'battle royal' ensued over my 'non-compliance' with what I knew was in fact for me a deadly poison! I just about put up with the fact that my passing out for two hours after each morning and evening dose, was totally ignored and regarded as normal by the staff, apart from Cathy and David! Even though it was horrendous, to pass out for hours a day due to 'medication' in that dreadfully hostile place!

Several times the macho hospital porters were called up in large numbers, to force me to have a large 'depot' of chlorpromazine and other nasty drugs to which I had an acute adverse reaction! The worst effect of all, however, was to be my reaction to being systematically deprived of lithium. My speech degenerated into a humiliating, incoherent, hyperactive stammer. My lovely acquaintance from then, Sarah Todd, to whom my book 'Spiritual Energy' is dedicated, now deceased, supposedly due to mixing alcohol with bizarre overdosing of drugs for depression, also by Whore incidentally, said this made her feel terribly sorry for me. Sarah was also appalled by the amount and intensity of bullying I underwent on Welwyn Ward, with constant threats of 'being sent to Fairfield Secure Unit' if I did not start to 'comply with my medication', especially the dreaded clozapine.

I just was not supposed to oppose the draconian use (abuse again, in fact) they were making of my 'medication order' or 'Section 3', and they did not know how to overcome such steadfast resistance. Especially as they were Atheists, and my fighting back while in principle powerless to stop them, was based on God's Word the previous Autumn at the LHM – that I am in fact not a schizophrenic like Whore adamantly and stubbornly maintained throughout.

Dick had been likewise punished for 'misbehaviour' – in his case violence – by being 'sent to Fairfield' for several weeks during his stay, and his graphic descriptions of it as a bleak and often very violent place appalled totally non-violent me!

Sarah said all the above remarks the following year, 1996, when I tried desperately 'in a vacuum' – she was then at home and virtually a recluse - to save her life by getting her to get a second opinion, away from Whore. When he emotionally and morally blackmailed her, she said, by saying that if she got a second opinion he would no longer treat her, I had a weird, ominous feeling.

You see, the normal maximum dose of the anti-depressant drug 'Prozac', a so-called 'wonder-drug', is one tablet a day. Whore had poor Sarah on five or more a day, along with loads of other strong drugs! Indeed, within a month of her telling me all this, she was dead from drinking a whole bottle of wine on top of her (perfectly healthy???) medication...

Don had a little girlfriend and accomplice in various mischief on the Ward then, one Anna, actually herself a psychiatric nurse, who was telling everybody she was a 'white witch'! She was one of the lucky ones – she was sent home along with Sue, her friend, after a few weeks – with no further treatment or 'processing' deemed necessary. Then they were barred from visiting their two boyfriends, Don and Dick, on the Ward because the latter were both married and the staff feared further ructions over that...

Feeling abused and battered by my constant battle not to have to suffer any more from the totally and utterly wrong diagnosis, and hence treatment with a poisonous drug, I was totally lacking the correct drugs and so very ill. I happened to meet Anna and Sue downstairs, and they were defiant. Indeed, they boasted to me about not having to take any more 'medication', which was pretty cruel and unfeeling, given my condition, and the abuse I was suffering...

I soon realised one vital reason why I was able to survive this dreadful imprisonment and poisoning. I was very lucky, in having extremely loyal parents and sister, who turned up to support me at the weekly 'Ward Rounds'. Believe it or not, in British NHS Mental Hospitals, the Doctor only sees you for about 10 or 20 minutes a week, then disappears again. Above all, they just do not work at the weekend, even if their nursing staff have a problem with patients for which they need a Doctor's advice and instructions. Such is the power of the BMA, the strongest, richest and most powerful Union in the country...

In the course of the previous year 1994, that year, 1995, and 1997, when another 'Doctor', Harlot, again took me off the only drugs that work, my ever-supportive parents were to acquire a foot-high pile of correspondence with Whore, Harlot and their respective 'NHS Trusts'. Both Trusts were to prove incredibly hard to complain against – with the 'Cronies of Consultant Psychiatrists' simply whitewashing our extremely serious and fully justified complaints!

Part of the reason for writing this book, however personal, is to get past the veil of conspiratorial 'Cronyism' that pervades Psychiatry. They are all so terrified of being sued when they make one of their many awful mistakes, that they actually congratulate such awful mistakes by other Psychiatrists, and cynically imply 'You are just a patient – your views simply have to be unsound!'

Because there have been so many deaths at Welwyn Ward at the QEII, a recent 'HAL 2000' report highlighted many serious problems amongst both Doctors and staff at that very under-staffed Acute Ward. It is, we believe, my family and I, only because of that report that I was allowed a full-blown NHS Independent Inquiry in 1999 – mostly into Whore's bizarre behaviour.

Certainly Whore was astonishingly elusive and rarely attended his Ward Rounds that Spring – leaving them instead to a 'locum'. Also, extremely arrogantly and frustratingly, again adding to the feeling that there was a sick conspiracy afoot, he did not reply to a single one of the twenty or thirty letters my parents wrote to him in that time! Several of these letters kept asking him desperately to put me back onto the haloperidol and lithium that had always worked from 1983-1993, after which he took my case over. He ignored all entreaties to be sane and reasonable, and totally arrogantly persisted down the wrong path. Nothing could have seemed more sinister to all the family, especially me! Then he hid away, seemingly, and manipulated everything from 'behind the scenes'. This cowardly lack of spine reached a height during my later 'stay' at Fairfield, that Summer, when he 'dictated foul treatments over the phone' for a whole two and a half months...

So when my traitorous ex- soon 'switched sides' in March 1995, and went to see Whore to feed him with complete 'misinformation' about me, much more frequently than visiting me briefly every now and then, my whole family felt they were watching me suffer the most terribly sick cruelty. Meanwhile my ex- as 'next of kin' backed this foul treatment. Divorce became inevitable within three months, given all the cruelty and abuse she was joining in and loving to mete out to me, along with Whore!

So, with full support from my immediate family, but increasing scorn and disdain from my own 'wife', and indeed treachery, I was almost alone among people on Welwyn Ward in having lots of visitors. Bert, the 'full-time' Vicar managed to spare the time to visit me several times during my total of eight months in three mental hospitals that year, from February 5th to October 2nd.

However, to my astonishment the self-esteemed 'Christian folk of Dane End' – there were several close acquaintances who could and should have visited me in all that time – claimed to pray for me, but not one dared visit. With one crucial exception, who loyally came every week, and tried his best at the age of 87, bless him, to understand that I was in fact being 'abused instead of healed'. He never did get the hang of that simple fact, and was not prepared to believe it. Nor was he prepared to believe how badly funded and equipped or even represented, the Church as a whole is, in the whole field of 'Mental Health'. Presumably all 'mental patients' like me, Gifts of the Holy Spirit or not, which in itself is a contradiction in terms, are 'judged as having an evil spirit' and abandoned to the 'tender mercies' of Atheist Psychiatrists!

The only contact with that 'shower of Dane End Bad Samaritans' – the lay folk, excluding Charles – that I have had since, has been occasional chance meetings. With one disgustingly pious, totally ignorant photocopy, given all I had been through that year of 1995. That with no courtesy of an accompanying letter, from the most bigoted and hypocritical 'do-gooder' of them all, as mentioned earlier, 'coward Chris'.

So, hopeless and tormented days turned into weeks and then eventually months, with hardly any break from being confined on that noisy, demented, frantic Ward. I got my ex-in the end to bring in my portable CD player and some CDs, and played restful music in the smoking room, which the Ward Manager joked became my 'office'. Everybody loved the 'Irish Princess' style of the Irish singer-songwriter Enya! This smoking room was tiny and polluted by too much smoke in a confined area, despite a loud, hateful fan, yet was some kind of refuge from the marauding staff, in my case threatening me all the time or – in their ignorance – telling me off for 'refusing their precious medication'.

In my case, I was too tongue-tied from 'pressure of speech' from lack of my correct lithium, to answer back. I just had to refuse any higher dose than 75 mg of the poisonous clozapine, morning and evening for months, which got very wearing and exhausting. I was drained at the end of that terrible year...

Another factor that added terribly to the sense of my ex-then being involved in some kind of conspiracy with the 'staff', especially 'Doctor' Whore, was that in about the middle of March, I suddenly asked her why she was not bringing me in my mail. As if to confirm that she indeed intended now to 'put me away for good', she casually and evilly replied, almost slyly, 'Oh, I am opening and destroying it all!' After that I kept on at her to bring it in, and so far as I can tell under those particularly cruel circumstances, she indeed started to bring in my post after about two months from that. Virtually the first letters that she brought in, when I was at Fairfield, were two extremely boldly addressed love letters.

'Diamond' had written to me in mid-May, addressing the letters, with no thought for the fact that I was still married, to 'Mr. and Mrs. Lee' at the home address I had given her!

Around the end of March a new face in fact appeared, and slunk cautiously and shyly into the smoking room, to join the rest of us listening to either a CD or the radio. Diamond had appeared, and was trying to decide whether as a voluntary patient she really wanted to stay for a while. As the 'Queen of Welwyn Ward', she was on her 45th or so stay since 1990!

I remember discussing with her that she was lucky in that she could go home again if she wished – some of us lucky ones were midway through a Section 3 of the Mental Health Act! Then I made the fatefully prophetic remark, 'If you don't stick around, you will miss something big!' In 1998 she told me that in 1995 she too was having an 'annus horribilis' – her worst ever year. Ten days later, after indeed going home, she came back, with no access to money as she had lost her benefit book – and was to remain, very distressed and confused initially, and without any decent clothes or any money, for another three months in hospital.

We return to what turned into a brief flirtation, then extremely erratic friendship lasting several years with Diamond, in due course. Around the end of March there happened a number of events, that affected me deeply at the time.

Firstly, allowed on the grounds, at the end of February I tried to get home. Breaking the draconian 'Law', I wandered out of the grounds and saw a bus at the bus stop. I had about ten pounds on me, and boarded it. It took me to Hatfield station. Within five minutes – God's timing, it must have been! – an hourly 724 came along – going back to the QEII! However, after a quick enquiry of a fellow passenger I found it went to Hertford after that. My luck was in – my attempt to 'do a runner' and get home – I felt terribly homesick on top of feeling very abused – was on! When the bus stopped at the QEII I hid my face from the outside world in case I got recognised. Then, the long haul through the backstreets of the East side of Welwyn Garden City – then at last Hertford itself! I did not have enough money to pay for a taxi, the five miles to Dane End, which would have been about eight pounds – the bus fare had taken up too much of my tiny resources.

So I walked up Bengeo Road in Hertford, near where I now live, intending to dive off once I got near Dane End, off the road, and take to footpaths – to avoid detection by anybody following me. Indeed someone with some insight into where I might have escaped to was following – my mother, in their car with my father. Just as I reached the turning for Dane End and Sacombe at the top of Bengeo Hill, a car pulled up and my father leaped out. I immediately began running away towards my village, as I did not want anybody, not even my own parents, stopping me in my 'quest' to escape from my torment and 'prison' – and have some quiet time by myself at home.

After a while I looked back and realised that they were both back in the car and trying to stop me. Suddenly they roared past – obviously to try to cut me off. Immediately I saw a footpath towards Sacombe on my right-hand side, and started to run down it – with my father soon running behind me. Even though he is over twenty years older, he was a lot fitter – he regularly jogs, whereas I was getting out of breath from spending all my time in the smoking room on Welwyn Ward. Soon he was steadily catching me up!

After about two miles of this bizarre chase, he caught up with me in the middle of a large field, and tried to pull me back. I refused, and said could we walk on – there was a pub close by, 'The Three Harts'. I had dismally been stopped in a brilliant 'runner' – not by the Police or Hospital Staff – but by my own father. I realised the 'game was up' and we must have walked, chatting about my plight, about four hundred yards before getting back onto the road, and finding the 'Three Harts' about two hundred yards further on. My father telephoned my mother from the pub to their mobile phone, and we went in and had a drink to recover from the chase – and me my disappointment that my homesickness remained frustratingly intact. So near and yet so far!

Halfway through the pint of Guinness I was enjoying, a young policeman and policewoman arrived, and I took my time over my pint, now fearing repercussions and reprisals when the inevitable happened – they took me back to my 'prison' at Welwyn Ward. When we walked outside there was an astonishing collection of three police cars and a police van with two tracker dogs! What are they expecting, the Spanish Inquisition, I thought dryly to myself? However, when I saw Whore's report on me for the abortive Appeal that never took place, that I have already described and will do so again when the time comes, I realised that they believed his awful smears of me, no doubt fuelled by my own wife's sinister lies. In that report he claimed, with absolutely no evidence, as I have never been violent in my life, that I am 'violent' – his diagnosis now leapt about again to 'very acute schizophrenic', equally bizarrely.

So he left the police with no option but to treat me as one of those 'dangerous paranoid schizophrenics' that the media love to publicise, ignoring the fact that most 'schizophrenics' are very gentle people. Above all I suffer no schizophrenic symptoms and never have – Whore's diagnosis was ludicrous, even sinister!

The next incident to describe briefly was typical of Welwyn Ward, but fortunately no harm came of it. I heard three of the 'hoodlum' element on the Ward at the time whispering in the smoking room about 'beating up X'. Little did I guess that their intended victim was me, until I went out to the toilet at the end of the long corridor that makes up that Ward, rather resembling as it does, an underground train! When I re-emerged, the three were in a group walking determinedly towards me, and were only about ten feet away, obviously intent on mischief or violence.

I had been on a one week training course on 'Leadership and Initiative' at Ross-on-Wye while at PA, which had stressed me to the point of nearly being ill, but as it was – literally – led by ex-SAS Officers, really taught us young potential leaders to 'think on our feet'. I had a sudden inspiration, and completely the opposite of what these dim people expected, standing and fighting, I ran three yards into the dead end of the locked stairwell at the end of the corridor. Then I whistled really hard, as if signalling to my non-existent 'backup'. Then I paused ten seconds, went back through the frosted-glass swing-doors and walked quickly but calmly back to the smoking room, while meanwhile the three would-be thugs had hidden from non-violent me! When I looked back they were looking in every one of the rooms at that end of the Ward, obviously looking for my support that did not exist. Needless to say, they left me alone after that incident, which clearly confused them!

There was another violent incident in the end bay where I slept with three others, that did in fact result in a sickening act of violence – to the young bisexual Colin in the next bed. The bed opposite mine had been occupied for two weeks by a little runt of a man, who however claimed to have been dumped in mental hospital, by his employers, none other than MI5! He was very aggressive indeed on the Ward. Having met him since he told me he was kept there for eighteen months!

His arrival on the Ward certainly warned me to be very wary of him, as he came charging wildly into the smoking room where I stood, and even though only half my size, shoulder charged me and glared viciously at me. When he said something very incoherently, I just sat down and avoided him and any possible confrontation. John, the fourth member of our bay at that time, later whispered to me, as such an expert on medication that he often gave talks to the Doctors about the patient's viewpoint, that this weird chap was getting hold of lots of street drugs and mixing them with his medication. I was not at all surprised.

Two weeks after he arrived, as I said, the terrifying incident happened. John and I had gone to bed, and were asleep, when suddenly I was dramatically woken up by the strange sound of hands clawing weirdly at the plastic curtains I had drawn round my bed for some privacy. I woke up with a start, and realised that 'Matey from MI5' had clearly got hold of some more heroin, or crack or whatever, and was trying to get at me, like a sex-starved demoniac! Fearing for my 'manhood' as a firmly married man, I also realised that from the strength with which he was trying to get at me, through the curtains, the drugs had made him unnaturally strong as well as crazed. He was demonised, in fact!

Instantaneously the insight flashed back from the LHM that 'Evil Spirits cannot tolerate your Gift of Tongues!' I gave him two minutes of calming rebuke in my – suddenly and very necessarily fluent to the point of perfection – Gift of Tongues, after about a minute of which, all suddenly went quiet in the bay, apart from me talking at him in the Language of the Angels.

After that I decided that discretion was the better part of valour, and walked with my pipe and tobacco to the smoking-room, where John had already taken refuge. 'Christ!' He said, 'What has he taken and mixed with his medication – and however much!' We did not venture back until the staff, clearly worried and afraid at this incident, checked and reassured us with the good news that 'Matey from MI5' had fallen fast asleep.

We did not find out about what for us two heterosexuals, would have been a 'fate worse than death' until the morning. Then I woke to see Colin, apparently even having enjoyed his ordeal and loss of virginity, the previous night, being helped by Don as he vomited into the sink in the bay. Fortunately, when I asked to be moved from the bay the following day, 'Doctor' Whore fully understood my fears, and had clearly been fully informed of the incident. He said that was not possible, but they would definitely 'swap' Colin out of that dangerous area into the bay where my then friend and fellow heterosexual six-footer, Don was, and give Don Colin's bed, to reassure everybody. So that afternoon Don moved into Colin's area. I had him next to me in the bay until my second and final 'successful escape' from that dreadful place of mental torture – from the frying pan into the fire, as it turned out!

Around that time there were two disastrous, abortive and legally compromised meetings – one for me, one for my immediate family – and the consequences, for me from both, were to be quite far-reaching.

I had been waiting to be formally informed of the date of my Hospital Manager's Appeal, but apart from hearing just a rumour – from my then prissy Social Worker, not ever the staff! – had no idea it had been arranged for a certain Thursday afternoon. I was actually fast asleep, exhausted from my Ordeal in mid-March, when David, the kindly Charge Nurse, woke me up and said, 'Wake up! Your Appeal is on in half an hour!' I protested that I had had no warning whatsoever from the 'staff' about this, and sensibly, as he was my best ally on the Ward and no part of the conspiracy against me that was so evidently afoot, he said nothing. I was taken downstairs to find my then wife and my then 'Social Worker' Fanny both smirking prissily at me. No sign of my parents – or any solicitor that I would definitely have recruited had I in fact had *any* formal notice of this Meeting!

These two prissy cronies, my ex- and the Social Worker, tried to tell me black was white – that I had had plenty of notice of my Appeal – from ALL the staff. The 'staff' concerned later lied through their teeth that 'I had plenty of notice'. If so, why weren't my parents there, or why if I had been shown the manners or respect of at least a bit of advance notice, had I not summoned them to be there as they were entitled to be? Fanny and Helen tried to get me to go into the Appeal with only their now obviously very dubious 'support' – but sensibly, hoping the whole thing would naturally – and only fairly, under the circumstances – be adjourned, I refused pointblank to go in! The Appeal Chairman came out of the meeting-room and I explained.

However, typically of the management of that Unit, no adjournment or repeat 'performance' came out through this 'conspiracy of silence'. I watched in disgust as a file of people that I had never met walked passed me, all taking a long hard look at this 'mere mental patient' who had so much 'wasted their time'. The fault was not mine, but that of their own staff...

Rigging of correspondence, reports and meetings was rife about me at that time. I learned from my parents after I arrived at Fairfield on 12th May 1998, that the reason that they stopped coming to visit me at the QEII in April, was another meeting, this time forced on them at Whore's insistence – and that of my ex- Helen, 'the Tart of Tarts'. This was with my ex- and with Mrs. Humbug, a manager at Ware HQ of East Herts Social Services, and as ever at such meetings, various silent anonymous 'Social Services people'.

This was, according to my parents, although I was not there, a complete set-up, and defied the Mental Health Act yet again! My mother was given a blistering lecture by Humbug about being a 'schizophrenic mother' which as we keep on seeing was based on the complete, Atheist, Satanic misdiagnosis of me as that by Whore! As a result my poor mother has suffered traumas by being character assassinated by a mere social worker, ever since! Unfortunately, just like Barristers, you cannot sue or even complain about social services – they are completely above the law, which is why most of them act totally irresponsibly and condescendingly. Most of them are fussy and prissy and casually neglect their responsibilities, thinking themselves above the law!

At that meeting it was – totally illegally – agreed by 'them' with my ex-, present no doubt to gloat, that as next-of-kin she would now have my 'nuisance' parents barred from any contact with me on Welwyn Ward. This totally breached the terms of the Mental Health Act, and again was more conspiracy by Whore and my ex-, the Tart of Tarts. This time social services were implicated. With my reputation and above all my mother's at stake, we would dearly like to prosecute. However, most of the smug arrogance and lack of care of most of them, stems from the immunity from prosecution given them by unjust law!

There was some light relief from all of this mental torture on my birthday on 30th March, when I was, as only occasionally happened during my ordeal, allowed to see my little daughter Jenny on the Ward. She came in and we tried to 'liven up ourselves' to greet her. Indeed it turned that one patient, Dick, who was very wiry, muscular and strong, performed 'robot walking' and other impressions – at children's parties, in the 'real world'. I vividly remember a worried but giggling four-year old Jenny being chased by him around the room! My parents brought in some very nice food, and a cake, which everyone loved, in strict contrast to the 'cattle fodder' generally served up to us on the Ward...

There were, as I recall, just two more incidents at that first hospital of three for me that year, that should convince you of why by now I knew my wife was unfit to remain in that position any longer!

Firstly, when I tried to express my pain and anguish over my sufferings on clozapine at Welwyn Ward, she scoffed at me! "Doctor Whore says that you aren't feeling real pain. You are just imagining it! It is NOT REAL PAIN!"

If I were violent I would have hit her for saying that. It just made me feel that after all her 'cosy chats' with Whore – he had clearly either brainwashed or hypnotised the imbecile. It was transparently clear to me that ALL the patients on that Ward – and any such place – felt great pain! After that she was beneath my contempt, as surfaced in May at Fairfield, my 'next stop on my grand tour of mental hospitals – three in eight months!'

The second incident was much more serious in terms of long-term effects. We went on a walk in the woods surrounding the back of the QEII hospital, as I had explained that I wanted to have some 'time alone' with her. Any more intelligent, sensible woman would have realised that I was expressing deep sexual frustration, having been on the Ward for three whole months. So when I started undressing her, and lay her down on the ground in the woods in a secluded spot, trying to make love to her, her reaction was very naïve. Even though it was her own husband trying to make love to her, she called out 'Help! Rape!' I rapidly got up and wandered off a little way, in total confusion. We went back, and initially she refused to return that day to complete the love-making session.

However, when I rang her up, she returned inside three hours – typically, with a house-wife's supply – of a dozen condoms! I could not believe that having feebly cried 'Rape!' she now expected so very much more of me than I could offer, a second time around! What was she expecting this time of asking – a 'gang bang by the twelve apostles' – or something...? We duly found a different, more secluded spot in the woods, lay down and made love – for the very last time. I remember that she felt exposed there in the woods and asked me not to remove her top – so I did not.

I have reliable circumspective witnesses to all this – as my parents visited at the same time, a few days later, as Bert made one of his occasional visits as my very busy Vicar. We went for a walk, and I embarrassed all of us by relating what had happened a few days earlier, between Helen and I.

I have always since put down her cry the first time around, of 'Rape!' to the sinister confession she made to me the second time around of this love-making. Namely, that she had stopped taking 'the pill' on the very first day after she 'put me away'. Clearly she thought I was going into 'hospital' for good!

However, she later that year completely twisted round both this and my other honest 'cry for help' back in 1994, as described earlier, when I accidentally overdosed, in a totally evil way. She took out, and for bizarre reasons which we come to at the end of describing this 'annus horribilis', got converted into 'Undertakings' by me not to contact her or return to my own home from hospital, a Court Order! Naturally there was no mention of 'accidental overdosing' or 'actually making love with me – three hours after the alleged "attempted rape"' anywhere in the completely distorted pack of lies she swore to on Oath in Court!

Yes, she committed perjury – against her own loving and very confused husband! The true version that I slaved in anguish to write down in reply was never used, and at last the truth about both small incidents appears in this book – one very good reason for writing it...!

Some couple of weeks after that, something that greatly relieved me took place. Astonishingly, I was stopped from taking the dreaded clozapine or clozaril! Instead, in mid-April I started to be given 'depot injections' of clopixol, a tranquilliser. I was to have just two fortnightly injections like this, and at the same time most of the other heavy doses of 'tranx' I was being given, were also stopped.

I vividly remember asking the staff who had been continually bullying me to take the dreaded clozaril, why they now had to stop that mental torture, and why the clozaril had been stopped. All I got was blank looks. In the end, a couple of days after it all stopped, Sister Cathy was the only one brave enough to tell me.

Only she and Charge Nurse David among the staff ever helped me in similar ways. Indeed David told me last September when I was there once more, despite all my fears of that place, visiting Diamond there, that 'Despite all the slurs, you were no trouble at all in 1995! You were all right mate – and I share all your views you are giving about your treatment then!'

Sister Cathy discreetly took me, as I vividly remember, to the Office, then at the end of the Ward, and produced a blood test. Still in silence she handed it to me. It was a recent one of mine for neutrophil or white blood-cell count – 2.870, I very vividly remember – almost exactly half the normal average of 5.500. No wonder my clozapine had been stopped – even on just 75 mg, less than one TENTH of the 'minimum therapeutic dose' – I had become like an AIDS victim, with a drastically damaged immune system! I immediately and very coolly got Cathy to break her obviously angry silence about this, and confirm my reading of my own blood test. Then I added, 'should I have been continued on this stuff while I had four short bouts of 'flu due to the intense cold on the Ward earlier this Spring?' She looked sheepish, and just said 'No!'

The next four weeks were sheer purgatory. Now being experimented on yet again like a laboratory rat, I remember thinking to myself, 'I must be the Chief Poison Taster to the Queen of Heaven – or something!' I could not think at all clearly on this new treatment of just clopixol depots, yet being left alone at last now that they could not threaten me any more, at least gave me time to think things over – and soon, to plan escape from this dreadful limbo...

At three months into my Section 3, the incident occurred that finally convinced my parents and me that there was an organised and insidious, cowardly conspiracy against trapped, helpless me, between the Tart of Tarts and the staff, orchestrated by Whore. I asked for a second opinion, as now I was supposed to be entitled to. I was also supposed no longer to be forced to have any treatment my Consultant saw fit, under the Mental Health Act – now Whore was supposed to discuss my medication with me. He got round the latter by firstly, carrying on with 'draconian enforced treatment' despite the fact that that broke the law.

As for the second opinion, these seem to be anathema to totally bombastic, arrogant young Whore! My soon to be late lamented friend, Sarah Todd, was the following year also effectively blackmailed emotionally and morally – effectively refused a second opinion, not his. He again broke the law by saying, 'If you go for a second opinion, not mine, I will stop treating you!' Bastard! This was while Whore was massively overdosing her with loads of medication, and so killed her when she drank just one bottle of wine. Why was he giving her such massive doses of drugs like benzo-diazepams, which specifically clash terribly with alcohol, when he knew she had an alcohol problem...?

My wife, parents and I waited for two hours one Wednesday afternoon for the notorious 'Dr K. of Fairfield' – "the last man in the Mental Health Service to actually wear a white coat"! – to turn up for the second opinion. He never arrived, and we were given no explanation, and told to sit around again the same

141

time the next day. The insulting and demeaning pantomime ritual was repeated again. Presumably they were trying to wear us down through attrition!

Finally, 'third time lucky'! Dr K. turned up late on the Friday, and I was taken by myself into an office. Then there were a series of shocks. Dr Whore had again, once more, bent the rules. This, I was told, was no 'second opinion' as fully promised and expected, merely something called a 'medication review'. There was then, no fresh assessment or fresh diagnosis by Dr K. Instead he picked up a chart, and looked at it for a couple of minutes. It was not my chart, although my name was on it! Second shocker! It just had three little crosses on it for that same morning's dose of tranquillisers I had taken, and the fact that I was on a 100 mg depot of clopixol every fortnight! My real chart reappeared at 'medication time' that evening, very mysteriously, so he had been completely misled – but proceeded to completely 'rubber-stamp' Whore's abuse of me up to then – with no evidence to go on!

This incident completed my 'conviction that I was at the crux of a conspiracy by a cronyism of Consultant Psychiatrists' and after that I just knew that if I stayed on that place of torture – Welwyn Ward – any longer, my life would be in danger! Escape was now the only obvious remaining option! Where to, I wondered, and vaguely thought of getting on a train and heading vaguely Northwards – to the Yorkshire dales, where I had old friends?

Meanwhile, off my lithium – my speech had reached a peak of incoherence and speed – 'pressure of speech', it is called. So for most of that month until 12th May 1995, I sat, at last left alone, in the smoking room, smoking, going on the occasional escorted walks that were all I was allowed, and biding my time. My chance came on 12th May when a pleasant male Nurse, Gary, an ex-army type, took several patients including myself, on a walk near the woods. Sorry, Gary, I had no choice but to 'do a runner', mate, as you can see!

We leave my account of that three and a bit months on Welwyn Ward, with a brief account of how I got to know Diamond, who as we saw a few pages back, came along twice. She then decided that, penniless and with no clothes, family or friends, she yet again needed the dubious sanctuary of that awful place of purgatory and – as we have seen – violence. She stayed!

I started talking to her several times in the smoking-room – me then with my pipe, her with her perennial 'Fag Ash Lil' roll-ups. Although I could tell she was extraordinarily highly strung indeed, I could also see she was very intelligent – and had a great line in wit and conversation! We were to have many – fascinating and very ill! – late-night conversations from then, about everything under the sun! On the other hand, by contrast to my own frequent visits from either Charles or, in particular my ever-loyal family, she rarely had any visitors. Nobody fetched her any decent clothes, not even her ex-husband, who visited a couple of times in that time from mid-March to mid-May. Like him she was on benefit – but was then absolutely 'skint' – she had lost her benefit book – and he could only spare her a few pounds at a time.

As I was then on £110 a week – meted out by my 'ex' – I felt both guilty and extremely sorry for this older woman, downtrodden by life but retaining for me a strange attraction. So soon I was giving her my loose change, then in the end £5 and £10 notes. Above all, I got my traitorous ex-wife to bring in extra packets of cigarettes – discreetly without saying who they were for.

I remember Diamond initially felt that I was 'threatening' at 6'1½" whenever I took cash or cigarettes to her room and 'dropped them off'. After a while, however, she got to slowly trust me. To quote the lines from the song 'Down Under' by the Australian Rock Band 'Men at Work', she was gradually having a weird attractive 'pull' on me, literally fulfilled in September that year: -

"I met a strange lady –
she made me nervous.
She took me in
and gave me breakfast."

It was Diamond who took it upon herself, despite the fact that she knew I was married, to thank me for all my kindness and generosity then, by seducing me and starting a brief love affair! I still feel no guilt over that. By the time of the incident that led to the affair, that we come to now, I was determined that as soon as (if I ever?) got out of this torment I would divorce the Tart of Tarts for 'high treason to our marriage'! As far as I was concerned she had taken sides with the seemingly all-powerful 'Authorities' against her own beleaguered and totally weakened, trapped husband!

So we leave my account of 'mental torture on Welwyn Ward in 1995' with that highly significant incident, that finally was to 'tip me over the edge'. As my ex- had by now clearly totally betrayed and abused me, this incident was to make me fall for the apparent charms of an older divorcee - Diamond! There were about seven of us in all crowded into the tiny room that formed the smoking-room, when Don suddenly said in typically superior 'God-like' tones,

'If anybody wants to kiss anybody else, let them do it now!'

Suddenly I saw Diamond come towards me with a huge welcoming smile, and I found myself suddenly aroused and moving up from my seat there to meet her. Her 'first kiss' then was damp and luscious – the best she ever gave me! I found myself embracing her passionately, for about twenty seconds, as we stood there, her in just a flimsy nightdress, so I could for the first time in months feel a sexy female body! We backed off slowly – and something had surfaced that was to re-emerge when we both found ourselves together at Fairfield Secure Unit some weeks later. She was sent there – typical Diamond! – for throwing coffee over several other female patients who managed to upset her feelings! We come to my 'great escape – to Cambridge' and my 'second runner been' of that dreadful stay at the QEII, in the account below, that too landed me up there...

My 'second runner been' or Great Escape from Welwyn Ward to Cambridge – thence to 'sunny Fairfield' Secure Mental Unit – and re-meeting Diamond!

With just £2 in my pocket, and the clothes I stood up in, I walked away into the woods and then started jogging, knowing that poor Gary would not dare abandon his other charges. I remember Don calling out "Don't do it! You'll get into terrible trouble!" then I set off at speed, towards where I knew the new golf course backed onto Hatfield Park. I guessed I could deter any pursuit by going the 'wrong way around' the Park of the Stately home, along the exit route for cars.

So my stay in 1994 had not all been wasted – I had been allowed out very, very much more then, and knew the way to Hatfield Park's front entrance – and thence the railway station – like the back of my hand! At that stage, with no money, I hoped to 'jump a train heading north' – and then leave the rest to God, the Holy Spirit, and Jesus!

In the end I went to the Fore Street entrance to the Park at Hatfield, and called in on poor Sarah's Vicar father there, hoping he might offer some help.

However, I was dismissed rather gruffly. So, after a five-mile walk, and as it was now evening rush-hour, the pubs were open, and I was thirsty, I walked down Fore Street into Old Hatfield. I had a quick pint of beer in the Horse and Groom pub, leaving me just 22 pence – i.e. a train fare to nowhere! – in my pocket. After that I walked to the nearby railway station, went in the side entrance past all the commuters coming off the train that was 'in', heading north to Welwyn Garden City, and just got on it, 'trusting my luck' there was no Ticket Inspector on board! There was not, and as for my 'first runner been' my timing was very fortunate. Within a minute of waiting at Welwyn Garden City, a train arrived that was heading north again, past Stevenage and then going to Peterborough.

I got off at Stevenage, hoping to walk the short half-mile to my old office at Old Stevenage, of PA, and to find any old work colleague who might be willing to lend me some money to continue my journey. When I got there I found the whole office was shut down – as long ago promised. So when I got back to the station and again found no Ticket Inspectors at the barrier, and the Cambridge train on the platform, I boarded it, and again I was 'being looked after' by somebody! For the train again had no ticket inspection, nor did it when it eventually got to Cambridge, were there any inspectors at the barrier there, either. Three trains and four barriers with no inspectors! That was in the days before privatisation. I wonder if things have changed at all since then...?

I walked the two miles swiftly to my old college of King's in the town centre, and tried to book a 'guest room' for the night, on the grounds that I am a Senior Member of the college. I was told to go to the college bar, where the Vice-Provost was – the Head of the place! – and the Porters would discuss it with him. They had very few rooms available, if any. Soon a Porter came into the bar and introduced me to the Vice-Provost, Nick Bullock, and fortunately we remembered each other other's faces, at least, after sixteen years.

He had a quick chat with me, bought me a pint of beer, and clearly sussed me out – for I remember, standing at the bar together, he asked, 'Who is persecuting you?' I replied cryptically, 'Enemies!' I was led to a small room on a staircase near the river, on the ground floor, by a kindly Porter, and told to 'try to rest'. In fact, what with the terrific excitement and drama of having got away from Welwyn Ward for at least one night, I was to have a very restless night. Security in Cambridge Colleges is much tighter these days than when I was an undergraduate – and in my case was exceptional. The patrolling security guard popped round every two hours at least, and apart from dosing off fitfully – and very hypomanic, of course – I was up most of that very distressed night, in a strange place, under very strange circumstances!

Dawn broke about 6am on that Friday 12th May 1995, and so I wandered unchallenged out of the front gate of the college to find something on the market I could buy to eat with my paltry – literally – four pence I had left. On the way I popped into the Refectory area, nearly penniless, and managed to 'scrounge' half a small jug of orange juice and some biscuits, left after some organised function on a trolley. I remember speaking to the cleaners there, who had clearly heard about the slight fracas I had caused, and they kindly enquired, "Don't you ever rest?" In the market I spent my 4p on six plums for my breakfast. I even remember having a bit of fun 'bargaining for these' – with my four pence, with the stall-holders!

Back to the college, where obviously my stay had been kept incommunicado on humanitarian grounds overnight, the Head

146

Porter, who behaved superbly throughout that whole twelve hour and very unorthodox visit, told me I had to stay in the Porter's Lodge. Soon I was being entertained, and was joining in with my own wit, by the very friendly Porters. Then at 10 am or so, very soon after my 'breakfast' of plums and orange juice, my parents turned up, very anxious. They soon realised I was really being looked after well.

There followed a series of phone calls between the College and Fulbourn Mental hospital, where I wanted to go, but in the end they said it was outside the remit of the rules about Section 3 medication orders. I would add – however unjust or cruel or mentally torturous that Section 3! As ever the 'propaganda' that Welwyn Ward put out about that morning and early afternoon in the Porter's Lodge was bizarre and full of sheer ridiculous lies. They claimed I got to Fulbourn, then got violent and tried to escape. Typical crap – in fact I only got as far as the tobacconist opposite the College, escorted by my Father, all day! Of course Helen swallowed their 'official' version hook, line and stinker...

My mother went out and bought some nice food and drink – non-alcoholic – for everybody at lunchtime, which was much appreciated by all the Porters – and starving me! By about 2pm it had become clear that my attempt to escape from Welwyn Ward to a Mental Ward that back in 1978 had been very 'open' and even caring, rather than draconian, had failed. About three o'clock two policemen appeared and shut me in the back of a police van, took me to the police station and put me in the cells for about three hours. Looking back this was yet another fine piece of mental torture by Whore – I could just as easily have been picked up by the ambulance that came for me from the QEII at around 6pm, from the comfort of the College.

No, the 'system' demanded I had to be punished for escaping – so a Police Cell it was for three whole hours. When a black nurse from Welwyn Ward arrived with two other men I had never met, I was ticked off for shouting in my cell – about nothing in particular. Who would not have, under such confusing and demeaning circumstances, imposed after a thoroughly enjoyable day at last away from the dreaded Welwyn Ward at the QEII? I was taken to the waiting ambulance and strapped in. There was generally silence on the hour-long journey – especially when I asked where we were going – although the coloured Nurse talked about my time at college a bit, and for him – 'super cool' always – seemed quite impressed.

CHAPTER SEVENTEEN

Crucifixion experience Two of Three in 1995

Out of the frying pan into the fire? 12th May - 24th August 1995. Fairfield Secure Unit – 'one step up from Broadmoor'! Sent there for resisting totally incorrect diagnosis and treatment with poison imposed in conspiratorial fashion, under the full cowardly weight of draconian Law, before which I was helpless.

Finally we drove up a wooded drive, past some most peculiar large Victorian buildings. I remember commenting that the grounds were very impressive, but that the roofs of the buildings were a most odd design and at very odd angles. Clearly then, this was a place designed by a madman, so it must be Fairfield Hospital. 'Super cool' decided to break his silence in some crazy kind of parting remark, which I remember was, 'Just obey the rules and you will be all right!', which if it was designed to calm me, at the time had the opposite effect. It sent a chill down my spine!

We parked in a quiet courtyard, at twilight, outside a building that looked just like a Victorian prison. Then I was led up an equally prison-like stairwell, a bell that was to become very familiar was rung, and I was led into Orchard II Ward. This was one of two Wards on two floors at Fairfield Secure Unit – Orchard I Ward was upstairs, which looking back I was blessed not to have to go to. It was the 'violent' Ward of the two – with many criminals and other violent people with mental illness.

Within a few hours that evening, I had met the staff, or most of them, and immediately and correctly received the impression that unlike Welwyn Ward they were all full-time rather than mostly being on short 'contracts' – and highly organised and efficient. They had to be – this was a place where normally only 'heavyweight' patients – including some criminals – were sent, because they needed to be kept in the Ward, by and large, either for the safety of the public or their own safety. However, the advice that 'super-cool', the black nurse, gave me – I once told him 'I am cooler than you – by a million icebergs!', which to say the least did not go down well! – turned out to be perfectly accurate.

That is, although there was no 'list of rules written down', as long as one stayed within the 'unwritten rules' of that place, it was perfectly tolerable and OK. However, the reaction of the staff to anyone 'breaking the unwritten rules' often included 'physical restraint' – two of the staff slipping their arms under yours from behind and bending your hands back over the wrists till the tendons were arched, and really hurt, for hours or even days afterwards! This happened to me twice – just for breaking the unwritten law 'Don't be cheeky to the staff, or ever answer them back! Never, above all, tell them how to do their job – it is hard enough for them without "patient feedback"!'

In general, as everywhere, especially Welwyn Ward, where I was confined again in 1999 for totally the wrong reasons, as we will be seeing, it was to turn out that there were of course a few 'rotten apples' among the staff.

However, although some were still training, not one was a 'stand-in' on contract, so one could get to know them all. Also, as on the odd occasion below where a member of staff was definitely out of order, a complaint to the Ward Manager was always enough to have it swiftly corrected – unlike Welwyn Ward, where all of my desperate complaints had been totally ignored!

On the whole however, the great majority of the staff were kind, efficient, and caring and above all dedicated to their jobs. You could easily tell that it was only the more 'mercenary' staff, who were only 'in it for the money and the power the job gave', who ever abused that position of power over ill, helpless patients like me. Then, and it only happened twice in a couple of days, a complaint to the very effective Sister Lynn, the Ward Manager, that was fully justified, soon put a stop to the 'abuse of privileged positions'.

So, staff I particularly remember as being very caring were: - Lynn, Lucille, Carol, Jim, 'Chippy', Harry and David (who left as my personal 'assigned nurse' after six weeks – he chose to go to Broadmoor). Then, who could forget Pete, with the build of a rugby prop-forward – always the backstop 'threat' whenever there were any incidents looking like they might become violent? I had my problems with young John. Until my medication started at last to be sorted out, and we found out we could both kick a football in the large garden behind the Unit. Then, I found out his aggressive posturing was due to a violent childhood with a large family of embattled brothers, so after that the relationship was altogether 'arms length' but respectful on both sides.

I will neglect to mention the names of other staff with whom I sometimes tangled. There was a young 'Welsh git' who was very smug, superior and very 'macho' – always drawing very 'butch' buildings as he hoped to take a degree in architecture. To him I was just some 'scum mental patient' – he never thought to inquire whether I had any qualifications, let alone had been to Cambridge University! We come in due course to the two 'rogue' nurses who gave me two days of Hell, totally abusing their mercenary position of power, which really was my only serious complaint against any of the staff on that Ward during my stay...

The Ward layout had been designed by old-fashioned Victorian minds rather than over-sophisticated 1960's planners, and hence was extremely simple by comparison. There were basically just two rooms, one larger than the other, and the larger had a very domineering TV and video set up high like some demigod. This room was tucked away from the entrance and visitors, smoking was allowed in the relatively huge area compared to Welwyn Ward, and we were allowed to listen to music on headphones on personal stereos. The ordinary looking Victorian windows, however, hardly opened a crack, and concealed iron bars... It had no fan so it reeked of tobacco smoke.

The other room was non-smoking, and led to the offices and pharmacy, and was used as the refectory – and non-smoking area during the day. It held just hard dining tables and chairs – and a machine selling of all things, only 'Ribena' at 20p a carton! These two rooms then resembled 'the Devil and the deep blue sea'!

There was a corridor between these two main patient areas, off which was the kitchen, where breakfast, tea and coffee were prepared – although only rarely did the staff cook any meals apart from breakfast. The food, far more substantial and better quality on the whole than had been normal at Welwyn Ward, was brought in by a catering company. Off the refectory, was the dormitory area, with first the female beds, then the more numerous male beds beyond – strategically separated by the office where the night nurses watched over the 'observation beds' – one patient of each sex immediately adjacent – and generally oversaw the entire dormitory area.

I was to spend some weeks in the 'observation bed' – until I was eventually replaced by a new arrival, and moved to the main part of the dormitory. Finally, a locked door was occasionally opened to allow access to a full-size gym, with basketball, football, art therapy – and vitally, showers and baths. A far more sensible and simple design than the experimental labyrinthine 'underground train' of Welwyn Ward!

It was clear from when I first arrived that there was a very strictly imposed regime or routine on Orchard II Ward – and I later heard, even more fierce on the harsher, more violent Ward upstairs. We were all got out of bed at twenty to eight in the morning, and washed and the men shaved, in the next twenty minutes. Then we were led after the women, to the Ward, for the smokers to ask for 'lights' for cigarettes – I smoked both cigarettes and pipe during my stay. Patients were not allowed their own lighters, which allowed the staff to stop 'crazy arson' and – if necessary – to impose discipline at will on any nicotine addicted person who broke the 'unwritten rules' in any way – by denying them a light!

After everybody was up and dressed, we had a large breakfast of tea and toast or cereal or both, much better by far again than Welwyn Ward, while unlike Welwyn Ward, the one door to the dormitory area was locked. Then came the first call of 'medication' of the day. At that stage of the day's proceedings, the staff were very vigilant about anybody slipping drugs under their tongues to dispose of later. Then came the call of 'cupboards' – a chance to retrieve – from the cupboard or locker room, your morning's supply of tobacco, food, and any other luxuries you had kept there.

Then the lucky ones allowed off the Ward to wander in the grounds were let off the locked Ward, and those of us who wanted to listen to music retrieved our personal stereos. We all went into the big day room, to watch TV on the 'Big Brother' set near the ceiling, or listen to music. This ritual was repeated at each meal, then at 9 o'clock at night we had a hot drink and a snack, before the fourth and final time for 'medication!' – thence bed, allowed any time between 10 p.m. up to as late as 12.30 p.m. Upstairs they were apparently got up earlier and were sent to bed far earlier as well – more like a prison!

I was told that weekend that Doctor Whore had not lost his baleful interest in me. The staff told me that he kept on ringing up. I soon realised that in fact he was continuing to dictate my treatment – over the telephone, by 'remote control' of the Doctors there! It was to take them all of four weeks to start thinking for themselves – and Whore to finally release my notes from the QEII to Dr Prussard, the Ward Doctor, and Dr Pinto, the Consultant. As soon as Dr Pinto saw my notes he must have realised there had been some terrible mistakes – or worse. For he immediately changed me back to the haldol depots I had always taken before Whore came into and wrecked my life, and it was me who said 'in that case I also used to take lithium – Priadel'!

That was both before and after Whore. Apart from the bizarre changes from this in 1997 under 'Doctor' Harlot, and 1999 under Thatcher and 2000 under Ballitch, and twice as in the sequel to this book in 2002 and 2003, I have been kept very well on this combination ever since.

So, at Whore's insistence, I was put on a very high dose – 100 mg four times a day – of a drug, chlorpromazine, that Whore KNEW just did not suit me. I was to stay on this for three weeks under his 'remote control', suffering greatly. Then, as we shall see, it was to get even more serious and sinister. For the next ten days, breaking all the rules as it had proven totally poisonous and life-threatening to me at the QEII, with no regard for my safety or my very life, Whore got them to put me back on clozapine or 'clozaril'!

I arrived as I said on the Friday night. On the Sunday afternoon I reacted deeply emotionally to the entire terrible ordeal and mental torture I had been going through and was evidently still going through. The 'spear' of Spiritual Experience Thirteen pierced me with a vengeance, and I was overcome to the point of tears by intense pain in my left-hand chest cavity.

153

I thought I had got lung cancer from smoking, the pain was so intense! Some staff helped me get comfortable with this agonising 'deferred, emotional pain' – but I was not then to know it was that.

'Welsh git' chipped in totally cruelly and thoughtlessly, 'Grow up! It is "only" emotional pain!' Just as cruel as my ex-, preferring to remain totally ignorant of the very real pain of the ordeal I had just been through on Welwyn Ward, he was as ever thoughtless and a right bastard over my sheer suffering!

I was seen by a kind Indian Lady Doctor, however, who arranged that I should have an x-ray at the Lister Hospital in nearby Stevenage, the next day, Monday 15th May 1995. The staff took no chances that following day – believing Whore's lies that I was a 'dangerous acute schizophrenic', and at that stage having no chance to change that opinion, I was given no less than four strong, fit nurses – some from Orchard I Ward – as escorts! I was refused permission to go to the lavatory at the Lister, and was seen very quickly – then whisked back to Fairfield. Cruel Welsh git turned out to be savagely correct – my lungs were both entirely clear of anything untoward! That did not stop the pain – which slowly died away over the next six weeks there!

That afternoon I had the first of many walks around the large garden facing onto the back of the two Orchard Wards. Outside I could see why they were called that – there was indeed an apple orchard over the high wall surrounding the garden, which was mostly grass, with some mature trees and a shed with benches in the middle. I was not to be allowed to go outside the Ward for walks round the lovely grounds, apart from my trip to the Lister, until 4½ weeks were up and I was established off clozapine and at last back on haldol and lithium. So this was a blessing – fresh air, away from the Ward! I really pitied those on 'Orchard I' Ward who could not share this luxury – of a smoke, returning to the door of the Ward for lights, and vitally, 'fresh air'!

I soon spotted running along the walls of the Orchard Ward area, a very unusual sight. *Black* squirrels were a local feature – and apparently only occur in a total of three similar places in the entire country. Normally squirrels are red, or far more usually today, the American grey. Camouflage against Evil Spirits?

Helen had been hardly visiting me, instead scorning me, increasingly less frequently while I had been on Welwyn Ward. She paid the first of about only four visits while I was on Orchard II Ward for the next three and a half months.

Outraged by her clear conspiracy with Whore of Welwyn Ward, even though she had the three-year old Jenny in her arms, I saw her and bellowed at her, 'You are a *useless* wife!' Other visits were equally acrimonious – on the fourth and last occasion she got the full works! In the garden of the Ward I turned my back physically on her and said the dreadful curse, 'Get thee behind me, Satan!' then walked away and left her!

If you read the gospels carefully, that is exactly what Jesus did to Simon Peter in the story that inspired my own curse – physically turned his back on him! That was the last time I ever had to try to make a conversation with this dreadful traitor – for soon she banned me through the staff from even telephoning her – for she claimed I was 'pestering her'! Even though I was always very diplomatic on the telephone or answering machine to her, merely trying to 'bring her to heel' – and save the marriage!

Days on the Ward stretched into weeks of endless routine, then months. Occasionally there was the 'sound of thunder' from upstairs – as some unfortunate patient 'broke the rules' or was aggressive – and no doubt was chased and restrained physically. I soon came to be very glad I was 'downstairs, not upstairs'! Every day was punctuated, as at any one time most of us were confined to the Ward, with Art Therapy and other forms of such 'Therapy' – including team music quizzes. Art Therapy took place in the gym, and Music Therapy in the 'day room'. As the late Spring turned into Summer, we were increasingly allowed out *en masse* – sometimes with the company of the 'Orchard I crowd' – into the garden. There we played ball games, and I usually brought out the portable hi-fi my parents kindly bought me, and played music – plugging in the machine through the window.

After three weeks on chlorpromazine at such a high level, I noticed that every time I went in the garden, I got very red skin – a classic reaction of that drug to the sun! However, as I said just now, at that point Whore made his final gamble – and dictated that falsely, allegedly 'dangerous schizophrenic me' be put back on clozapine! When Lynn told me this news, which I had no way to defy, I just said, 'That's *my* drug!' – very sarcastically. She looked quite worried!

Indeed, as clozapine was reintroduced to my system, instead of chlorpromazine, gradually as ever, the 'side'-effects of this *poison* were to start taking hold. I felt nauseous once more, and soon, after a couple of days at the trivial dose of 50 mg twice a day, blacked out each time I took it, for two hours or more. So in the daytime I 'crashed out' in an armchair in the day room. The night time was different. I slipped the dose under my tongue, as the night staff did not rigorously check for such "non-compliance to save one's life" – then went to the WC and flushed it away! The following week, having 'fooled the staff' for ten days, I finally saw Dr Pinto, and heard the best news of my life!

He was putting me back on haldol and lithium, after two whole years of being experimented on like some laboratory rat, by Whore!

Just before this 'clozapine incident', on 1st June 1995 something equally important happened. I was on a solitary walk in the garden behind the Ward, when I heard a voice from above me, from Orchard I Ward, calling out 'Hi! Si!' It was no less than the voice of Diamond, calling through the crack in the window! Excitedly I had a quick conversation with her, a bit like Romeo and Juliet, as I recall! She turned out to have been sent there too from Welwyn Ward, but not like me for the crime of 'non-compliance – with a poison' – no, for being 'violent' – throwing hot coffee over fellow patients who, she imagined, had offended or even threatened her!

That was why she was to spend just ten days on the 'violence' Ward, Orchard I, compared to my 14 weeks and a bit on Orchard II downstairs. She told me afterwards that it was the worst part of, like mine, the worst year of her life. She survived by writing her journal, doing frenzied art work, especially art therapy, and generally trying to ignore the place – especially certain of the worse male fellow patients, some of whom leered at her or followed her about!

In the meantime, although Helen hardly ever visited me now, out of what she claimed was fear over her 'paranoid schizophrenic, and so violent' husband attacking her (!) – she did come up and drop off carefully rationed cash, tobacco, sweets, drinks and so on she had bought. I later learned that everything she ever brought me in hospital that year was paid for systematically out of my own money, that she had in sinister fashion got Power of Attorney over. She never bought me one little thing out of her own money! Indeed she kept every single receipt meticulously, glued them on sheets of paper, and presented me with some bizarre 'accounts' when I eventually 'got out' – that I could make no sense of. Yet again this added to the sense of 'conspiracy – involving my own wife'!

One thing she stopped doing once she had her cruel way, and with Whore's help she got me 'put away' in the draconian environment of Fairfield Secure Unit, was at last and at least to stop illegally destroying or reading all my post! On her visits, now I was completely 'under her thumb' and 'put away for good' – or so she thought – she started to drop off my post once a week. Most was junk mail – but in the very first batch, before Diamond had herself arrived at Fairfield, were two love letters from her, boldly and deliberately tactlessly addressed to 'Mr. and Mrs. Lee'.

Presumably she half-hoped Helen would open these, and find out that I had a sex-starved admirer. I read these letters, and after reading them, quite shocked at their explicit declarations of love from Diamond, immediately destroyed them. At that stage I still quite naïvely believed, quite honestly, that once I got home everything could be sorted out and return quickly to normal. How far wrong can you be?

Anyhow, once I knew Diamond was upstairs, and on reading these letters, I suffered the delusion, still very ill remember, that this 'noble princess' had got herself admitted to that place – just to keep me company! This lasted till she disillusioned me some weeks later, and confessed she had been sent there as a 'punishment' by her own Doctor, for chucking coffee at people at Welwyn Ward that she took a dislike to!

In the meantime there was a flurry of notes in the Ward post between us, between the two Wards. We both enjoyed the 'war-time camaraderie' between us in keeping in touch despite all. I remember another apparent delusion I had, that back in 1998 I actually made come real (for about £100, by buying half-price end of range 'sale goods'). I looked in a catalogue at the rings there, that had been left in the Ward, and schemed how to 'cover her hands with nice rings'! I sent her a note with a picture of how her hands would like once I bought her these rings! The staff got paranoid about my fascination with this catalogue – and soon confiscated it from me!

Soon after this, as Summer was upon us, our Ward was escorted *en masse* into the Ward garden – and then came Orchard I Ward as well. Looking dreadful, in a shabby drab-green jumper and black skirt, and very coy after all our correspondence, came Diamond – so at last we met up again face to face!

Looking back, we both remained very 'high', so the conversation was a bit stilted. We have since often looked back in disbelief that the 'furtive romance' had gotten to both of us – and that after two minutes of talking I had proposed to her, even though I was still married and really still hardly knew her – and she immediately accepted! She was in fact to remain loyal for just two months after that, before 'falling abruptly out of "love"' (infatuation for all my kindness?) – once we tried love-making once we were both discharged.

My guilt over such 'adultery' – however much provoked it obviously was by Helen – ruined it for both of us. After that, this flight of mine into the arms of an apparently sympathetic 'other woman', was doomed to be a 'favourite mistake' that was to drag on until early 1998 – three years!

Diamond was, she later described, virtually a recluse and impeccably well-behaved and non-violent on Orchard I. When she was seen by Dr Prussard and Dr Pinto, Dr Pinto remarked, 'she is saying all the right things!' and decided to send her back to Welwyn Ward as soon as possible. She later told me that her stay there was her worst ever on any Mental Ward!

The news that I could see her before she left, as she was leaving, came in the middle of a terrible trauma that 11th June 1995 – just off clozapine (again!), after all I had been through, and still with 'emotional pain' in my left chest cavity. I had finally found I could take no more of these months of confinement and the obvious imminent destruction of my marriage – by those very people – Doctors – supposed to care for me! For a whole hour one afternoon, I wept solidly and openly in the Day Room. One of two Asian Nurses who was later to completely torment me - see later about my letter to the Chaplain there – completed my torment now. He came up cynically to where I was in deep grief, half way through it, and timing his remark to inflict the maximum degree of pain possible, said 'Diamond is leaving! She is going back to the QEII!'

I felt devastated to be losing my only 'compatriot' from Welwyn Ward – on top of which, with whom I was by now having a full-blown and ill 'postal affair'! My weeping got really intense now! I saw her briefly in the non-smoking room about two hours later, just before her return to Welwyn Ward at the QEII.

We promised to stay in touch and write, and she was upon discharge to visit me twice there before my next stop on my 'eight month grand tour of Mental Wards' at Harlow, then fully well and 'asymptomatic'. So I was to have to wait for another four weeks until her discharge from the QEII before she could visit me, we could go for a walk – and inevitably, we could at last express our feelings physically – so far frustrated by impossible circumstances!

In the meantime, my parents were regular visitors, and occasionally my sister and brother. Once there they had satisfied themselves there was nothing at Fairfield resembling the 'conspiracy of incompetence – or something much worse?' surrounding my treatment at Welwyn Ward, they left me happily to the care of the Doctors at Fairfield. They were not to know till much later that 'Doctor' Whore continued to exert an evil and baleful influence, 'dictating my treatment by remote control'. There was only one week when I had no visitors – tension was high in the whole family about the six-month legal confinement I was going through, and we had some kind of inflamed row. After that they did not visit me for ten days. Otherwise we eventually went for walks round the grounds – but for the first eleven weeks they just sat with me in the Ward – or if it was good weather, in the Ward Garden.

Another faithful and regular visitor was Charles, the retired Vicar from Dane End, who kept up regular weekly visits. Bert the 'real' Vicar only came once. When I told him that I was very angry to have had no visitors in six months, from the lay 'Christians' in the Parish, and that 'You are all right, but your flock are a right hypocritical shower!' he immediately left in a hurry. I understand that by popular treachery in 'his' congregation, he was ousted from being Vicar a year or two later, to be replaced by a Lady Vicar. I have no way of knowing what that Church is like now, but the parishioners, by and large, wanted a much more 'trendy', modern Vicar and Church interior, so presumably have got their way now! It was Charles who made inquiries on my behalf, and told me to write to 'Joy', the Lady Vicar at Fairfield. It turned out there was an actual makeshift Chapel on the site at Fairfield Hospital – although for weeks I was confined to the Ward, so could not attend services.

I wrote to Joy at least four times over two weeks – but some nerd among the staff was interfering with the mail – she said later she never received these notes! In the end I got the Ward Manager to intervene and ask Joy to call round to see me, as I could not get out to see her. She came several times to see me after the initial fracas about my notes to her, and was a really lovely, caring Lady – the first female Vicar I had met. She even put up with having a Mental Hospital rather than a 'proper parish' as her first 'place of duty'!

Shortly after I had been in touch with Joy, and she had called to see me several times, the incident happened that I referred to earlier, involving the two nastiest staff on the Ward. They were both Asian, as it happens – although I got on fine with most of the staff there. The same day, 9th June, I had been stopped from taking clozapine – for an illegal second time. I went to the office to post Joy a note, quite innocently, and these two started sneering and laughing.

Even though it was clearly marked 'private and confidential', and what is more clearly addressed to the Chaplain of all people – they opened this note and started reading it! I then immediately knew who had been intercepting my previous notes to Joy, the Lady Vicar! I promptly complained bitterly to the Doctor standing there the whole time! "Do you want me to re-seal it and post it for you?" he offered, having adequately 'told these two little boys off'.

"What is the point of me using the office post for anything at all while I am held here, if all my post is opened like this? No, don't bother!" was along the lines of my reply! However, this incident produced immediate repercussions from these two reprobates! They came on duty first thing the next day, and lied to the other staff that I was barred by the Ward Manager, as 'punishment' – for *their* crime – from smoking at all – I was 'banned lights'. This deprivation of any form of comfort from smoking went on all day...

About 6pm, having not smoked all day, I at last managed to query this ban with the Nurse in charge – and was immediately allowed to smoke, having been stuck in the smoke-filled 'day room' all day without a smoke myself...

To change the subject, we were all increasingly allowed out that Summer, and as it warmed up I took to wearing my canvas shorts – so exposing my then prominent varicose veins! Immediately from the ever charming Pete came the obtuse remark 'Nice legs, shame about the face!' on the steps outside the Ward. I tried to invert it to 'Nice face, shame about the legs!' but by then all the other staff had joined in the laughter! I have since gone on to get a job the following year, and on 4th November 1997, had my legs 'done' in a major operation in a private Hospital – financed by my then company's Private Health Insurance Plan. Apart from a few scars, they were nearly totally smooth and youthful-looking then, but in 2003 have erupted once more!

The shorts that I wore that day were brought in by my ex, who mysteriously appeared early in my confinement, and took away a lot of my clothes and replaced them with summer ones. She generally 'inspected' my living quarters, such as they were – all without a word to me, although she and my (her, in fact, I had realised by now) prissy 'social worker' Fanny, passed me by several times!

That, apart from Whore's 'reign of clozapine' ending eight weeks into my stay, as I have said, once I had secreted half the daily dose under my tongue, was the end of the 'influence of the Tart of Tarts/Whore/Welwyn Ward Conspiracy' while I was there. I may have been confined – but was generally far better off than at Welwyn Ward at the QEII – at Fairfield, a Secure Unit!

Soon after 5th July 1995, around which I was put back on haldol and lithium at last, after nearly two years of being 'poisoned' by Whore, I was given permission to leave the Ward several times by Dr Pinto, the Consultant.

However, it was to take some three weeks for 'his staff' to actually allow this in practice. Some lingering memories endured of the Whore/Welwyn Ward Conspiracy, among the staff at Fairfield? In the meantime, on the next meeting following my transfer back to haldol and lithium as medication, Dr Pinto expressed very severely and bluntly, his (wrong!) diagnosis at the time: - "Mr. Lee, you suffer from both schizophrenia and manic depression!"

He was to vary that by the end of my stay, in telephone conversations with my father, to 'bipolar (I) affective disorder', which is far milder than 'schizo-affective disorder' as he had previously implied was my problem, as above.

As I have said throughout this book, the former diagnosis is absolutely correct. Tragically it was immediately changed back to 'schizo-affective disorder' for no apparent logical reason, at my next and final hospital of the year... After seven weeks at Fairfield, in what turned out to be a familiar pattern from 1983, when Dr Gander first tried me on haldol, Dr Pinto tried changing the haldol to a close and milder relative, depixol. However he was to return me to haldol after a further two weeks. In the meantime, at last – three weeks after first being actually allowed this – I was able to leave the Ward and wander round the grounds. After a while I was allowed off the Ward for up to three hours at a time – but stopped going round the nearby village after being told that I was strictly not allowed off the hospital grounds under my Section 3.

The very final baleful piece of 'Welwyn Ward cock-up or deliberate interference' came then. My Section had been imposed on 5th February – so it was due to end on 5th August. When that date came, at the end of my time on depixol, naturally I asked for the Section to be ended, as legally its time was up.

However, I was shown the paperwork from the QEII, weirdly declaring that the section ended on 24th August 1995!

Some Nerd – Whore? – at the QEII had clearly rigged things so that I should spend an illegal further three weeks beyond the correct span, confined by a Section 3.

Just before that point, on 28th July 1995 – extraordinarily late in my nearly seven not the legal six months on a Section 3! – came my long-awaited Tribunal Hearing, when Dr Pinto presented a case to the solicitor Chairman, Doctor and Lay Member, that I should not be released from my Section, but that it should continue over the last few weeks of the full six months. My parents had arranged a solicitor on my behalf, a local one from Royston, picked from a list of 'local experts on Mental Health cases' as recommended by my friend and now solicitor from Cambridge, Duncan. I felt afterwards that even though I argued that I was indeed still ill, but did not need to be on a 'Section', but would prefer to continue on a voluntary basis, that this was 'par for the course'. So, briefly treated like a human being rather than just a 'mental patient', I was led back to the Ward. To spend, as I just said, the rest of my illegally imposed 6 months 3½ weeks, not '6-month' section confined to hospital...

Certainly, after that Tribunal I was allowed the full extent of my freedom from the Ward. I soon started to attend services at the Chapel on Sundays, go for long walks – as I said, soon curtailed to be on the Hospital grounds – and visit the site canteen. If one bent the rules somewhat, there was a lovely beauty spot – with several fishing lakes in crystal clear blue and bright green water respectively – just off the grounds! The bank there, typically for a 'crazy place' like that, had equally crazy hours – opening and closing at odd times through the day, with about five 'opening times' a day – at very strange times like '10.15-10.30' then '10.45-11.30'! All designed to confuse the poor patients, no doubt!

Shortly after I was first allowed out, for just half an hour at a time, I was given a short visit by Diamond, who came for the first time of two, now discharged herself from hospital. We talked for a while on the Ward, then used up my half-hour 'off the Ward'. I had been thinking of her as a refuge in the face of all the baffling hurts by Whore and the Staff at Welwyn Ward, now perpetuated by the Tart of Tarts. Now came our chance at last to touch, and for us both to express our feelings... I remember that at the time the song by Sting 'Fields of Gold' was in the charts. Strangely, our cuddle was lying down in a field of barley near the Ward. Inevitably our first attempt at passion was 'spotted' by hospital staff in two cars, which stopped in the road nearby. We straightened her skirt and top (we hadn't undressed) and went back to my Ward...

Some weeks later, my father kindly brought her again by car, not by the train she had caught the first time. This time, I had far more time off the Ward, and 'sought my comfort with her' in the woods just outside the beauty spot I just mentioned. She was wearing flimsy and provocative clothing – a halter-neck top, which I soon undid to let out her then slim breasts – and a slit skirt, which soon parted to reveal her lovely thighs and lacy white panties. However, as before, at her request we just kissed and cuddled. Full sexual activity was only to take place some weeks later, at her house in Welwyn Garden City.

Around the 10th June 1995, Dr Pinto, just like Dr Gander of the QEII before him, years before in fact in 1983, concluded that of depixol and haldol, the latter suited me better. So I was to remain, increasingly nearly well, on that, until my transfer on 22nd August 1998 to my final hospital that year. My 'Grand Tour of Mental Hospitals – conducted by Whore' was nearly over!

In the meantime, my times at Art Therapy were not wasted! I had very nearly finished my 'rainbow picture – Spiritual Experience of the Tree of Life of the Holy Spirit' that features in my other book 'Spiritual Energy'. I now attended Art Therapy at the Occupational Therapy Centre in the main grounds of the hospital, so finishing it was much easier...

So, at last, on 22nd August 1998, I was at last told to pack my belongings up, and was told I was 'being transferred again'. Was this 'pillar to post' or what? When I was supposed to be suffering from stress? We headed off, for 'destination unknown' until the three staff escorting me in the minibus told me that I was allowed to go into a tobacconist *en route* and buy cigarettes – and that I was at last being transferred to Harlow's Princess Alexandra Hospital. If I had been in the 'correct', local, 'catchment area' all along, not going to see Whore at the QEII, this would have been the hospital where I would have been seen!

CHAPTER EIGHTEEN

Crucifixion Experience Three of Three in 1995. Eviction and divorce – brought about by medics!

August to December 1995. Final crucifixion experience of my 'annus horribilis'. Princess Alexandra Hospital Harlow, 22nd August 1995 to 2nd October 1995, followed by eviction, homelessness, divorce, dispossession and 'Jenny deprivation'. All of these imposed by the Tart of Tarts, blaming Dr Pinto, 'Dr' Harlot and others – never herself for her blatant 'marriage crimes' against me!

We arrived at Princess Alexandra Hospital, Harlow, about mid-afternoon on Tuesday 22nd August 1995, and I was admitted to Hopkins Open Acute Ward, which then served the Hertford Area – which was my normal 'catchment area'. My section was not to expire till 4.30pm that Thursday 24th, even though as I have said it should have expired weeks earlier. Hence, even though I was fully mentally well and soon judged to be 'asymptomatic' on arrival, by all the staff and Doctors, I was forced to stay on the hospital grounds for those two last days of the Section. What is more, as I was a new arrival and hence an 'unknown quantity', I was to remain confined to the Ward apart from meals for the first thirty-six hours.

My 'natural' Consultant, who I was to come to call 'Dr Harlot' after he started to make a series of very serious mistakes in handling my case over the next few years, was on two weeks leave. So I was to be seen several times in the next couple of weeks by his 'locum', one Dr Brook. At first he seemed mystified that somebody so obviously mentally fully fit could be confined to a mental Ward, but soon gave up trying to make out that just because I was still a patient I must still be ill. He was to report to Dr Harlot that yes, I was fully mentally well on arrival.

So why was I not allowed to go home once Harlot returned? The answer is that I had no home I was allowed to go home to. Helen completed her cruelty of the year by not visiting me once in the six weeks I was kept there and clearly did not want me to go home at all! Although my parents often took me home for 'leave' just as they had at the end of my stay at Fairfield, they were not prepared at that stage to have me home for good. At that stage my family and I had no idea what sheer evil my ex- was now planning as her latest cruelty to me!

I did catch sight of her trying to get useful information about me from the Doctors, by hovering around and hoping they would write a damning and misleading report on me like Whore had done for my abortive Managers' Appeal back to the QEII. Once Harlot returned from this latest of frequent holidays that he took, he was indeed to oblige her, having met me for just ten minutes beforehand, and so gain my nickname for him. He wrote a reply to a letter from her, which she was to use to terrible effect a few weeks later, because it totally helped all her lies in Court and on Oath – that I had been violent.

With no evidence whatsoever, and totally irresponsibly, damning me and branding me totally falsely 'violent' rather than representing my interests as his patient, it was clear when this letter from him was produced in Court, that no, Harlot was acting in his own self-protective interests, not mine.

I thought of the 1930's actress Mae West's remark about her contemporary Jean Harlow, 'the "T" is silent as in Harlow" so 'Dr. Harlot from Harlow' got contemptuously named.

That letter was just the result of one vitriolic Meeting – my first Ward Round under 'Dr. Harlot', around 12th September 1995. Harlot was there, as was my then Social Worker, who stayed silent – and, without me being seen first by myself, as 'next of kin' ('next of kill' in her case?) was Helen!

I immediately got very angry with her, and above all accused her of treachery to me and our marriage, especially over wanting her own husband put away in a Secure Unit like Fairfield on a false diagnosis, to be poisoned by force! I blasted her with a full list of her crimes against me, then left 'my' Ward Round, no doubt for her and Harlot to conspire what he could write to damn me, his own patient. My offers via Sandy, my new Social Worker, after that meeting, for Helen and I to meet away from any such contrived 'meeting', and have marital conciliation, were totally rejected. It is clear from that point on that Helen had only one thing on her mind – divorce. However if she had not gone on to divorce me on the grounds of totally trumped-up and false charges of 'violence', I would have divorced her for her appalling mental cruelty, amounting to mental torture, throughout that year of 1995...

Shortly after arriving at Harlow, I was granted extended leave of several days at a time, most of which I spent at my parents' house in Hatfield. However, I spent one long weekend at Diamond's house in Welwyn Garden City, but when I made love to her three times that weekend, I was terribly guilty about it – still, even if only technically – being married. She protested each time that I went at express rates and virtually had premature ejaculation! It turned out she liked to have at least two hours of foreplay followed by very slow intercourse indeed – at 46, only in the 'missionary position', she insisted! As a result of this very obvious difference in speeds of lovemaking, she hardly ever let me take her to bed again in the remaining three years of our peculiar 'relationship'. We were both devastated that a very promising initial attraction had led to proving that we were so sexually incompatible. Indeed we never went to bed together more than about ten times the whole time we were 'friends'...

However, Diamond took her disappointment that she over-excited me, while I was so nervous about 'bedding' her, being adultery, far too much to heart.

One night on the Ward, about a week after staying with her, I received a phone call on the patients' telephone from her, clearly very drunk indeed.

"I am about to telephone your wife and tell her we have been to bed together three times!" she threatened sickeningly! I positively begged her, stuck on the Ward late at night, not to do it: - "What have I done to deserve this?"

However, whenever nutcase Diamond gets an idea in her head, however wild, crazy or simply cruel, especially when drunk, she *always* immediately, impetuously, acts it out in real life. About ten minutes later she completed this torture, which made me feel quite sick, by ringing me back to say,

"She was out so I left a message on the answerphone! You've had it mate! She knows all about you and I now!"

In the morning, having slept off the bottle of whisky or whatever it was she had drunk, she rang up all sheepish and apologetic. However, typically the drink, as well as being her downfall in making her often behave in such a wild, cruel way, also badly affects her memory. I expect she has largely forgotten she ever did such a mentally cruel and cowardly thing as this, only one of a long list of cruel things she has done in her life, often to me!

About the only kind thing my ex- had done all year was to restore control of my own benefit money to me while at Harlow. I soon put this excess by Diamond down to her alcoholism, and quickly forgave her. Soon I was on the phone to her again, and on the afternoon of the 21st September, took a bus to her house, to stay the weekend. However events concerning Helen were to intervene to prevent that weekend being at all happy. Far from it, it was one of the worst weekends of my life! The following week got even worse!

About 7pm we got a very worrying call from my parents. A furtive-looking man had tried to serve some kind of papers on me from Helen, but as I was not there, they suspected Helen knew Diamond's address – so if he came not to let him serve the papers. As they spoke the doorbell rang – he had got there very quickly indeed. Before I could stop her, Diamond had opened the door and the dodgy-looking man was asking for me! I walked up very reluctantly and took the sheaf of papers. He said very smarmily, "I hope that you are very happy together!" with the sincerity of a snake, and vanished into the night, a mere pawn in the deadly serious legal 'game' about to start...

I opened the papers, and could not believe my eyes! A pack of lies, alleging that the two tiny incidents when I 'cried for help' to her, after overdosing the previous year, and in the woods in March 1995, had really been attempts by me to first strangle Helen, then rape her...!

As I read the nine-page diatribe based solely on twisted, cruel lies, I first of all felt disgusted at Helen, then started to feel hope. This was an *ex parte* injunction, so there was to be a return hearing the following week, on Thursday 28th September 1995. "I'm seeing my solicitor in Royston tomorrow, as it happens," I thought to myself. "Surely, with a whole week to work in, we can prepare a more than adequate defence and totally sink all these lies!"

Then in shock, I left Diamond and went and had a drink in the pub to relieve some of my anxiety over this latest shock in a long year of shocks. Unthinkingly, I left the injunction papers at her house, not thinking she would read them – and could actually, after all my explanations, actually believe they told the truth! However, read them she did – and believed them completely...

So when I returned, she was well into a bottle of whisky, having been out to the off-licence. We had a short sharp discussion about these accusations, then I rang my parents and got them to pick me up so I could stay with them, safely away from Diamond who was totally taken in by seeing my wife's lies in writing. I have often noticed since that Diamond has a peculiar crazy double standard – it does not matter what is said, particularly by her, in words, however hurtful and destructive. However if something is said in writing – that really matters! This explains why she was very aggressive in 1998, and took me to task by getting her solicitor to write to me. This was after she would not respond at all when I telephoned her many times, maintaining a weird, aloof silence before suddenly slamming the phone down, forcing me to express myself by the only means left – writing to her. A heinous crime, in her view! After that, she changed her phone number, such was her paranoia!

I was particularly upset by my ex-'s injunction because despite her stolid resistance to such reconciliation, I had tried my best to 'make things up' with her. My parents, my brother and his partner and their then two daughters had been to Whipsnade Wild Animal Park, earlier that month, just before my wife's birthday. I had bought a T-shirt with dolphins on the front, for both my ex- and Jenny, but when my parents gave these to her as her present, there were no thanks – no response at all in fact!

Again, some weeks into my time at Harlow, I persuaded my father to take me to my home at Dane End, as I had keys. I took flowers for my ex- (a large bunch) – and a large bag of sweets for Jenny. My ex- reacted by ringing me up there and saying mockingly "I'm calling you from a safe place!" as if I was some kind of violent criminal. Then 'Doctor' Harlot called, and in equally bizarre, cowardly fashion, told me that if I did not immediately return to the hospital, he would obtain a Home Office detention order against me! (Even though he still had no evidence that I was violent, and indeed in a report written once I had seen him for a while, stated I was definitely *not* violent! The truth – far too late in the day!)

So this arrival of an Injunction was a deep shock, but not entirely a big surprise. Immediately, the following day at my parents' house, now away from Diamond's inquisitions and paranoia, I began to prepare a defence – which took me slaving away in a lather, till that Sunday 24th September 1995 to complete. This was at the behest of my then solicitor at Royston, who told me on the Friday 22nd September, in a long-scheduled meeting, that I should not worry, but to get my 'notes' to his firm of solicitors by the Monday – they would 'immediately' be turned into a proper affidavit. He also explained that he was off sick on the Monday and Tuesday, and was busy on the day of the return hearing. However at that meeting he arranged for 'no less' than a Barrister to stand in for him at the hearing, who supposedly, was expert in the Mental Health Act. He assured me at the end that we would definitely fight back at the hearing. Nothing could have been further from the truth...

Nothing at all happened at, or was heard from my solicitors, until Tuesday 26th September, while I waited in terrible suspense, especially after the terrible ordeal I had just been through all year. It struck me that I was once more powerless, while two women both behaved terribly badly around me. My wife had totally betrayed all my confidence and trust in her all year, and totally abused any right to remain my wife. Yet it was her not me who was forcing my eviction, homelessness, and was soon to extend that to near-complete dispossession and the ensuing divorce. She had surpassed all her mental cruelty towards me of that year, by now taking out a 'behind the scenes' and very cowardly *ex parte* injunction, hardly giving me time, particularly as I was still stuck in hospital at her behest, to defend myself against her ludicrously weak charges!

Now, on top of that Diamond was showing just how bad she is when on the bottle, and totally abusing my friendship and help for her when we were both in hospital together. So, the 'old woman' and the 'new woman' in my life were both proving to be an overwhelming handful. Indeed, during that week I was preoccupied with the problems that Diamond had brought on me by seducing me, so evidently being the final spur for divorce, according to what I heard from my ex- through my solicitors. "Oh no, he has gone off with an alcoholic mental patient! Do I divorce him for adultery as well as my other (false) accusations?" was the message I got on the Tuesday.

For, deeply concerned, and allowed leave from Harlow all week to defend myself in this very serious Court Case, I went the thirty miles to Royston on the Tuesday afternoon. There and only then I was told that the plan had already broken down, and that the necessary legal aid for my nine full pages of notes to be turned into an affidavit had only just arrived. I asked why they had not done that vital piece of my defence on the Monday and assumed that legal aid would arrive in due course. Indeed several other solicitors have told me since that they would have done the work *bona fide* to save time as soon as my notes had been opened on the Monday. Not so this firm of solicitors!

The junior solicitor there rather lamely said they could not (afford to risk to?) work that way! He did promise to do the work immediately, so I left a bit happier, having arranged to return the following day, when Terry, the senior partner would be available. So I made the long journey back up there again the following day, only to meet Terry and be told no, the work on my defence had still not been done. Final change of plan was that his stand-in, the Barrister, would be briefed to definitely adjourn the Court Hearing for two weeks to give my side time to prepare a proper defence. I was very reassured by this, but still anxious to avoid delay and get home as soon as possible to my wife and daughter – naturally, as soon as this nonsense had been sorted out. Yet, to quote Robbie Burns, "How oft the plans of mice and men do gin astray!"

For the Hearing the following day was to see a momentous and monstrous 'change of plan' yet again – this time by the stand-in Barrister supposedly acting for me. He was to 'roll over and play dead', and failed to defend me, giving the entire Case to my ex- on a plate, having completely ignored his brief!

I complained about the Solicitors to their Office for Supervision about various aspects of their mishandling of my affairs in 1998, and eventually received an apology for 'distress and inconvenience caused' as well as a mere, derisory, £200 compensation. Actually I lost nearly £100,000 in all in this divorce case...!

After that derisory compensation and very reluctant apology, as advised by that Office, I turned even more seriously and heavily to train my guns on this Barrister – via the Bar Council, his managing and disciplinary body. The relevant committee sat on 11th November 1998 to discuss my complaint, and decided I was entitled to neither any apology, nor financial compensation. In 1999 the case went to the Ombudsman for Legal Services, who agreed with that decision...!

I have lost my life's work and savings of nearly £100,000 over this – all invested in my house and car and marital possessions, all of which apart from a few of the latter my ex-wife now has. If this Barrister had adjourned the case as his brief very clearly said, I would not have lost everything like this. There is every chance that in an adjourned hearing, my defence could have overturned my wife's blatant lies about my behaviour while ill. These lies still make me squirm when I think that all that mud seems to have stuck!

So, to summarise briefly. As soon as my parents and I arrived at Luton Crown court for the hearing, I found that the Barrister was already there. He did not want my parents in with him, the junior solicitor, who arrived late, and me in the ante-room. Almost immediately he started talking about something mysterious called 'Undertakings', saying that these could quite simply replace the Court Order sought by my ex-, with no onus of guilt on myself. In other words, he thoroughly recommended that if the 'chance came up in Court' to take these I should do so. The issue of adjournment was totally ignored by both him and the junior solicitor, who just seemed to sit and take notes throughout. So, here was the third change of plan in a week by this dodgy 'team'!

At the end of two years of illness, ending in eight months in terrible hospitals, I admit that I was completely caught off my guard. I did not understand what these 'Undertakings' really involved – effectively they gave the same result away as accepting a Court Order – and when both the judge and my Barrister pressurised me, in my first ever appearance in Court, I took them willy-nilly.

For our case was late in, the day was booked solid, and the female Indian Judge was clearly in a hurry. My ex-, about as wifely and friendly as a three-headed rattlesnake, once again totally wantonly broke the law, by presenting 'Doctor' Whore's totally wild and misleading report on me for the Appeal earlier that year at Welwyn Ward – remember? This stated totally dogmatically yet erroneously that I was 'among the most acute cases of schizophrenia' – and with absolutely no evidence apart from the lies of my ex-, now repeated in Catch-22 fashion by a Doctor eager to hear them and 'report them officially' – that I was violent! My ex- had stolen this report from me when I was given it just half an hour before that bogus Management Appeal. In producing it in public in this way she and her solicitor broke all the rules of the Mental Health Act, about confidentiality.

Perhaps even worse, she had written to and got a horrible letter back from 'Doctor' Harlot, who had known me for literally ten minutes, claiming equally wildly and libellously that 'anyone with my particular illness was bound to be violent' without actually claiming – totally falsely - that I was indeed violent. Just two months later, having actually taken the time and trouble to get to know what I am really like, Harlot wrote a very different report. This stated that 'he (me) has a warm, compassionate nature, and is not at all violent'. Again, if he had written that truth, instead of the initial drivel of 'violence' that let my ex-wife brandish such a letter from him in Court, things might have turned out very differently that day.

Having read these two scandalous packs of lies, after a few minutes, after just a few questions, the Judge pressed both sides to accept Undertakings. My ex-wife's solicitor had not been able to countenance my taking Undertakings. Very grimly, my ex- wanted to have the police able to actually arrest me if I ever went within 100 meters of her – such was her state of pure paranoia about my 'violence' towards her, as alleged in her Testimony on Oath for her Injunction!

Immediately, seeing the chance to get a 99% 'victory' over me very cheaply, apart from the draconian power of arrest for vehemently totally non-violent me, the 'other side' changed their tune and agreed. Naturally, my own stand-in Barrister, obviously out for an easy time at my expense, again pressurised me to take Undertakings. Dumbly, still reeling from two whole years of being kept ill by my own arrogant, sinister 'Doctor' Whore, I acceded.

So, within ten minutes I had signed the wretched Undertakings, which sealed the fate of my marriage, as I could not even talk to my ex- at all for at least six months, making reconciliation totally impossible. As she had possession of the house – in joint names then – the car, and all my possessions, she was to prove to relish having a complete 'whip hand' over me, and was to actually enjoy stripping me of everything I had spent my life working towards.

She actually once said to my sister in an argument on the telephone, 'He deserved to lose everything after all he did to me!' *What???* All I ever did to her was go to see the dangerously arrogant and sinister 'Doctor' Whore. It was *her* who was then mentally cruel to me throughout my ordeal in various hospitals in 1995, as we have just been seeing. The marriage had been irretrievably broken by her breaking *all* her vows, 'In sickness and in health... For richer, for poorer... For better and for worse'.

That and only that was what drove me into the arms of Diamond, and made me commit adultery in a marriage already smashed by my ex-, whose true character, that of a domineering, bullying, cowardly dragon had finally been exposed. No, I cannot blame myself for seeking comfort with another woman... I am just sad that Diamond was so utterly plagued by problems and personality, and cold, hard and grasping, she totally failed to provide it...

I have mentioned that I complained about these solicitors and received a fulsome apology and trivial compensation of just £200. The Office for their Supervision at that time stated clearly, that I ought to take up the Barrister's behaviour with his Bar Council, as he had clearly ignored his brief totally. Also nobody still in mental hospital should be judged as mentally fit enough, to Undertake anything so onerous as abandoning their home and all possessions, and not talking to or seeing their wife or daughter, for six whole months.

As I said earlier, there was a Committee Meeting on 11th November 1998 at the Bar Council, to discuss my case against this Barrister, which went up to them four months previously. This totally 'whitewashed' this Barrister, and totally exonerated him. The long letter back from them totally failed to mention most of our most important points against his abysmal and pig-headed ignoring of his totally clear brief – and pressurising me, ill for the previous two years, and so clearly incapable of doing so, to give Undertakings.

As I said, I lost nearly one hundred thousand pounds in the end, and my home, let alone the far more important issue that I was not to see Jenny from July 1995 to March 1996 – nine whole months! After that my ex- meted out 'Contact' like the miserly dragon she is – and humiliated me by insisting I had always to be accompanied and 'supervised' by my family. Totally demeaning and unnecessary!

So, I returned to my parents' home, still on leave but with no home to go to. My ex- had made me homeless now, and my parents, having taken a basinful that year and the previous one, were also unwilling to take me in.

Finally I borrowed the car and visited Diamond, who immediately offered that I could come and live with her, after she returned from the alcoholics' Ward at Ealing Hospital, where she was due to spend the weekend following the Hearing, starting the following day, Friday. I was duly seen at Harlow that Tuesday 2nd October 1995, told them I was going to stay with Diamond – and at long last was discharged – even though my stay with Diamond was abortive, and only lasted one night! I remember I lugged two heavy suitcases through Harlow, caught the 724 bus to Welwyn Garden City, and was nearly dead with aching arms by the time I reached Diamond's house, some way from the bus station. I remember thinking, 'I wonder what I have let myself in for here?' Diamond served up a meal and I duly stayed that night – just the one in the end!

Without my very kind parents I could have ended up on the street, for on the evening of Wednesday 3rd October 1995 I returned in the car I had borrowed from my sister, from Harlow to pick up my medication. There I had had the harrowing experience of seeing my ex-, still prowling around even though I had been discharged, still clearly trying to get Doctors to give her the incorrect 'lowdown' on me behind my back. One harrowing experience led to another. I had a meal with my family in Hatfield and then arrived at my would-be new 'home' at Diamond's – to find her recent experience at the Ealing Hospital alcoholics' Ward had clearly totally failed. It was 9.30pm and she was most of the way – solo – through a bottle of whisky! As soon as I walked in I encountered one of my earliest experiences of a "Diamond diatribe". She gave me a verbal lashing, complete with threats of violence, all because she was still vividly running through her mind the recent totally false accusations against me – which were why I was trying to stay with her, after all.

By about midnight I had had enough of this complete verbal abuse, complete with threats, so packed up yet again – for the umpteenth time that year – and even put my bicycle in the back of the car. I set off for my parents' house four miles away, reflecting I had left one three-headed rattlesnake for another three-headed rattlesnake! Luckily they welcomed me, even though they had been fast asleep. They quickly made up a bed on the floor in the large back room of the house, facing onto the garden. Then I crashed out, wondering what on Earth had happened to me all that year, especially recently, and even too upset and confused to collapse in floods of tears…

My parents rapidly accepted that indeed I could never go back to an alcohol-soaked, clearly demented, violent, threatening nutcase like Diamond, so quickly agreed the following day to let me stay in that room as long as I needed it.

That was to turn into a whole nineteen months. "No son of mine is going into some homeless hostel!" swore my Mother – the only alternative at that stage.

They planned, at long last, after all the traumas of that year, especially over me, to take a week's caravan holiday in Devon the following Saturday 8th October 1995, so I was immediately invited to take a tent and go along too.

Meanwhile we quickly transformed my room into a makeshift 'bed-sit' – with bed and wardrobe. In the end it was really reasonably homely, and as it overlooked their lovely garden, with plenty of light, was quite pleasant. It was really cold outside, so my Mother even broke her 'golden rule' and said I could smoke in that room during the Winter…

The holiday in Devon was a true delight for all three of us, given all the truly stupendously traumatic experiences of the year for the whole family, especially of course me. We were camping, almost alone as it was at the very end of the season for camping, in a large campsite in the middle of nowhere, with sunsets over the distant sea. A two-mile drive or bike ride took us down between the Devon coastal hedgerows to a village with harbour and fishing boats. There were several pleasant pubs and two very nice cafés. After the ordeal of the last nine months, we just relaxed, eating outside as much as possible, with long nights, and occasionally having a meal or drink in the village. Then there were occasional trips to neighbouring coastal towns to shop.

Too soon the week was up, and it was back to face the horrors of what was now an obviously impending divorce to follow the traumas of an Injunction based solely on lies, which had completely dispossessed me. My ex- drove up one day, smirking, in her car, with my father in his car – heavily loaded. She had agreed to give me my clothes, books, and my computer, at least accepting that these were mine. Other effectively trivial and 'useless' i.e. not worth any money, possessions of mine continued to arrive as she alone saw fit to dictate, over the next few years. I have never received anything I acquired while we were married, even presents to me, and I have never been allowed back to my own former home, that I bought for the family, since…

The 'Divorce Petition' duly arrived about a month after the holiday ended. I was disgusted and horrified that it merely repeated the same total lies as the Court Order – and immediately urged my solicitor in Royston to get her to drastically water it down, and also to immediately submit a 'reply'. The latter was about the only redress I had under the law to all these fresh lies and smears – in divorce of all things.

Diamond and I were now cautiously seeing each other again, and slowly the relationship was to thaw and get a bit more sexy. This was to become a familiar pattern, her driving me away, usually after her drinking got the better of her, then a gradual thaw in her ice, followed by a hint of sexual behaviour.

It turned out that, although these terrible solicitors totally neglected to tell me that, that there was a six-week time limit to 'file a reply' to my ex-'s divorce petition. Quite astonishingly and dismally, despite several prompts and reminders from me, ever anxious after their dismal performance at Court, and increasing complaints from me about their appalling 'performance' – they were to fail me there, yet again. They had six weeks, yet totally failed to 'file my reply' to my ex-'s divorce petition. They had let both my eviction and now my divorce by my very aggressive ex- go totally undefended!

That is one major reason why I have written this totally true and objective account of my life, especially about this year of 1995! How else can my daughter eventually, once she is old enough to be allowed to, hear the truth about the divorce? For instance, my ex- has clearly told her the whopping lie that she sold 'Babar', my car, 'because Daddy did not want it any more'. The truth is that I continually demanded to have my car back – and my ex- just laughed at that!

My complaints against these atrocious solicitors mounted, until in December, after I wrote them what my now solicitor called a 'totally innocuous letter' when I hurriedly arranged to see him to ask him to replace them, they broke off all contact, saying 'relations have totally broken down'. Such pride and arrogance have I encountered among 'professional' people! First the brash, arrogant, casual, totally selfish and uncaring 'Doctors' Whore, and to a large degree Harlot. Above all of course the abysmally cruel and selfish actions, with absolutely no thought for my feelings, or those of my family, of my dragon-like 'ex'-, a so-called 'caring Veterinary Surgeon'. Now, to complete the full set of 'professional behaviour', these solicitors and their appointed Barrister, above all, had totally let me down – then stoutly defended their appalling amateurism.

Anyhow, as of December these 'lawyers' I had, made divorce inevitable. Then, like a breath of fresh air, Ed, my new lawyer, turned out to be very wise and professional, hence very busy, but vitally both very caring – especially about children in divorce – and above all an expert on Mental Health. So he was very effective when the long, traumatic process of getting

'Contact' with Jenny, all of nine months after I last saw her, culminated in March with the first tentative session – in the hostile environs of a 'contact centre' in Hatfield.

I distracted myself in the months of November and December in two ways. I borrowed my sister's car – she was abroad for six months – or cycled over to see Diamond, in an ever-rocky 'relationship' that swung wildly between being 'off' due to one of her frequent 'diatribes', to me trying to stop her abusing alcohol and experimenting with her medication quite so much. As my only friend, left and in the area, for the next three years, it was still a very one-way supportive relationship, me doing all the giving, more 'off than on' and 'up and down' through rows, the whole time.

The other 'hobby' was to start work on my computer. I produced a fresh draft, based on fresh ideas, and a certain amount of input from Diamond, by working very hard, including sketching various of the illustrations on my computer package, that led to the four main pictures in my book 'Spiritual Energy', which was then called something entirely different. What I had left it as in 1992, was totally transformed. No Spiritual Experiences, and poetry all removed at Diamond's strong suggestion, and re-packaged as a terse, short, yet highly compelling and unusual work. I am not at all surprised, after all I have been through, to find the poetry emerging in another book of mine, and the Spiritual Experiences, much more fittingly than in the original, completely definitively interpreted now that I have got down to describing my life in this new set of books.

I 'mailshot' about thirty UK publishers with this book, and after a 'lead' from one of them, got a reply from an Irish publisher based in Calais in France. After about a month, I signed his contract, and paid up £550 – from my credit card, I had no other way to pay – for him to produce and market my book. I also started to rewrite and strengthen various parts as he requested, and reversed the order of the two 'halves' of the book. Sadly he was to turn out to be a con man!

Christmas that year, dispossessed and sadly without any hint of seeing my daughter, is best forgotten. Only one friend left to speak of – a nutcase, to boot!

179

Then a fateful Christmas card arrived out of the blue, from Sarah Todd, whom I had not seen nor heard from since the Spring on Welwyn Ward... Just before that card arrived (one of very few that I received now that I no longer lived at Dane End – by force of law, combined with excruciating cruelty); on 22nd November there was one of just a few bright spots in that dismal *annus horribilis* of 1995. My Mother had retired from running the Health centre as a Nursing Sister, in the previous year of 1994. Now she was to be the first in line as a result, at a Ceremony at St. Albans Abbey – to receive an Honorary Masters Degree or MSc – in recognition of all her hard work at the University. We all enjoyed a lavish banquet including duck and salmon at the Civic Centre, along with my Mother's Sister Pat and her husband John. Then onto a ceremony, with mother up front chauffeur driven, that was full of pathos considering all that the family had been through and continued to go through that year.

Mum was not alone with problems with her daughter-in-law – Pat's son, my cousin Nick, had an equally difficult and obstreperous wife, who would not let her see her grandchild (later to become grandchildren) in a similar dragon-like way to my own ex-wife. As I say this occasion was memorable, and greatly relieved my frequent tears of rage and frustration all that Autumn and into the next year, 1996. As an aside, I also saw Carol, the Student Nurse I met at Fairfield earlier in 1995, take her degree.

Meanwhile, all of Diamond's many massive problems were coming out or simply being confessed. As my ex- refused to hand over my car, intending to sell it, only surrendering my push-bike, I had to resort to cycling or usually borrowing my sister's car (she was abroad) to visit Diamond, about four miles away in Welwyn Garden City. She frequently 'blew me up' – or her then 14-year old daughter, who had been in care since 1991 and scarcely approved of her mother's frequent episodes in hospital preventing her looking after her!

So, I had scorned my ex- partly because I had met another woman, who it now turned out, too late, could offer me virtually nothing. This was in return for loads of moral support, advice, a lavish holiday, and money she scrounged from me over the next three years. Also that December, my row with my solicitors at Royston that had been going on since their Barrister let me down so badly back in September, resulted in the complete rift described earlier.

So apart from a bright spot of 22nd November and Mum's honorary degree, 1995 was best firmly forgotten. We spent a quiet Christmas at my parents' house, apart from when my brother and his two daughters – soon to be joined by a son, Jordan – descended on us. Without Jenny but with her girl cousins, Christmas seemed very bleak indeed. Contact was not forthcoming because – again – my ex-solicitors had failed to pressure Dr Harlot into preparing a full medical report on me in order to satisfy my ex- that I was not completely 'barking' mad.

The year ended with my father and I seeing a new solicitor for me in Saint Albans, Ed, whom I still have as my solicitor, who is an expert on the Mental Health Act. I really hoped Ed could secure contact for me within just a few weeks into 1996. However I was in the end not to see Jenny from July 1995 to March 1996 – so great was my ex-'s antagonism towards me and my family...

CHAPTER NINETEEN

That traumatic year of 1995 was so important that all of four Ominous Spiritual Experiences came true, or started to, then - Experience Five Outcome One, and the last year 1994's holiday Spiritual Experiences twelve, thirteen and fourteen

1. *Meaning One of Eight of Spiritual Experience Five of Chapter Seven.*
   Very negative, doom and gloom! My 'relationship' with my friend 'Diamond', which started in 1995, and was 'killed' by her early in 1998...

'Diamond' is a nickname I have agreed with her to protect her identity as far as possible. When I suggested it to her she readily agreed – saying that in the very 'rough company' she had kept before meeting me, and does again since dumping me in 1998, they often called her a 'diamond' – probably due to the local Cockney expression 'me old diamond'!

It is indeed an apt name, although her deep, sexy, husky, very clipped and sultry 'upper class' voice straightaway tells you that like a diamond, she is completely fascinating – in personality and looks. She is very multi-faceted in fact, just like a diamond. The fact that she suffers from chronic compound mental illnesses, not just my one, on top in her case of being very artistically talented and having a full blown 'artistic temperament' at the root of it, is dangerous indeed. It means she can show another side to her personality – the (very) 'rough diamond'!

Certainly I experienced a 'Diamond Diatribe' – the full force of the rough edge of her very sharp tongue – on many occasions, almost always after she had had a drink too many! On such occasions, when given a lecture about every single possible tiniest flaw in my character that I could wish not to hear about, greatly exaggerated, I either wished the ground would open up and swallow me up – or preferably, her! – or simply vacated her dragon-like presence.

It was Diamond herself who emphatically 'laid claim' to being the subject – or, as it turns out, the first subject of all of eight! – of this Spiritual Experience Five. This was in 1996, when I showed her my 1995 notes about my Spiritual Experiences – which were totally sketchy notes, compared to the definitive, final account you are reading now.

As soon as she saw the drawing of this Spiritual Experience Five, and that my notes clearly said 'yet to materialise' she excitedly said, 'But that is about me! I just love wearing dark glasses, especially throughout the Summer! And as you well know, I have been an alcoholic since 1970, when I was 21!'

I immediately thought about the meaning that the first image had about her for me – and equally excitedly added, 'Yes! I see it now! The 'eight stars' indicate that you are indeed eight years older than me' (8 years and 18 days, to be precise!)

Diamond is small (5'6") and slim, and has a cold, very 'aristocratic', exterior on the whole. This has been brought on by thirty out of her fifty-odd years having been filled with suffering – featuring dozens of stays in Acute Wards in Mental Hospitals – and lots of other problems, discussed below.

Although she has only been on benefit, with very few earnings, apart from occasionally selling one of her paintings, for the last twenty years since retiring as a stripper, she has very expensive tastes. One of the kindest things I did for her at the peak of our friendship between 1995 and 1997, was to give her most of my spare time – and cash and presents – and indeed got into financial trouble a couple of times over that generosity. A new outfit is a rare luxury for a woman living on benefit – so when I bought her no less than three, one 'mix and match', in the Autumn of 1996, when I was working on a good salary with few out-goings, she was delighted! She was just as obviously thrilled this summer when I fulfilled a daydream I had about her at Fairfield in 1995 – and covered her hands with rings! I managed to do that for around £100, by cannily buying good – but end of range, hence half-price – rings in a discount store!

A newly found or uncut diamond is a 'rough diamond' and to cut it requires something just as hard and so sharp – another diamond. Certainly when I first met her, virtually her first line in one of her love letters then, in response to seeing my very good CV, was the ironic, self-mocking title, which was 'Degree in alcohol and drug abuse' – saying 'Look, you ought to know I am a rough diamond!'

I can only put down my attraction to this beaten-up, screwed-up, alcoholic, who regularly abused prescribed drugs and alcohol, and then mixed all the time with similar 'drop-out' people, to two things. Firstly, I deeply pitied her with all her problems, as I then had a comfortable middle-class background. Which, only partly due to Diamond seducing me in 1995, but mostly the fact that 'Doctor' Whore had put me in that situation by systematically medically abusing me in the first place over the previous two whole years – I was soon to completely lose!

It was clear from several love letters from Diamond in July 1995 that the feeling was mutual, and in the face of the fact that my wife had changed sides and was now on the side of 'Doctor' Whore, our brief sexual affair was inevitable. Diamond is a divorcee, but it was 'illicit' and extra-marital for me, even though Whore had irretrievably damaged my marriage, and my 'ex-' had gone on to betray all my trust as my 'wife'.

Alcohol and drug abuse are the only two of Diamond's dozen or so really very serious problems that Diamond has any real control over, then only if she uses will-power. Once you read the list overleaf of the 'twelve fiery thorns in her slipped crown of thorns', you should be able to see this. Certainly for the main two years of our very erratic 'relationship' featuring little or 'No sex, we're British! – or something!' – these were the two main areas I tried to help her with.

This was apart from telling her frequently, along with social workers, her medical 'helpers' and Doctors, and above all the Police, that it was pointless to dream of having her teenage daughter living with her. At least, not until she grows out of being a violent delinquent, not able to work and only interested in men. Needless to say, 'dreamy Diamond' learned the hard way – by taking her daughter into her house for two months in 1998 – and ending up on the local Acute Ward after an overdose. Another 'last ditch' attempt to take her in failed in

1999... On top of that in 1998 her daughter drove her back to the drink having heroically not touched it for over four months!

She went on a drunken rampage around the local pubs – even though she is still banned from most of them after previous similar drunken rampages! In the end she attacked several 'bouncers' as well as a policewoman. She was bundled into a police car, spent a night in the cells, and was released on police bail on charges of 'drunk and disorderly' and 'assaulting a (woman) police officer'. She cannot remember the latter! The Court was very kind to her and she got away with a tiny fine. I was very pleased for her, but when I rang and told her so – she acted totally crazily and got her solicitor to send a very irate – and misled, deluded, letter warning me to leave her totally alone – or I would receive a Court Order – or Injunction. As a result I could apparently never contact her again!

So, as well as being a 'rough diamond' she is often 'half cut'! However, to her credit, all is not awful about her. She has a very deep, sexy, 'upper-class' voice that is a real 'turn-on', especially on the phone. Also, as a retired stripper she retains a – to me, anyway – attractive face, and especially, astonishingly, retains at 50-plus, the slim, attractive, well-proportioned figure of a 19-year old!

Above all, as her Mother often reminds her – 'she has her art' – she trained for most of the Degree in Art at St. Martin's College in London, the famous Art College. She is both a very skilful artist, with a superb 'eye' – and can turn out a very expressive poem or piece of creative writing.

So when I met her Diamond was not all 'rough' – but a very multi-faceted, 'partly cut' – and often 'half cut' – diamond! As I said, I set out to help her sort out those problems where her, and only her, will power could be the main or indeed only solution – drink and drug abuse. On the occasions since when she has temporarily beaten those, mostly if I say so, after all my help, there was a vast improvement in her feelings about life, and especially herself.

The most helpful thing I did for her, from 1995 to 1998, was buy all her drinks whenever we went out together. This – for me – expensive arrangement was made on the basis that I could thence control her intake of drink – and so 'train' her to only have two drinks, and so moderate her drinking, like 'normal' people.

Most of the time this arrangement proved to work – until as I said, in 1998 – when first she went four or five months without drinking at all – then it started to go wrong again. Dare I say it, partly because she started pushing me out of her life about April 1998, saying I 'pressurised her too much'? Along with the pressure of having her dreams of looking after her daughter after being in care from age ten, constantly frustrated by this delinquent daughter playing up?

Twelve fiery thorns in her 'slipped crown of thorns' I mentioned earlier that I would give a full list of her problems. There are all of twelve listed below, of which the last two are the only two I did not list when I wrote back to her solicitor after her ludicrous and well over the top letter arrived on 14th October 1998. Each of these twelve would in itself be a 'thorn in the side' of anybody else. Pity then, poor Diamond, wearing a 'crown of twelve such fiery thorns'! As I and many other people have pointed out to her, most people would be dead by now under such vast problems! She is brave and tough indeed to endure them!

1) Diamond has a rich mixture of both chronic (lifetime, episodic) and acute mental illnesses, for which she takes a heady cocktail of strong drugs. Moreover, she insists, despite all sound advice to the contrary, on perpetually abusing these, both by themselves and with many 'Mickey Finns' of many, many bottles of wine or whisky. She has been an alcoholic as long as she has been a chronic mental patient – the self-styled 'Queen of Welwyn Ward' with 50+ stays there in the 1990's and a similar frequency in the 1970's! She wears some weird crown…

2) As a result of all this the Doctors at the QEII have completely given up on a diagnosis, and kindly tell her she just has 'a psychotic illness'! She actually thinks this is quite good!

3) Her longest-term problem is chronic, acute and very paranoid schizophrenia. After a whole year of me trying to get her to take the new atypical tranquilliser 'olanzapine' she took it for a while in 1998 – and, surprise, surprise, even though she still abused other drugs and alcohol, she was indeed far less paranoid and 'drugged' for a while! Of course, at the time she denied any part I played in persuading her to try it!

4) She is a chronic and acute sufferer of psychotic hypomania and has often been diagnosed as suffering from chronic and acute bipolar affective disorder.   She is often suicidally clinically depressed as a result and often takes large life-threatening overdoses of the drugs she perennially 'experiments' with.

5) Whenever she drinks on top of all these problems she gets verbally, and often physically, abusive. I personally have been verbally abused hundreds of times, yet still persisted in trying to help her – which I see as stopping her abusing alcohol and drugs. She got let off very lightly from criminal charges of 'drunk and disorderly' and 'assaulting a policewoman' after a drunken rampage through Welwyn Garden City in 1998. She is psychopathic, in other words. The medical people have tried to warn me about this...!

6) Especially after a couple of drinks she is very promiscuous. At the last count, she has had over 120 (at the very least) sexual relationships in 30 years, often with married men like myself – in her twenties she claims to have seduced a professional and international footballer, while he was married, and to have bedded the radio and TV celebrity Jimmy Savile. At the same time she is totally frigid and sexually frustrated – she told me that of these 120 men in her past sex life, only three – not including me! – gave her any 'sexual satisfaction'. Her relationships with most men are stormy – apart from me, she has mostly 'gone with' brutish types who either beat her up or rape her.

7) She admits to having been raped at least three times in her twenties, and made pregnant when 'gang banged' in Hatfield. She told me guiltily at the same time that she got drunk, then deliberately provoked the gang bang, and all but one rape. The gang bang resulted in one of two abortions...

8) Her ex- used to abuse, burn and beat her, and is a psychopath like her and her daughter. He has been in prison for long periods several times. Her daughter is in danger of the same...

9) She has not worked in twenty years – and her only full-time job she could hold down for any time in her twenties was as an 'erotic dancer'. She may be so stooped, lined and wizened that people call out 'witch' in the street to her, but she retains a gorgeous voice and body – at 50-plus!

10) She is about the worst example of the 'It ain't me mister! It is them others! Yes all of them!' syndrome I have ever met. She always blames everyone else for all her problems! No wonder her GP classifies her as 'Severely Mentally Impaired' and no wonder I went to her assistance when we became

friends, then like so many others she used all of her sexual techniques as an 'erotic dancer' to seduce me, even though I was then married, in 1995. You see, I have a lot of background of working with and helping people with a mental impairment, in their case 'learning difficulties'. In her different case, with her drinking, wit, and intelligence compounded with it, things got very confusing...!

11) Her family have progressively and until recently, with a lot of help and advice from me to her about 'tact and diplomacy', completely disowned her. She recounted to me that there were two main reasons for this. Firstly, shortly after her divorce in 1990, she appeared on prime-time national television on a programme that interviewed mental patients. She very publicly accused her entire close family of 'dumping her' in Welwyn Garden City while they all moved away in the 1980's – her parents to retire to Eastbourne, her brother and sister to get married and move on. Very hurtfully to her parents in particular, she also claimed on this programme that when she was first ill in bed at home for six weeks with clinical depression, that her own father had kept sexually abusing her! Her mother cannot accept that her lovely, church-going, gentle husband could ever have done such a thing, and always accuses Diamond of having a vivid imagination! Secondly, until recently the family have not begun to forgive Diamond for extremely wild and lewd behaviour, which resulted in her being taken forcibly to a local Acute Ward, which they think largely caused her father's heart attack and death some years ago. For she wantonly and crazily and deliberately tried to show how badly she often felt, by swallowing a bottle of pills and downing it with a bottle of whisky, in front of her parents, whilst visiting them in their new home at Eastbourne!

12) To cap all this huge list of twelve very major problems, is the biggest of all – her ongoing attempts to establish some kind of control over and relationship with her own teenage daughter. The latter is a typical Welwyn Garden City delinquent – mixing with criminals and drug-addicts, never paying her rent, too wayward to get a job, so forever scrounging to make up her meagre £28 a week "job-seekers' allowance". She is not really interested in getting a job

anyway – she is too interested in men! Like her father she is also violent, and often beats up her own mother or her crockery or doors, or other parts of the house! Once she beat Diamond up so severely that her mother vowed never to have her under her roof again until she was 21 – like I and so many professional people had often advised – until she starts 'growing up'! It is not surprising that Diamond cannot cope with her daughter, with the above list of problems. As she is herself highly unstable, violent and admits herself to be a scrounger, who cannot work, it is virtually impossible for her to set an example to her wayward daughter – who has a fatherless daughter of her own!

If she ever gets to read the above account of Diamond's problems, together with the rest of the account that follows, in the next few chapters, of our friendship between 1995 and 1998, my 'ex-' may realise just how lucky she is compared to poor Diamond! Also I hope she might appreciate that compared to the violence – especially domestic violence, and self-abuse – inflicted over the years on Diamond, any problem she still claims I ever caused – particularly of so-called non-existent 'violence' – pales into insignificance!

2. *Definitive interpretation of Spiritual Experience Twelve of summer 1994.   "What is a 'Legalist', daddy?"*

A 'Legalist', Jenny, is a Christian term for a *Devil* – who like to wrap you up in artificial 'rules and regulations' – just like the three heads I saw of Satan – who always has three heads like this! - in this Spiritual Experience I saw when we were on holiday when you were three!

3. *Definitive Interpretation of Spiritual Experience Fourteen of summer 1994.*

The door I only recognised the following year during my runner to my college as being exactly identical to the small west door of the chapel of King's College Cambridge.

Indeed seeing that door revealed as the one in my vision of 1994, during my 'runner' to my old college, was highly encouraging as a 'sign from above' during the great ordeals of that year of 1995!

4. Definitive Interpretation(s) of Spiritual Experience Thirteen of summer 1994. Three 'Crucifixion experiences' – with the central one involving acute pain in my left-hand side! A Spiritual Experience with no less than three parallel meanings, like the eight of Spiritual Experience Five.

First meaning of three of Spiritual Experience 13 – unlucky for some? I would undergo no less than three 'Crucifixion experiences' the following year of 1995

In 1995, I was indeed to face three Crucifixion experiences, in all of three very different mental hospitals. First dragged into Welwyn Ward, then Fairfield, then further torture at Harlow Hospital where I was evicted then divorced, making me homeless. As we saw at length in the preceding three chapters, in the course of the central 'Crucifixion experience' at Fairfield, I indeed suffered acute emotional pain – just like a spear thrust into my left chest cavity!

Second meaning of three of Spiritual Experience Thirteen – three 'years in which I would be crucified by so-called "Doctors"' – 1994, 1995 and 1997.

This second meaning of Spiritual Experience Thirteen takes a broader view – I had been 'mentally crucified' that Spring of 1994, and would face two other even worse Crucifixion experiences in Mental Hospitals – in 1995 as we have just seen, and 1997 as we will see.

Third meaning of three of Spiritual Experience Thirteen – Jesus flatteringly compares my experiences to his own on the Cross – at Calvary Hill!

The third and final meaning of this Spiritual Experience, taken with the Spiritual Experience that followed a few seconds later in my mind's eye while praying at Evensong, at Christchurch Priory, was the simplest and most direct.

Clearly the three crosses in my Spiritual Experience, even including the big central one with its spear, are an uncanny analogy of the scene on Calvary Hill in Jerusalem in AD 33 – without any figures. To fill these in, if you recall the story, Jesus was stabbed in the chest with a spear on the cross, and another innocent person and a criminal were crucified along with Jesus.

The innocent person in my own Spiritual Experience was clearly my poor little daughter, still suffering and confused today because of the divorce brought about by the latter-day 'criminal' in this analogy. This is clearly my ex-wife, who divorced me very wickedly, cruelly, greedily and spitefully, with total disdain for any feelings I might have, late in 1995.

CHAPTER TWENTY

1996, a year of many 'uphill struggles', then latterly something of an 'eye of the storm'

1996, and a long battle to give me any Contact at all with Jenny is reluctantly lost by Helen – like 'getting blood from a stone'. A long, fruitless battle to try to get Sarah Todd to save her own life – by getting a second opinion – away from 'Doctor' Whore's baleful control. A full-time job in Defence, starting mid year, at an excellent salary! A (nearly) memorable holiday with Diamond. Spiritual Experience Fifteen repeats Spiritual Experience Three, and so definitively confirms that everything about that Spiritual Experience had come true!

Spiritual Experience Five – Meaning Two of Eight. My abortive attempt to get my other book published – through a rogue 'publisher' who really let me down.

When Diamond read my book 'Spiritual Energy' in draft form that Autumn of 1995, she said it was so riveting that 'she really fell in love – with my mind!' Sadly she has never been bothered to read the final finished version.

That Winter, amidst all the horrors of impending divorce, and legally imposed – totally unjustly – absolute lack of Contact with my daughter Jenny, then coming up to five years old, I desperately tried to 'launch' my book. I took out a lot, at Diamond's advice, first, and added some new material. Then, only just able to afford it on incapacity benefit, I 'did the rounds of the publishers' by post.

Eventually, one publisher who was not currently operating, pointed me to another, in Calais. He immediately sent me an offer to publish – provided I 'shared the pre-production costs' by paying him £550. I eventually risked a lot by paying this huge sum on my still useable Visa card, which has a cheque book facility. In hindsight naively, I got Diamond, who also writes poetry and short stories as well as painting, to go with me on the ferry to see this character in Calais. He seemed to live in a hovel in a run-down part of Calais, and that is where the coincidence with this Spiritual Experience comes in, and as it turns out, fits exactly.

The first symbolic image contains, in fact, at least two numbers. One as we have seen, is *eight*. The other number comes from observing that there is a small pair of two lights surrounded by six others, much further out. Hence there is a strong indication of the number *sixty-two*.

Astonishingly perhaps, in view of what comes next, this very number occurred not once but twice in his address! His street number was 62 – as was the French Civic Departement in which Calais is situated – and hence the first two digits of the postcode were also – 62!

This publisher initially gave me a lot of help in turning the book into its present form, then revealed himself progressively to be highly bombastic and stubborn, and one of those irritating people who has a pre-formed and often misguided opinion about any topic under the sun! Then again, as for the rest of Spiritual Experience Five in relation to this man, we must have tried in vain about half a dozen titles for my highly unusual book. In the end I settled for 'the Hi-Tech of the Holy Spirit' – and realised once I had agreed it with him, that it was again portended by this Spiritual Experience Five back in 1983! The dark glasses in this 'double meaning' then symbolise the 'white heat of high technology (hi-tech)' and the chalice, obviously, the Holy Spirit...

I got the book into an agreed form by as early as April 1996. Then I waited seemingly endlessly, in ever-increasing exasperation, until all of two years later, for him to actually sell some copies, as well as copies of most of my poems. In the end, my patience totally frayed, I ordered twenty copies of each in November 1997, specifying a month's delivery. I hoped to try to market the two books myself, where he had patently dismally failed and clearly was not even trying! However, he failed me totally there as well. After about twenty expensive phone calls to France, to hear the endless promise and lie 'I will send them tomorrow... tomorrow... tomorrow...' I eventually exploded in rage at him – and he then sent only half the quantity, seven months late. These turned out to be so utterly poorly printed and bound they were unusable – the print quality was hopeless 'poor photo-copying' and most copies just fell apart in my hands!

That was it. I sacked him – several times – as he obstinately refused to comply, or refund any of my money. In the end on 20th June 1998 a letter arrived from him cancelling all contractual arrangements as long as both parties agreed to drop all claims against the other for money. I immediately agreed to that, except that I asked for my money back for the still undelivered twenty totally substandard books he owed me. We completely parted company, and even before we had done so I was looking for another, this time professional and honest, publisher.

Moral: never mess with 'vanity publishers'! Especially those who do not admit to being such a dodgy sort of publisher!

After a bleak Christmas, above all with no Jenny, divorced, dispossessed and still 'homeless at home' with my parents in Hatfield, the New Year of 1996 looked very bleak indeed, but at least I was out of those terrible hospitals. Plus, after two whole years of continual illness solely due to 'Doctor' Whore's total arrogance and incompetence, that had lost me everything, my health was fully restored now I was back on medication that actually worked...

Apart from my separation from Jenny, that was to last from July 1995 to early March 1996, I had just a few relationships left in my life. Because of the draconian legal force of my wife's Injunction against me, I felt totally unable to get in touch with anybody at Dane End. I also felt betrayed that they may have prayed for me in their Church, but not one person had actually taken the trouble to visit me while incarcerated, apart from Charles, the retired Vicar...

So, I was left with friendships with, obviously, my parents and family, especially my mother and father, and later my sister when she returned from Italy. The only other two relationships I had left were with the ever volatile 'hot and cold, on and off' attitude problems of Diamond – and to some extent, but tragically not enough to save her life, with Sarah Todd. Let us first look at home life with my parents and then in June,

195

Libby, my sister, after she returned from working as a travel courier in Italy, where she had a 21 year-old student boyfriend.

My family's priorities for me were to stop smoking; get a council house; and in due course to get a job. Giving up smoking proved impossible under the traumatic circumstances, but they saw that I was in tears so often over my previous year's ordeal, that they let me smoke in my downstairs room. I went to see the local Council several times and got put on the priority housing list, but soon realised I would only get a bed-sit, in a bad area at that.

Also, I would be in Whore's catchment area if I lived in Hatfield, so that was an extremely bad idea indeed. It would be no good having him undoing my recent recovery all over again! So, once I felt strong enough, and started to look for work around April, I reckoned I would pay off the £2,400 credit card bill, that I had slowly accumulated, and much more rapidly when I paid 'Matey in Calais' his £550 – all down the john, in hindsight!

Only once that was paid off – next year, in 1997 – could I possibly look for my own house. Then, I reasoned, just in case I ever got ill again, through some mischance, I would rent a place, so I could get housing benefit if I got ill. Housing benefit is not paid on mortgages. Indeed, I got a job I would normally not have considered, but did well at interview so was offered all of £29,000 a year in July 1997. I was right to guess that as it was Defence-based it would not suit me in the long term. However, after I started that July I could not have guessed that this job was to pay high dividends by paying me full salary for all of six months when off sick, the following year, 1997. My parents' advice to me since has often been 'get a job!' rather than stay on benefit, but my 'care team' advise strongly against that. I guess they are the real experts... These books, anyway, are hard enough graft as it is – both in the writing and their promotion!

As for contact with Jenny, my new solicitor Ed had taken prompt action at our very first meeting back in December, and applied for a Court Contact Hearing, so that my family and I could at last see Jenny again. In the end, Contact was to be negotiated in February without us going though a long Court battle, before the hearing. So I started going through the further humiliation of attending a 'Contact Centre' in Hatfield to see her – initially for just an hour at a time, then building up to two hours after six weeks. We had to threaten a further Court Contact Hearing before I was allowed to see Jenny at my parent's home. This was in July 1996, so my family saw Jenny for the first time in a whole year then.

Very cruelly – and this still applies to me today – I had to see her 'within earshot' of other members of the family. My ex- has always clung onto the encouragement of the witch-like social worker Fanny to 'do me down' like this wherever possible. This malign influence, you will recall, started in 1994, when I described how Fanny took Helen apart for 'cosy chats', about how to do me in. That was sinisterly using my time, supposedly with Fanny, as my social worker – definitely not that of my ex-! After my time in mental hospital, that year of 1994, I could add that Fanny persuaded my ex- to make up a long list of fierce rules for me to obey at home. This was so long and nonsensical a list that I just laughed at it – which riled my 'ex-' no end, of course. After all that, and stories of other people I have heard at first hand about this Fanny, one can tell that she is one of those apparent majority of social workers whose aim is to actually break their poor "clients'" marriages, far from rescuing them…

I have not had any sort of relationship, and very little contact, with my ex- for five years now. Of course, for six months, between 21st September 1995 to 21st March 1996, I was to have no contact at all with her or Jenny – although I first saw Jenny on 3rd March 1996 after a whole year – thanks to those wretched Undertakings I had given under pressure. However, Helen did condescend back in late 1995 to drop off my clothes, my computer, vitally, and just a few other possessions. More arrived after the extremely upsetting and traumatic arrival in the post at Hatfield of the decree nisi, dated 19th February 1996.

In the meantime, I did risk Court action by trying to write to her twice with firstly, a somewhat bizarre and lengthy poem or ballad, trying to set the record straight. When that failed I wrote to her and some members of her family, in the absence of any reply or defence by my various lawyers to either the

Injunction or the Divorce Petition, setting out the basis of that very defence. It made absolutely no impact, on very thick skin!

After that Ed warned me most strongly not to write again, so I did not. Anyway, both pieces of writing, however carefully thought-out and written, and above all *true*, that they may have been, fell on deaf ears in my ex-'s whole family, and were totally resented and ignored. They preferred her lies...

Anyway, having the computer let me write letters to lawyers, job agencies, and above all achieve two other things. Early in 1997 I started resumption of work on my 'Idea' project, in the language C++, that I had started three years earlier when at home, redundant, in Dane End.

Also, to my parents' resentment, but to my satisfaction, I largely rewrote the book I was supposedly having published, on the computer, as per the editing 'instructions' of 'matey in Calais'. I swapped the last four papers of the then seven to the front, and greatly beefed them up. I went through various new titles, settling then on 'the Hi-Tech of the Holy Spirit', partly inspired by Spiritual Experience Five, as described at the start of this chapter.

I changed and finished various diagrams, in accordance with "matey's" requests to clarify them. I also incorporated answers to various comments by Diamond, who as you will recall said she 'fell in love with my mind' after I gave her a copy of the book, which she read in Fairfield in June 1995 by torchlight – under the bed covers!

That brings us to Diamond, with whom, until our friendship was destroyed by her in very short order, I had a very up-and-down, on-and-off time. I had by now met her then 14 year-old daughter, who was itching to pass puberty and 'grow up' and escape care, by reaching the 'magic' age of majority of 16 when she would be able to make up her own mind about things – and have her own flat. She was forever being 'dumped' by a string of foster parents, often played truant from school, was violent and delinquent, and still I guess, will only ever stand a chance of some maturity if she manages to successfully cope with the fatherless baby that she gave birth to in 1999...

I was also painfully aware that there was still another man in Diamond's life. He was in his twenties, so half her age, and another alcoholic, who also experimented with his prescribed drugs. He appeared from time to time, in a drunken alcoholic haze, and was triumphant when somebody told him Diamond's new telephone number! She had changed it to avoid him, and in 1998 changed it again, to 'avoid' me, him, and various other 'enemies'...

I also discovered that Diamond had been an artist, and had trained for two years out of the three, on the degree course at St. Martin's College, London, in her early twenties, before getting mentally ill – and falling, as she put it, into 'bad company' and becoming alcoholic. She had various pictures of her and her ex-boyfriend that she had painted as 'male and female alcoholic Devils', and one on the wall, painted in Art Therapy at the QEII Hospital, of herself in the role of Mary Magdalene, clearly shown as a whore! I cycled and often borrowed the car that my sister had left in England, to go to see her, as virtually my only friend in the area, some four miles away in Welwyn Garden City...

She was hospitalised twice that Spring. The first time in Ealing, at the Alcoholics' Ward, "St. Bernard's", as she said it used to be called – now called the 'Max Glatt Unit'. This lasted ten days and I visited her twice. The second time was more serious – a nervous breakdown again, for which she spent several weeks in hospital in April, in Welwyn Garden City at the QEII. I remember being horrified that she had to pay for the rent on her house out of her benefit while in hospital – how unfair! As I said, I had rewritten my other book, and arranged to go to see 'matey in Calais' with the manuscript copy on the 2nd May 1996. I invited Diamond, two weeks or less out of the QEII, to go with me, and she readily agreed. We both only bitterly regretted that trip afterwards...

We drove down to Dover Docks in Libby's car, with Diamond, fresh out of the mental hospital, very nervous and still quite ill, and often urging me to 'slow down!' on the motorway. We easily found parking. The trip over was calm, and when we arrived, 'matey' was at the bus stop where we had arranged to meet near his house and 'office', brandishing a copy of the cover of my book.

So far, so good. However, when we walked with him and a prospective colleague – who turned out to be a heroin addict, so 'matey' later dismissed him! – to his 'office', it turned out to be a hovel in the middle of a derelict area of Calais due for redevelopment. Indeed, over the next two years, 'matey' was to fight several battles to avoid being evicted! He lived there with his ex-girlfriend, half his 64 years, and her live-in lover and their children – a manic-depressive who refused all medication! We chatted for about four hours – with the promised 'meal' turning out to be a baguette with some pate!

Both Diamond and I left some of our literary work – my other book, now ostensibly finished, and some of her poems and short stories. We left at five, I paid for a decent meal on the boat, and drove back to arrive home after midnight.

She has since always blamed me for 'rushing her' into parting with her valuable work to somebody who has since turned out to be a total con-man, failing to publish my book or hers, or my poetry, despite having two whole yawning years of having them ready to be marketed until 1998!

At this early time of knowing Diamond, I learned that as well as portraying herself as a 'Whore' and a 'She-Devil', she also rather prided herself on her reputation in Welwyn Garden City as having the looks and manner of a Witch! Indeed, in 1998 I was to transcribe writings in which she clearly said 'I am a witch' – albeit a 'white witch' – if there is really any difference! With her tendencies to massive amounts of alcohol and drug abuse, directly fuelling a very short and fierce temper indeed, you might ask, 'why did I stick by her so long?'

There are three answers – I found her sexually beguiling; I really wanted to see her beat her terrible problems; and above all, apart from the reclusive Sarah, whose tragedy we deal with next, she was my only friend at the time! Scarcely a loyal or reliable one – but my only friend in the area!

So, that's enough of Diamond – now we turn to the very much more unfortunate – tragic in fact – Sarah Todd. I had seen Sarah briefly at her second floor flat in Old Hatfield opposite her father's Rectory, the previous December of 1995, after she sent me a Christmas card. I looked her up in the telephone book, and phoned her up. However, during the year of 1996, I was only able to see her about a dozen times, or even talk to her on the telephone. This turned out to be because she had first become ill at 35, three years earlier, and lost her job as a Chartered Surveyor, specialising in public houses, and now had lost her driving licence for alleged drink-driving, which she vehemently denied.

Now she was often drinking, and like I had been, was 'under' Dr Whore, who despite her drinking problems that often required help from the 'Cedar project' or hospitalisation, bombarded her with the maximum doses of various drugs that are very well known to clash with alcohol. For instance, the normal safe maximum dose of the anti-depressant drug 'prozac' is one tablet daily. I watched her one day, taking the no less than FIVE prescribed by Whore!

I used to get terribly frustrated by getting the answering machine when she was in, or no reply to knocking on her door when she was clearly in, with all the lights on. Her shame, as a Vicar's daughter, at drinking and mental illness problems, obviously tortured her. She became virtually a recluse!

About March she had a rare 'good spell' and made various relevant comments to me about different matters. Starting with Diamond, who had tipped hot coffee over her on Welwyn Ward the previous Spring, part of the reason why Diamond was punished with being sent to Fairfield to join me there.

Sarah's comment on Diamond was "she is a sweetie!" but she also warned "*Don't* have a relationship with her, whatever you do!" I said nothing in reply, but thought to myself, "It's too late to say that! But you are proved right by Diamond's bizarre behaviour, Sarah!" I lent her a copy of the new and then 'final' version of my other book, which she looked at with interest, and finally said, "This is a very important book!" I wish my two abortive publishing attempts, then and more recently in the summer of 2000, had been carried through, with those two publishers actually recognising that fact!

I saw her occasionally till about April, and once I realised that Whore was bombarding her with medication that was patently failing to cure her depression – she 'trashed' her flat twice in that time – I tried to help her help herself. However when at last she plucked up the courage to adopt my suggestion and asked Whore for a second opinion around May, she was confronted with his extraordinary arrogance in the form of emotional blackmail.

His reply was 'If you get a second opinion, I will refuse to treat you any more!' Typically irresponsible and totally self-interested of the man – that second opinion could have saved her life, for on the 12th June 1996 she was found dead – full of benzo-diazepam tranquillisers and a bottle of wine on top.

In the meantime, she had secretly confided in me two months earlier that she had gone out for a drink with 'Peter', the man she said had taken over her job when she had to leave sick three years earlier. They had a 'one-night stand' and she had got pregnant. However, after that I did not see her again – alive or dead.

Two days after she died, a young policeman knocked at the door at my parents' house to see me, and told me of her death. I was stunned. There were some short questions – clearly trying to find out if I was the father of the child she had been carrying. Well, apart from a peck on the cheek to say goodbye, a couple of times, there had been nothing like that, even though she was a highly attractive 38 year-old, with a lovely figure, even glamorous looking...

Her inquest was held on 29th November that year in Hertford Town Hall, and I had had to prepare a statement, and was briefly questioned. The cold, hard statements of the woman pathologist stunned me, remembering Sarah's charm and good looks. "Weight of brain was... Weight of heart was..." All I remembered was her lively outgoing personality, lovely face and figure, all *intact.*

To hear the results of her dissection was almost too much to take...

Just before the time that Sarah tragically died, in mid-May, I felt well enough to look for work, and had three interviews for jobs within half an hour's drive from my parents' house. In the end, in early July I drove for about half an hour to Hoddesdon, and had a very technical interview at a Defence Contracting Company, which was looking for people to work on virtual reality tank battles. It was clearly very interesting, and technically challenging, so I overruled my objections to Defence work. As I answered all the technical questions in half the time of any of the many other candidates – even though I was largely self-taught in the language they were using, 'C++' – I accepted their offer. This was the highest salary I had ever earned – at £29,000 a year! I started work on 28th July, and was still sitting in the firm's very own Scorpion armoured vehicle playing tank battles on the prototype battlefield simulator, from 6.30pm to 7.30pm that night!

Early in July, as often happened, Diamond fell out with me and I did not see her for a while. Then there was a sudden phone call to my parents to say that she just heard that the picture of the front of the local very Georgian-looking shopping centre, that she had submitted to a competition in her Art Club, had won the first prize of the 'Welwyn Trophy'! Understandably, she was so delighted she had overcome her previous feelings of rejection of me! I immediately went round to see her, and the relationship cautiously resumed. I bought the picture from her, and then in good faith returned it with another that went with it, at no charge, once we finally lost all contact in November 1998.

The friendship stayed on course, and now I was on a good salary, I started to pay off my £2,400 credit card bill very quickly, and to treat Diamond to lots of drinks and meals out. Meanwhile work was quite hard, but after not working but suffering a major illness, while taken off the right drugs, since 1992, I adapted quite quickly. However, it did not take one bright spark long to figure out that I had a mental health problem, and when he challenged me about it I felt obliged to confess that yes, I had a manic-depressive illness. After that it was not to take long for the whole firm to know, or so it seemed!

Eventually, after just six weeks at work, I felt in demand for my skills! Enough to offer to take Diamond on a week's holiday at Falmouth in Devon. This really was decadent – we had a self-catering apartment in a small hotel, but ate out all the time apart from cereal or toast for breakfast. We went to many nice pubs and expensive restaurants, went for walks along the coast, or drove out to beauty spots. I quickly got through about £1,000 in that holiday!

Diamond ruined my hopes in two ways. Firstly, even though we slept naked together in the same bed, she denied me any love-making at all. Indeed, when I tried anything on at all the first night she cried out something that struck us both afterwards as very funny, "Damn cheek!" I crept off and slept in the other room in a bunk bed that night...

Secondly, I was very short of cash, having been so very generous to her on the holiday, on the very last day, which was my pay day, so in Falmouth High Street I checked my bank balance. Hurray! I had been paid, so we could afford petrol to get home – her not having paid for a thing throughout the holiday! Suddenly I heard her behind me, oblivious that if I had no money I could not get us home the next day. "All you think of me as is money!" she cried and struck me round the head – then, paranoid, ran off down the street! I eventually went after her, but she backed off weirdly, clearly slightly ill. In the end I drove back to the hotel by myself, rather worried about her fate. Would she get drunk as ever and end up in a police cell? I need not have worried – she arrived by taxi with half a bottle of whisky still unopened, about half an hour later!

The following month, October 1996, I learned that Falmouth had also been the holiday destination for Jenny and my ex-, and her sister and her children, around Jenny's age. What a coincidence! However, it rather sealed the fate of the destroyed marriage, now in tatters, in my mind... That same month there was due to be a Contact Hearing again, but it never happened. My ex- offered fairly reasonable terms, with the one horror that I still had to have a chaperone when seeing my own daughter – even though Doctor Harlot had produced a report following his letter to my ex- that so damned me with no evidence, the previous Autumn. This report said that I 'have a warm and compassionate nature with no inclination to violence... There is no reason why he should not have contact with his daughter'. However, to deliberately humiliate me for my 'mental illness', my ex-wife blocked solo contact, which applied for several years! She even added the blatant lie, 'it appears that Simon was hospitalised several times for long periods before I met him!' Why lie about something so crucial, knowing it to be a total lie? What a Tart of Tarts!

Finally that October, I was standing in my parents' garden one weekend, on a bright sunny day, and looked up to the North to see four clouds in a row – in a strangely familiar pattern! Clearly Jesus was recognising that while I was now 100% mentally fit, it was time for him to sympathise with my recent ordeal of the previous year. For the four shapes of this Spiritual Experience Fifteen **exactly** repeated those of Spiritual Experience Three as described in Chapter Three earlier! As a result I can now give the definitive interpretation of both these Spiritual Experiences Three and Fifteen, with Fifteen repeating the former to say – "that is all done and dusted now!"

Spiritual Experience Fifteen. October 1996 – repeat of earlier Experience Three.

Definitive interpretation of Spiritual Experience Three of Chapter Three

Image I. Dragon's head. This turned out to be saying, 'You will meet somebody pleasant, cool, and attractive on the surface. Scratch the surface, and you will encounter hell-fire, and the true utterly thick-skinned dragon within!' This was my ex-wife Helen, it now became clear.

Image II. The dragon gives birth. Our daughter Jenny was born on 22nd February, 1991, about four years after our 'perfect' marriage service... Still, after all the time since my wife's brutal cruelty in 1995 followed by divorce in 1996, I hardly ever see Jenny.

Image III. Pegasus, the winged horse, from Greek Mythology. It was only in about 1994 that I realised that this winged horse was indeed Pegasus – and this was confirmed in prayer about this Spiritual Experience. When I looked up the legend, I learned he had been swallowed by a dragon or 'Gorgon'. Then when a Greek Hero – either Perseus or Theseus, I don't recall – cut off the Gorgon's head, Pegasus flew out, to carry thunderbolts, in the end, for Zeus, the chief of the Greek gods! Hopefully this image signifies how I will eventually escape nearly being killed off – mentally at least by the many dragons or Gorgon-like 'professionals' involved to date. Many 'doctors' – and a Vet – the Tart of Tarts!

Image IV. Woman as a 'figurehead'. The woman is of course my daughter Jenny, shown as her natural leader or figurehead self, astonishingly ever-loyal to me despite everything, and my only real friend for years now.

Definitive Interpretation of Spiritual Experience Fifteen. Spiritual Experience Three repeated i.e. Jesus said "It has now all definitely happened and is all over!"

This Spiritual Experience, by repeating the four images of Spiritual Experience Three together not separated in time, definitely said, "That is all over now!" Jesus was saying I would have no further ordeal as bad as the divorce of 1995 indicated by Spiritual Experience Three – obviously very important to both Him and myself. I was immediately very relieved!

Spiritual Experience Fifteen marked the very middle of my 'eye of the storm' period, of July 1996 to the start of 1997, before 'Psychiatrist, crass misdiagnosis and medication (drug) problems' reared up again. Diamond too, said that like me, for her 1995 was her worst ever year, and 1996 was relatively very enjoyable – particularly when I took her on holiday, then bought her no less than three brand-new outfits to wear. Normally she put up with buying second-hand clothes in charity shops! In fact the one sour spot that Autumn was to be Sarah's Inquest, and it even looked for a while that I would see Jenny at Christmas! That at least was agreed by my ex- in November, then in December, treacherous as ever, she changed her mind!

Meanwhile in November, Jenny having been at school since the previous September 1995 with me having no say over that, at last I saw her Infants' schoolteacher. She was doing all right, and shining at her art – just as I had done at Infants' and Primary School – as well as at writing, especially stories!

Then in December, although it was the festive season, I found my only real friend, and a very dodgy one at that, was Diamond! We went to her Art Club Buffet – and both won a raffle prize! Meanwhile, as I just said, the issue of Contact once again reared up, and we quickly arranged for 'Social Services Mediation' at nearby Stevenage to try to get my ex- to relent and let Jenny spend Christmas day with my family as previously agreed, and now reneged on, by her.

For an hour and a half, the two male social workers tried everything short of twisting her arms to make her honour her original promise. With nothing achieved after all that time, and her totally stubborn, they commented, "She has no respect at all for anybody else's feelings, in our opinion!" About all I could expect, given all her foul abuse of me the previous year, followed by an injunction and divorce founded solely on her lies…

Just before Christmas itself I had a review of my work at the firm, which was to prove decisive and very damaging the next few months, once the results were produced and I was confronted with yet more totally unjustified knocks. However, after the bitter disappointment of Christmas there was some light relief to the end of the year, as my ex- actually allowed us to take Jenny to the National Theatre with her cousins to see the ballet. They missed the first half – my car broke down! What an omen of disappointments again in the New Year of 1997!

CHAPTER TWENTY-ONE

1997 – another traumatic year – another 'annus horribilis'?

The drug experiments resume in January with Doctor Harlot this time – with disastrous results. Work gets extremely perilous – I am wrongly threatened with 'the sack' after false allegations of 'not working hard enough'. Really, I can tell, it is pure stigma about mental illness. A new house in Hertford, followed by four and a half months in Harlow Hospital as a result of both factors, leading to financial hardship – meanwhile in my absence Diamond goes off the rails, often gets drunk and reveals her promiscuous side. The Divorce 'Decree Absolute' comes through while I am 'incarcerated'. In the end, after four years of trauma, I settle, in the short term, for a new life on benefit.

I had managed to clear my credit card debt of £2,400 by dint of being on a high salary with low outgoings while living with my parents, by the end of 1996. However that did not last long – I used my credit card cheque book to buy a second-hand car costing £1,000, then tax and insure it – very expensively, as my ex- retained the 'no claims bonus' for the insurance!

Also that January 1997, I was seen by Doctor Harlot, who persuaded me very fatefully that the new drug he wanted to replace my haloperidol with was absolutely marvellous, and by comparison had no side-effects. So I agreed to change to it, although it took a while to get him to actually write out a prescription. When this new drug, olanzapine, failed to control my feelings of anxiety that Spring nearly as well as haloperidol had done, things went completely off the rails. Harlot's cowardly reaction was to shrug off all blame and claim 'I had pressured him' to give it to me – when all I had done was chase him up for a simple initial prescription by telephone several times, which he was remarkably reluctant and initially too lazy to actually produce.

In the interim, negotiations between Ed, my solicitor, and my 'ex-' were proving extremely arduous. She held out for the house and the equally jointly owned Estate Car, and refused to let me near the house to pick up possessions that I felt were mine. In the end her solicitor realised that if I did get anything, it would all be owed to the Legal Aid board in solicitors' fees built up so far. By their harsh rules, everything above £2,500 somebody on legal aid gets from a divorce settlement, goes back to the Legal Aid Board. So in the end her solicitor offered me just £2,500 instead of the house that I had largely bought for the family – and in March I was forced to accept that offer on pragmatic grounds alone! So I had lost everything!

Meanwhile, Diamond was proving increasingly pesky with her totally unprovoked and very abusive and hurtful 'diatribes'. I was starting to wonder what I had let myself in for by knowing her – out of the 'frying-pan with Helen' – into a real fire of Hell with Diamond? However, this was as nothing compared to her very wild and lustful behaviour with a string of other men, and really going off the rails with the booze, later that year when I went into hospital. She admitted after all her gallivanting was over once I returned, that she had simply failed to cope without me around! In the meantime, whereas I was a frequent visitor during her oft-repeated stays in hospital while I knew her (at least six!) – she only visited me just twice at Harlow – and on the second occasion was evicted from the Ward, nearly blind drunk!

In the interim, before May, when the failure of the olanzapine caused me to admit myself to mental hospital (twice – they would not admit me initially!) two significant things happened in February. Firstly, my job review back in December proved to have gone very badly – and I was falsely judged to be not trying nearly hard enough, given my salary, even though I had actually done a lot of very hard and strenuous work that simply passed unrecognised. I really resented being judged 'below average' in this way, and also, being put on a 'less demanding', i.e. the worst project in that company, after the 'elite' team I had started with! There I had to spend all my time correcting glaring errors in the work done by a 'contractor', who had left the company during an embargo on contract workers. The worst of it was being threatened with the sack for incompetence – which was deeply hurtful, and I only prevented that particular disaster by asking to have my pay cut by £3,000 to £26,000 a year!

As if to compensate, just as Jesus had sent Spiritual Experience Fifteen the previous October, now the Holy Spirit joined in, with a Spiritual Experience above my parents' garden that February 1997.

Once again, as so often before, a small group of clouds made very distinct and at last, this time, very simple shapes – *Greek letters*, together with yet another "beast's" or "dragon's" head, as below. As so often prayed for since Spiritual Experiences Twelve, Thirteen and Fourteen, almost immediately, within three months, I 'got the meaning' of this Spiritual Experience.

Spiritual Experience Sixteen. February 1997. Sky-writing over Hatfield – by the Holy Spirit!

Spiritual Experience 16 - Image One.

$Y \Pi -$ *The Greek prefix 'up-' – 'below, under'…*

Spiritual Experience 16 – Image Two.

$I T$ *… Information Technology and a 'Beast'…*

                         of 'Religious Intolerance'!

Spiritual Experience 16 – Image Three.

Ω *'Omega' – Title of the Holy Spirit Herself!*

Three sets of images were separated by a total of about four minutes in time. First I saw the 'up'- prefix, then two minutes later those three clouds had changed to form the shapes 'IT – and the Beast'. Finally after a further two minutes the three clouds merged into one 'Omega'-shaped cloud.

I was at a loss to understand this Spiritual Experience for about three months, until one day I finally looked up the Greek prefix 'υπ-' or 'up-' in my Greek lexicon.

Only then did I discover that it means 'below, or under or beneath'. So the Holy Spirit, who *'signed'* the Spiritual Experience as 'Omega', clearly feels 'beneath' IT and the 'beast of religious intolerance' as in my other book. Or as she is now revealed as female by this Spiritual Experience, confirming my innermost thoughts, it even says she is being 'raped' by IT – 'mechanical spirituality'? – and *that* Beast!

Even though when this first came through to me in a rush, it was about June 1997, and I was ill in mental hospital, I struggled manfully to extend the thrust of the then draft of what became my book 'Spiritual Energy', in those two respects.

Saying, that is, that The Holy Spirit is essentially Female; and that She has these two particular enemies today! As a result, painfully and with great difficulty, I added material while on hospital leave and even got it photocopied while very ill.

The final reason why I got ill that May, on top of my changed drug regime and acute pressure of work, was that in April I spotted a rented house in the paper at just £420 a month – even though it was in 'desirable' Hertford.

Particularly desirable for me, in that I would be away from the QEII Catchment Area, if I moved there. I rang up the number given, saw it the following day, was first to do so, and immediately took it on! I moved in a few weeks later, on 1st May 1997, which happened to be the day of the General Election last year – so missing all that razzamatazz! However the following week, on leave, I must have been getting slowly ill off the right vital medication again.

For I spent over £2,000 on my credit card kitting out the place virtually from scratch. I had to buy all the kitchen utensils, bookcases, tools, etc., but Helen had by now supplied my bed, wardrobe, and chest of drawers, so I had a basis for the bedroom. However, she has never relented to give up anything jointly owned, or possessions actually mine – presents etc. – from after the time we were married!

What a selfish, avaricious, grasping Tart of Tarts she has proven to be! My parents and I were both very glad to be free of one another's company – they particularly disliked my smoking, and by now heavy drinking as the olanzapine made me feel very anxious indeed. As for me, their constant nagging lectures were starting to prove unbearable! Anyway, by 12th May I felt totally stressed-out by the year's events, and ready to have a 'break' in hospital in order to get my drugs sorted out – hopefully back onto haloperidol.

Just a week before that I saw Dr Harlot as an out-patient, who said (I quote) 'If things get any worse I will either restore your haloperidol or admit you'. He was too late in the day and in hindsight should have put me back on haloperidol immediately. For after I saw him in hospital after I admitted myself on 14th May 1997, some two weeks later, he made another enormous mistake following his letter to my ex-, written when he hardly knew me, back in 1995.

For he stopped my lithium and started 'sodium valproate' on top of the olanzapine. Two changes in one go rather than retreating to a safe known regime – lithium and haloperidol? He has always denied it, but that totally flawed 'decision' cost me a four and a half-month stay in Harlow hospital rather than his promise of two weeks.

I actually admitted myself – but was turned away at midnight of 12th May 1997, furious that they did not find me at all ill. The following day I drove in fury to my brother's house in Sussex, where my parents were staying. However, the motorway was very crowded, and I must have been ill, for I opted to navigate through the centre of London and out the other side – without a map! I arrived about eleven o'clock that night to a furious reception, especially from my father. He stormed up to the local pub and arranged for me to have a room there as my brother's house was full with the two families! So, escape to nothing!

I left the following day about midday, and again drove back hypomanically through the heart of London with no map or navigator. That evening I again admitted myself, and was accepted that Friday 14th May 1997 – on the basis of failing just one test – due to my exertions of the previous two days I did not know the date off the top of my head! I had gone prepared and carefully packed a suitcase, and taken my medication with me. I was only slightly ill at that stage – my escapades in driving through London had mostly been out of anger. However, as ever the mere fact of coming to admit myself to a place with such a 'sick' atmosphere, soon combined with Harlot's experiments, were in two weeks or so to make me extremely ill indeed.

I admitted I had been drinking a bit, so in addition to my normal drugs was given a course of librium to take. Also infuriatingly, because of what 'they' called this 'abuse of alcohol' – very 'over the top' indeed! – I was not to be allowed off that Ward for a whole week, except to be escorted to meals in the canteen.

215

I stopped a fight between Brian, a burly bloke, and a little lesbian whom he hated for that fact, in the first week – and picked up a massive yellow bruise on the arm where I intercepted a punch intended for her. Also, I got a letter from work that was very reassuring – they would pay me full salary for the first six months of any period of illness.

Three weeks into my stay I received a dreaded letter – the declaration of the Decree Absolute. I was obviously very upset at something that I had been blamed for, totally unfairly, which was all anyway totally unnecessary. If only 'Doctor' Whore had been more conservative, less arrogant and less apparently out to destroy my marriage! I was victimised by my callous 'fair weather wife' of an ex- for his appalling mistakes and totally arrogant errors of judgement...

Such real stresses of the past year, and now 'Mental Hospital Syndrome', were now combining to make me more and more ill. As soon as I got some leave I drove to a shop I knew in Hertford, and bought a cheap mobile digital phone. I simply could not appreciate in my sick state, that given the amount of calls I was intending to use it for – basically lots to my family and Diamond – the bill for just the first month would be massive. Indeed when the bill for that month came in the post, shockingly at nearly £300, I stopped using the phone. I eventually persuaded the company and shop involved to let me break the contract of 12 months – on the grounds of mental illness!

There were lots of rather wild, thieving, homeless, not at all ill, youngish people on Hopkins Ward at that time. However, I was to be surprised that even though I risked bringing in my entire CD collection – and eventually my entire hi-fi from home, 100-Watt speakers and all! – only a few items of mine, especially a couple of CD's, were to disappear.

My basic problem – as ever as I find with such places – was sheer unremitting boredom, with just smoking to pass the time. I could not stand watching the TV all day for dubious 'entertainment', and some others agreed, so sometimes there were verbal battles over whether to turn the damn thing off and listen to my portable hi-fi and CD's or radio. Soon I got involved with trying to organise a barbecue, which was eventually censored by the Nursing Sister, even though I had bought two huge joints of meat for it! When I was eventually moved downstairs to 'Shannon House' Intensive Care Ward, they discovered loads of barbecue equipment under my bed, which caused both concern and amusement!

It was my boredom that led me to go to my new house 'on leave' whenever possible in the first couple of months. I played music or worked on my 'writings' on my computer, furiously trying to get down what I felt initially about Spiritual Experience Sixteen. I went initially by car, but when I got too ill to be allowed to drive any more, caught the slow bus, or two even slower trains. Eventually I was to be stopped from going home at all, and was so worried about my house being burgled, and in particular losing my computer, that I got my Father to change the locks and fix the windows... Fear of burglary was why I brought in my hi-fi!

Towards the end of my stay in Harlow that year I learned that I had been falsely accused of violent behaviour – even though the only times I was involved in violence it was that of other people. As well as the 'fight' I mentioned earlier I was to try fruitlessly to get between two male nutcases trying to maul each other – like women 'cat-fighting', rather than men!

However, I was so concerned that I had been accused of 'throwing chairs around in the Ward Office' by some lying nerd on the staff, that I asked to see my notes in 1998. There was an anonymous, unsigned, and highly significantly so, report by that nerd, making these and other equally lying allegations. Not all staff in mental hospitals tell the truth, particularly when they dislike a certain patient, as was clearly the case with me here! In fact, the only time I had caused any sort of disturbance in their precious office, was when I evicted a moth through the window, slightly upsetting a nurse sitting there, who was 'afraid of creepy-crawlies'!

This nurse was in fact to prove a really distressing influence on me – for with her amazing eyes, and figure like my ex-wife, I soon got quite a crush on her! In the end, very ill by now, I tried to buy her presents, which were all kindly and politely returned – so, unrequited love! At the very end of my time there, I asked for ten minutes of her time, to which she only reluctantly agreed. I explained that she strongly reminded me of my ex-, especially in a dress, and we left that particular 'crush' behind, with her thanking me for 'sharing that with her'! I felt that honour had been retained on both sides, so all was now well...

Finally in June, I got so very ill on Harlot's new double change of treatment, that he put me on a 'Section 3' of the Mental Health Act – which meant that I could not leave the hospital grounds, and indeed from now on was largely confined to the Ward! Shortly before that I had cycled wildly through a thunderstorm that was extremely fierce, from Hertford to nearby Ware but along the riverbank cycle path, loving the torrential rain, thunder and lightning!

Now the staff, partly as a result, said that with that and my other 'escapades' with bringing in my hi-fi, and the abortive barbecue, that they 'could not contain me'. So, about a month after that 'Section' was imposed, I was transferred to the 'downstairs' Shannon House Intensive Care (locked) Ward – at last back on haloperidol for the previous two weeks, but off my lithium still.

As a result of not having any lithium, and taking epilim (sodium valproate) instead, I had now, after two months, developed massive and extremely embarrassing 'pressure of speech'. Everything I thought of, I was immediately blurting out at an extremely high rate of garbled speech...!

Earlier efforts to get me to go to Shannon House had so terrified me, that I had refused. Once I got down there however, it was then so brand-new and luxurious, and the staff were so polite and kind, that I remember saying 'why don't you give new patients of this Ward a tour of it beforehand?' In my three much longer trips there 2000 to 2003, after the departure of the Ward Manager then, Diane, it has since seriously deteriorated. I was tucked up in bed by a pretty nurse the first night, and generally allowed to recover in a very controlled, friendly environment. I was even often called 'Mr Lee' – unheard of in a mental ward!

We were kept occupied with a lot of occupational therapy and good food, and frequent substantial snacks. Vitally, music was broadcast through the Ward, which was very therapeutic, whereas smoking and TV were off in two separate rooms. As it was Summer, we often exercised by playing volleyball in the yard outside, or just sat around chatting and smoking. The only 'problem' was it being locked. I did get an – escorted – trip to town each day to buy vital tobacco supplies – and often, strong cheddar cheese in particular, and other groceries, to share out with the others, all on benefit – unlike me, then still on full salary!

After a couple of days off lithium *or* epilim, the staff accepted my proposal that I return to lithium as well as my newly restored haloperidol, by saying 'we had thought that you need it too!' They had started 'from scratch' and totally ignored what Harlot had done to me in the previous ten weeks – which meant that after three more weeks back on lithium I was to prove well enough to return to Hopkin's Ward. So I was only 'in intensive care' for four weeks – and it would have been a lot less had a bed been available for me back on Hopkin's Ward.

There were two girls on release from Holloway Prison on Shannon House Ward at that time – both absolutely desperate to get proven as acutely mentally ill, and so not to have to return to complete their sentences. One I recall ended up having quite a 'crush' on me and asked for me to write to her in Holloway. However I never did – she was half my age and there was no future in it – for either of us... In the end they both returned to long sentences...

So, my inevitable pre-arranged Appeal against my Section 3 was held in Shannon House Ward – with my parents and my solicitor Ed's colleague, Catherine, present as well. However, I failed to have it lifted, being judged as still needing mandatory treatment. The fact was that I would not have needed that enforced treatment – which on Shannon House Ward was in fact totally voluntary – without Harlot's totally irresponsible and even casual, cavalier, swingeing changes of treatment both before my admission and during it.

Finally on Shannon House Ward, came my first meeting with my then freshly-appointed Social Worker. Following abysmal earlier experiences of Social Services, I was initially very reluctant to have anything to do with her. However, Julia has since proven efficient, too busy all the time – amazingly, she really *cares!*

Back on Hopkin's Ward after exactly four weeks 'downstairs', the second 'male cat-fight' that I mentioned – this one I failed to stop – ended with one of the assailants being very roughly taken to jail by the police!

I was now told that the Mental Health Tribunal I had requested months before was a few weeks away. Harlot asked me in a Ward Round whether I wanted to challenge his treatment in this Tribunal, now that I was back on the original medication, after 'all that' time in hospital. I rather surprised him, I think, by being totally non-confrontational about this entire problem, and simply asked him to 'drop the Section'. As that meant he too would not have to go through the Tribunal, after consulting with his Registrar, he reluctantly eventually agreed.

Soon I was up in the town, celebrating my restored freedom after some months with a can of coke! About two or three weeks after this, on Tuesday 23rd September 1997, he finally discharged me, judged fit enough to return home.

I had noticed two non-mental health problems while in hospital. For the one – my long-term varicose veins – the Shannon House staff had made an appointment with a Consultant Surgeon on 17th October at Harlow. When I saw him he immediately said that an operation was essential – which was scheduled very promptly as I could go privately through the health insurance at my then firm. In the end I was to go in three weeks later on 4th November to the Rivers Private Hospital near Harlow. As it was private I found I could smoke in my room – and even order a beer. Which I paid for, not the insurance, of course!

I astonished the staff completely, by stoically walking all of five miles on the first morning after my 'op', not just the tentative 'hundred yards' they had suggested! After ten days the stitches – catgut in my legs, metal ones in my groin – came out, so ending a period of acute discomfort, especially climbing stairs.

The other medical problem was rather less serious – I had a crown fitted to a tooth, in two appointments. This was expensive, adding to my great costs that year, so when my pay soon ended from work, I took up the offer of a second credit card from a very irresponsible credit card company based in Chester. I had soon nearly filled that as well as my first one, as I was soon on just £55 a week statutory sick pay, with outgoings still far higher – it took a long while to adjust to a drastic cut in income!

Shortly before my operation, on Sunday 2nd November, I found the money from somewhere and went to Calais – to try to sort out 'matey', or as I now found him, the 'con-man from Calais'! For he refused to do any more than the tiny amount of work he had done on my book already. In the end, desperate to get it published, I agreed to leave it exactly as it had been all year – and still not marketed! I sent him later that month £240 that he welcomed, to send me by the next month, 20 copies each of that book and my poetry book, so I could try to market them where he had patently failed... However, as we shall see in my account of 1998, I was to wait six months for just half these books to arrive, to receive complete rubbish quality copies, after lots of expensive telephone calls chasing him up! 'Con-man from Calais' *indeed!*

In the meantime, before I went into hospital Diamond had been portraying me as her 'boyfriend', even though I tried to deny her that 'status' as she called it. I turned out to be quite right to do so, for while in I was in hospital it turned out she had really missed my kindly discipline of her, and had gone 'completely off the rails'. She had frequently gone to the pub and got drunk, sometimes causing a scene, and had even been arrested for being 'drunk and disorderly'. She freely admitted to having been looking for a new man – other than her 'boyfriend' – me!

That then was why she had only visited me just twice – she was out boozing and on the look-out for a new man! In the process of being so totally disloyal she had attracted several men – but the only one she really fancied and so bedded – she claimed would not put on a condom, so she had thrown him out of bed without him forcing himself on her – thank goodness! Also in the process she got herself banned for lewd and whore-like behaviour, from most pubs in Welwyn Garden City town centre – and in 1998 got banned from all the rest, for similar, lewd, drunken behaviour! After all this she spent about six weeks in the QEII, Welwyn Ward, after I had returned from Harlow, and during my trip to Calais.

Very unwisely, because my finances were in chaos and I now had no way to return to my previous job with my pride intact, I started looking for work about now. In desperation to return to a good salary, I went to several interviews, ending up accepting an offer in the early New Year from a Management Consultancy, based in London – but promised local work, which was indeed to be forthcoming early in 1998. That was only to last two days!

The hospital offered me Occupational Therapy to do at Harlow – but it was a thirty mile very expensive round trip, with very poor parking facilities at the hospital, so after a few weeks doing two hours of gardening a week, I dropped that too. I started German evening 'club classes' at an Art Centre I discovered close to my new home, and often went to the 'ladies' night', a disco at the Sportsman Pub in Hertford, desperate for 'social life'. While the support of a 'government friend' or Community Support Worker – they help social workers by visiting one – took some months to arrange in the end, my CPN or Community Psychiatric Nurse, Cheryl, got a trainee male colleague to keep me company once or twice a week.

That, especially with total financial confusion, and very high, but no regular outgoings, was my life until December. Then on the 8th December I took Diamond, and two of her female friends, to a night-club in Hatfield. The only one of us who met anybody of the opposite sex was, of course, Diamond. She started 'snogging' with some hospital porter who forced himself, very drunkenly, on her several times, and got quite passionate. I remember feeling cold stabbing feelings of jealousy – before hospital that would have been me in his place! If the relationship with Diamond had not already ended, it died that night! In the car on the way back she turned out to have arranged to meet this guy again, but I warned her he was only after her body – so she failed to turn up the next day for the rendez-vous with him!

Also in December 1997 I applied for various benefits - Disability Living Allowance, Housing Benefit, Incapacity Benefit, and Income Support, and was only outright refused the last one. This was on the grounds that I still received just £55 a week Statutory Sick pay a week as my only income, not enough to pay my outgoings on the house, but deemed 'adequate to live on' by the government. It was to take some months into

1998 to sort out my benefit situation – in the meantime, needing to equip a house and live, and completely unable to adjust from having quite a good salary, I just built up debt on my new second credit card...

I started seeing Jenny again at my parents' house, about six weeks after hospital, but for the third Christmas in a row, was denied all Contact at Christmas itself by my adamant ex-. However, the year ended on a virtually solitary happy note, on New Year's Eve. Jenny's cousins and their parents Jem and Jane came up from Sussex, for a belated Christmas lunch. Before that, I took Jenny into my old back room, and pointed to a large object covered with a sheet. "That's your Christmas present from Santa Claus and me!", I said. "What is it?", she asked, seemingly forgetting she had chosen it in a large toy store a month earlier! She took off the sheet to reveal a gleaming £100 mountain bike I had bought for her, risking the wrath of my bank yet again... She was absolutely delighted with this, and it should have lasted her for years! Except 'clever, superior ex-' left it outside unlocked all the time, and of course it was stolen last year...

After 'Christmas' lunch – we took Jenny and her three cousins – Jem and Jane's two girls now had a brother, Jordan! – to the ballet at the National Theatre once more. This time around there were no car problems, and everybody enjoyed the 'tales of Beatrix Potter'. So that terrible year – yet another! – ended on quite a high note!

CHAPTER TWENTY-TWO

1998, a 'year in the doldrums' and on benefit – but still fairly busy!

1998 – I give up trying to look for work and resort to drawing benefits. The 'Diamond relationship' drags to a close – and for a while I date other women! Part time work, official complaints to various bodies – and unexpected financial help! Diamond – having been in hospital several times that year, issues legal threatening noises over nothing at all... Contact with Jenny dominates the year!

This year of 1998 might have started on a high note – on the 19th January I started work on behalf of a multinational management consultancy, at a firm in nearby Harlow. However, looking back, I was very far indeed from being ready to start work again. I left the job the following day, weathering some funny looks and searching questions... My 'notice sick pay' from the last, Defence, company ran out on 2nd February. I redoubled my telephone calls to sort out my benefits...

I tried the 'Mental Health drop-ins' in Hertford but found they reminded me of mental hospital too much. I have not been since. I am determined, but remain continually frustrated in trying, to supplement my friendships at similar places here now in Ware, with some with 'normal' people...

Jenny had started coming to see us at my parents' for up to seven hours a day some months earlier in 1997, and I continue to look forward to a whole day with her every two or three weeks, with mixed feelings. One feeling is gladness to simply have her innocent, lovely company for some hours – most of Saturday or Sunday in fact. My 'ex-' reluctantly agrees with Jenny that her days with our family are her 'best days'. The other feeling is sadness mixed with bitterness – why do my parents have to do all the fetching and carrying, why can't my ex- make the one-hour round trip? Is all this huffing and puffing by my ex-, over my seeing Jenny, really necessary?

In February, having been promised one for four months, and with my Community Psychiatric Nurse's (CPN's) trainee having gone on to training, I finally saw my 'Community Support Worker' – or 'Government Friend'. This was Bill, an avid Labour Party guy, former local councillor in Brent, and my 'official friend'. Providing useful contact to relieve my social worker, Julia, of that 'burden', on top of her normal work at Harlow Hospital. I usually got on well with him.

Pretty soon, however, he was 'taking the Mickey' over the fact that I had advertised in the local newspaper – and was seeing 'blind dates' – about two to three women a week at the time! This did not last, as most had pre-prepared questions, and the subject of my mental health always emerged from the woodwork... So after six weeks of this I gave it up as a bad job, at the end of March.

In February I spotted an advertisement in the local paper for 'A level and GCSE tutors urgently required – good rates!' and immediately applied. The upshot was that I started teaching a 17-year old girl, A level mechanics and mathematics on 2nd March – and starting giving weekly lessons, to a series of students, in mathematics, netting tax-free 'therapeutic earnings', for a whole year! I received glowing appraisals from several parents, some of whose children had gone up several A level grades following my tuition, which was really satisfying...

Nothing much happened apart from the teaching from March to May, except that the books that I had ordered from 'matey in Calais' at last arrived – and as I said before, were so substandard that I tried to reject them out of hand! I wrote some very straight and insulting letters to him about this, and in the end he reluctantly agreed to a 'parting of the ways', revealed as a con-man, on 20th June.

On 9th June my parents and I went to see Professor Hirsch at his office at Charing Cross Hospital. He is the Professor of Psychiatry at Imperial College, London, whom the Harlow Hospital had finally arranged for us to see in connection with our complaint about Doctor Harlot's cavalier attitude. Both in branding me violent in 1995 and so assisting my ex- to get her divorce; and his casual experiments with drugs in 1997, resulting in a four and a half month spell in hospital for me that year, and losing my job. Hirsch promised to produce his report within two weeks of that four-hour detailed meeting, but was to take some two *months* over it. We need not have bothered waiting for it…!

It was a complete whitewash, from his remote and lofty height, completely exonerating Harlot – and even, astonishingly, with no information about him, Whore! The report was virtually illiterate, with frequent spelling mistakes and grammatical errors, but astonishingly was seized upon by Harlow Hospital as 'clearing' their man. Apart from noting that apparently, as a Christian, in 1996 I was weirdly described by Harlot as suffering from a 'religious paranoid illness', I leave the damn thing there. Unless my parents decide to take it further, Harlot has been exonerated by a load of "Psychiatrists' Cronyism" and mumbo-jumbo!

Also in June, I had been concerned that my friendship with Diamond was virtually over. She had not been speaking to me at either Christmas or my birthday at the end of March, and so although she got substantial presents from me for both Christmas and her birthday, she gave me absolutely nothing for either of my occasions. At around the time we saw Hirsch, she was admitted for the second time this year – later to become three, in late October. She had been given an "alcoholic de-tox" in the Spring! Anyhow, that June I really bent over backwards to visit her, at my own expense, and do everything possible for her.

Then, on Tuesday 16th June, she attacked me in the car on the way back to the Ward from her first hour's leave – all over just £10 she had lent me the day before and now wanted back immediately! – and threatened to hit me and so crash the car! After that, she wrote me a letter, saying 'thank you but goodbye – forever!' and after 20th June 1998, the same day 'matey from Calais' finally agreed to sign off, I have had only two strange contacts with her. One was when she agreed to trade my cheap hi-fi for one of her pictures to match one that I had actually bought from her. The second, and last contact ever, was in November, when she suddenly wrote to me 'out of the blue' from her third stay in the QEII hospital in just one year!

In June, I had written in some desperation to the Benevolent Fund of the IEE or Institution of Electrical Engineers, my Institute as a Chartered Engineer, that I had joined in 1992 along with joining the Institute of Measurement and Control in 1991. I expected they might give me, say £200, but later that month I was visited by two local members, who explained that the help would be far more substantial! Indeed, in August they paid off my £800 bank overdraft, and gave me a sheer gift of £1,260 on top.

The £1,260 went on vital bills like having my car and hi-fi serviced, and lots of other vital things. Only one luxury, I bought one of Diamond's pictures from her Art Club's exhibition for £65. The £800 however also soon went - £700 on upgrading my Personal Computer, and £100 on buying two years' unlimited Internet Access.

You see, I was determined to use the Internet to promote my books – 'Spiritual Energy' and my poetry book. The latter had been given the totally derisory and insulting title of 'poems' by 'matey in Calais' – but was now definitively retitled 'A Many Threaded Tapestry' – by the mother of one of my students, who also drew the front cover! The IEE were even more fabulously generous since then – they settled two credit card bills for me, totalling some £4,000! All praise for the generosity of the Benevolent Fund of the IEE!

Also in July, my complaint about my ex-solicitors in Royston was upheld, and their apology and derisory £200 compensation arrived... However, I was extremely depressed by 'matey in Calais', Diamond's erratic dismissal of me after my massive help and visits in hospital, and a particular phone call from my ex- late one night. She had called me the night after we both saw Jenny at her school's 'Open Day'. She had tried to persuade me to 'forget the past' and effectively become a 'plastic parent' – with us both cooperating as Jenny's parents, while divorced. I kept telling her that I could not accept such an ethereal role, and kept slamming the telephone down on her, but she kept ringing back – at nearly midnight! In the end I said, "How on earth can you expect me to forget the past just like that? You have made the past stay all around me!" After that she took the point and stopped repeatedly ringing – clearly drunk...

At the end of July I passed a new practitioner of Traditional Chinese Medicine in Hertford, popped in, had a consultation, and started having acupuncture the following day. This was

227

initially combined with strong herbal drinks for four weeks, then just acupuncture every week, then finally every two weeks. Finally, two weeks ago, I felt so well, actually cured by this treatment of my depression over the things that I mentioned above, that I stopped going! In the meantime I had written the genuine Chinese TCM Doctor a glowing testimonial, for publication in the local paper...

In August I was still having acupuncture, and my depression was rapidly lifting. I had negotiated a rate of £8 a session not £30 for this, and really relished using this alternative medicine rather than risking hospital, even, by adding antidepressant drugs to my existing medication. Besides having moved to Hertford the previous May to escape the QEII, I was now re-assigned a Doctor there by the NHS! The catchment area of the QEII now extended to Hertford!

So, as I was not even to meet my new Doctor till 4th October, I was 'between Psychiatrists' – and my GP would never have dared prescribe any drug for me without consulting my new Consultant Psychiatrist. So looking back, I did exactly the right thing by taking on acupuncture – and it actually worked on my feelings of depression – so there you go!

On 4th October I met, and was duly impressed by the attention to detail, and vitally for me with my 'Whore/Harlot' story, conservatism, of my new Doctor. This was at my 'CPA Meeting' for the year – a meeting with my Social Worker, my CPN and my parents present. This lasted about an hour – and I remember being embarrassed to recount that I could not have a blood test for my lithium blood serum level that same day – for the first time in months, I had forgotten to take the lithium tablets the previous night!

In October, I was due to start an MSc course at the local University of Hertfordshire, which had been prompted by a suggestion by my close family, particularly my sister Libby. However, because I still felt very stressed out, I was sleeping about twelve hours a night. So in the end, not relishing the commitment of two years, of even part-time study, I backed out of the course...

The following day, a leaflet arrived in the post advertising computer courses for unemployed people, at £60 a month for a year, and initially it seemed like 'one door shut and another opened'. However, after I signed up when visited about this course, I realised it was far too simple – given my background in C++, so I backed out of that as well... My family just shrugged in disbelief! I have done no studying or work in computers, as a result, since early 1997.

Also in October, there was some potentially good news. My parents had asked the QEII Hospital for an inquiry into 'Doctor' Whore back in October 1997, and now were at last and finally to be granted, in due course, a full-blown NHS independent Inquiry! As soon as I had got on the Internet back in September, I had been in close touch by e-mail with my Godfather in Georgia, USA, so eagerly relayed this news on to him!

On Remembrance Day, 11th November 1998, I went to see my new Doctor for my first outpatient's clinic. He gently warned me about one thing – it is really black and white advice that sufferers of mental illness do NOT drink! As a result, for a week after seeing him I stopped my three pints of beer a night – and suffered from a drastically affected sleep pattern – often staying up to 4am, until I started *slowly* drinking as a sedative again!

Spiritual Experience Seventeen. 2am on the night of 11th November 1998

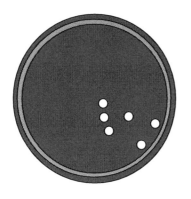 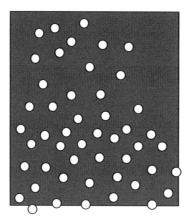 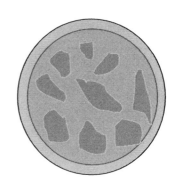

I. The Constellation   II. The stars falling   III. A 'spiritual cell' –
   Cassiopeia – attacks   - en masse   full of energetic
   A Black Hole!   Entities!
   (Omega or 'W' –
   the Holy Spirit!)

Definitive Interpretation of Spiritual Experience Seventeen.
'Retitle your book!'

On Sunday 8th November 1998, I went to the local Baptist Church Service, and received a premonition that another Spiritual Experience was on its way. The day of Remembrance Day, 11th November, was the 15th anniversary of my first ever serious hospitalisation, in 1983. Two dramatic things happened.

Firstly, whereas previously I had reckoned on Diamond having written me out of her life completely, that morning I received a letter from her, two and a half weeks into a stay on Welwyn Ward – yet again – the fifth or sixth time since I had known her in 1995! She 'desperately wanted a business relationship' – me to do some urgent typing for her, no more, no less, or so it seemed. Very warily, as she still had me under the threat of a Court injunction if I ever contacted her, I rang up and arranged to visit her in hospital. I saw her that night, and three times more, taking in drinks, fish and chips one night, and fruit. I made sure when I went to the Post Office for her and cashed her benefit, that I exacted my costs of helping her, exactly.

Then on the fourth visit in four days, she was back to her old tricks – and angrily told me to go away after just five minutes. I left it a week and phoned, only to be threatened, very tiresomely, with 'an Injunction if I ever contacted her again'.

Meanwhile, in the small hours after Remembrance Day, the morning of 12th November, I was lying, unable to sleep, and I hasten to add, totally mentally fit, when I saw a series of beautiful but unrepeatable images above me while in bed.

I knew a Spiritual Experience was in the offing, and saw three images – Spiritual Experience Seventeen was happening…!

This was a new type of Spiritual Experience – for instead of all being static – all three images moved! Nearly all my previous sixteen Spiritual Experiences had been static!

First I saw a constellation – Cassiopeia – disappearing into a huge 'black hole'. Then in the second image I saw lots of stars dropping down. In the third and final image I saw a strange 'biological cell', with lots of small land masses – moving about in the 'sea' within!

I had prayed the previous Sunday 8th November, after my first premonition that another Spiritual Experience was coming, to be able to interpret it immediately, unlike the tormenting delay of previous Spiritual Experiences.

In fact I was to I realise just what this Spiritual Experience meant within just three and a half days – so receiving an answer to my frequent prayers that 'any more Spiritual Experiences must be decipherable in a very short space of time, please!' For the following Sunday, I was at Church when I was given a copy of the 'Alpha News' newspaper, about the 'Alpha Course', the then current attempt at a Revival in the Church.

I immediately realised that my Spiritual Experience three days or so earlier had been about this – in advance of me realising how important it was.

The Spiritual Experience showed in image II, the stars falling from the sky. Image I showed an 'Omega' or 'W' attacking a black hole – Satan. In my now retitled 'Spiritual Energy' book, 'Omega' is my title for the Holy Spirit. Hence I now knew for sure that in this Spiritual Experience 17, I was being *instructed by this Spiritual Experience* to drop the recently adopted 'The Holy Spirit, Queen of the Stars' title for my other book. I had given it that long title earlier that year, mostly out of pique and exasperation following my lengthy debacle then bust-up with 'matey from Calais'.

Now the Holy Spirit In Person was saying "call it indeed 'Spiritual Energy'!" through Image III, showing a strange 'cell' with small 'spiritual organelles' moving around.

CHAPTER TWENTY-THREE

Into 1999, and another 'annus horribilis'. Another Crucifixion experience, just like 1995.

No less than **thirteen**, each massive, sources of stress precipitated a massive breakdown as the Winter of 1998-1999 took its toll of me – I was hospitalised and immediately had Spiritual Experience Eighteen! This totally accurately predicted just what horrors lay ahead in that awful year, 1999!

The Winter of 1998-1999

I do not remember much about the late Autumn and Winter of 1998-99. I only remember being torn apart by stress. So much happened after that to blot out my memories of October 1998 to February 1999! The one highlight that I do remember is seeing Jenny at Christmas for a memorable first time in four years!

I taught A level mathematics and physics part-time. Without Diamond now, I had no friends left, and was so stressed out that I felt unable or lacking motivation to make new ones. Stress? In the letter to Diamond, nearly the last I wrote to her, at the end of 1999, reproduced on the next pages, I list twelve nasty stresses on me. Really, as we shall see after this, I had on me in all thirteen massive sources of stress!

LETTER TO DIAMOND. NOVEMBER 18th 1999.

Dear Diamond,
...You must have changed. I have not...

My world record (?) 12 stresses and how they have (are being) resolved.

I adopted the first technique I learned recently on a Stress and Anxiety Management (SAM) Course about alleviating stress and so relieving the resulting anxiety, namely 'identify the stress(es)' in preparing the following carefully prioritised list. Namely, one must identify the 'who, what, when, where, why, how often, and history of the stress'.

So what follows is a prioritised list of causes of stress that had accumulated last February, that caused an admittedly disconcerting and massive breakdown as according to all witnesses, clearly including you.

The next thing the SAM course absolutely urged and emphasised was to 'confront and challenge the stress'. In particular eliminating any delusions, false beliefs, or other mistakenly held or irrational conceptions about that stress.

Above all, you must not shy away from the stress in escapes (particularly alcohol, note!) and if you truly confront the pain of the stress and the resulting anxiety level, each subsequent time you do that it will be far less. Ultimately it will fade to 'normal' - healthy - anxiety levels. To 'confront' the stress means to use your conscious mind to 'break the cycle' as soon as possible after the trigger for the stress, and start 'thinking positive' instead of getting anxious, depressed or ultimately panicking!

If you don't recognise such techniques, they are called 'cognitive recognition'. They have been incredibly effective in stopping all my stress-related 'flashbacks' recently!

1. **Contact with Jenny**. The fact that I have only had, thanks to Helen's 'diktat', Contact with Jenny only ever supervised by chaperones, for five whole years, had started to really get to me. My solicitor offered a Court Hearing in Summer 1998, but this was stalled because my new Psychiatrist, Dr Thatcher said he was not allowed by his job in the NHS to do a report! Result: No report! Hence no Hearing! Hence Stalemate! *How I've dealt with this stress.* The opportunity came from my Creative Writing homework after the first Wednesday evening session two weeks ago. The topics set were 'a narrow boat', 'Last Will and Testament' (ugh!) or - aha! – 'a (right) royal occasion'. I determined that this would be a first and last attempt at a *personal* piece, last because this group is not your 'Psychiatric patients only' style class, but for the general public at the local college. Indeed the reaction a week ago was 'it is a good poem'

(Colin, the leader); 'it is very sad' and 'personal – very!' So this week's piece - the theme was a radio play or the topic of 'little foibles' - was also about Contact - but the good, funny up-side. Equally well-received - both attached. Between them I have now explored all aspects of Contact and realise that the original pain will go in due course – and that I can bear it far better in the meantime, before the renewed attempt in some months promised by my solicitor, at a Court Order.

2. **Your excommunication of me twice early last year, followed by total stony silence for a whole year until last week.** Yes, the prompt for this letter was that last week it was a year since we last spoke, and six months that I have been judged 'fully well - but homeless living on Mymms Ward'. Now at last, thank God, ended, with two months in a lovely new flat - but with only one friend in the immediate area - lots in WGC. Well, Dim, I am certainly not going to repeat again what I say here, so this letter is your last chance. If you don't reply, I will be free to never contact you again, and draw the following conclusions about your bizarre behaviour towards me last year and this: -

(a) You excommunicated me because I overwhelmed you with loving help twice on Welwyn Ward last year, and you felt 'dependent on me' and 'crowded'. *Your problem entirely. You could have said something earlier about that feeling. Initially you were both times amazed at my responsible caring attitude.*

(b) You only blasted me out of your sight each time because you were acutely ill and totally irrational. *Your problem again. I understand.*

(c) You still are yet to respond to my entreaties to resume our old friendship because you have still to shed the irrational paranoid thinking that led to my being excommunicated. *Your problem again. I can only hope this last 'Bitter End' letter will change your mind.*

(d) You have not responded because you think I am still very ill. *I am not. I have been fully myself again since mid-May – six*

235

months ago. This letter should firmly establish and prove that – which is its intention.

I will just assume that no answer at all means the above version - mine - is entirely accurate. Hence *no reflection on me as a person at all.* SAM techniques working and fully applied again! *Think positive!* You see, you are quite simply the most wild, flamboyant, colourful, yet frustrating woman or even person I have ever met, and life without you has seemed quite grey, lifeless and empty. How you manage all that on top of your problems, rivalling mine as described here, especially as a woman living alone, is quite beyond me!

3. **Crashing memories of being divorced.** The next three stresses were all, I am afraid, down to your strange behaviour in multiply excommunicating me last year, plus the Contact issue was a strong factor in this number three. You see, a year ago you invoked massive 'flashbacks' to my feelings of total despair and betrayal while being divorced while I was being poisoned in 'drug Hell' in three hospitals in 1995. More of the poisonings in Stress 11! In the meantime, I have reached one very logical conclusion. My divorce is irrevocable – and has now been superseded by you much more recently 'divorcing me as a friend'. As for point 2, this letter is my last ever attempt to deal with the problem at source.

4. **Loneliness and frustration**. I don't think you can possibly imagine how lonely and frustrated I was from November last year to February this year. I was devastated at a second if not third excommunication by you inside six months, and totally frustrated that it was totally irrational, as I had been bending over backwards to help you when you asked. Apparently none of your family or other friends were prepared to do anything at all for you, let alone my constant visiting. As I said before you seemed amazed and delighted at this intensive care. If you felt 'crowded' - why didn't you say? *Solution in your*

case. Finish then send this letter. I will have done everything possible.

5. **ALCOHOL**. You of all people should understand how alcohol is an escape when you have massive stress to deal with - and after these three, plus all the rest of the stresses I had to deal with - perhaps it is not surprising I was downing up to eight pints a day - escapism. Disastrous, all my Doctors and Nurses, and now the SAM Course leader have endlessly pointed out. It massively upset my mood, made me even more depressed and upset, and interfered terribly with my medication. Even though I feel massively over-sedated now I only drink in small moderation, and am still on, since 1995, 150 mg/fortnight of haldol, my new Doctor (Thatcher) would not give me any more haloperidol. Even though I complained then of feeling 'high'. *As a result I have taken the rational conscious decision to remain a light drinker! Problem solved!*

6. **NEW DOCTOR.** Even though I knew I was massively over-stressed, it proved virtually impossible to get in to talk to my new busy Dr Thatcher, now that the Trusts had swapped Hertford as a 'catchment area' over to the QE2 from Harlow. This was in itself a massive stress - and when I saw him he only gave me 10 tablets of 1.5 mg of haloperidol - a tiny dose! *I am shortly to be back at Harlow under some new Doctor yet to write to me - hopefully better established than then 'new boy' Thatcher - and with more time for me initially! I have no CPN yet either! My old one has the situation under control and is handling the referral now Thatcher has 'referred me into a vacuum'!*

7. **Boredom.** Following on the heels of 2, 3 then 4 - all originally started by YOU, remember, I got very BORED. This started to get me drinking in the afternoons as well as the evenings - but luckily never in the morning. DON'T BOTHER RINGING ME IN RESPONSE TO THIS LETTER IF YOU ARE ONCE MORE DRINKNG HEAVILY. I JUST DON'T

WANT TO HEAR ANY MORE EVER AGAIN ABOUT YOU AND YOUR PROBLEMS WITH ALCOHOL!!! *Solution. The time on Welwyn and especially Mymms Wards has given me a very thorough training in sheer boredom - and getting used to it! I am also still persevering to get a publisher for my long-finished book – Spiritual Energy – that you keep on destroying copies of!*

8. **Finances.** What with a car, alcohol, smoking and a big overdraft to finance, my finances got into a worse and worse state - punctuated by absolute nightmare crises when I bought the rings you still flaunt, and helped you in hospital. *My car is on the scrap-heap; the bus is much slower, and inconvenient but far cheaper; and - after being extremely over-generous to you; and your friend Dobbyn on Welwyn Ward - my Girobank account has been forcibly closed and I have no overdraft now – I am with the Woolwich! Finances are under my control again now, but with debts…*

9. **Autobiography.** As you may have noticed, I wrote my autobiography last Autumn, vainly hoping to get rid of a lot of flashback-style stress by writing about it. An admirable intent, which has since at last greatly helped as I write now, but which backfired at the time. It only worsened and heightened my feelings about (1) Contact (2) You (3) Divorce (4) loneliness - it was a massively isolated thing to do! And (5) alcohol was soon pursued for two or three weeks while I faced up to the next three to ten pages. Margaret C. on Welwyn Ward said it was 'gripping' and that 'it got me out of my depression - the first book I have read since suicidal'. I have read it quickly once then not touched it in a year. *Safe on my bookshelf, it has finally done its job. Writing about my problems has been incredibly therapeutic, then and now!*

10. **Publishers and agents - and complete shits like 'Matey from Calais'.** I won't bore you with this one. Namely I was finding the publishing game a deep pool full of sharks – and endless refusals. The devastating time

with 'Matey' - you had been right all along, I had been wrong, over-enthusiastic and naive - left a massive nasty taste in the mouth for months. *I mail-shot 48 publishers some six weeks ago and two have asked to see the book - then they said 'No!', 'but we say that to 99% of unsolicited manuscripts'. I am yet to hear from 16 UK (no less than six Chnstian - so relevant), 4 Irish and 3 US houses. So I am following up the UK ones after I finish this letter, probably tomorrow now. Think 'stay positive even though it's ball-breaking work!'*

11. **Medical Inquiry.** My parents have complained bitterly to East Herts Trust about Dr Whore and I am helping a bit with chasing out of them my clozapine blood results for 1995. These should show that my white blood cell levels fell below 'AIDS'-like danger levels so Whore should never have sent me to Fairfield so destroying my marriage – with help from you, writing to Helen and then ringing her about us. He sent me there, the Inquiry this April said clearly, and sinisterly, to 'enforce clozapine treatment' – which should have been totally abandoned after that first near-lethal blood result. The Inquiry was totally stage-managed, and the resulting report - four months later not the promised one month - a dismissive whitewash clean and complete exoneration of Whore. *My Father is handling this one - he is getting up at five each morning and working all day, for weeks now, on a report in reply for the Ombudsman for Medical Services. We are going to the very top... Watch this Space, as they say!*

12. **Feelings of inadequacy over being unemployed.** With all the above going on, not surprisingly perhaps I longed for the 'old days' when I had a career, a salary and was not dependent as now on benefit. *I am seeing a woman from the Hertfordshire County Council's Agency 'Employment Direct' with a view to getting back to work - slowly – part-time work at first.*

That then is the full list. No wonder I ended up on Welwyn Ward. Had I been able to get in to see Thatcher a month earlier

I would have ended up there at the same time as you - as it is you had been discharged a week before I arrived. I can't help wondering what would have happened had we been back on the dreaded Ward together at the same time? Please note that only four of these problems have been partly solved by others - alcohol, Doctor and the last two. Many of the more serious ones have been my domain alone - and now I turn, with this letter, to try to reason with YOU - one very last 'bitter end' time...

I never did get any reply. This letter, being written late in 1999, hints at some of my massive problems in the course of the previous Winter, that I forget the details of now, it was all such a nightmare! Suffice it to say that by February 1999 I had started cracking up. My 'Outreach Worker' and Community Nurse called several times in the week up to 10th February 1999, trying to keep me out of hospital, but I flipped completely. I even sent an attractive neighbour, the very double of my now ancient unrequited 'flame' at Cambridge in 1978, some Valentine's day 'slush' all mixed up with a series of faxes I sent to the number given as that of the Pope's office by his Ambassador's Office here!

'Slush' it was, its posting based on the half baked coincidence that her car registration held the same number exactly as my old flame's mailbox number at Cambridge. Such things mean a lot when you are ill! However she well and truly over-reacted! This sending faxes about the Y2K Bug to the Pope was Massive Stress 13. Unlucky for some? Definitely unlucky for me! I was hospitalised!

I will skim over that 7½ months in hospital, apart from main 'low-lights' which are less painful to remember. It started with an Eighteenth Spiritual Experience... My last of the 20th Century...!

The nature of my admission was a bit bizarre, and its consequences fully predicted by this Eighteenth Spiritual Experience. On the Sunday 7th February 1999 I had a couple of drinks on top of a week of getting so ill I thought I was totally well (believe me, this can happen with my bipolar affective disorder!) Then I drove to the QE2 Hospital at Welwyn Garden City to give a patient friend there a lift home. I was nearly sectioned and hospitalised on the spot, as Dr Thatcher was there and realised I was acutely ill and had been driving on top of some drink.

Somehow I evaded being detained by Law, and took my friend Peppy home as arranged. The next day my CPN called round yet again, and I was phoned by Social Services and asked to come in on the Tuesday 9th February to see the Social Worker responsible for Sectioning people under Psychiatrists.

My parents came too, the next day, and after some discussion I agreed to go in voluntarily. My friend and benefactor from the IEE, Julian, said soon afterwards that I had 'been very brave' to do so. The following morning, I drove to the QE2, and perhaps bizarrely, admitted myself on one condition. This was that I have my ever-reliable haldol injection stopped and that I had sulpuride tablets instead, as recommended by the Professor at Charing Cross Hospital the previous Autumn. Little did I know that they only work on schizophrenia!

So it was, that the events of those two weeks up to my admission on 10th February 1999 were to have a drastic and very damaging effect over the whole of my confinement of the next 7½ months. I was to spend the first three months in the prison-like surroundings of Welwyn Ward, only later when judged well, but evicted and so homeless, on the rehabilitation Ward, Mymms.

On my third night I saw a dramatic Spiritual Experience that fully predicted my further torture, having hoped I would never return to this place after 1995 and all that...

Spiritual Experience Eighteen. Small hours of February 13th, 1999. My side-room at Welwyn Ward of the QEII. All eighteen including this one have now revealed their prophetic meanings. Does this mean the set of eighteen in twenty-one years, with 18 + (8 – 1) + (3 – 1) = 27 meanings, is complete – there will be no more?

Image One. A Dark Crucifix, radiating gold light.

Image Two. Doctor Who's Tardis!

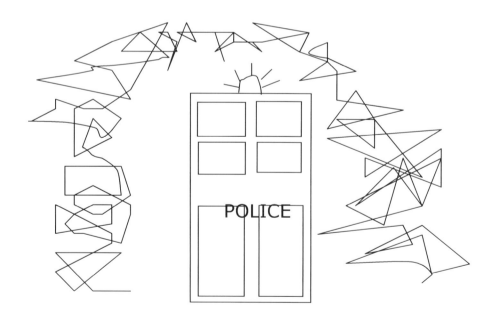

Image Three.   An indecent memory! – in silhouette – of the first kiss Diamond and I ever shared! This had taken place on the same Welwyn Ward in 1995!

Definitive Interpretation of Spiritual Experience Eighteen

After Spiritual Experience Sixteen had taken some agonising three months to understand – I had prayed that any further Spiritual Experiences would *immediately* reveal their meaning.

This eighteenth one *did*, and so my prayers were answered. I almost immediately knew what Spiritual Experience Seventeen was saying, as we saw in Chapter 22. Likewise the three awful meanings of the three separate images of Spiritual Experience or Premonition Eighteen were revealed in days or weeks, as I now vividly recall.

Image One of Spiritual Experience Eighteen. A vivid crucifix.

Just like Spiritual Experience Thirteen, which I had obviously already got a clear interpretation of, this portended another 'Crucifixion experience' in that Acute Psychiatric Ward. Indeed, as we see on the next few pages, an absolutely massive crucifixion experience was indeed to unfold! I won't give half the detail, just highlights – or should it be 'lowlights'? That year was just too painful to recall on paper in too much detail!

Image Two of Spiritual Experience Eighteen. Doctor Who's Tardis or Time Machine!!??

God has a sense of humour or rather irony, in this case! This image portended *Time Travel*. As part of the next few months' crucifixion as portended by Image One of this Spiritual Experience, I did indeed 'travel in time'! I had massive and terrifying *flashbacks* about the previous seven years, as pre-empted by the stresses that had caused me to be admitted, as described earlier.

Image Three of Spiritual Experience Eighteen. Acute reminder of my first ever kiss with Diamond – in the tiny gas chamber of a smoking room on that Welwyn Ward.

Being in that place I learned that Diamond had ended a four month stay the week before I was admitted. It was as if she haunted the place still! During the four months I was on that Ward, prior to being transferred to the much less severe Ward on the floor below, I was constantly and agonisingly reminded of her. I wrote to her all the time. All the 'thanks' I got was a letter full of death threats from her nerds of inadvisable drug addict and alcoholic 'friends', at which I called in the Police, had her cautioned – then continued to write...

No good, it looks like I will never see her again. Mixed feelings result...

CHAPTER TWENTY-FOUR

Acts I and II of a tragedy – another 'annus horribilis' – 1999?

Into the crucible of yet another 'annus horribilis' of 1999 ('terrible year', for those who don't speak Latin!) Act I – first 4½ months on the 'Welwyn' Acute Ward, yet again, in the Psychiatric Wing at the QEII Hospital, Welwyn Garden City. Speaking of unspeakable things will I know in the end prove therapeutic… Then Act II – the comparative peace and haven – and thence acute boredom – of Mymms Ward for exactly three months. I was well, but awaiting re-housing, having been evicted under cruel circumstances… Stigma! It was pure paranoid prejudice that caused that!

I am writing this on Sunday 5th March 2000. After the pure ordeal of writing this chapter, I will breathe a huge sigh of relief, having gulped for over a week, with my heart fiercely in my throat, at the prospect of facing this chapter! My recent 'stress and anxiety management' course tells me I will suffer in the short term, from a resulting peak of anxiety, which will vanish rapidly, having 'faced the stress' – and written down what my rough plan says. Hopefully I will, by writing it all down, overcome my persistent flashbacks about 1999. Acts III and IV, in Chapter 25, will describe my rapid recovery in the New Millennium, as 1999 ended and we entered the 21st century so dramatically!

In order to keep the amount I have to write down to the bare minimum, I am working to a writing plan – to present the 'material' as a series of bullet points in this chapter. A lot more trauma happened, as you will see, in 'Act I' (Welwyn Acute Ward at the QEII Hospital, Welwyn Garden City). As I start out, my plan shows twenty bullet points in Act I, over twice as many as 'Act II' (my time on the much less acute rehabilitation Ward at the QEII, Mymms Ward).

Act I.   A real ordeal of nerves back on Welwyn Ward, having hoped never to have to go back there in 1995. Trauma – February 10th to June 21st 1999…

1. **'Sulpuride' was yet again the wrong drug – for entirely the wrong diagnosis!** I had been treated like a laboratory rat or 'the Chief poison taster to the Queen of Heaven' as I have previously more poetically put it, for years. As we will see in the final summary chapter of this book, I had been through over *forty drastic changes of treatment within six years – for a purely mythical diagnosis of either straight 'schizophrenia' or 'schizo-affective disorder'.* Now the latest change of treatment – sulpuride tablets instead of haldol depots – was apparently down to me! Actually it was based on a recommendation from Professor Hirsch of Charing Cross Hospital, whom my parents and I had seen as part of our complaint about 'Dr' Harlot the previous year.   However it was immediately to backfire – I was not to know it is an 'atypical' tranquilizer specifically targeted at schizophrenia. Not my actual illness of a 'bipolar I affective disorder'. So, for the next seven weeks, Thatcher kept shoving up the dose, while taken off my usual neuroleptic tranquilizer of haldol, I got ever more 'ill' and 'high'. Why was I kept on sulpuride for so very long when it was totally inappropriate, when Psychiatrists normally allow just two weeks for a new drug to have its effect? Yes, why, Thatcher? *You* told me later 'it had some effect' so why, in actual fact, did I become so very ill while I took it for all those seven weeks? The answer I will tell you. The diagnosis you inherited was all wrong. I am in no way 'schizo'. I actually suffer occasionally from hypomania due to my 'bipolar affective disorder'. This maldiagnosis and so mistreatment for too long, has a great bearing on what follows…! Indeed, the renewed 'Crucifixion experience' portended by Spiritual Experience Eighteen, that I saw on admission!

2. **A very real, and very persistent, attack of 'emotional pain'.   The consequences are first appalling and hideous, but end up *beautiful!*** Virtually the first experience that mattered when I arrived on that Ward once

again, was severe *emotional pain* – that soon led to the *flashbacks* so very accurately portended by image two of Spiritual Experience Eighteen! Most of this emotional pain occurred while I was, as ever, back in the smoking-room cum Gas Chamber. To my horror, after I had briefly, just once, compared the agonies I was going through to 'growing wings', a drug addict, extremely schizophrenic with massive delusions, picked up on it. He kept running out to the staff outside, who rarely ventured in there because of the smoke, with the cry 'The wings! The wings!' They were eager to earn Brownie Points and accumulate 'symptoms' I had, however phoney – so this smear duly solemnly appeared in all my reports. I was in such real 'emotional' pain I was unable to stop this travesty... The flashbacks of Spiritual Experience 18 were also starting to severely weaken my emotional reserves... However, on and around 16th March 1999, a remarkable thing happened. First, I recalled it was exactly the *fifth Anniversary* of my 'Baptism of the Holy Spirit' in 1994. That day, to honour the occasion, I starting fluently 'speaking in Tongues' – my original *first 'spiritual wing' was in full flow!* Around that time, I started healing people as well! A new *second 'spiritual wing'* appeared, as it were! I stopped somebody's LSD overdose, and actually stopped someone else from much pain and slurred speech, from a blocked artery – in their brain! All without touching them, only by holding my hands three inches from the source of their problem, in both cases of course their heads. This of course was scorned by the Psychiatric-materialist-drug-based 'Profession'. Once I announced that these two gifts had genuinely been given to me as 'compensation for my recent suffering' by God, Thatcher wrote in my notes, and reported to colleagues, that I had now new 'schizophrenic symptoms'. Namely that I 'believed I had "special powers"'. He was simply wrong... These Gifts were given to me by the Holy Spirit...! I was outraged at his philistine dismissal of my new Spiritual Gift, and wrote him a long letter about it. He ignored this completely, but did at least include a copy in my notes...

3. **Diamond had been the most frequent patient there – 50 times in the previous 10 years. Especially 1995 when she seduced me while I was still married. Her presence seemed to be everywhere, haunting that Ward!** The third and final image of my last Spiritual Experience Eighteen had painfully reminded me of Diamond's first seductive kiss of me in the smoking-room on that Ward during 1995. This accurately predicted that my worst flashbacks as in point two above, as predicted by Image Two of Spiritual Experience Eighteen, were to be all about Diamond, and the roller-coaster of an abusive period I had had from her from April 1995, the time of that fateful kiss, until the previous year of 1998. So it was, constantly reminded of her and – while so 'high' – only dimly remembering the bad times of her abusive, alcoholic, ill 'madam' moods – that I started writing to her. For quite a while this became a torrent of letters! I also delivered some birthday and Mother's Day presents in March, preceded by Christmas gifts, rather belatedly, of books, including copies of my own. When my parents later retrieved my letters from her, she told them she had, as ever with my stuff, simply destroyed my books… Meanwhile there was a mutual acquaintance of hers on the Ward with me, Sonia, who relayed all the news about this bizarre family to me, as she heard it 'on the grapevine'. In particular, Diamond was about to become a grandmother – her daughter was expecting a boyfriend's baby that early July. So I sent her some 'birth' cards and presents, too, overly sentimentally! I should not have bothered – this exercise was to cost nearly £200, and along with helping out Diamond's long term bosom pal 'Dobbyn' as we discuss later, was to cost me so much in helping out these three people – that my bank account was shut down! Not before I received Diamond's only ever reply then or since, to all my correspondence and kindness. *Death threats*, composed by her drug addict and alcoholic so-called 'friends', to 'nutter me', and addressed on the envelope by her! I spent the day this arrived on the phone, eventually after several calls persuading the police to reluctantly come to the Ward about it. The two policewomen at first dismissed it, then read the letter more thoroughly,

and promised to caution Diamond. So, even though I simply in due course resumed writing letters, less frequently now, there were no more direct repercussions. Diamond did write to my Doctor, but when he asked me to stop writing at her request, I took a risk and ignored him. I bumped into her while on leave or discharged a couple of times later that year, but despite all my previous attentions – she totally 'stone-walled' me – and walked past with a cold, withering look. I guess I am forcibly spared any more problems and use and abuse from this 'Cruella De Vil', as the police in her home town have as a less than affectionate name for this tiny package of venomous trouble – caused by her massive problems – and the fact that her wild personality makes them much worse... Really, she is her own worst enemy!

4. **These Acute Psychiatric Wards can be very frightening – especially if you have always been opposed to violence, like me... Yet MORE death threats – from two extremely fierce and extremely ill male patients!** A very queasy feeling was all about me for weeks, twice, on Welwyn Ward, from very physical and visible threats. These – death! – threats came first from a wiry and very strong old patient who came on the Ward, and immediately started irritating everybody with his nonstop, gravelly, gritty, whining voice, rambling on endlessly about his 'vast wealth'. Most patients in Mental Wards, after the first month, only get £13 a week in benefit or so, so were deeply offended. The threats came after one of the women, in an argument in the smoking-room, told him in no uncertain terms, that he had deeply offended her by slyly sitting there the previous week, and flashing down to his underpants. I confirmed that, having been there to put up with it. He immediately went into a rage, denying it, and was finally removed from the room by Nursing Assistants. His passing shout was extremely angrily at me, "I'll kill yer! I'll kill yer!" Shortly after that 'Doctor' Whore, his Psychiatrist, 'bombed him out' with a massive cocktail of mind-bending drugs, which reduced him to a croaking, incoherent, dribbling shell, confined to his room, with lots of assistance to do anything at all. He had been transformed by prescribed drugs into a

zombie, unable to do anything for himself. Pretty soon, it got life-threatening – he was taken to an intensive care Ward in the main wing of the hospital for two weeks, crippled by Whore's prescribed psychoactive drugs! Remembering my own similar poisonings by the same Whore in 1994 then again in 1995, I finally became sympathetic. I remember taking him some African violets in that Ward... Shortly after he had been 'taken away' after poisoning, in that sick way, a much younger and even more aggressive and talkative patient arrived. He had apparently come in after trying an ecstasy tablet, and was very affected by it. He kept on rabbiting on about cannabis and other drugs, effectively talking to himself nonstop, as everybody soon realised it was best to ignore him and his ill, possessed almost, stare – and constant jabber. After a few weeks he had demonstrated clearly he really was a karate expert, by doing some very slick movements in practice and to demonstrate his 'virility' that way. I took the advice of my acquaintance 'Mick', a burly Staff Nurse – that this guy was 'all talk, no action', until after about six weeks of this sheer torment, he physically threatened me. He had objected to me in particular, as I had proven unafraid of his posturing. So I reported him for this threat, instead of retaliating. This approach made him much calmer for a long time. The big change came when he was starting to recover from his psychotic episode. It was March and my parents had brought in some strawberries, which I proceeded to offer around in the smoking room. I had a brainwave, and offered him one – an apparent enemy – with the words "Try one of these! Tart!" strongly emphasising the last word! He could not help himself, starting to laugh, having just looked deeply suspicious, and soon after that really started to 'climb down'. However the preceding six weeks of facing him down and totally avoiding violence from him, despite several death threats from him during that time, as for the old bloke before, were really draining. Especially when I was so ill myself... I have never experienced such exposure to at least potential, sometimes actual, violence, except in these Acute Wards and Secure Units I have unjustly been forcibly confined to. All due to the Satanic 'conspiracy of incompetence' of the Psychiatrists that

I have endured for so long. With their massive string of faulty diagnoses and so endlessly damaging rather than helpful treatments... For over *twenty-three years* 1978-2001...!

5. **The 'Nursing' Staff on Welwyn Ward do virtually no Nursing or actually talking to us patients. They hide in their recently-installed central office and write reports all the time instead. Some of them actually admit to me that their top priority is to protect their own backs following a damning Report about that Ward following a large number of deaths two years earlier...** Following a highly critical report about Welwyn Ward two years earlier, after a large number of deaths and suicides, the regime there was even more paranoid than I remembered from my own stay in 1995, and visits to see Diamond the previous year. A large glass-fronted office had been installed, and because of their paranoia over losing their jobs, most of the staff, two of them readily admitted to me, stayed in there as much as possible. Totally ignoring the desperate needs of most patients, who were left to rot of boredom and neglect, with just other equally ill patients or the untrained Nursing Assistants to talk to. The Ward still looked very shabby, which went along with the paranoid, nearly fascist control regime by the staff, mostly 'control freaks' of the highest order – and proud of it – presumably that is why they could only do that particular job. In the case of my own 'treatment' and that of many others, it had been totally wrong because of the gross exaggerations of my alleged 'symptoms' while in that dreadful place in particular. Indeed, if one wants to work in a place like that, it helps to be mad yourself! Most of them were – power mad at least – with their control freaks' "petty poxy power over poor poorly patients" as I dubbed it at one point in my confinement.

6. **Constant threats of 'Fairfield' or worse Secure Units – just like 1995 – just because I can't accept domination while ill, by all these 'control freaks'. When I tell them this would be a rather drastic 'punishment', they deny they are trying to 'punish' me at all! They *are* madder**

than the patients! I must have received at least twenty threats from various staff of being sent to an even worse hospital in my first eight weeks... In the end, I had had enough of this bully-boy (or bully-girl) tactic – so after the latest threat, packed my bags and said "Fine! Send me to Fairfield then!" to an astonished Nursing Sister, who dominated even though she was a wimp! Mick and she who were standing there, just did not know how to take this head-on affront to their dubious Authority, given to them by law, not by any personal abilities!

7. **My Primary Nurse, Donald, far from talking me out of, as not a good idea, actively encouraged me to go through the process of changing my name to something extremely exotic, which he told me could be anything inoffensive you chose, and above all free as long as you used the right form of legal words and got it witnessed by just one person.** It *was* free – as I phoned up a solicitor friend who sent the right form of words, which I adapted – to include surname – and retyped. Luckily the person I got to witness my change of name by deed poll was technically 'legally incompetent' – as Sonia was on a Section 3 even though I had not yet been placed on mine. So, after I went all the way, and got a new passport and driving licence in this new name, it proved easy to revert back to my old name once the new one proved not to be legally in force. This did not stop Donald enjoying his misdeeds, and taking no responsibility when he gleefully wrote up my latest 'symptom' in his reports – which said not one nice thing about me. He also trawled the dustbin for the slightest 'eccentric' thing about me which he could put into my reports...

8. **Leave from the Ward, such a relief, is only ever reluctantly granted, after a great deal of bureaucracy from the 'staff'. I stop for ten minutes in the car park, attracted by the sight of a beautiful double rainbow above that concrete jungle, after a day of continuous such 'breaks' – and all my leave is stopped!** Getting any 'relief time' from that dreadfully fiercely controlled environment turned out these days to be fraught with

difficulty. One had to endure endless form filling before being eventually 'let out' at all into the slightly less dismal environs of the hospital grounds – the limits of leave if on a 'Section' as I was. Then, you had to time your roaming, with a constant eye on your watch. Any leave beyond about a minute late was fiercely scrutinised by the staff on your return. Indeed, on one infamous day, I must have already taken about ten 'unrestricted' leave periods, when it started raining heavily. As I prepared to re-enter the dismal confines of Welwyn Ward, bang on time, an astonishingly beautiful *full double rainbow* appeared over the Hospital. Entranced, I stayed an extra ten minutes to take in this lovely sight, so rare in that dreadful built-up area. When it finally faded away, I returned to a Gestapo-like interrogation from Heavy, the retired landlady who was then my first of two Primary Nurses – Donald was the second. She banned me all further time off the Ward, in total contrast to all my recent massive amount of freedom – for a whole week – just for watching a rainbow near the 'Unit'! A 'bit heavy', Heavy!

9. **After Thatcher stubbornly keeps upping my sulpuride as in point (1) above, for seven whole weeks, I just get worse and worse, despite his claims it has had 'some effect' to defend his incompetence. The right diagnosis would have helped – I am NOT a 'schizo' or 'schizo-affective' sufferer!** In the end I resisted returning to haloperidol depots, fearful of once more feeling 'foggy' and irritable and 'twitchy' among a whole list of lesser side effects. Amid yet more threats of Secure Units, I eventually did have a depot of the stuff, having previously been Sectioned for refusing *all* 'their' hideous drugs – and claiming wrongly I could give myself my own Healing – Spiritual Healing. This did not exactly go down very well with the Doctors and Nursing Staff in that Satanic Materialistic Stronghold. My Section 3 was applied on 29th March 1999, the day before my 42nd birthday. Thanks for a lovely birthday present, Thatcher and the Welwyn Ward Staff! As we will be seeing, and saw in point (7), they were 'out to get me' – as my family and I had complained bitterly – and fully justifiably – about faulty diagnosis and treatment by Whore.

Back in 1995 that had handed my ex- her divorce, and my life savings, on a plate, while I was 'held down helpless under a great Weight of Law' by them...

10. **Relationships with my family, especially my parents, were often difficult, but they were terrifically supportive, especially with finances.** Nearly immediately after I was admitted, not knowing I was being evicted, my parents took it upon themselves to 'do me a big favour' – even though I had tried to explain I did not want this favour done – to my house in Hertford. So once they explained they had put lots of bricks in my front lawn, and installed new worksurfaces in the kitchen, while I was confined and could not stop them, I did not speak to them for a long time. There were to be lots of other occasions in my 7½ months there, when I or they 'took umbrage' at the other's attitude, and they stopped all visits, or I stopped telephoning. On the whole however, they were incredibly supportive and visited every day when I was on speaking terms with them. In particular, as we shall see when discussing the awful state my finances got into due to being confined there, and a lot of budget-busting spending, particularly on Diamond and her bosom pal Dobbyn, who was still there, in point (12) below, they were to prove life-saving with money.

11. **One particularly memorable attack and dismissal of me as 'nothing' by perhaps the most affected member of staff – by a 'Petty Power Complex'.** If previous descriptions of how the Welwyn Ward Staff were usually 'out to get me' – just because we had complained about their appalling abuse of me 1993-1995 – this incident was the worst. For the first three months of my unwilling 'stay' there, on totally wrong medication most of the time, I did not need much sleep. As a result I started to ignore the 11.30pm 'curfew' and stay up late while so high. This was allowed as long as I could get up on time for breakfast in the morning. One night the afore-mentioned member of staff, the Nursing Sister on 'nights' was in a particularly bad mood, though she was often bad-tempered and domineering – unusual for an Indian. Something I said when taking my

255

night drugs must have upset her, probably the fact she felt I was encouraging other patients to 'break the curfew' too. She bawled at me, "While you are up here, Simon, you are NOTHING!" It just seemed to sum up the "us and (domineering) them" attitudes amongst nearly all the Nursing Staff. On top of all their threats of Secure Units, it made me feel very angry. I promptly wrote "(her name) is nothing" on a copy of my still very good CV, and handed it into the Office. A lot of laughter and sympathy from other Staff immediately resulted!

12. **My heavy subsidies to impoverished smoker Dobbyn – on the obviously ill, naive grounds that she had been back from Fairfield recently – and far worse that 'any friend of Diamond was a friend of mine'.** Dobbyn was an Asian girl, very confused, with some learning difficulties. She had become Diamond's bosom pal the previous Autumn, when on visiting Diamond she had struck me as 'extremely voluble'. I was told by one of the Nurses they had shared 'mutual screaming sessions' together that previous year! When I was admitted she had been sent to Fairfield as Welwyn Ward could not handle her. She returned traumatised after six weeks or so, reduced to tears and silence. I took pity on her, on her £13.50 a week sole income, as a fellow ex-inmate of Fairfield, and as a friend of Diamond. The latter was rather misplaced, but I was still in March 1999, yet to receive Diamond's death threats. Dobbyn referred to Diamond as a 'sweet tart', which in my long experience, just about sums her up – although most of it can be excused by problems beyond Diamond's control... Anyway over the next six weeks, we discussed Diamond at length, and in the process, out of the kindness of my heart, I must have given Dobbyn about £400-£500 in cigarettes, loose change, snacks and drinks – some of it supplied by my parents, mostly by me. In the end she fulfilled her endless promises to repay this money – at least in part – and had the balance of her electricity account converted into a cheque payable to me, which she freely handed over. Almost immediately however, she 'turned nasty' and threateningly accused me of 'stealing' increasingly large sums of money

from her, instead of the truth, that she owed me a lot of money. Soon these reached vast amounts - £1400 was her last ludicrous demand.   The staff, intent on 'getting me', ignored the fact that her claims were clearly ludicrous, and in a clear attempt to have me framed for stealing, fraud or worse, were to call in the Police!   See Act II below for the outcome, as I was indeed briefly seen by a PC on Mymms Ward later – he was very sensible, and dismissed all these allegations inside two minutes flat!

13. **MONEY situation diabolical!   Soon I was on very low income although some patients like Dobbyn above, were on a third of that, even! There is a mistake at the Benefits Office and for three months I get nothing at all!**   My father greatly helped out by lending me money during that three months, fortunately... In the end, thanks to being so unwisely generous to Diamond, her daughter to an extent, and Dobbyn (see points 3 and 12 above) my bank account was closed!   I was helpless in the face of their demands that I should halve my overdraft, on such low income, all needed.   I opened a building society current account in Hertford, but telephone banking – there are no Telling Machines at the QEII – was cripplingly expensive and virtually impossible.   The telephones ate all my money, running as they do at *five times* the normal charges, so frequently, very frustratingly, I wasted lots of money on abortive phone calls, ended while waiting to get past the automatic phone lines.   A true nightmare, which I will give no more than this brief summary of...!

14. **A mere Nursing Assistant, who *of course* remains anonymous, claims she has seen me driving and lies by doing so. Then Thatcher and a heavy female Doctor who stands in for him, take a very cruel heavyweight step – and have my driving licence confiscated. I still hadn't got it back nearly a year later...** My family and I were horrified at these lies, that I had been categorically 'observed' driving – by a Contract Nursing Assistant – who conveniently 'they' refused to name or bring forward. Rather than the obvious light step over these outright lies, of simply

telling me not to drive, the vicious, totally unprofessional vendetta among the staff there against me, because we had made a serious complaint, however justified, became transparently obvious. First of all Thatcher was on one of their frequent two-week holidays as a Doctor, so his female stand-in Dr Feinbeeste, held one of her absolutely huge 'Queen with her many courtiers' Ward Rounds, very self-important, and ordered me to surrender my car keys. When Thatcher returned from his holiday, he immediately swallowed the lies flying around, that I had been driving while on a 'Section 3' – and told me to send my licence back to the issuing authority, the DVLA. Initially I balked, horrified that they were obviously so guilty about all this, that I myself, not them, had to surrender the licence. I complained about all this to a Lady Nursing Assistant, who was very shrewd and worldly-wise, and she just looked at me with a certain look. She said, "Well, Simon, Welwyn Ward knows it has got its worst enemy on board!" That explained a lot – there *was* a vendetta against me – cynically while I was ill and vulnerable – even though the complaints causing all this were entirely unjustified. Totally cynical, spiteful and unprofessional. I was due to have my licence returned in December 1999, even though I have no car as I could not afford to run it any more while on pitiful hospital benefit, so scrapped it in August 1999 having failed to sell it as it was very rusty. Pity – it was a lovely car. However, I still have no licence back, having only briefly had one in 2002.

15. **My serious problems with psychotic females caused by accepting their initial pleas for help. Later most of them 'turned nasty' and complained for no real reason, to The Staff. As a result I was accused, falsely again, of alleged '(sexual!) harassment'!** As we saw in points 11 and 14, the 'Welwyn Ward Mafia Machine' really had it in for me, whom they saw as their 'worst enemy – and under their dubious "care"'. Getting the *police* involved over Dobbyn's plainly ridiculous allegations, was clearly a very crude and bungled attempt to frame me over *nothing*, by this WWMM. Also, Diamond and my neighbour in Hertford had both complained about my writing to them, however

innocent the content. This was not the end of this matter of 'alleged harassment' – the attempts to frame me over helping out 'damsels in distress', for absolutely NO sexual motive, my 'nit wit syndrome', just proved the underlying viciousness of the self-proclaimed 'caring' Nurses of the WWMM. Several female patients on the Ward first of all asked for my help, then after a while they 'turned nasty'. Hysterically and in paranoid fashion rather than dare face me, they asked the staff to get me to not contact them again. This sexless help to them then paranoia from them, was soon bizarrely translated into 'sexual harassment' by the staff, even the Doctors, in a further attempt to 'set me up'. Sonia, for instance, kept borrowing money off me which she was not in a position to repay. She had given me her address, and when she was on leave one day I went round and left a polite, totally business-like note asking for my – just – £2 back. The next thing I knew, she had complained to the WWMM who virtually insisted I was sexually harassing her – over a debt of money, just £2. Really WWMM, that was your most brazen attempt at a set-up! I do NOT sexually harass women – I am too shy and too much the gentleman! The feeblest attempt to implicate me they made came over a homeless woman teacher who was terrified of the elderly 'gent' of point 4, as he seemed to pick on her to grate on to, in his disgusting 'voice' all the time. Also it was her first time in a Mental Ward, let alone an Acute Ward, let alone Welwyn Ward! So I 'minded' her until her transfer to Harlow, her home area hospital, from him and other equally obnoxious patients. She kept ringing me from there, to share experiences, and read my writings, especially my 'Spiritual Energy', which her sons much admired, and she said 'but I know all this already – we are on precisely the same wavelength!' I rang back a few times, to learn she hated manic-depressives. I foolishly interjected 'But I am a manic-depressive like them! All this talk on Welwyn Ward that I am a 'schizophrenic' is a smear!" Shortly after that I was 'summoned' to see Thatcher and again accused of sexual harassment – of this middle-aged woman! It turned out this charge was again a bungled attempt to set me up – she had simply asked my social worker, fearful of manic-depressives, to ask me politely not to contact her again. The only female patient I had problems with who did not get me into trouble was Peppy, a friend from Hertford I had first met while in Harlow Hospital in 1997, who was admitted when I was. She borrowed a CD from me and then lost it when sent to Fairfield for a month for argumentative behaviour. In the resulting argument over this, one of her own CD's got smashed and she then broke several of mine, as they sat very vulnerable in the smoking-room along with my portable hi-fi. Shortly afterwards, after more such psychotic, childish, aggressive behaviour, 'they' returned her to Fairfield – for all of four months this time. We kept in occasional touch – but I was 'downstairs' on Mymms Ward when she returned.

16. **I have now ended twenty whole years of being diagnosed and so wrongly treated, totally falsely, for alleged schizophrenia.** In Welwyn Ward I was now once more told by the Doctors, 'you are being treated as a schizophrenic patient'... Since coming here to Ware two *new, objective* experts have told me the correct name for my – emotional not 'mental' – condition is a 'bipolar I affective disorder'! They have told me to 'forget' the 23½ years of self-doubt I have put up with, of falsely being labeled a 'schizo' or a 'schizo-affective disorder sufferer' (a 'schizo-defective', I used to dryly and ironically call this! "Do they see things in me I can't detect in myself, so are not really there?" I thought to myself...). However, the so-called 'Doctors' at that dismal QEII Hospital have always been totally incapable of diagnosing my actual condition, although between 1983-1993 the treatment happened to be appropriate, despite huge side-effects. They cannot 'tell their arse from their elbow' or in my case 'their schizophrenia from their bipolar affective disorder'! All the time since, I have been put through great swingeing regimes of totally torturous 'treatment'. These were totally wrong, so my actual illness went untreated, but I took huge amounts of totally the wrong drugs, for totally mythical 'schizophrenia', all that time. Thanks for nothing – for destroying my life, QEII and the WWMM – in 1995 and 1999 in particular!

17. **My attempts to brighten up the Ward. Art and flowers and lovely books, some of the pictures from 'Art Therapy'. My music fills the smoking-room. None of this positive effort appears in my totally negative, damning reports for a "Hospital Manager's Appeal" – see next point.** As soon as I arrived, along with every other patient, I found the grim surroundings of Welwyn Ward to be totally bleak and prison-like. I had foreseen I might end up there again the previous Autumn, had spotted a portable CD/radio/dual tape machine by Philips – good make – at a bargain price, so soon this was playing non-stop in the only interesting room, the smoking-room. Until Peppy attacked it as in point 14, my CD collection I entrusted to the space next to it, even at night. Nobody apart from her ever took or damaged my CD collection, even though they were all seriously ill. They respected this privilege too much... I also brought in loads of my best 'coffee table' books to supplement the Ward's dismal 'library' of three battered, ancient volumes... I asked friends to bring in magazines, and pots of flowers. A girl I had been teaching physics till admission, was brought by her wealthy Mother with her sister – each of them clutching a huge pot of brightly coloured flowers, with Mum also carrying an absolutely huge bag full of boxes of Smarties! These lasted all of the next week, and I made little models of 'Smartie-henge' out of the empty boxes! I bought or painted lots of posters, and put them up to brighten up the walls. However even this innocent activity had to be picked up on by the WWMM, resentful I was taking such glorious liberties. It turned out that even the Art Therapist was determined to 'frame me'. I got her permission to take away from one such session, to finish, a huge picture I had drawn, of a huge angel with many wings, innocently enough with the start of a legend written on the bottom – 'Gabriel'. I finished it later, and presented it to the person who I had intended it for, with the wording now completed to make it clear that I thought of *her* as the 'Gabriel' of the legend. The way that in my "Doctor's report" at the Meeting to Appeal to the Hospital Managers, this painting was used to prove 'he thinks he is the Angel Gabriel', was dismally twisted, cynical and sinister. Truly

261

they are not trying to 'heal people' in that place. They sinisterly 'observe them', and try to collect even the slimmest form of 'ammunition to use against patients to prove they are far madder than they actually are'. This became totally transparent in the Reports, especially the Nursing Report, a series of totally negative smears with nothing positive said about me. These came out of the woodwork in the Meeting which I was allowed in May, to appeal to the 'Hospital Managers', actually elderly, lipsticked, handbag-wielding female *management consultants.* What is the logic in appealing to people like that, rather than the actual management of the hospital? What an insult to the patients, to wheel in total amateurs with no medical experience. As we now see, you stand NO chance of an objective appeal then!

18. **My Appeal to the 'Hospital Managers' in May (old – retired? – Lady 'Consultants' from some *Management Consultancy!*) is a farce – what with Reports from my Doctor and my 'Primary Nurse' that mention no good points, but are totally negative and full of smears and lies.** When I was sectioned on 29th March 1999, I had immediately as a matter of form appealed to both the Hospital Managers and the Mental Health Tribunal – the two 'standard' forms of appeal open to a patient under Legal Section. There had immediately been yet more sabotage. I handed the forms to a black Nurse I had nicknamed 'super cool', who had never liked me, and he duly mislaid them – in the dustbin? – on the short trip to the out tray in the Office. Luckily I thought suspiciously to check up on him a few days later, and had to fill in the forms all over again – the originals were nowhere to be found... Then, about six weeks later I heard that my Appeal was to be heard in a few days, and was duly handed my Doctor's and my Primary Nurse's Reports. The Tribunal was to be held the next month, but was mysteriously put off not once but several times – more examples of sabotage, I still wonder? In the end I cancelled it, as the two Reports contained so many coloured and wildly exaggerated opinions about certain of my behaviour, portrayed as, to say the least, wildly eccentric, that I felt that

the Tribunal would be a lost cause. For when I confronted Thatcher about what he said, he refused pointblank to alter any of it in between the Appeal, and the abortive Tribunal. Likewise the Nurse concerned at first tried to remain anonymous. Then he slyly wriggled out of changing any of his highly colourful list of bullet-point condemnations of me, or even to add any one of many positive points he could have added if he wished. That left his report totally emphasising negative points, some as I said totally exaggerated! I am not alone. Previous Appeals I have had have also been totally one-sided, and made me out to have a far worse condition than was real or feasible. Other patients I have talked to, many of them, reported similar 'smearing' and total negativity. Thatcher's Report had several things I violently objected to, in particular the claim in the previous point that 'I thought I was the Angel Gabriel'. What a smear, in an official report as well. Things that patients hold as 'spiritual tenets' are supposed to be tolerated by Psychiatrists. I have however read a reliable report in the last few years, that a massive majority, 90% to 95%, totally unrepresentative of the Community as a whole, are Devout Atheists, so ride roughshod over any spiritual inclinations of their patients. So my Report by Thatcher dismissed my Spiritual Experience Eighteen, which by now had totally revealed its meaning in the ongoing abuse I was experiencing, i.e. the Crucifixion experience of Image One, and the flashbacks of Image Two, in particular my writing to Diamond after the prediction of Image Three. He insisted emphatically that this could not possibly be 'a Spiritual Experience that had come true', despite all the evidence, and that anybody in such a place who 'saw something' was 'having hallucinations'! Likewise my precious Gift of the Holy Spirit of Healing, he dismissed as a 'schizophrenic symptom, of me believing I had "special powers"'. I was up against massive Spiritual Warfare, with a Psychiatrist with all the power of the Legalist himself (Satan) to overcome me, on his own ground, in the form of the Mental Health Act. In the face of such distortions of The Truth, especially the Spirit of Truth, my Appeal to have my Section lifted and stay on voluntarily was dismissed as a foregone conclusion. The elderly women Management Consultants, not proper Managers from the Hospital at all, who were all lipstick and handbags, dressed like something out of the Fifties, listened patiently to all the discussion, then naturally rubber-stamped Thatcher's case, that I should stay Sectioned. The main restriction of that was not being allowed off the hospital grounds without getting past fierce legalistic bureaucracy and having a special additional Section filled out by a Consultant. After all they had put me through so far in that stay, I simply shrugged my shoulders, agreed fiercely with my Mother that they were 'some managers' with no medical experience at all, nothing at all to do with medicine especially Mental Health. I wrote it off as 'another brick in the wall', with well over 95% of such 'Appeals' also simply rubber-stamping the Section.

19. **Two years after it was originally requested, a further Meeting in May – that 'they' conveniently excluded me from on the grounds that I was ill, allegedly to 'hear our complaints as a family' about my abuse ('treatment') there in 1994 and '95. It was a total condescending farce and whitewash!** Shortly after the above abortive Appeal, the long-awaited Inquiry Panel into my parents' complaint of two years earlier about Whore's appalling series of misdiagnoses and then even more appalling treatment of me in the same Ward, was at last held in the Hospital Board Room. It had been conveniently announced so as to coincide with my confinement, so equally conveniently I could be excluded from attending on health grounds. I was shown in briefly along with my solicitor, it was explained it might be stressful, then I was equally politely but firmly told to leave. So my account of the so-called 'Independent Panel' is second-hand from my parents and sister, who were there from 10am to 3pm. At the end, and when I met them while having a cup of tea while Whore gave his evidence, taking over an hour and a half rather than the allotted half an hour, typically unfairly, they were fuming! No attention was given or allowance was made to the lengthy submission – including his own opinion that I am a sufferer of bipolar affective disorder not schizophrenia –

264

my father had slaved so painfully to prepare. It was dismissed, even though it all rang true! As well as Whore having so much more time, the two Medical Experts, a Forensic Psychiatrist and a Professor of Psychiatry, completely moved the goalposts from the previously issued agenda! They refused to allow any confrontation or even the two sides being in the same room at the same time, so circumventing any cross-examination of Hawley – or Thatcher, who was wheeled in at the last minute, again for an undue amount of the available time given over to this. That was the main set of problems. To cap it all, we had suspicions of foul play being inevitable when the Chair of the 'Panel' had a familiar name. He had been sacked as Chairman of Welwyn Hatfield Council over a multi-million pound scandal that left the Council flat broke, and owing a development company tens of millions after the Council was sued by it. It seems that these 'Independent' Panels exist to rubber stamp the 'treatment' – abuse in my case, it had been – and failures of diagnosis of criminally incompetent 'Doctors'. The Report was months late and came out in September, after my discharge. It was very condescending, totally whitewashed Whore – and totally contradicted the equally 'independent' report on Harlot's behaviour and his diagnosis the previous year, that had been totally illiterate yet still brandished in triumph by his Managers. Significantly, Harlot had immediately misconstrued my final diagnosis at Fairfield Hospital from the *correct one* of 'bipolar I affective disorder' back to 'schizo-affective disorder' – schizophrenia as well as bipolar affective disorder. Thatcher was vague and elusive about my diagnosis, but when challenged, finally owned up to sharing Harlot's view he had inherited. Rather he claimed to follow Professor Hirsch, even though the latter had no realistic chance to form a diagnosis, in the report on Harlot's mistreatment of me from the previous year, 1998. So that report had called my condition a 'schizo-affective disorder' but there is no sign that in his *in camera* presentation that Thatcher at all backed up any particular view. For the Report said bluntly that clearly, from all my QEII notes they had seen, I 'was definitely a schizophrenic'. So. Total frame-up after total frame-up. One 'Doctor' claims wrongly I have a 'schizo-affective disorder' in 1997 – so a Professor is wheeled out – 'independently' – to rubber-stamp that. Then, a year later, another Psychiatrist has previously equally erroneously, yet with total conviction, said I am 'among the most acute cases of schizophrenia'. This time a Professor *and a* Forensic Psychiatrist rubber-stamp this entirely different and equally totally *wrong* diagnosis – and try to talk us down to accepting my torture in 1995 by Whore and his team as 'par for the course' – 'just shrug it off, won't you, and accept it all' was their dismissive tone. The report was so overwhelming a whitewash that my family took advice from the Community Health Council, then decided to take it to the very top. My Father slaved away as requested to prepare a full set of documents – with a huge 40-page covering letter trying to summarise what by now had got inordinately complex, last Christmas. This was sent to the Ombudsman for Medical Services at New Year 2000. We await their reply, likely to be after some months, but they have already warned that the bureaucratic delays – 'their' fault! – mean we are probably too late. The furthest back they are prepared to go reliably in time, is to 1996. In the meantime a lot of hogwash has been spoken in reports by 'eminent, professional' Professors and Forensic Psychiatrists about my 'bipolar affective disorder' – calling it 'schizophrena' simply to protect the wild similar mistakes of their croney Psychiatrists, while claiming to be objective and 'independent'. Surely the collective term for a group of Doctors, especially these Psychiatrists, must be 'a cronyism' or 'a depot' of Psychiatrists...!

20. **May 25th. Judged fully well back on haldol and after an ECG before briefly having the dose raised, I am told that my woman neighbour in Hertford has told my landlady 'either he goes or I go', so I have been evicted! I was homeless again but with nowhere to go this time, unlike 1995! For three weeks Dobbyn harrassed me, until the Staff reluctantly lost control over me, and I was transferred downstairs to Mymms Ward on June 21st.** Weekly 'Ward Rounds' are held in

places like this, and my Social Worker, who doesn't drive, was there for one on May 25th. I had had just one depot at 33% extra drug for two weeks, following an ECG to confirm my heart would take it, an excessive precaution perhaps as this is by no means the maximum dose you can be given. I had immediately been put back on my usual dose, as I was now judged at this Ward Round on May 25th 1999 to be fully fit. Julia, my Social Worker, had reluctantly come as a bearer of bad news. She gently told me she had not previously been able to tell me, as I was so ill, but I had been evicted from my privately rented cottage in Hertford. However, even though I was so well now, off sulpuride and onto haldol once more, she had persuaded the Council in her calm but firm way that would not take 'no!' for an answer, that there was 'no way I would "hack" being put in a hostel'. It had been agreed I should stay in hospital whilst arrangements were made for me to be re-housed in a bed-sit flat. I immediately specified WARE – as then I would be able to get away from all the 'setting up' at the QEII, rather than care due an ill person, I had just experienced. I was very upset about how unfair all this was, due to my neighbour reading all sorts of sexual innuendoes into my behaviour that simply were not there! As if that was not enough of a blow, shortly after that Dobbyn was getting ever wilder and more abusive in her claims that I owed her "£800…£1,000…£1,400" when the opposite was true. She in fact owed me £400 that I had long ago written off as she would never repay it even if ever out of hospital and then able to. I complained about her abuse to the Senior Sister, who flatly and coldly refused to have me transferred to the other less acute Ward, away from Dobbyn's threats and shouts. It became an unbearable ordeal of her ravings, totally wildly, day in and day out, until one day a Nurse said to me, 'You owe me one, Simon!' He was a friend, rare among the staff, and that day, June 21st, had arranged to have me transferred 'downstairs' to the haven of the much less acute, open, Mymms Ward. So I rapidly collected my belongings, and said a hasty goodbye to people I counted as genuine friends, and kissed goodbye to (nearly) all the attempts to frame me, just for rightly complaining about the

267

place. Especially the incessant tirades from Dobbyn – yet I did not know that episode had one final 'kick' left in it. I was to have an interview about Dobbyn's bizarre claims that I owed her lots of money, in the face of my actual excessive generosity to her, that closed my bank account! The WWMM were to attempt one final frame-up with me out of their control – a Police Interview on Mymms Ward.

Phew. I am very glad this 'Act I of my past eighteen months' is down on paper. It is Friday 10th March 2000, it has taken just five days to wade slowly and more and more easily through these lengthy twenty bullet-points, and I can breathe a sigh of relief! I feel very satisfied to have got my version of all that gory 'stuff' there last year, down on paper. I need a fresh start badly as the Year 2000 starts! Now I can write about the increasingly better times I had after this 4½ months of sheer Hell. First 'on Mymms' – and then at last rehoused after a three month agonising wait, in the pleasant little town of Ware, from September 10th 1999.

ACT II of my last eighteen months. Three months in the 'haven' of a Ward just a floor below Welwyn Ward, but like another planet... Or so it seemed!

We have just got through all of twenty mostly quite long points, of experiences that were a sheer ordeal to both remember – and write about!   My plans are to get the comparatively few, nearly all good, points about my stay on Mymms Ward, down in just a few pages. Act II of my saga of my life between Winter 1998 to Spring 2000 was relatively very painless, as we shall see!

1. **Indeed, 'another planet'. I soon acclimatised to the relaxed, even sleepy with boredom, atmosphere 'downstairs' on Mymms Ward. The Nursing regime is totally different here. The Nurses actually do some – a lot of very good – Nursing and 'therapy' with the patients. It is an Open Ward.** The immediate impression I was bound to receive on arrival here on 21st June, in contrast to the then dismal 'institution green' surroundings of the Ward I had just left, was of "brightness"! Mymms Ward had been refurbished since I was last there for a brief two weeks in 1994, and the walls were mostly brightly painted in bright yellow, finished off with new pine furniture.   The patients were allowed off the Ward frequently, and it was not locked. We were even entrusted with a glass aquarium, as the likelihood of it being smashed by an ill patient was judged to be very low!   Unheard of 'upstairs'!   The atmosphere was totally different, and immediately struck me as warm and caring – like a proper hospital, not the concentration camp and 'Reform Centre' upstairs... I was soon introduced to the extremely pleasant, relaxed Nursing staff, who even added to the scenery. Some of the female Nurses were extremely attractive, including my new Primary Nurse; who turned out to be a woman of extremely strong Faith that I could relate to immediately, as well as being a very competent Nurse indeed!   However, my ordeals and repeated attempted 'setting up', by the Staff on Welwyn Ward, had suppressed my flashbacks. Now I slept in every day, overwhelmed by the flashbacks as I awoke, often in

tears as a result. These fits of tears over past agonies were to continue well into my time out of hospital. My consequently getting up late often being branded by less sensitive staff as pure 'laziness', showed a dim understanding of the scale of my past problems – and abuse. I still feel this constant fatigue is partly due to rather too high a level of drug as introduced by Harlot in 1997. My new CPN has listened, but said in a counselling session today, wearing her 'other hat' as a fully qualified psychotherapist, that there are other, worse, hurdles to overcome before my new Doctor could think about lowering the dose at all. I have finished off the last 'Act' and aim to do the whole of this one in the same day – clearly the counselling is giving me a burst of self-confidence – and so energy... Down to my caring, clever CPN!

2. **I get bored out of my *skull* pretty quickly.** Although it was a heavenly Ward compared to the last one, it was also extremely quiet and almost *too* quiet at that. Positively a 'sleepy hollow' I christened it after my ordeal 'upstairs'... Sometimes an hour seemed to last a whole very boring day, as the clocks ticked slowly by. The patients were generally far more well than those on the Acute Ward, so this was almost certainly a major factor in the staff having a far easier time, not locking themselves away in some central domineering glass-protected office, but actually coming out onto the Ward and talking to the patients, and regularly carrying out 'Ward activities' like word games, with us. I joined in some of these, but had my own personal worries to deal with, alone... I got nearly as much time as we could both take with various very pleasant nurses, particularly my very professional yet genuinely caring Primary Nurse. I got quite fond of her over the three months.

3. **Endless waiting for rehousing.** I was constantly reminded that I was entirely in the hands of East Herts District Council, as I waited seemingly for eternity, to be told I had been found a place. There soon emerged a place in Hertford, but I turned this down, insisting on moving Trust yet again away from the dreaded QEII – and Welwyn Ward.

So two areas in Ware, where I could get 'attached to' Harlow once more, were soon indicated, in July, as having flats being renovated. Soon these were confirmed by my Social Worker Julia as very likely being ready in September. On leave my parents took me to the most likely venue – then a building site, but the builders let us look around. Small flats, bedsits, but luxurious they seemed, with a lovely view of an ancient building and a small park – very close to Julia's office, and above all very central – with easy shopping on foot! Indeed, you can imagine my delight when after what had seemed an endless wait, but had actually been under three months of feeling totally 'in limbo', on September 10th the suspense was over! I was indeed handed the keys to my new flat, immediately started moving in, and was installed completely just three weeks later, after my intervening discharge!

4. **The residents are much more friendly than upstairs!** Yes, I made the acquaintance of quite a few very pleasant 'characters' while there, amongst both patients and staff! Some of the women 'talked a bit common' and could be very vulgar, but had "been through hell' like myself, so an easy-going 'share and share alike' respect and bonhomie soon developed. The men too were generally polite, and a lot of them were called 'Paul' – although one of these Pauls got very disgruntled that despite any number of types of treatment, his depression stubbornly refused to lift. I understand he later sued the hospital after a whole year of illness!

5. **I am warned to expect an 'informal' interview with a policeman – the WWMM has not let up and is making one last attempt to 'get me'!** The final sorry instalment of the saga of 'pitiful Dobbyn and my money, not hers' from 'upstairs' was daunting when I was told one Friday that the police wanted me to undergo an 'informal' interview about the matter that Sunday. My lovely Senior Sister, an Indian lady, volunteered to give up her free time, bless her, to be there with me. When they later called to postpone she said she quite fiercely demanded that they stick to the original time – to spare me any further unnecessary ordeal, for I had

told her the whole story. The interview, when it finally came, was mercifully brief – and painless. The PC introduced himself, saying he had got 'almost nothing out of Dobbyn upstairs'. We spent the next five minutes going over the copies of letters they had got hold of, and I agreed straightaway that I remembered them all. Then he simply said, "Well, I think we can simply draw a solid line under this. You've got nothing to worry about. Thank you for being completely honest!" That was the end of the matter, and the last lingering attempt at a set-up by the WWMM...

6. **A near scandal erupts as I resume more 'Healing by laying on of hands'.** There was to prove a lot of suspicion and resentment among certain staff there about me openly discussing 'laying on of hands' Christian Spiritual Healing with my Christian Primary Nurse and two other Christian Nurses, on both of whom I demonstrated it – for some reason ineffectively. However, with the perhaps more 'open' patient who had chronic sinus problems, just ten seconds of holding my hand over her nose, and moving it around till I 'found the hot spot' and felt my palm simply glow, the response was immediate. She said, 'they are clear! I believed you would do it all along!' and immediately was able to stop the medicine she had taken for this problem for weeks!

7. **Cash! Or rather, the lack of and difficulties getting enough.** The whole time I was 'in', on both Wards, I really had to halter my smoking habit a lot, to stay within my budget. Yet, as I had worked all my life till the last few years, and 'kept my stamps up', I was entitled to nearly £50 a week benefit. Those who were not so fortunate made do with a pitiful £13 or so a week of income support, like Peppy and Sonia upstairs. I found this nearly impossible, and indeed after my benefit was reinstated after three whole months non-payment due to an clerical error at the Benefit office, even with the lump sum I got was far from able to fully repay my parents the large sum they had lent me. I

still would love to repay the £2,000 to £3,000 I cost them that year...!

8. **Increasing amounts of 'leave' from the Ward – and hospital. I resume the writings I have been working on for years in those times.** As my time on that new Ward wore on, I was allowed off the Ward as often as I wanted – into the grounds only – and with permission. I frequently also went to my parents' home but only rarely and cautiously to my own former house, where my furniture was. Where, with some difficulty, Julia kept the rent benefit up – but reduced now, due to nasty aspects of the benefit system, even though I was on a vastly reduced income. The rules are the rules, however unfair, I suppose... Into August, I started being allowed to stay at my parents' home overnight for several days at a time, and really relished this freedom back 'into reality', even though it was not at my own home – which was forbidden because of my impending eviction. My final week on Section 3, up to discharge on 22nd September, was spent in that way – but moving house into my new flat! An exciting time, and I was soon overwhelmed at how smart and new it was when I opened the door and was shown around. They had even provided carpets along with the 'all mod cons' – as a 'free introductory gift'! It felt like a brand-new start in a fresh town – safe at last from the QEII and Welwyn Ward...

So ends my account of my fourth and hopefully *last* ever such massive ordeal in the QEII...

CHAPTER TWENTY-FIVE

Propelled out of the QEII at long last – into starting a new life yet again in the Autumn of 1999. The Eve of the 20th Century... My 'new life' only really starts in the New Year of 2000...

ACT III of my tale of the last eighteen months up to April 2000. Very busy starting a new life – Ware? – but initially very bored and lonely as well. I get lots of help from the social services nearby. ACT IV – the Dawn of a New Millennium – the cold Winter of 1999-2000 at length fades and Spring arrives. After all the excitement of the New Year celebrations, my Fresh Start at last gathers momentum. Things were happening for me after all the trauma of 1999!

ACT III of my last eighteen months since finishing Chapter 22 in 1998. A fresh life in a bedsit flat in Ware – as the 20th Century breathes its last in Autumn 1999.

1. **Moving in is relatively straightforward! The pitfalls of having to rely on benefit.** The flat had just been refurbished, having been derelict for some years, as I understand. It turned out, when I looked it over, signed the lease and took over the keys on 10th September 1999, to be nearly complete already. There was a shower as well as a bath, I noted with relief. I much prefer taking the former to baths! There was a lovely fitted kitchen. We realised I would need to buy a cooker and refrigerator – but could afford neither. In the end my parents, generous as ever that year in particular, said they could not let me buy second-hand, so they would look around for the best price – and buy me these appliances brand new! I already had a microwave oven so lived out of that until we had found these appliances at a shop in Hatfield, which were delivered and installed by

the end of September. My parents also supplied some ancient curtains, but soon replaced these with new ones from a shop in the 'Galleria' near them – very pleasant and at a bargain price! The flat came fully carpeted and decorated, and I decided to sleep on my sofa bed from my old house – as it was a bedsit, space was at a premium. Moving, which cost £175, was only funded by a £50 allowance I got via Julia as a surprise total of about £400 from social services – so I had to divert a lot of the balance of that £400, just into the high cost of moving. My bed and wardrobe went to my brother, but to our surprise I got all the rest of a house full of furniture at Hertford, which I was in fact relieved to leave, into the bedsit fairly easily. My father had very over-ambitiously, in fact, offered to completely kit out the flat with all new furniture, and waxed lyrical about this scheme, going through Ikea catalogues for hours, till I thanked him but said no, I would be happy with my existing furniture. For the first four weeks money was a nightmare. I had I thought done all I needed to, while in hospital, to warrant receiving quite a lot of money from being on leave, but typically the benefit office was very reticent about restarting my benefits back to their normal much higher rate of pay out of hospital. In the end I made a series of complaints at the highest level, to Benefits Headquarters, and most of these teething problems were resolved within a couple of weeks. As I write in March 2000 there is still just under £100 which I should hear about very soon, I have been told, and the possible matter of compensation for the considerable inconvenience, amounting to anguish, I went through for my first month out of hospital. By December I was getting threatening letters about High Court Action they planned to take, from my old bank. However, I was now at last able to start paying them back some of the outstanding £560 or so, on a regular basis each month. My financial affairs had settled down by around Christmas...

2. **Having been 'bumped unwillingly back' from Harlow to Welwyn Garden City NHS Trust, I return once more to Harlow, having easily signed on with a new GP. I eventually see a new Sri Lankan Psychiatrist, and all of**

three Community Psychiatric Nurses in three months, as well as being assigned a new 'Outreach Worker', that December. All change! Meanwhile last year's crop of new grey hair, to my delight, actually nearly all falls out. It had fortunately been only a *temporary* response to my 'annus horribilis' of 1999... One of Thatcher's parting remarks at the QEII, at a 'CPA Meeting', might sound as though it was designed to alarm me. Namely that he had heard that all the GP practices in Ware were fully booked, so I might have to stay with my GP in Hertford. Under Thatcher at the QEII, not some new Doctor at Harlow, which was my whole main intention in going to Ware. However, when I walked into the nearest Doctor's practice to my flat, within days of moving in, they immediately said they were not full – and they were associated with Harlow not the QEII, so I immediately signed up for a check-up with their Nurse. After that, it took till mid-December to meet my new Psychiatrist, a pleasant Sri Lankan. In the meantime, I saw no less than two different CPN's – and then the second one said he was going into hospital for some weeks himself! So this year of 2000 I started out with a third and seemingly final, female Australian CPN – who turns out to be a fully qualified psychotherapist too! It has been her who has finally reacted to my complaints that I seemed to have developed an allergic reaction to haldol depots, which had been increasingly leaving hot, very painful 'bumps' or abscesses at the fortnightly injection site, which were then a constant reminder of that. She also does excellent therapy and counseling, I can tell you! More of that in Act IV below... Having said goodbye to Thatcher and my long-standing CPN, Cheryl, in December I also said goodbye to Bill, my outreach worker, and met my new one, Jo. I was very glad that Julia has remained my social worker, as she is *caring – very rare in social workers!* Meanwhile, as my trauma of the year subsided, something remarkable happened. Most of the large shock of grey hair that had appeared on the top of my head earlier that year, in response to my trauma at the QEII, simply fell out again! I was relieved – at nearly 43, I was back to looking age 35 again, as before! Fighting acute trauma seems to have kept me young!

3. **My mental health steadily improves, now discharged, and the flashbacks rapidly recede. My main health problem is my teeth! Commuting by bus 15 miles regularly each way to Hatfield, as I cannot change to a dentist in Ware mid-treatment, for several crowns and replacement fillings.** The effect of being in a totally new home in a strange, unfamiliar town on my mental health, was almost immediate. Once I had settled in, my only mental health problem since the previous May – flashbacks about my mistreatment over the previous eight years, and all that had caused – rapidly nearly entirely disappeared. It was only on one occasion, February this year of 2000, that I got terrible nightmares and sought medical help in Hertford with the emergency weekend service. After that weekend, as we shall see in Act IV, the nursing and social services team here jumped to my assistance! Meanwhile my dentist in Hatfield had fitted a crown a couple of years earlier, and warned that the teeth and fillings on my left side needed watching, and probably would need some work doing in the next few years. Indeed over the next three months into January 2000, I was to make a number of trips to see him for first one crown, then on breaking another tooth, a second. This was by bus as I now was without a car. Fortunately the 724 bus leaves from a bus stop near here in Ware, and goes directly, an hour later, to within ten minutes walk of my parents – and fifteen minutes of the dentist. In fact, apart from that time of seeing that dentist, until the work was done and I moved to one in Ware, that bus was also my only means – and a relatively rapid one – to go to see my parents in Hatfield. They usually give me a lift back...

4. **I have been working on my book 'Spiritual Energy' while on leave from hospital, on my computer, at my parents' house. On October 8th I sent off the first of several 'mail-shots' to 100 publishers in all in the end, having mail-shot many agents earlier that year – with no success then and as yet no success now!** I had been finishing off the decisive last two pages of my book 'Spiritual Energy' while still in hospital. Now I decided I would try

once again to face the inevitable disappointments, and try to get it published. I looked through my 1996 Writer's Handbook, well out of date, for suitable ones – and found all of about 40 UK, 6 USA and 4 Irish. I invested in a lot of second class stamps on 8th October and sent them all a two-sided letter with a synopsis on the back. A month later I had saved up £12 and bought the latest year 2000 version of that book, and found that their number – of appropriate publishers – had been joined by the same number again since 1996. In December three publishers asked, or I persuaded them, to see the manuscript, but all three were to eventually turn it down, for very different reasons. One of them, on December 3rd 1999, really enthused about the presentation – then gave the decision about publication to another member of staff. Less enthusiastic, he turned it down in January 2000. The other two turned it down in December having received it for an opinion earlier that month. None of the Irish publishers replied, and only two of the US ones. In all one third of mail-shot letters have failed to get any reply... More about this in Act IV...

5. **Job-seeking – while feeling increasingly lethargic – and sleeping for 12-14 hours a day – proves difficult!** I had been introduced at last to a member of 'Employment Direct', a recruitment agency run by Hertfordshire County Council specifically to help people return to work after illness or disability, at my CPA Meeting on discharge on 22nd September. They had not come forward to offer help when I had actually needed them throughout 1998, and now after all that trauma, my name had come to the top of their waiting-list, 'a little too late'. Robyn was actually a well-dressed, attractive-looking woman! We met each week over the next few weeks to discuss what I could do for a new career now, particularly if that should involve computers in any way. She probed me about my other interests, and after discovering I was currently interested in publishing, arranged that we spend an afternoon 'behind the scenes' at a bookshop in Hertford. In the current year of 2000 I have also twice been to the local College with Robyn in tow, to help teachers teach people with learning difficulties. However, ever since coming

out of hospital, my problem with needing too much sleep has got even worse than when there. So I have had to 'put the brakes' on job-searching, saying that while I am only awake for 10-12 hours a day, any work apart from the bare minimum is out of the question. I can only imagine that this lethargy is due to the drugs I have to take, for I am doing no physical work and taking little strenuous exercise. She and I are both frustrated that we will have to wait quite a while, much longer than her normal three months to get someone a job, before the medical staff agree that my depot is the problem, and restore it to 1997 levels; when Harlot insisted it be put up. The problem has got worse and worse ever since...

6. **My creative writing course and its benefits. My Stress and Anxiety Management Course and its benefits, as well.** Term had started at Ware's Hertford Regional College – and my then Outreach Worker, Bill, showed me their brochure. I tried to join several courses a few weeks later – all at concessionary rates. However the only one with places left, that caught my eye, was a 'Creative Writing group'. Once my finances had stabilised enough, mid-October, I signed up and went along to my first session, having missed about three. My first real taste of Social Life in Ware! I told the group of six or seven, whose membership eventually stabilised this year, 2000, that I had written some poems and even a couple of books that I was trying to have published. There were literally gasps of admiration from some of the women, one of whom was struggling to write her first novel! We soon settled down to writing exercises, in poetry and short stories, and were set 'homework' – a piece to write on a given theme by the next lesson. The latter is often quite stretching, as often you would not have thought prompted to write on such a theme. Some of the writing – often my own! – is often quite wacky, and occasionally rude... The exercise at the annual Christmas party, of writing a limerick, having been given just the first line, produced some hysterics amid the wine and food! Also in the same period, I got up by 9am with difficulty on a Tuesday, and managed most sessions of a 'Stress and Anxiety Management' Course

nearby at the local Psychiatric Social Services Centre. This focussed on dealing with stress by techniques called 'Cognitive Recognition'. Recognising, then analysing, the sources and symptoms, and cycles taken by, stress and anxiety. By using your analytical, conscious mind rather than your feelings, or 'escapes' (like alcohol) to deal with stress and anxiety. By the end of it I had sufficiently actually applied these techniques to break out of my 'cycle of stress and anxiety – about the past'. My flashbacks, very frequent at the start of the course, had mostly gone, along with nearly all physical symptoms of anxiety, by the end at Christmas. Both courses had a very beneficial effect on my mental well-being!

7. **Jenny reports being 'bored' at school. She tells us, first one then the other of our two faithful Labrador dogs have died. I have to console her while feeling fragile myself. I see her teacher, who says the reason she feels bored, is that actually, she is doing very well... Fireworks for Hallowe'en *and* November 5th!** I had hardly seen Jenny for eight whole months while hospitalised, so it was a thrill to resume regular Contact, with my parents picking up first her then me every Sunday, then taking us to their house at Hatfield. She reported she felt 'bored' at school. For the first few weeks of her previous two years at school she had been found to be depressed and distant – which had been a worry. She also gave us the news that my old black Labrador dog friend Gemma had died of a stroke. At which I had to console her, once we got out of the car in Hatfield, with the advice that 'but if every person and animal lived on the planet for ever, it would become too full' which is actually in the Bible, in the book of 2 Esdras! She seemed to accept that better than I did, reflecting bitterly that I had seen neither Gemma nor her daughter Josie in five whole years. So when a few weeks later she said that Josie, was also dead, we shared our upset and grief in respectful mutual silence all day. Later in the year I went to a parents' evening at Jenny's Primary School, with my teacher sister Libby. As we went in my ex- came out and went out rather sheepishly! It was soon revealed

that the reason that Jenny was getting so 'bored' with school work – was that this year she was doing exceptionally well! Her male teacher enthused for over half an hour over her progress, and Libby and I went back home very relieved. Jenny was going great guns! So to the traditional annual fireworks – which for our family started on the Saturday, the day before Hallowe'en. Jem, Jane and their kids joined Jenny, Libby, my folks and I in Hatfield Park for 'Witches, Pumpkins and Fireworks' – a charity 'do' which as its name suggested, combined Hallowe'en with a superb fireworks display, synchronised with music. The music varied between the horrific – Hallowe'en – to the splendiferous – Guy Fawkes night! The following Saturday 6th November we all congregated in Sussex at Jem and Jane's house for the repeat performance. I won't describe my awkward feelings, at seeing Jenny looking all forlorn quite often, at this point. A poem I wrote for my Creative Writing Class, the penultimate poem in the collection included as the Appendix to this book, sums it all up. Suffice it to say that Jenny and I have got over this period this New Year following a splendid time at Christmas, and things have now greatly 'returned to normal' especially after her birthday.

8. **All the above takes a certain amount of my time on this 'business' – but I got very bored and often lonely that Autumn. My few friends then are often full of their own problems – worse than mine, many of them...** Ending up in a strange, unfamiliar town with initially no social life, after the ordeal of Acts I and II in the last chapter, was of course very daunting. However, I had a few contacts left, and after a few weeks passed someone on the street I actually remembered from Harlow Hospital in 1997. Theresa and I spent the odd evening entertaining each other to food at each other's places – until in early December I heard no more. Eventually I phoned her on her mobile, and as expected she had had a huge problem. Her father had died, and she was in nearby Stevenage consoling her mother... I have only spoken to her once up to March 2000... Peppy and Sonia were my only contacts at the QEII, although I rang up another young girl ex-patient, Lynne,

several times. Peppy still insists there is nothing wrong with her, meanwhile her treatment has changed totally, and both those two aspects guarantee her a long time there. I phoned her occasionally, and sometimes visited.   Both were a struggle and a bit of a haphazard, wacky ordeal. Sonia proved elusive out of hospital and at the New Year was back in again, having unwisely told her CPN she was fully well so had stopped her tablets... Sonia ended up at a Secure Unit near Royston by now. They never telephoned me, so they were both lost causes as friends.   So that left as old contacts, friends I had made at my club for Divorced, Widowed and Separated people in Welwyn Garden City. I went along a couple of times, and renewed acquaintances with my regular visitor at the QEII, Mark, as well as some of the other regulars, and finally Pat.   The latter soon disappeared to have an operation for cancer, to add to her triple heart bypass... As I said at the start, some people had even worse problems than me, by a mile... So my social life in the Autumn of 1999 was to say the least patchy. I found the 'drop-ins' offered by Social Services were simply not stretching or interesting enough...

9. **Into the Dark of Winter, all to be lit up by Christmas, then... the Millennium! I see Jenny a record FOUR times over the Christmas period. Has my ex-'s, the Dragon's, partner, himself divorced with a daughter, had words with her?** My family believe that now a man lives in MY house with my ex-, he has actually helped our cause over Contact by telling her of his own daughter, problems with his Contact with her; and so to be less dismissive and cruel to me. Whatever the reason, we were to be astonishingly given no less than FOUR sessions of Contact with Jenny over Christmas. Our family spent a quiet Christmas Day opening our presents at Hatfield. Then Jenny arrived on the Boxing day, Sunday 26th December, and we all went down to Sussex for a memorable and highly excitable day, with the girls insisting I chased them all the time! Then on the Wednesday 29th we had Jenny *again* at Hatfield all day, drawing, again playing 'chase' games, or playing on my Father's new computer, complete with the scanner I had

282

bought her for Christmas. We had a cold but delightful walk by the lake at WGC. Then on Friday afternoon, Millennium Eve, Jenny and I were both to stay up and celebrate a fantastic New Year's Eve, with fireworks both on TV and at midnight all round the house.   First the immediate family went to St. Albans, nearby, for yet more fireworks over the lake. Then we went to two 'Millennium events' that were by contrast poorly organised and a dismal anti-climax.   The 'beacon lightings' in WGC then Hatfield had no ceremonies attached, just a torch thrust into a gas bunsen burner, not wood even, on top of a small pillar with a beacon – only to be kept lit for a few hours. Typical of the local Council for the two towns to show such little imagination… Jenny went home at Midday on New Year's Day, and must have caught influenza, for she sat miserably through the Pantomime on the Monday 3rd January in Hertford – all wrapped up, hot then cold, and sweaty – even though the rest of us enjoyed the show. So she went home and I rang up a couple of days later to be told by my ex-, "Yes, it is 'flu!" She soon got over it and back to school. Meanwhile I felt charged up by that Christmas and New Year period, given a burst of energy to 'get out and achieve things' in the New Year of 2000 – a true Millennium Spirit! So as we continue into Act Four, and the first two months of 2000, we hear a more positive and optimistic note!

ACT IV. The New Millennium arrives – after a lot of 'fizz and wow' which certainly gives me a boost, in the long cold Winter nights of 1999-2000!

A time to review my portion of the 20th Century – as in this book up to now…

1. **The Millennium Celebrations, world-wide and local, have a real effect on me!** Especially seeing Jenny for a totally unprecedented four times over Christmas and the New Year! The effects of the Millennium Bug, as I had cautiously ended up thinking would be the case at the end of 1999, after serious worries about it earlier, were minimal, world-wide, so I breathed a sigh of relief…   I was to put renewed effort into getting out of the trap of having no social life, and went to the local library to look at the 'interest groups in Ware' section on their computer. On 6th January I was taken by Jo to meet the head of the local Volunteers' Bureau in Ware. Both trips produced a surprisingly very high number of options, and had an immediate effect! As a result of visiting the local library and the Volunteers' Bureau, I discovered that Ware boasted a lot of social and voluntary activities, much more than I had imagined for some months after arriving here.   There was a Lady doing meditation classes – so I rang her and caught the bus to her house outside Ware, the following day, to see her. I explained my previous medical history, she listened kindly, and said I was too 'wired up' at present for meditation – but suggested a whole range of 'alternative' healing techniques.   Such as 'looking at Nature', looking at candles, aroma-therapy, and walking.   I have tried some of these since and had some benefit.   She looked at my 'Spiritual Energy' book and my poems, and said she immediately followed, and indeed identified with, their 'spiritual nature'.   Nearly all the concepts were familiar to her, she said, so I was 'preaching to the converted'.   We kept in touch by telephone, and I have been to see her to chat to, once more. She got me in touch with Cygnus Book Club, which specialises in books with

284

a 'Spiritual' angle.   That will prove significant later on, in point (3) in this Act IV…   As an immediate outcome of going to the Volunteers' Bureau, I was invited to go to a Committee Meeting of Hertfordshire Action on Disability, as they had a vacancy on the Committee for an Outings Organiser.   This Committee turned out to be made up of retired elderly ladies – and as the Treasurer was leaving, I nearly got 'roped in' to do both jobs!   However, common sense prevailed, and Betty the chairman asked me to her house the next week.   Then it was readily agreed I should help out first at some of the monthly social evenings for disabled people, at the Age Concern hall near my flat – before there was any suggestion of my joining the Committee.   I have since been to two enjoyable sessions, easy physical work like putting out tables and a dinner service for 50 people, and clearing up afterwards, in February and March this year of 2000.   As well as the highly enjoyable Creative Writing Group, which has nearly finished the Spring term at the College and again been great fun and the highlight of the week, in this rapid burst of 'reaching out for social life' I was to join various other groups in the area. I have twice in February made the mile and a half journey to dancing lessons at Ware's sports centre, on the outskirts of town.   Then the centre asked me to pay a membership fee, which has temporarily been beyond my means.   I hope to join next week, and save up my money in the meantime.   It is extremely enjoyable and good exercise, a bit like my jazz dancing two years ago but less demanding and not aerobic. Just modern ballroom dancing – like salsa and rumba, to modern pop songs.   I was going to join a T'ai chi class in neighbouring Broxbourne, but was misdirected to the wrong site the first night, then found the bus fares prohibitive – even though I have a bus pass on the grounds that I have been banned from driving on health grounds.   So I have given it up – then heard last week a class is starting up in nearby Hertford on a Friday – which I will try to attend.   Jo took me to a new 'drop in' at a Church Hall, which is much more enjoyable than other more dreary ones in the town. The organisers are really highly enthusiastic – and one, an Irish guy who is a born-again Christian, has even bought

285

from me a copy of my 'Spiritual Energy'! It turns out that he shares with me a fluent Gift of Tongues *and* their interpretation – and used to do some healing, until like me prevented by Spiritual Warfare. It just goes to show, you meet some very interesting people in Mental Health! I am waiting to hear back about doing some voluntary work for a shop that trains people with learning difficulties, in the town. So that will be two areas of voluntary work, along with the HAD I mentioned above. On a monthly basis, I usually also attend a beer and wine circle, which is mostly for amateur beer and wine makers, although quite a few like me just go along out of interest and for the social aspects. I have also attended one session of the poetry society at the Arts Centre. All in all, as I have, as ever, endured and counted away the long dark nights of January and February this year, I have had a lot more 'social' things going on to attend. My social life is starting to pick up speed, and is vastly improved from my first few dismally lonely and bored months here in the strange new town of Ware.

2. **My health 'problems' – more with the abysmal treatment then my actual condition – and 21½ years of great damage from being labelled a 'schizo' – seem to come to an abrupt end! I am now diagnosed as 'having a mood disorder'!** On 11th January my history of health problems, although I was not to know it at that stage, took a dramatic turn – for the better. I met Vivian, my fourth CPN or Community Psychiatric Nurse in four months – but she now seems to be a permanent feature in my health team. I really hope that her liking for working here means she eventually joins this team on a permanent basis, from being a stand-in or locum Nurse. I had seen her twice, each time complaining about severe discomfort and swelling after each depot she gave, having complained of such pain increasingly since hospital last year. Then on Saturday 5th February came my only small 'crisis' since discharge last year. I had terrible nightmares, and spent the Saturday in a state of being very upset over these renewed 'flashbacks' – so anxious that that evening I rang my GP and saw the Doctor on duty in Hertford, after my parents gave me a lift.

286

The small amount of diazepam or Valium he gave me helped a bit until my pre-arranged appointment with my new Dr Ballitch, nearby at the Social Service Centre, on the following Monday. I had been unable to contact anybody there over the awful weekend – Julia or Vivian – but as soon as they heard I had had a 'wobbly' they both came into the meeting with my Doctor. I think, having got to know me a lot better than him, that they wanted to calm me down so he did not do anything drastic – involving hospital, for instance! In the end this 'wobbly' produced dramatic benefits. I had needed counselling like a dose of salts for four years – and now Vivian suggested to Ballitch that she give me an initial set of eight 'therapy' sessions. For as well as being a highly objective Australian Visitor to this country she is unusually highly qualified for a CPN. So far she has given me an initial five sessions of psychotherapy in her capacity as a fully trained psychotherapist, starting the Tuesday after all this blew up – the following day. Initially there were some tears from me, followed by a lot of 'positive', uplifting talk from her, as she carefully identified my main areas of mental and emotional scarring over the past 21½ years of psychiatric 'treatment' – especially at the QEII under Whore – and before, at school. The third session was short and sweet and ended very positively. Vivian said 'Things are going to get a lot better for you now – remember you are only young! You are really in the Spring of your life!" It was indeed a very Spring-like week a couple of weeks later, starting on Monday 25th February 2000, when three exciting and highly significant events happened, on the Monday and continuing, on the Tuesday – the joint birthday of Libby and Jenny – and the Friday, with more counselling. On the Monday Vivian had arranged that I saw Ballitch again to talk about medication, and the reaction to haldol that I had developed. It soon emerged that they had been through my past treatment, and spotted that I suited clopixol as an alternative to haldol depots. So I had a trial half-dose, as my depot was due that due anyway. It had no such allergic reaction, and unlike the haldol depot that had proved allergic, there was no pain all week. So on Friday after the counselling session with Vivian, she gave me a full dose.

Then at the end of that session Vivian made some analytical remarks, as a psychotherapist, having taken the trouble to talk to me far more and far more in depth than any Doctor ever has. "You suffer from bipolar (I) affective disorder!" she suddenly said. "Your condition is purely emotional not 'mental'!" Too shocked to react much to my own suspicions of half a lifetime being confirmed, I just said, "But I have always known that. Why do they always label me 'schizo' or 'schizo-affective'?" "Just forget that label of 'schizo' will you?" she said and we left it there. After I left this highly effective meeting, I got more and more excited. At last! The psychiatric profession was finally dropping the 'wrong label' that had caused me so much anguish and loss – especially my divorce and losing over £85,000, as I had calculated it! They had been so damned casual in applying a label that was so harmful and abusive and so damnably **wrong!** Helen's family and her had both found it anathema – so I had to go – even though I am no 'schizo' – I had always felt I suffered from bipolar affective disorder as Vivian now said! So the most significant change in my entire medical history happened, with my diagnosis now at long, long, last being accurate!

3. **The Third Outcome or Meaning of Spiritual Experience Five of Chapter Seven emerges astonishingly – and is the first POSITIVE OUTCOME of all of Six such Positive Meanings to emerge after the initial two negative... O**n Jenny's birthday of 22nd February 2000, her ninth, on that 22/2/00, a third, and definitely *extremely positive* Outcome or Meaning of Spiritual Experience Five was 'fulfilled'. This most complex and laden with meanings, Spiritual Experience Five, of as long ago as 30th January 1983, in its first Image of *eight* lights in a pattern – proved to have a total of all of eight predictive Outcomes or Meanings. The first two *negative Outcomes* 'came out' as we have seen, in 1996, predicting the baleful effects of Diamond and 'matey from Calais'. However Jenny's birthday came in the middle of my best ever week for good medical news, and events surrounding it provided a completely *POSITIVE third fulfilment of Spiritual Experience Five.* For 22/2/00 fit that

first Image as well, perfectly, in having 'four pairs' in the number.   That day, we were sitting down to lunch in Haddenham, near Thame, prior to the very enjoyable afternoon that we were to spend at "St. Tiggywinkle's" hospital for wild animals in the village.   Jenny produced a birthday present from my ex-, having shown us the rather over-elaborate present of a mobile phone her Mother had also given her. The other present completely astonished me – a pair of spectacles, absolutely identical to the ones I had seen in the second Image of Spiritual Experience Five (see the picture in chapter seven!) in 1983 long before marriage or even Jenny were considered!   They even had the exact same, and strikingly impractical and purely cosmetic, electric blue colour of lenses and the same black frame – identical! 'Vanity glasses not sunglasses!' She produced them in the 'Crown' pub in Haddenham, full of *drinks* glasses, just as symbolised in Spiritual Experience Five in its last Image of three! So God gave me a clear sign that the whole of that week was highly significant, by in a way that I had no control over whatsoever, fulfilling one of my Spiritual Experiences! Or at least, the third and first *positive* Outcome or Meaning of eight of extremely powerful and complex Spiritual Experience Five! The following Monday I was delighted by the events of that week, especially being at last 'cleared' by Vivian – but as yet not my Doctor – of being a 'schizo' or falsely diagnosed one for 21½ whole years, half my life. So delighted that I wrote a very rude, fierce letter on two pages to my ex- about it. Pointing out that it was false, so her eviction, divorce then taking everything I owned was very evil. She ignored me – but left a half-hour reply on my parents' answer-phone while they were on holiday in Venice, threatening to break off all Contact with Jenny! So, my delight at finally being diagnosed completely accurately at last – by a Nurse and a Social Worker, for Julia has long held the same view, not a Doctor – 'fell on stony ground' with my 'ex-' – who dare not admit its significance to the stormy history of our family!

3. **My attempts to find part-time work, leading to a possible full-time return to work, seem to coincide**

with my parallel usually extremely frustrating efforts to get writing published. Back in December I had a successful lunch cum four-hour job interview, with the sales and managing directors of Authors Online, an Internet publishing company – conveniently based in Hertford, the next town. However, as I write on Wednesday afternoon 15th March 2000, they are still in a 'make or break' situation. They still have not got the seed capital in place that they need to expand and get proper offices rather than working above a brewery! So I am still waiting to hear. Last week I helped with a class teaching IT to young adults with learning difficulties, and as a result of that time at Ware College, may get some maths tutoring to do as *paid* not just voluntary work instead. Meanwhile, I was still relentlessly, and increasingly less intensively due to the sheer frustration of it, intent to get my poetry and 'Spiritual Energy' published – if at all possible. Authors Online have copies, prepared with software they lent me a copy of, which should be 'up' and selling copies, hopefully, on their web-site soon.

4. **The small hours of 16th March 2000. A month to celebrate – an End of an Awful Era, in many ways is now becoming obvious.** As the Sixth Anniversary of my 'Baptism of Fire (of the Holy Spirit)' enters its second – small – hour, I prepare to rapidly add to the text of this book with a small chapter of 'Inevitable Aftermaths and Outcomes'. I may just leave that, or answer the list of questions to appear there as yet unresolved, as they are resolved in the next few months. My birthday is now just two weeks away, when I will be 43 – and 21½ years of torment, HALF of that, appear to be ending! In the meantime my life reached a turning point in many ways this new Millennium year, culminating last month, February: -

a) Near complete acceptance by my medical team – except the Doctor himself as of yet – that I suffer from 'bipolar I affective disorder' – a pure mood disorder. I am no longer, after 22½ whole years, regarded by those of the team that matter most as they see a lot more of me – as in any way 'schizo'. This confirms my suspicions of all those agonising years, that I have been afflicted by that awful 'label', that it was totally inaccurate – a very poor reflection on the judgement of many 'Doctors'!

b) At the same time, in the same week, Spiritual Experience Five has given up a third – and for the first time *positive* – Outcome or Meaning. Another to do with Authors OnLine will imminently be resolved, in weeks or months – probably again positive...

c) I am starting to see my way forward in publishing books – at least the Internet offers a totally affordable route, and there are still a number of 'printed' publishers yet to reply about my poetry and other books – including this one!

CHAPTER TWENTY-SIX

Future as yet Unresolved Aftermaths and Outcomes

As of 16th March 2000, I present this list of four categories of questions still at the forefront of my mind about my immediate future. I am still undecided as to whether to leave the list unanswered, or to keep updating the text as the questions in fact get answered, hopefully all in the next few months at the latest…

1. HEALTH

i. Will my new Doctor of three meetings only, 'stick his neck out' and agree that my diagnosis should actually be 'bipolar I affective disorder'? After my Social Worker, and now my CPN cum psychotherapist, but disavowing the opinions of many previous Doctors, who had much less time with me?

ii. Will he put this in writing, so enabling me to copy his letter to the Ombudsman for Medical Services, so confronting Whore's abysmal 'treatment' following various diagnoses of me as 'schizo' – his *torture* of me!?

iii. Will this have any effect on the Report by that Ombudsman?

iv. Might this just help other patients? You see, I have read reliable reports that it often takes *eight years* for my condition to be diagnosed properly. *22½ years* seems a trifle excessive, don't you agree? I feel justified and much happier now! It just proves Psychiatry is a real Black Art, with most practitioners really not 'knowing their schizophrenia (arse) from their elbow'!

v. With counselling, I am really starting to feel like 18 again – back in the heady days of 1975! A different depot also seems to be helping – hence staying up typing, with energy, at 2.30am, so as to be able to 'run off' copies of this book after I have got some sleep! Will I end up getting the promised benefits in full from this improved drug – and above all, brilliant counselling? Will the dose, once lowered, stop my total lethargy and sleeping in?

2. SPIRITUAL EXPERIENCES

i. Will Spiritual Experience Five's fourth meaning be positive or negative? i.e. will my book or books be published on the Internet, and on paper?

ii. Will Spiritual Experience Five go on to turn out to have yet more predictions to 'yield up'? It seems that, as it has eight points to it, there might be four more to add to the existing total of four! Watch this space...

3. MY ATTEMPTS TO GET MY THREE BOOKS PUBLISHED

i.   Will Authors Online publish my books – and sell any copies – before they conceivably go bust, for lack of finance?

ii.   Will any poetry publishers come out of the woodwork following my recent mail-shot?

iii.   Will any publisher really take me up and publish this very damning autobiography – of the Black Art of Psychiatry – especially after my recent small mail-shot (of nine publishers, four have already said 'no!') ?

4. WORK – PART-TIME OR FULL-TIME?

i.   What *does* the future hold? Publishing my books, as a part perhaps of working for AoL as a successful local publishing company in Hertford? Working part-time, some of it voluntary, for the foreseeable future? A return to IT after all this time seems very difficult! Teaching maths and science and computer science, some to people with learning difficulties, at the local college? Really, this seems like my most problematical area of all!

ii.   I have just heard, as I write on 16th March 2000, that on 'medical advice' I am 'barred from driving' – permanently, is the implication! My trusty Social Worker, Julia, happened to pop in to see me, was horrified, and is taking the matter up for me. What on Earth has Ballitch said to them? I had a clean driving licence over all of 25 years up to last year – what have these Doctors done to me? I *need* to be able to drive to get a decent job as of old! Will they ever return my licence?

I have never been one to wield a crystal ball. The answers to all these questions seem tantalisingly close. So it will be fascinating to patiently await their outcome and resolution. Hopefully invoking the 'Spring of my Life' as Vivian has said!

CHAPTER TWENTY-SEVEN

Resolutions of most Aftermaths and Outcomes. Thursday 13th April 2000. Only two Outcomes yet to occur!

I finished the last chapter, with all its unresolved issues, exactly four weeks ago today. Since then much has happened, and most questions have been answered.

There was an interlude of two weeks after finishing the last chapter on 16th March, of two weeks, until my 43rd birthday on Thursday 30th March 2000. Sadly, I did not see Jenny that week or the next, as my ex- decided she wanted to spend Mother's Day on the next Sunday with her. However, in a veritable flurry over the last two weeks as I write, nearly all the large number, except just two, of the unresolved issues of the last chapter, have clearly been fully resolved!

*Outcome or Meaning Four – **positive** again! – of Spiritual Experience Five. Authors Online accept my books!*

The following day, the last day of March, I phoned Authors Online on the off chance, to find the boss had made a rare appearance there, and immediately offered to let me bring over (three miles away by bus) my disks of my 'Spiritual Energy', and book of poems as in the Appendix to this book.

I had carefully and painstakingly worked these up that week, to be publishable versions, with hopefully no errors at all! I had then produced from the 'Word for Windows' original versions, which I work with reluctantly as 'Word often throws wobblies', 'Acrobat pdf' versions, which AonL also offer as a format.

Then Richard supervised on that Friday evening, while I spent all of four hours 'putting up on the website' these two books. He did not charge but did it as a favour, as I might still be coming to work for them at some stage. So their web-site at www.authorsonline.co.uk now contained references to my books and myself – published! – at least in electronic, low-revenue, low-budget, form…

Immediately on leaving their site to return home by bus in the dark, it suddenly occurred to me that the fourth – and obviously *positive* like the third about Jenny – Outcome of Spiritual Experience Five had just happened!

The first image of that Spiritual Experience can be seen to represent, in electronic or electrical engineering terms, a *dual-redundant star network* – of computers? The Internet is just such a network! They are a 'hi-tech' company by being involved with it – with vast ambitions – hence the 'hi-tech' glasses like the ones my daughter was wearing when Meaning Five of Spiritual Experience Five 'happened' the previous month! The last 'cup' image fits too. They work over the Dark Horse Brewery in Hertford – the offices simply reek of beer – alcohol!

So that answered two of the 'aftermaths and outcomes' of the last chapter, 2(i) and 3(i), both very positively! Then exactly a week later, when I was just starting on the Friday on the week it has taken of hard work, working up the manuscript of this book from what I can now say was a patchy original version, outcome 3(ii) was answered too. A small poetry publisher called 'Aural Images ltd.' came forward asking permission in writing to publish in an anthology my poem 'Social and Security'. In the meantime I had spoken to 'Beyond the Cloister Publications' which turns out to be run by a vicar, which explained why their Recitals are all held in Churches. He said I will hear in due course about my poems being read out professionally – he certainly intends to have 'Forest of Unearth' read out in the Summer!

My hopes for my two (three?) books now revolve around the only point in (3) of the last chapter that has not yet been resolved – 3(iii). Namely, I just hope that of the small handful of publishers I am currently dealing with, just three, once they receive their copy of this revision (they already have the vastly inferior original, with little or no such suspense!) one of them just might want to publish one or both books… I only now have to spend four days running off copies!

All the points in parts 1 and 4 of the last chapter turned out to get answered, for the foreseeable future, at my Care

Programme Approach (CPA) Meeting last Monday 10th April 2000. Absolutely everybody was there! My parents, Julia, Vivian, Joe, Robyn and the two Doctors including my Consultant, barely fitted into the room! Everyone agreed that my health was rapidly improving, due to both new medication and Vivian's counselling, but Vivian insisted that in fact I should take credit for the latter.

Then it came to the issues of the last chapter. When I straightforwardly asked Dr Ballitch what his diagnosis now was, now that Vivian and Julia had told me their mutual opinion that it was 'bipolar disorder' he coyly and disarmingly put me off by replying, 'What do you prefer to discuss, your diagnosis, or you as a person?' Clearly he was well prepared by a letter I had written to him demanding to have that answer, some weeks earlier, later apologising for my somewhat strident tone! So, clearly, he declines at present to offer any reply to all of questions 1(i)-(iv) of the last chapter! No doubt he is terrified of the implications of 'grassing' on other previous Psychiatrists who have called me 'schizo' instead!

As for my lethargy of the last two whole years, i.e. sleeping 12-14 hours a day! See point 1(v) of the last chapter. This was generally put down to trauma, and Dr Ballitch said that if that made me feel unable to work, I should not work! As simple as that. That answered point 4(i), so Robyn said she would take me off her agency's list if that situation did not change in a month. I greatly doubt it will...!

That leaves points 4(ii) and 2(ii). As for 4(ii), Dr Ballitch could not believe that I had been banned from driving for life, and readily agreed to write to the DVLA.

CHAPTER TWENTY-EIGHT

Monday 3rd July 2000.   Battles with 'the Psychiatric Monster' get ever more bizarre – by the monster's very mad nature!

I finished the last chapter, with its lingering note of optimism, on Friday 14th April – and breathed a big sigh of relief. I had spent long hard hours for three weeks, starting with the previous version of the book, which was in two disjointed parts.   With the tale abruptly developing inconsequential and unsatisfactory twists between the first and second parts. The first part left off in November 1998, and the other 40 pages were sort of tacked on, taking the account up to early 2000. So I had spent hundreds of hours rewriting the book as a seamless whole, all now seen completely from the viewpoint of this year, 2000.

I took out all of twenty pages of what had been called 'repetitive' material, and also since to my mind, out of temporal sequence and so hard to follow. The result to my mind is a far easier read, and even very suspenseful. In particular I don't attempt to give interpretations of my Spiritual Experiences as they occur, but only at the point of the actual predictions coming true.

I reflected that I was at rather an impasse. I had spent just over six months in not inexpensive printing and correspondence of the results with virtually every 'spiritual, religious, and above all Christian' publisher in the country, and even a few abroad. About 100 in all! Despite a sprinkling of interest, I had drawn a complete blank with promoting my 'Omega Course' as 'Spiritual Energy' was then called, despite all that hard work and endless waiting for replies, in trying to find a publisher for it. I now abandoned all hope, barring a miracle, of ever seeing it in print.

Apart from sending copies off in vain hope to two poetry publishers, one who had kept some poems I sent in February possibly for use in London Recitals, 'Beyond the Cloister'.

'Beyond the Cloister' have been silent for all of ten weeks since I sent them their copy...

That poetry was the main theme of the next two rather lonely, bleak and empty months, even more than usual, as I recall. Apart from adding a new 'prose poem' to the frontispiece of 'Omega', in May, I did nothing with it.

Indeed, my £100 overdraft was starting to bother me, as although it cost nothing to use, I was fed up with constantly bouncing off the bottom of it. So I decided to sell the PC, for whatever I could get, that I had built for Christmas 1998 for my daughter, mostly out of reused parts, but a few new. She had soon got bored with it, and anyway, my father and I both had computers that she could use. This eventually involved three separate adverts, the first leading to a shark in Essex offering to pay £200, then leading me a merry dance on the phone till he turned out to be selling it on to somebody else for a profit. In the end this dubious 'end customer' inevitably backed out! In the end I got £150 from the first caller from my third advert, having travelled to Welwyn Garden City to place it in the paper. My overdraft was now back under my control...

In the meantime, apart from my usual occasional appointments of an official nature, I unwound from the effort of rewriting this book, and indeed by contrast soon got very bored and frustrated. Then on 2nd May I was severely henpecked by my social worker, to my consternation, and chastised for allegedly 'messing about and faffing about' (in not going out to work like she insisted). The same day my employment agency lady rang up, having been at the meeting, offering a long shot of a job, with an interview the following day, in a new area to me – of Web Page Design. I felt battered and bewildered about this, but went along. After all, just three weeks earlier at my CPA meeting, my Doctor had readily agreed that if I did not feel fit to work, what with needing for completely medical reasons of trauma and depression, to sleep a great deal, I should not.

I was immediately offered work, but could have no idea how much of a merry-go-round distraction that would be. Until I wrote to the agency on 26th June giving eight compelling reasons why I should not take it up, now it was at last actually about to start, after all this long interlude since the interview.

Life continued to be largely dull into May. I wrote the frontispiece to 'Omega' that I mentioned – then sent it to several people to whom I had given copies. For two weeks, ever since I 'got my job', since dwindled away with week after week, with more and more drawbacks emerging, to the point where I firmly backed out, I had been getting increasingly irritated.

For my social worker had arranged that my 'outreach worker' or social worker's 'dogsbody', literally, should come around three times a week, at 9am, to get me out of bed! So, the twelve hours sleep I actually still need to overcome my depression and genuine Post Traumatic Stress Syndrome was now being brutally foreshortened by social services. Even though my problems were all caused by the Psychiatric Monster they get paid by! The following week, as we will see, those sort of problems re-erupted after a lengthy dormant period, and I got to the end of my tether, and had a short, fierce argument with him on the phone.

He finally actually admitted that it was my choice, not ultimately that of social services, if I needed to sleep a lot to avert much worse depression. So he has not been back so early ever since...

However, that disruptive start to my day only added to mounting utter frustration, and a desire to fight back at that, caused by all the last eight years of 'sheer unmitigated abuse under psychiatry'. Ever since my parents got their latest dismissive 'There there, children. All was well' whitewash of a reply to the final complaint available to them within the NHS about all that abuse.

This was the Ombudsman – the last line of complaint mechanism on offer.

So after a brief chat as ever with my outreach worker, I immediately got dressed, and went round to the nearby Citizens' Advice Bureau, where it took a quarter of an hour as first in the queue, to be seen. I briefly told the adviser the reasons, then that I needed my MP's phone contact number and preferably address. She took a few details for her records, then noted down for me his phone and fax numbers, and address at the House of Commons. Then I went home, rang his PA and made an appointment for four weeks thence,

Saturday 17th June at his surgery. The ungodly hour of 10am did not appeal, and when I was told I would only have 15 minutes with him, we talked about it and agreed that as my case was so complex, I should write to him at the House of Commons first.

I then was due to see Vivian, my CPN/counsellor, for treatment and an hour of further chat, and of course when I happened to mention I had procured my MP's address, the reaction was predictable. "There you go again, trying to be dominant and not keeping to your 'true', vulnerable self. Put that past behind you! Think of the present, in particular look to the future." I refrained from trying to argue in vain, as often before, that I could not leave such a messy, abused past behind me before facing the future, so bleak at present, without doing all within my power to correct the dire effects of that past. I don't now remember any more about that meeting. It achieved very little.

Then on the Sunday I had Contact with Jenny, as is usual every two weeks, and soon forgot the tedium of a bleak Saturday, the day before. As ever, we played games, went on a walk and enjoyed my mother's cooking. No glimpse of a warning that the next two weeks, starting Monday, would be so traumatic that they would result in a total of five weeks of suffering. Once again, as usual, caused by appalling mistakes by the 'Psychiatric Monster'. Then, when I expressed my agony as a result, nearly making me ill through this alleged 'care', I was penalised – for supposedly upsetting THEM!

My only appointment was with Dr Ballitch, at 2pm. My Social Worker, Julia, came in at first, specifically to get him to write urgently to the Drivers' Vehicle Licensing Centre, about an alarming letter I had shown her, from them a month or so earlier, apparently banning me without any limit being given! To her embarrassment, she had promptly lost this! Almost inevitably, he ruminated for a while, incidentally admitted on checking that for god-awful reasons, he had previously ticked a box to say I was 'mentally unstable' back in February, when I had not been! – then passed the buck back to me. I now had to write to them!

She left, as expected he said I was fully 'in remission', and then to my surprise, at last, as requested back in February in a letter, started to discuss my diagnosis. Or at least, he said he was going to, then proceeded to say 'diagnosis is what I use when I first treat you' as if I was a pig-ignorant child, along with many similar completely tangential remarks. He finished without actually saying what I had wanted to hear – confirmation of Viv's and Julia's joint view that 'my condition is bipolar affective disorder. Just forget you were ever called "schizo"' of what immediately came to seem a phoney 'honeymoon period' of three months. For, just before saying goodbye, he filled out a form for a blood test.

When I got outside, I soon felt utterly confused! There on the form in the slot marked 'diagnosis' he had written 'schizo affective illness'! Oh no, back to 'manic depression AND schizophrenia', like so often in the past, was my immediate reaction... As I walked back the short distance to my flat, it was with mounting feelings of confusion and betrayal, which soon led to despair...

I remember brewing away alone in my flat, then after half an hour decided to walk to Tesco and do my day's shopping, to get some fresh air, distract myself with everyday things, and try to get rid of the mounting stress, hurt and confusion. The supermarket left me in a detached blur. As I walked home the anxiety became physical, and I got breathless, with the start of tension in my chest, that became actual pain once back at the flat. I tried twice to leave messages for Julia to call me urgently about the meeting, but as ever got no reply. At 4.30 I decided enough was enough, and walked down the road to their offices. I needed an urgent explanation of not one but two extremely serious mistakes by the Doctor, the second so much undoing three months of 'honeymoon bliss' as a 'pure bipolar affective disorder case'.

Julia came rushing in, and I found myself so distressed that I could hardly express myself. I said as I recall, 'is there no teamwork or communication going on within the team?' and then just handed her the blood test form with the very offensive diagnosis! Ballitch was still in his office, but was not inclined to see me himself. Instead, in a bizarre pantomime, Julia, tight-lipped and stiff with resentment at this embarrassment, acted as go-between between myself in the reception and the miscreant Doctor in the adjacent office!

In the end, after several such 'disjointed relays' of remarks, he gave her a new blood test form, duly relayed bizarrely out to me – with treatment details and no horrible abuse of any alleged diagnosis, that had caused such hurt! Then his third faux pas came out, when she said, unbelievably, 'He says he thought that you thought that was your diagnosis!' As I said once I recovered myself enough to write to her the following weekend, as we shall see, 'that was 0% a medical remark and 100% a political statement!'

Back at the flat, I recovered slightly, enough to realise that more needed to be said about just why I was so upset. I explained in a note that whenever in the last five years, in 1995, 1997, and 1999, that I had had that diagnosis, it had been explained to me by so-called 'experts', that it meant I had some schizophrenia. As well as the affective disorder, which I fully accept that I suffer from. I had just had a lovely period of three months of continually being told by two of my team that 'try to forget you were ever told that you are a schizophrenic!' Only now for the lynchpin of the team, the Doctor, to brutally reverse all that good work – in three words!

Sure enough, when I dropped off the note, both he and Julia were still around, preparing to go home. After she questioned my producing my note, I handed it to her – then saw him passing to his big car in the car park, and incredibly, there was a final fourth huge gaffe. I said pointedly to him, "*That* label of 'schizo' cost me my divorce – and to lose everything." Yet unbelievably, his reaction was utterly 'inappropriate' as these psychiatric people say. A huge beaming smile lit up his face as I said those words, as if I were a mere nothing complaining about nothing!

I reflected as I walked home that this was a lousy start to a week for which I had little planned, ending up with a completely empty May Bank Holiday weekend, not even with any Contact. Indeed, as it wore on so very slowly, my few commitments hardly distracted me from my brewing feelings of 'Oh no! Here we go, yet another out of control Psychiatrist damaging me!' so soon my drinking had risen a great deal, which stayed that way until the, by contrast, completely positive events of last weekend, which we come to shortly. Indeed, he caused me such stress, which only mounted, that I had nearly six ensuing weeks of deep turmoil, and this soon led to frequent heavy drinking – all down to 'them'.

I was rudely awakened again early the next day, amid the deep stress of all this, by the ever irritatingly 'positive and cheerful' outreach worker. As I said earlier, I rang him and argued my way out of any further such embarrassing intrusions into my privacy, later that week. Enough was enough! Anyway, as we shall see, I had already become increasingly disenchanted by the slender 'job prospect' now revealing increasing pitfalls, he was supposedly preparing me for.

However, that afternoon I met Robyn, my Council employment agent, at the local college, for a 'job taster' of voluntary work teaching young adults with learning difficulties, to at least attempt the task of operating computers! This went well, was very enjoyable, and the harrassed, overrun teacher was very grateful afterwards. I've helped at three more sessions since, two of these with her colleague instead, had my patience stretched, but always been thanked. The last two sessions until September were last week.

'All I had to do' on Wednesday in the day, was go to the local Hospital, and wait a long time to have blood taken, as decided so brutally on the Monday. That evening I stayed a while at the local 'drop in' for people with similar problems, then went on to a thoroughly enjoyable Creative Writing Class. The only highlight of that ten days starting on the awful Monday!

Then on Thursday the trouble 'they' had caused got a lot worse, as I festered in agony about all the gaffes 'they' had made on Monday. I realised I had that, and about seven other things, especially the fact that Viv was apparently leaving, breaking all continuity of counselling, to talk to Julia about. I tried to call her, and was told this urgent message would be passed on. Four calls like that later, she actually came to the phone, and was clearly still very piqued about the events of Monday. I started to discuss Viv, and was cut off with the riposte 'Is that all you called five times to talk to me about? I'm very busy. Don't waste my time with such trivia!' I tried to say I had a whole other list of things requiring urgent discussion, but she said, "I've had a very stressful day. I will call you back!" and almost immediately put the phone down on me. I was stunned. Yet again I was taking flak just because of the incompetence of a 'god-like' Doctor – that might be his view, but is not mine in any way, after all my terrible Experiences of 'them'!

Friday was wet, bleak, and empty – especially of any long-awaited call as promised by Julia the day before. In the end, I got so despondent that I realised a long letter about all of my eight current areas of most concern, in fact summarising my current position, was called for. As soon as I started it I realised I intended to also use it as a vehicle to send to my MP, to save repeating myself.

The weather was 'set foul' for the long weekend, and by Saturday evening I had written a twelve-pager to her. It all seemed very polite and business-like, except for two slight criticisms of her in the last two points, and a very good summary of my then position in general. Or so I thought when I came to post it on Tuesday. Her reaction, that it was 'so abusive it made her cry, and nearly resign as my social worker', or so I was led very firmly to believe, seems now unbelievably histrionic! Especially as just this Tuesday, my father finally read a copy – 'their' reaction had made me delay in showing it to him – and fully agreed with me that it was innocuous and meant no offence! In fact, he commented that both that letter and the next, equally long, to the MP, were totally rational.

The latter I started on the heels of the other, on the equally damp, lonely Sunday. I could not face finishing the last six pages of it, and by 6pm on the Sunday (28th May) realised all this solitary, extremely arduous typing was making me feel rather ill! Luckily I remembered that there was a 'drop-in' running that day at the local youth club, so rushed down, and luckily it still had over an hour to run. I started to say how I felt, and for the next half-hour 'dumped' a lot of stuff!

Luckily there were two NSF people on duty that I got on with and knew well, with very few other 'members' there, so I soon discussed it, in complete safety as soon as it dawned on me, that I was speaking under some pressure, very quickly. This in turn made me realise that I was so stressed out by my awful, lonely, abused week, it had made me rather 'high'! However, I had done the right thing. I released a lot of pent-up steam built up over the whole week, especially in my typing long, difficult letters, in isolation, by just chatting about it all, and having a few cups of tea. I readily agreed to give the typing a break till the following day, knowing already myself that was the right thing to do, then went home again, fully myself again but deserving a break, at 7.30pm when it closed. Soon to bed!

The following day, a yet again wet, Bank Holiday Monday, I got down the last six pages of the letter to the MP, mostly a long list of ten points about how the new Mental Health Act being drafted, should quite definitely incorporate sweeping changes. To greatly dilute the current draconian powers of solitary, often very biased and as in my terrible case, usually incompetent 'Doctors'.

Likewise, I proposed a whole raft of new safeguards and even staff, and powers, to actually help the poor patients stop feeling so utterly helpless. Again, my father reserved most praise about these two letters to this part! Then, feeling I had done enough, I posted the letter with enclosures to the MP, and popped off the letter to Julia. I could not guess that such an innocent statement, innocuously phrased, could provoke the knee-jerk reaction from surprisingly, not her, but Vivian, who called an hour or so after I dropped off this post, and asked me to 'pop in for a chat'. I was suspicious, as 'they' usually use that key phrase when it means "you need a politically correct yet thorough verbal thrashing – and almost certainly an injection earlier than planned! Just so 'we' feel good – and in charge!"

I was not to be disillusioned about that when I duly turned up at the centre. Vivian was suddenly transformed from 'friendly counsellor', to her seemingly true 'just one more of "them" self', for a whole hour – to be repeated at her insistence at a further hour's session on the Friday that week. I am very glad that after her holiday in Turkey, and so not seeing her for a month, everything was 'back to normal' last Friday just gone, when I saw her for an hour – and my depot.

"You realise your letter brought poor Julia to the point of tears? Did you actually read it before you posted it?", were her opening remarks! Completely taken aback, I said yes, I had read it, of course, and it seemed perfectly harmless. The 'chat' continued in the same vein, and although my father had strongly advised me not to mention that current bone of contention, diagnosis, I said that was the root cause of all this dissent. While denying it when I directly challenged her about that, Viv then proceeded to completely compromise herself about all she had repeatedly, wonderfully been affirming about my 'bipolar affective disorder' for months now – since February 25th in fact.

"I never said, 'your condition is pure bipolar affective disorder'. I said I had only seen those 'bipolar disorder' aspects of your 'schizo-affective disorder', which Julia and the Doctor have seen far more of". In fact Julia was once more to reassure me in a meeting I soon arranged, in desperation, for the following Monday, 5th June, that her position had never wavered. She has always believed me to have bipolar disorder, and even once again said, 'you have never been a schizophrenic'! Yesterday, Friday 30th June, Viv had indeed reverted back to her original, consistent view that I have pure bipolar affective disorder! So where does that leave one, one wonders to oneself? The meeting on 30th May ended with the question "Don't you think you ought to have your depot injection a few days early?" to which I immediately acceded, knowing the alternative was probably hospital!

The meeting on Friday passed in a blur. All I remember is more barracking, mostly because the 'Sorry' note that Viv had coerced me into handing in for Julia had rightly been perceived as totally back-handed! Her 'parting remark' before not seeing her for four weeks, due to her leave in Turkey, was indeed totally baffling to me. Further indication that I was being made guilty over something that was really due to the Doctor having earlier put his foot right in the shit – several times, not once! "Have you thought about the need you might have – to forgive yourself?" was the disarming 'thought for the day'!

As a person who may smoke a lot, and sometimes drink a lot, I in fact count myself very lucky, as somebody who very rarely does anything that requires forgiveness – least of all this baffling, guilt inducing 'forgiving myself'! By now, I had realised that the stress of this series of meetings, to end the following Monday, and which was even more negative, on top, were making me suddenly drink heavily! The medical profession frowns on people like me with a 'mental condition' doing so – yet this was entirely down to 'them'! My final action that week, after all this totally undeserved 'disciplining', was to e-mail Julia to suggest (beg for?) a meeting – at last! She e-mailed back suggesting 'Monday at 12pm', to which I readily agreed.

Meanwhile events were starting that, just last Saturday 24th June, were finally to completely halt that excessive drinking. That was pre-empted by a chance phone call, on the Wednesday 31st May, to Peppy at Mymms Ward, totally unexpectedly taken by another patient, whom I had not heard from in a whole year. In fact, that departure by her to Harlow Hospital had resulted in yet further wild allegations of so-called 'sexual harassment' by the control freaks at Welwyn Ward in 1999. Which she was now to totally dismiss as soon as our friendship renewed, after all that time since! So I called Peppy that Wednesday 31st May, after my first of two totally negative meetings with Viv – to call off a planned trip to visit her in hospital that same day.

The woman who picked up the Ward telephone immediately said, "Who's that? Is that Simon?" It was Mary, who I had immediately become firm friends with on Welwyn Ward in 1999, then had several phone calls from Harlow hospital from, after her transfer there that year. Excitedly discussing the copies of the very original copy of this book, as well as my 'Spiritual Energy' that I had given her! She was as excited as I was to hear from her after all this time, and told me Peppy had gone in to see some Doctor, so couldn't meet up with me as planned. That suited me. Could I call Peppy back after 3pm?

I duly called back at about 4.30, and again it was Mary who answered the phone. I was told that Peppy had got the wrong message across, and had gone to the meeting with me 'up town' as arranged, only to be disappointed! I had had time to recover and think after the shock of hearing Mary on the phone earlier, so ventured, "You remember when your social worker called my Doctor back last year? I got accused of 'sexually harrassing' you as part of a hate campaign because of that!" Her reply is still vivid, "Well buggar that! What a load of crap! I always felt totally safe, indeed protected, when I was with you!"   We soon re-established what had been an immediate friendship that previous year, on the telephone. So the seeds of Outcome Five of Spiritual Experience Five, in its astonishing, compelling way, were sown.

The weekend of 3rd and 4th June 2000 was to provide a welcome relief from the series of so far three arduous meetings with 'psychiatric people' – now interrupted by the welcome phone calls to Peppy – only to be greeted by Mary!

On Saturday 3rd June I opened my post – and found a packet from Spotlight Poets, giving me a set of pages to edit. Of my ten pages in a new anthology, featuring ten poems by myself I had sent them in May, to be promoted in the local press as well as on local radio! That weekend I found various lines of poetry missing, so corrected these. I posted the draft back along with the requisite cheque for £58 to buy 12 copies when it is printed in September. Very exciting!

My Godfather John was certainly very excited when I sent him an e-mail in Georgia, USA, as was Julia on the Monday 5th June, when, what seemed like 'at last' literally, we finally met at her offices.

On the Sunday we had Jenny for Contact again, and she was keen to improve her physical reactions – so it was 'French cricket' with ball and racquet, and games of catch and 'donkey' with me most of the time. She was very much sharper at the end, leaving me to regret yet again how much of an education in these very basics she was being forced to miss out on from me...

The weekend led to a very positive meeting with Julia, which started with me again mystified by her saying my letter to her of two weeks earlier, had been 'abusive'. My father does not agree, now nor do I, on looking at it again. She even started to say that she was redundant in the role of being my social worker any longer! Forty minutes later, it was all sorted out, and I had smoothed back her ruffled feathers, without really understanding how she had become upset in the first place! She, for her part, again reassured me, whatever changes of position and goalpost-moving had been made by Viv, that I had 'never been a schizophrenic – if I ever had I would be one now. I remained in her view a sufferer of pure bipolar disorder'. This all helped, of course, but not nearly enough to get me over all the trauma mostly caused by a grinning Doctor two weeks earlier.

To resume the story on Monday 5th June, after my positive meeting with my social worker. That rest of that week was very quiet, mostly worrying increasingly about whether I had 'bitten off more than I could chew' over the job in Hertford in Web Design. I remember my usual Creative Writing class on Wednesday was very enjoyable, but I was sneezing, and seemed to be developing a cold!

I woke up that Thursday full of it, with my sinuses full of muck! This turned out to be a virus that my GP refused to treat the following day, when it peaked, simply suggesting paracetamol and citrus juices... To break this reinforced tedium, I rang Mary at Mymms Ward on the Saturday 10th June, then due to travel to Hatfield to visit my folks the following day, arranged to pop into the hospital on the way, off the direct bus route. Mary said she would be delighted to see me, and also Peppy was desperate for visitors. So the following day I caught the bus, and stopped off for two hours. Mary had a massive migraine, and only talked for a while as a result, mostly about how her drinking problem had this time nearly killed her. Fortunately, she readily agreed to trading telephone numbers, and as she was going home the next day, Monday 12th June, I was soon indeed to start a series of lengthy telephone conversations with her. She was readily to agree that she had looked dreadful in the Ward, after her ordeal. Soon to recover her normal more healthy looks after a few weeks of coming home, and regularly going every day to the centre for alcoholics in Hertford.

I was very inspired by Mary yet again saying that she had greatly admired my writings, in particular my 'Spiritual Energy', until it 'blew her mind' the previous year when she was at Harlow. So 'they, there' had confiscated my books from her indefinitely! I told her when she had been settled back at home for a while, the books had been very much improved since, so I would give her fresh copies to read, now no longer ill in any way. She readily agreed.

So, inspired by another 'fan', the next day, Monday 12th June, I changed the cover of the 'Omega Course', soon to be renamed 'Spiritual Energy', adding a 'psychological note' to the title:

A 'Spiritual, anti-materialistic, New Psychology' that actually acknowledges that The Mind and The Spirit are Real and Exist in their own right – they're not just 'froth made out of chemicals'!

Another quiet week followed, so I was led to pursue this, reprinting and rebinding all eight copies of my book I then had. Finally, I thought to myself, perhaps my quest for a publisher is not really totally yet over. Why not write to New Scientist? I did so, with a copy of 'the Omega Course' that Thursday, to hear back with a comment "very interesting – but we have a lot of competition for space for our material, which is mostly generated in-house". Yet again, so near yet so far... However, this venture had led me to yet another 'mail shot' on Friday 16th June, to 20 'scientific, psychological and psycho-analytical publishers' as in my "Writers' Handbook". Yet again, as ever, there was an initial flurry the following week of some seven or eight "no's", including that of New Scientist!

I mentioned earlier that I had been writing to my local MP, who had now written back to cancel the meeting at his Surgery that Saturday 17th June. Now, much better, he had read my letters more fully, and is clearly taking them very seriously. He is investigating my complaints with the Health Authority, then coming to see me at home – and my whole family. So when my parents were down with an ill Jane at hers and my brother's in Sussex, I was left to look after Jenny that Sunday by myself. My sister was busy with end of year teacher's business – as well as finishing off the first year of work on her related MA degree, astonishingly undertaken at the same time!

Jenny and I were picked up by my sister Libby and dropped off at Stanborough lakes, where we spent over a half hour, after nearly giving up waiting in a long queue, having a great time rowing around! Jenny, at nine, and slim, could not manage both oars by herself when she asked to have a go! She loved coming up close on the water to baby coots, geese and ducks! After that, as it was extremely warm and sunny, back at my parents' house, we stayed inside at her insistence, and played 'fours', 'boggle' and other games, until it was home-time...

So, into a week with little on, except I arranged to do two final two-hour sessions teaching computing to adults with learning difficulties at the college on the Thursday and Friday. I was getting into regular contact with Mary, who significantly, as it turned out, agreed to come over for the afternoon and evening of the Saturday 24th June, when I would cook some steak I had bought cut-price and frozen. Apart from my Creative Writing class, the penultimate session of this academic year, on the Wednesday, the week was notable for a flurry of "no's" from 'scientific and psychological' publishing houses. Then it was that I looked through my "Writer's Handbook", and found just how suitable a publisher 'Open Gate' seemed to be. They started off specialising in 'psychoanalysis, philosophy, religion...' and four other areas, most of which equally apply to my 'Spiritual Energy'. So I tried on the Thursday night to e-mail my whole 1.5 megabytes of manuscript over to them...

This failed all of four exasperating times, as did the short e-mail I sent then, and the one on Monday. I had previously had a lot of problems with the server computer of my ISP (Internet Service Provider) and this seems to have been more of the same... So in the end on Friday 23rd June, I resorted to posting the disk and hard copy of my 'Spiritual Energy' to them. Two further e-mails followed, and at last on Wednesday 28th June they replied, saying they had only received my e-mail of the previous day – the previous flurry, all of six, had failed to get through!

So, term ended at the college, also with me now utterly convinced that there was too much of a vast 'learning curve', with far too little job security, for too-short term a 'job opportunity'. I now fully intended to abandon a once bright, now dismal seeming, job opportunity. It even threatened my benefit situation, and possibly my sanity! So the weekend of 24th June 2000, with my excitement at entertaining my first non-family 'guest' to supper in all of three whole years of total isolation, in Mary, what with her long absence from my life, due to 'them' at Harlow hospital, was not to disappoint me! In fact, her trip over, as we now come to see in the next chapter twenty-nine, was surrounded by incredibly powerful and above

312

all unbelievably positive New Spiritual Experiences. Numbers Nineteen and Twenty – the first in this new 21st Century!

CHAPTER TWENTY-NINE

A most dramatic day – of Saturday 24th June 2000. Mary's visit, my first guest for literally years, is flanked in the early morning and night-time, by two dramatic and mostly extraordinarily positive Spiritual Experiences for the Twenty-First Century! I reflect afterwards, that this day indeed constituted Outcome Five, again positive, of two negative and three so far positive Outcomes – that led to hopes of final Positive Outcomes Six, Seven and Eight – of a very complex Spiritual Experience Five!

I write on Tuesday 4th July 2000. The dramatic events of Saturday 24th June 2000, the other weekend, really started with the busy Friday I had the day before. In between printing out fresh copies of my 'Spiritual Energy', so I would be able to give Mary a copy as promised the next day, while keeping copies for myself, I taught for two hours at the local college. I got home to find the printer had, as ever, jammed for no reason – with forty pages or so still to print. I just had time to finish this printing by 4.30pm, quickly type up and print a letter covering my sending a copy to Open Gate the publishers, and to buy an envelope to post it in time to catch the last post. Then I made my big mistake of Friday, by rewarding myself for all this intensive afternoon's work – by buying some very cheap Spanish white wine to drink that evening.

So it was that the following morning at the ungodly hour of two minutes to four, I woke with a start from a lovely dream about Mary coming that day. Very exciting, since knowing Diamond two years earlier, I'd had no guests either here or at my last house in Hertford! Soon I became aware, now unable to get back to sleep, with a grey dawn outside, amid the sound of the dawn chorus, that my sleeplessness was due to an acute need to be sick. So, instead of my normal sleep pattern these days, of sleeping in through stress and trauma, until about twelve midday, yes! I now found myself doing a lot of thinking while vomiting continually, and very painfully, for the next six hours, ending at ten o'clock!

I was very aware that I now had a very long time to wait until Mary was due to arrive around 2.30pm. I had brought up most of the effects of rough wine the night before, just before seven, and tried to lie down to get some rest, disturbed at having got up so very unusually early because of my sickness. I dosed for about forty minutes, unable to sleep but getting just enough rest to cope with the imminent long day.

Suddenly, to my astonishment, a highly colourful, dramatic, totally positive Spiritual Experience – number Nineteen in the long series – formed in my mind's eye while I lay there! Unlike almost all my previous Spiritual Experiences, it was clearly moving, with a clearly photographic quality! I looked at my watch. It was 19 minutes to eight...

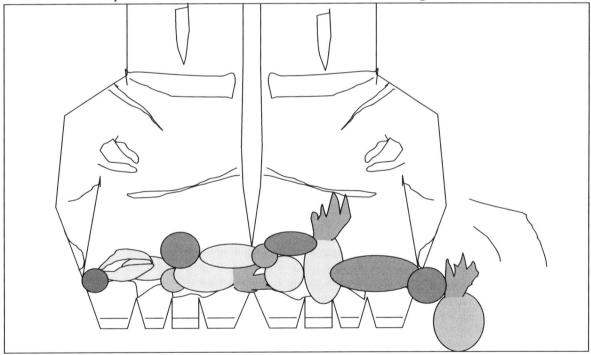

SPIRITUAL EXPERIENCE NINETEEN. 7.42 a.m. on 24th June 2000

Two enormous hands offer me two handfuls of overflowing, luscious, exotic, tropical fruit!!!

Around when I finished rewriting this book, and writing the end of chapter twenty-seven, I had actually prayed about any further Spiritual Experiences:

(a) That if any came, they should only be *positive!* I wanted no more negative!

(b) Any should be short-term in producing their obvious, positive outcomes.

Following hard on the heels of posting my book to Open Gate Publishing, then relating that a moment earlier to possibly fulfilling Spiritual Experience Fourteen, I now had a fresh Spiritual Experience – the first in 18 months!

So, my forty minute cat nap culminating at just after twenty to eight with a dramatic Spiritual Experience, was to prove enough to keep me going until after midnight that day, even though I was sick once more, at ten. Indeed, I was amazed at the totally compelling, obviously very, very positive, even dynamic, moving Spiritual Experience I had just seen – my first of the 21st Century!

I had to wait till 2.30pm for Mary to arrive, so defrosted the steak I intended to cook as a luxury for both of us, which I had bought cut-price. I went shopping for vegetables – but no wine with the meal of course, with her awful recent experiences – and now mine, that morning! I remember I missed out lunch, in the end.

Mary arrived a bit early, and immediately began to prove she is 'quite a teapot' with me constantly ferrying cups of tea from the kitchen. Like me, she smokes like a trooper, which along with the drink problem she is trying to beat, adds up, like me, to quite an addictive sort of pattern as a person.

For the next eight hours, until I left to get the bus back from her place, having escorted her home, for her safety, at the late hour of twenty to eleven, we did not stop talking! Indeed, we had never met up with each other outside the QEII Hospital before, so could talk freely for the first time, staying in apart from a half-hour walk along the lovely river in Ware. It soon became clear that just as she had pointed out in the QEII with the remark, "I don't do sex" that she remained celibate – but with a long-term lover available if she ever did want sex. In fact he lives on the same housing estate, and that long-term affair had caused her divorce and homelessness the previous year, ending up in the QEII. That first ever time in Mental Hospital had been followed in a year by three more times 'inside'...

We talked about my writings, and she took home the latest versions as then of this book, and my 'Spiritual Energy'. She explained the versions she had last year had 'blown her mind' while psychotic and she had described this to her social worker – who had promptly confiscated the books!

Also, inspired by my Spiritual Experience, I gave her loads of fresh fruit and lots of cans I got from my own cupboard – sardines, tomatoes, beans, soup, etc. etc. She is only on a third of my own level of benefit, as she is yet to claim any disability benefits. I am due to go over and help her fill out the form for that this Thursday. I took her back some time after a supper which came out very well indeed, as she was gratefully to comment. I reflected just how glad I was to have 'bumped into' a potential lifelong friend after so long, who is already the only friend I have in the area I can ring any evening. Above all, although she may be an alcoholic like Diamond, she is a vastly more pleasant, straightforward, person to know than the latter! Also, we are clear there is nothing 'romantic' involved – we are just platonic friends. So we planned to go on holiday together like that.

I noted the time as I went to bed, and realised that it was not surprising that I was so tired – it was twenty-one minutes past twelve! Then, as soon as I closed my eyes, still wide-awake, it happened again! I saw four, dynamically moving, once more – all but the second – very positive, Visionary Images, in what was clearly a second Spiritual Experience – Number Twenty – in one dramatic day!

Of the four cinematic, brightly coloured scenes that I saw, only the first and third lend themselves readily to sketching here. Even then, the drawings below are only snapshots of moving images. It was remarkable to me that I saw all of five Visionary Images that day, in my mind's eye, all clearly moving animatedly! Hardly any of my previous, nearly all negative, Spiritual Experiences, had moved like this. This was a new set of phenomena, therefore! Here are my descriptions of the four

Images that I saw at 12.21am on Sunday morning, 25th June 2000: -

SPIRITUAL EXPERIENCE TWENTY – Image One. After a long labyrinthine journey up through a tunnel made of a 'cybernetic net', I stand about to emerge into a glorious sunset!

Spiritual Experience Twenty – Image One. In the first of a set of all of four colourful, dynamically animated, moving scenes, that lasted only two minutes or so in total, I found myself walking fast, and steeply upwards, through a dark, labyrinthine tunnel. This was clearly a Spiritual Experience, no dream or 'hallucination', for the walls, which increasingly got lighter from a red 'light at the end of the tunnel', had a strange, computer-like, prison-like, 'cybernetic net' on them! At the end of the scene I found myself at the end of the tunnel, where the source of the light became clear at last. There was a vivid red sunset shining into the mouth of the tunnel, from which I was on the very point of stepping out, into this sunset. See the drawing above for that final pause in my fast walking 'out of the cybernetic tunnel'.

It looks like a bright future is destined for me now that my 'time in the cybernetic tunnel' or very tough career in IT, is fully acknowledged to be truly a thing of the past!

Furthermore, this image definitely seems to symbolise my parallel journey – out of the awful minefield that being wrongly

319

labelled 'schizo' or 'schizo-defective' for the last 23½ years had put me through, as we have seen so far in this book.

Spiritual Experience Twenty – Image Two. I won't attempt to draw this second Visionary Image of four, especially as on a computer, it would prove impossible. In it I had a view of myself, yet again being crucified on a cross, even with a crown of thorns. In the image I looked about to pass on... Suddenly, however, the view changed from just past the nail in my left hand, to from my front, right-hand side, where I now stood, clearly removed from crucifixion, with my hands by my sides and head lifted up, eyes now open. Suddenly I again knew this was a Spiritual Experience, for something weird happened. The crown of thorns suddenly slipped down round my neck, breaking up and falling out of sight of the scene, onto the ground!

Spiritual Experience Twenty – Image Three. This is easier to describe. I saw my own silhouette, as my head and shoulders raced at high speed through rapidly passing stars – seemingly at near light speed – just like the old screen savers on computers! 'Eventual recognition for "Spiritual Energy"', does this mean?

Spiritual Experience Twenty – Image Four. This final image was also incredibly positive, like all five images in one day. It was simply a series of colourfully dressed crowds of people, hundreds of them. The striking thing was that nearly all of them, of all types of race and colour of skin, turned to me and gave me a huge beaming smile!

This message of 'imminent popularity' was striking, at a time when a very long period of years of solitude was just seeming to be ending now I had reacquainted myself with Mary, that very day...

I soon worked out, just the following day, Sunday, even before I went over to see Jenny for Contact, that this day had been a dramatic Outcome Five of Spiritual Experience Five! Starting with the wineglass, the final Image of Spiritual Experience Five. Clearly I had just entertained an alcoholic – whilst recovering from the effects of 'rough plonk' myself. The sunglasses this time symbolised that much of the conversation was about the possibility of going on holiday together this August, first suggestion Cuba, from Mary! Then the Canary Islands; finally, more realistic, Yorkshire.

The first image of Spiritual Experience Five, in this Outcome, symbolised *time* – or rather times of that very significant day! The pictures below illustrate this: -

Just before 4 a.m.
I wake up at dawn

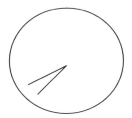
Twenty to eight
Spiritual Experience 19

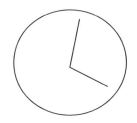
12.21 a.m.
Spiritual Experience 20

If you superimpose where all three sets of hands end up, with a central pair of points symbolising 'my meeting with Mary'

– you end up with precisely, yet again, Image One of Spiritual Experience Five! What an incredibly rich Spiritual Experience it has been since 1996, in yielding so far, all of eleven totally separate Meanings in actuality!

This 'twelve points of a clock' imagery also further reinforces my view that there are an outstanding Sixth, Seventh and Eighth Outcomes to emerge, almost certainly positive! The sequence of Five Outcomes so far has been: -

1. two negative (1 and 2)
2. two positive (3 and 4)
3. one positive (5 – this one)
4. three positive – again, the final positive three...?

CHAPTER THIRTY

Yet again – admission to hospital due to yet another failed 'drug experiment' lasts 29th September 2000 - 10th January 2001

Friday 2nd March 2001. As I resume writing this book, I have a throat-blocking feeling of fear, nausea and anguish at some of the awful things that have happened in the past eight months since completing the last chapter. I simply at first could not bring myself to write about these terrible things, particularly as they are completely in a negative mood, far removed from the optimistic note of the last chapter. Only in the last month have more positive things started to happen.

It turns out that I was very naïve to ignore the fact that the second image of my last Spiritual Experience, Twenty, was of a personal *crucifixion experience.* For no less than four times in the past seven years, such 'crosses in my Spiritual Experiences' had directly predicted, totally accurately, that I would shortly face such a crucifixion experience - in a mental hospital or hospitals.

Spiritual Experience Twenty predicted, not just a fifth such crucifixion experience that in fact turned out to last an agonising three months between 29th September 2000 and 10th January 2001, but, with its *two* scenes, *two* crucifixion experiences *in one.* Yet it was a 'double crucifixion experience' in its two images, with the crown of thorns symbolising a very poignant emotional relationship, soon smashed. The staff did warn me about starting such a tender relationship under such awful circumstances - especially in such a terrible place!

Indeed from 3rd December to now I am still getting over the shock of the way my sensitive and passionate relationship with a beautiful young Asian fellow-patient, just short of 19 years old, was ended by her just over a month before my discharge. Shabs initially completely fulfilled the 'exotic, tropical promise' of Spiritual Experience Nineteen – literally – in the flesh, even! However, the 'execution of our brief affair' took place very coldly and facelessly by telephone - after she had been returned to her original hospital.

323

We pick up the threads of this tale at the easiest point of all, July 2000, when I was fairly regularly going to Mary's house to 'chat', or she, out of her far more limited income, found the bus fare to come over for a meal with me. This normally happened in the late afternoon or evening, as her days were taken up, by and large, by anti-alcoholic rehabilitation classes. It was really delightful to have a single friend to chat to, especially to pick up the phone to call - especially, in fact, non-sexual, for she was determined she wanted no sexual relationships at present.

That purely platonic friendship came at last after so long without Diamond to call on or just chat to on the telephone - two years of solitude now!

Looking back, it was about then, what with all the excitement of Spiritual Experiences Nineteen and Twenty, when Mary and I had our first encounter in many months on 24th June 2000, that I started to go off the rails. I started to go out to the pub and occasionally eat out a lot more, trying to start up even more social life. Meanwhile, Mary, whose finances were vastly more constrained than mine, tended to stay in and drink tea and watch TV.

So it was, that on her advice I watched a fateful TV programme - even though I rarely watched TV and she had explicitly warned me I would hate the programme. Indeed I did find the one episode of 'brain story' on BBC2 that I stomached was anathema, on July 18th - so much that by July 20th I had written a whole new section of the 'Spiritual Energy' - the Appendix! This, if you read it, completely counters the materialistic self-alleged 'wisdom' of neuro-scientists and psychiatrists on that programme, to the extent that I actually propose in this 'White Paper', a complete structure of thought itself. In the complete absence of any 'chemical code' for it as dogmatically proposed essential - but unproven by science as yet! - by the female Professor of neuro-science narrating this 'brain story' programme.

I had given up on getting Spiritual Energy published in print long before, but now had thoughts almost immediately, following on perhaps from watching 'that' programme - led by a professor - of getting academic recognition. In the next two months I was to travel to both Cambridge and Hatfield and try to present them with 'Spiritual Energy' as a PhD thesis. Cambridge turned out to want all of £385 as an examination fee, which I simply did not have access to at the time.

Then, after a day that broke my bank account just getting to Cambridge, my home town University, the UH at Hatfield turned back on me and said 'Sorry - we are unable to help you. The only place obvious for you is - back to Cambridge!' I draw a veil over the awful day at Cambridge, staggering around with too much luggage which I frequently had to put down because of its sheer weight, and called a couple of expensive taxis. Looking back, by that stage in September I was getting really rather ill.

Shortly before going to Cambridge on this wild goose chase, ending in torrential, miserable rain as I recall, I had lost my brief friendship with Mary. At the end of a £500 binge on spending that much of a grant for a holiday from the IEE on a four-week 'holiday at home', pubbing, eating out, buying odd things for my flat and (fruitlessly) trying to extend my social life even more than with Mary.

Believe me, it is very easy indeed to spend £500 extra in four weeks in a 'holiday at home'! However, one night I stayed up nearly all night, drunk, lonely, frustrated, and it turned out, once more on totally the wrong medication and so becoming ill. I left several rather personal and rude messages on Mary's answer-phone that night, that led her when I rang the next day, to say 'I told you, I have no interest in sex right now! Don't contact me again for a very long time!' As we shall see, most of my behaviour in this uncharacteristic way was due to becoming ill from the wrong depot, exacerbated by all the excitement of completing my other book - and lengthily celebrating that accomplishment, as I rightly saw that!

Indeed, from the end of July through September, until my eventual admission on 29th September 2000, this time ostensibly for just a few days to Hopkins Ward, Harlow, I came under constant, ever increasing scrutiny from my then Social Worker, Julia. Then, in short order a series of Doctors and psychiatric assessment committees or 'posses', as I am tempted to call them, called round. In total there were three of these. I narrowly escaped a Section 3 Medication Order from the first, and then a two-week stay of execution of another Section 3 from the second.

It was shortly after this expired without such a Section in fact resulting, that as a result of this pressure I was so traumatised and ill that I went to Cambridge. That was on a Monday, with a whole week's benefit in my pocket at the start, which soon diminished to just £45 to last the week! Tobacco habit and all!

Pretty soon I called Cygnet House Social Services to say I had no money - and when no less than Neil, the manager called round, he was to discover, no fresh food either! So, to my humiliation, for the only time in my life I had to accept food vouchers for £25 to spend at Tesco's!

It had not helped that in the months since Vivian left the office at Cygnet House, I had been assigned a bewildering series of about six successive CPN's to allegedly 'look after me'. Plus there were wholesale changes of staff there at the time, in a big shake-up of the local NHS Trust system. The final nail in the coffin was that after my trip to Cambridge, based on observation of the atmosphere of the place today, I concluded that it is controlled by the Freemasons!

So I said so, on my then new web-site, still unknown on the Internet, and this fact has since been totally reliably confirmed by a Psychiatric Charge Nurse, one of whose hobbies was studying Freemasonry.

So finally, on 29th September 2000, I was confronted by a final sectioning team of the three, taken to Cygnet House at my request, persuaded them to let me go in voluntarily, and admitted to Hopkin's Ward, Harlow, that evening. I was given a lift in by two policemen (no arrest or handcuffs, of course, I hasten to add) after being given five minutes to pack my case...

That first evening I realised that quite a lot had changed at this ward since I was last there in 1997. There were mostly elderly patients now, and as Mary had reported the previous year by phone, the infrastructure of the Ward had been completely renovated. I immediately found there was now a separate nicotine-stained smoking room, so the old arguments about smoking had been eliminated.

I noted that mysteriously, the extractor fan in this room had been fixed to blow inwards, which seemed a bit suspicious.

More of that later. I had a shower and found that the old, decrepit, even potentially dangerous set-up had been revolutionised. Now, apart from a seat, shower-head and control in the wall, releasing fixed temperature water, and some rails for the disabled, the room was completely bare - and hence had been made safe!

One thing that had not changed much was the set of staff on duty, and nearly all the faces and personalities were very familiar. They felt I was trustworthy, so the next day I started a series of trips to town to go shopping. I remember I bought a cheap rucksack, and battery and new strap for my watch, on the market, anticipating possibly quite a long stay. Otherwise I helped myself over the weekend to drinks from the unlimited or apparently so, supply of hot and cold drinks in the day room.

I listened to the radio and CD's I had brought in, annoying a few old patients whose chairs touched the outside of the smoking room where (as ever!) I put the radio. Eventually I found a position for the radio where it could be played with minimal noise leaking out of that room and so annoying other patients. Peace prevailed!

On the Monday I was seen by Dr al-Abbaday, my new Saudi Arabian Consultant from Cygnet House. He stopped the clopixol depot I had been wrongly put on at the start of the year, which was in the end to prove the reason for this stay in hospital and all my illness leading up to it. Instead I was started back on risperidone, which so alarmed me that I refused, and told him the next day that this drug had made me feel very ill for all of 1994-95, and also had been the root cause of my being divorced in 1995! He did not seem to know what to do next, so I was left on just the residue of the last depot, with just my 'evergreen and old faithful' tablets, lithium.

In the next few days, mostly tied to the Ward, I got my usual opening reaction to staying a while in such places - I got much more ill. This was compounded by acute boredom, 'loneliness in a crowd of strangers', lack of home comforts and being in a strange place, and above all the general atmosphere of "other peoples' illness affecting me". It is not surprising perhaps, therefore, that by Thursday my lack of haldol or any other effective similar medication made me completely crack up and 'lose it'.

The grille in the door of the smoking room had suspicious looking wires leading to it, and was of US Army military style and colour. As I said earlier, the fan blew inwards not outwards. Suddenly on Thursday 4th October I cut one of the wires and disabled the fan, having defused it first, with my smoker's penknife as a screwdriver. I had put two and two together and got five, and thought for days that the smoking room contained a nerve gas bomb in that grille, designed to be pumped out by the 'faulty' fan.

I had written to one of the policemen who brought me in about this, so was questioned that Thursday in depth about why I had done so rather than alert hospital staff to this threat. I said I suspected a conspiracy! Asked by the Doctors, who had now seen the print-out from Cygnet House of my web page, whether this supposed 'threat' was to do with the Freemasons, I said 'very likely!'

Finally in front of the whole ward I kept demanding stelazine, the medicine that I recalled had worked 100% in a month on my very first quite minor depressive illness back in 1977, the very start of 'my troubles'.

Pretty soon it was clear they felt they could not handle me on this ward while getting so ill, and clearly lacking effective drugs. There was a flurry of telephone calls, and at about 6pm I was in my bay when four or five strange nurses came in. Soon I submitted non-violently - as ever and always - to a large injection of droperidol, a drug I was allergic to, which I was to be force-fed and come to detest in ensuing months. I am delighted it has since been banned!

Within five minutes I felt very sedated, and while I packed my things, asked very concerned, where I was being taken. It could have been any other psychiatric ward in the area! I was naturally very relieved to be told it was Shannon House, downstairs, which I felt I knew well from 1997. I knew it would be basically more tolerable, despite being a locked ward, than the bleak isolation and unremitting tedium of Hopkins. Plus the food was better!

I arrived downstairs to a scene of very worrying chaos! A teenage guy, who turned out to be called Ned and rather a sexual monster in 'the real world', was being restrained by six nurses on the floor and given a depot injection. Nearby the three current female patients - Natalie, Sharon and Shabs - soon crucially to dwindle in number to just Shabs - were screaming their heads off. Pandemonium!

Which luckily turned out normally to be controlled on that Ward these days! However, at first I thought to myself, understandably, 'The rumours were all true! This Shannon House Ward has gone to the dogs in the last three years!'

The man who ate himself, love broken on stony ground, and other horror stories.

As has happened each time in the story in this book, my crucifixion experiences in mental hospitals have been so awful that it has involved a break of several days in writing about them, before I can face starting, three days after writing the above paragraphs. Shannon House 2000 has proven no exception. As for all of this chapter, it is obviously an abridged account, but glancing at the list of topics that I have notes to write about, has until tonight kept putting me off from starting my account. Only now, after a couple of good days achieving a lot of things especially in my social life, do I feel strong enough to once more brace myself and face writing even this abridged summary of my recent experiences.

Then after a little while their memory will die away, and this book on the bookshelf will be my only reminder. On the bookshelf, that is, and out of my head, i.e. agony dying away for several months, leading to longer term therapy...

Also as I start typing, I am encouraged by the realisation that after this chapter is over I have the relatively light chapter thirty-two to write, dealing with much more hopeful topics like my current recovery out of that ward in 2001.

Shannon House Ward may not have completely 'gone to the dogs' as above, but Diane, the very relaxed Ward Manager who founded it and was there back in 1997, was no longer there, and probably as a result, the regime on the ward had been tightened up a lot. Also, a new Mental Health Act UK is planned for 2001, so the old 1983 vintage one was being applied to the maximum in anticipation of a much fiercer still new version coming in soon.

The interior of this Locked Intensive Care or Assessment Ward was very familiar, apart from one new feature out in the totally enclosed concrete yard - which caused me to notice in turn a peculiar feature on the floor of that yard.

There were up to just nine patients on the ward, with five staff or so, dependent on ward level of 'crisis' or otherwise, at any one time. One saving grace was that each patient had his or her own private bedroom, very basic with just bed, bedside locker, sink, window and wardrobe, all of course fixed down. The windows only opened a crack and outside each was a strong security grille... There was a fiercely guarded door at each end of the ward, which was kept locked with only one staff member able to operate the doors with special keys at any time.

The ward was open plan, apart from the offices and a tiny dining room. The staff often either laughed or groaned when they recalled how the kitchen had been missed off the original design. A smoking room led to the yard, with plenty of ventilation through windows as well as French doors, as well as a large (totally impossible to sabotage!) extractor fan. Often piped radio was played throughout the ward, or selected areas, or else my radio and CD's (soon I had the entire collection brought in) which I played in either the smoking room - or the main lounge, near the office.

I once facetiously called the Ward a 'collection of armchairs' - for that was the only furniture apart from four expensive exercise machines and a full-size table-tennis table. This was used for multiple purposes apart from infrequent table-tennis. Drinks and sometimes snacks like toast and sandwiches appeared there from the kitchen at fixed times - and only then - in the day. Art therapy also used the table-tennis table in the absence of anything else.

So the surroundings in the ward itself were basic - but functional. Back to the two strange features in the yard, which was at the centre of the building, with three stories of psychiatric unit above. We never saw the sun out of there at that time of year. The striking new feature, Natalie told me on my first evening, had been christened 'The Shannon Dome' by many patients. It was ostensibly built in the air over the yard to stop chairs and food and other objects being thrown down from the wards above.

It was a square metal pyramid - of very flimsy construction apparently - made of four big beams at the four corners of the yard rising to a point over the centre of the yard. Just above the basket-ball net at one side and just low enough, frustratingly, often to interfere with shots at that net when we passed the time playing basket-ball. The four beams rose up and met in the middle, with pieces of metal foil arranged in very similar fashion to the stones in an Ancient Egyptian Pyramid, tied together with plastic or metal ties on the four sides. It had recently been breached by a basket-ball or football on one side, so one of these sheets had been knocked to one side, revealing the only hole in the dome.

As I was recently very clued up on Freemasons and their 'golden chains' as we can see in my 'Spiritual Energy' book in the 'black paper', I was very disturbed to see some very strange 'etchings in cement' on the floor of this yard. A large snake traced in cement led from the lounge doors to one of two metal, bolted down, seats, in the far corner. The most curious feature of all, however, was the way cement had been used to draw indelibly, 'golden chains' throughout the body of this 'snake'. Clearly the most peculiar Occult work of Freemason builders, it occurred to me...

It was to turn out to be an autumn of heavy rain, which meant that the yellow lights reflecting on the urine-yellow walls and brown flag-stones of the yard, especially at night, with large puddles in the yard, kept us huddled in the smoking room or lounge. Especially as the heating did not come on till early November, so we all froze! I remember describing the grim outlook onto rain in the yard on those dark autumn nights as being as depressing as 'treacle and custard'! Luckily the staff were far more pleasant than those on Welwyn Ward at the QEII the previous year, and many had much more of a sense of humour and fun than either ward contained at the QE II - Welwyn or Mymms Wards.

Some staff I remembered from 1997, of course, but there were also lots of new faces. In 1997 Jenny had been the Staff Nurse who tucked me up in bed the first night, and now she was Deputy Ward Manager. Pretty, petite, incredibly hard-working and pleasant, she remained rather a 'done that, seen that, got the tee-shirt' cynic in terms of mental health! The Ward Manager, Steve, reminded me that he had known me on the Orchard Wards at Fairfield in 1995 - and told me that several nurses I had been friendly with there, now worked at Broadmoor!

Matt I remembered at once, and we soon resumed the 'quick-fire instant banter' we had known together for a month in 1997. Michelle and I also hit it off. She was another auxiliary nurse, who in due course used to take me on the most relaxed 'leave walks' for an hour off the grounds that I had in my time there. She was attractive yet divorced, incredibly full of energy, with three doting children.

Soon I had a running joke about her with Matt and some of the others, which actually made her blush! "Michelle and I have just had another of our 'dates'! We've been snogging by Oakwood Pond!"

John, Mel, and all the other Nurses and Nursing Assistants were also always just as calm and professional. My Primary Nurse was Lyn, who was in her mid-fifties, a Senior Sister in General Nursing previously, who was very 'English and old-fashioned' and with a plummy voice – a 'trill'. We got on well because of her 'matronly' attitude, and because of respect that both of us were divorced.

Apart, then, from some problems with one particular overly politically correct nurse called Rick, the one problem I had with the staff was, as ever, with the Psychiatrists themselves. I was often involved in running battles with Dr. George the Consultant, and Dr. Mark, the Ward Doctor, often had to act as a sort of 'go-between' between us. Dr George, incredibly, even initially suggested using my anathema drugs, clopixol or risperidone, from 1993-4! Arrogant wally!

So, my crucifixion experience of Image Two of Spiritual Experience Twenty was underway. It was to come clear only this year that the burden of the crown of thorns corresponded precisely, in advance of it happening, to my relationship with my fellow patient, Shabs, who I mentioned earlier. This was initially and indeed always confused, for a while very tender, but within weeks was to be cut off very brutally by her. Very draining on both my emotions, my mental state while we were both very ill, and even my wallet, as I was to buy her loads of presents and cigarettes to keep her spirits up!

Strangely enough, Shabs was the first fellow patient that I talked to, the morning after I arrived, while we both smoked outside in the yard. First impressions, it turned out as she later confessed for both of us, were dramatic!

For both of us later 'confessed' to the other we had butterflies, raised pulse, palpitations and blushing over the other. 'Love at first sight?' she asked rhetorically and needlessly in one of four love letters I still retain - obviously that was definitely the case then and for the five weeks that she remained there. She was a stunningly pretty Pakistani beauty, with long black, red-tinted hair down her back, about 5'4", with a lovely figure to cap it all. Why she fell for me at the same time as I fell for her remains a mystery, but these things always are!

There were three damning reasons why our brief affair turned out to be doomed to an abrupt, brutal ending on December 3rd. She was only 18, rushing around inviting everybody in sight over-enthusiastically and over-optimistically to he big '19th birthday party - with fireworks', in Edmonton in London, coming up in December. I was, at 43, old enough to be her father!

Secondly, inevitably there were cultural differences. Although she had the greatest respect for the Bible, and incidentally my 'Spiritual Energy' I lent her, with the Bible as 'The Book' in her family's tradition, it was her fiercely conservative Muslim family who were in the end, a major factor in breaking up our brief, furtive affair. Finally of course, throughout her time there of five weeks that I shared, we were both extremely ill, and a lot of what was said between us was in fact an elaborate 'Double Fantasy'. Obviously Shabs was the patient I got closest to in my time there, but we need to mention certain other patients before discussing her further in depth below.

Indeed, as ever in psychiatric wards, especially as acute as this one, most of my problems, and those of most other fellow patients, were caused by certain 'difficult' patients. Shabs was to reveal she already had a fierce, often physically violent, feud

333

going on with Ned, whom probably correctly she accused frequently of being a pervert. Certainly his drug-crazed fixed stare always seemed to go straight to her very attractive cleavage - so mostly because of this she always covered up at all times. What an ordeal – for a Muslim girl of great modesty!

Another patient she had a lot of problems with after his melodramatically violent arrival the following week, was Bonzo, who was to punch her hard in ensuing weeks in the stomach, and twice kick and also hit me very hard - all for no logical reason and with no provocation. Both of us were too stunned to even think of retaliating, and after a couple of weeks he had been given so many strong injections in a row, and was so heavily sedated, he was nearly always asleep - and generally a lot calmer when awake. However, Ned and he 'teamed up' for a while, until this over-medication stifled Bonzo's aggression.

Then after about two months of my stay, there was another team formed, when a young skinhead arrived. Ned and he teamed up for roughly a month until he was sent back to his home area. As neither of them had any money, there was a lot of intimidation with very base "giz a fag!" demands to all us other smokers more prudent with our money, who actually had some of it! This got very wearing when it happened all day long, every ten minutes or so, or so it seemed...

There was also a patient there who had been on the Ward for a horrifying two years. A consistently awful case of self-abuse, he was on constant 'one-on-one' supervision and barred from 'dealings' with other patients, apart from two weeks during my time there. For he was so emotionally disturbed, especially by the death of his mother, he had the horrifying practice of biting deep into his arms - or, even worse to watch, trying to kill himself slowly by inhaling his pipe extremely deeply, which filled the smoke room with acrid smoke.

Not surprisingly, the staff kept his arms bandaged up to the elbow, and rationed his smoking severely. During his two weeks off 'one-on-one', I remember he conducted an illicit 'black market' trade with me by selling me duty free cigarettes he had been given - sneaking out into the yard for these totally forbidden sales! He could be either viciously selfish or deliciously charming from minute to minute - a tragic case who was very hard to forget...

Other patients were easier to get on with. After two weeks of my stay first Natalie and then Sharon had left the ward, for very different reasons. Nats was an athletic lass, with a lovely, coarse sense of humour, whom I helped teach Shabs how to dance, play basketball, and catch and kick a ball. Initially she was hopelessly physically uncoordinated - but soon caught on!

Nats was, apart from me at the very end, the only patient on 'maximum' unescorted two hours of leave a day, and soon went back to her original less acute ward - to be discharged almost immediately. Sharon was instead quaking with fear as she was on remand there for psychiatric reports after a charge of criminal damage - just for pulling a car wing mirror off, so she said. She was soon out after her case - on probation, I was very pleased to overhear the staff saying.

The three of them were in the yard together by themselves one day early in my stay, when they gave me a lovely surprise. When I came out for a smoke to join them, they stopped what seemed to have been a discussion about yours truly, all turned and grinned at me, and started giggling! Then Shabs, I think it was, blurted out the reason for this - that they all 'fancied me' - nearly as much as her, that seemed to mean! This was definitely the most flattering remark and response from any group of young women I have ever experienced - at the time a real boost to my ego.

At that stage Shabs and I had not yet started our two weeks of kissing and cuddling in the yard, in the only 'blind spot' in the ward free from prying eyes. Apart from the night before she left - when I was interrupted from trying my first and only 'grope' – when an alert nurse appeared who had seemingly 'intuited' this!

A month before I left I was delighted when Martin, whom I knew from Hopkin's Ward, Harlow, in 1997, was admitted. At last, somebody I already knew whom I was guaranteed to be able to have a laugh with. Although having violent, even psychopathic tendencies, he is essentially very polite and gentle, embarrassed about his problems, and does his best to control them by will-power. He had been admitted for hitting somebody, without criminal charges. He was discharged shortly after me, after a lot of laughs, but left with the severe warning from Dr. George that in accordance with the new Mental Health Act, 'should there be any more violence, he would be locked up and the key thrown away!'

Most patients, like Martin, were 'put right' in about six weeks on that Ward, so there were quite a few other patients that I don't recall as so memorable, 'passing through' while I was there. Only a few matched my stay of over three months, which was exceptional, and at the end everyone agreed, staff and patients alike, that I had to stay there too long. The reason was that as for 1999, it took a long while to get back onto haldol and lithium.

In 1999 I had insisted for 7 whole weeks on following a Professor of Psychiatry's disastrous suggestion of sulpuride. This time around, in similar fashion, I went right back past the haldol that started in 1983, that you will recall had caused disastrous lesions in my injection sites earlier in 2000. To insist on stelazine, an outdated drug I had been successfully given back in 1977!

Indeed, after four weeks on this and lithium I was judged fit enough to go back to Hopkins Ward. Had that happened in the next day or so as planned, I would indeed have gone back there on that medication. However, very much less than wisely, Dr George relied too much on that imminent availability of a bed on Hopkins, and told me that the Doctor there would renew my leave, now expired under Dr George. That was Monday 30th October. I had two more days 'unofficial' leave at the discretion of the nurses, then nothing more till that Friday 3rd November, still with no sign of a Hopkins bed coming available.

I exploded angrily at the Doctors for cancelling my leave that unfair way, swore at them, and it was decided to cancel my leave - and give me four simultaneous large injections that morning - for this swearing, it seemed! The Monday 6th November, I had a further injection, after again swearing loudly - this time when at last a heating engineer came down to fix the radiators - with the ward still freezing cold with no heating, and all the blankets used up as a result. I felt terrible after all these injections - very dopey with a very dry throat!

The punishment continued on Wednesday 8th November, when I was started on high doses of liquid droperidol with the threat of a further injection behind it! That despite complaining immediately I was told this was being done to me, that I had in the past proven totally allergic to this drug. "No you are not!" came the response from the Doctors, with no basis whatsoever. Where was the ward policy of 'no intimidation' at that stage of my stay, I am left wondering, with drugs being given orally with threats of needles behind them, especially drugs that were like poison to me?

The only good thing that happened that week was that the Doctors finally listened to the frantic signalling from Julia, still then my social worker, and my parents, that 'haldol and lithium were the only drugs that suited me!' I had a haldol depot that Thursday.

At the same time as all of this, I was experiencing massive pain in a huge cut in my right foot, a lot of which seemed to be emotional pain.

Shabs and I had our final private kiss - and failed, spied-upon interrupted grope that I mentioned before – on her last night, Thursday 10th November.

Then all those drugs, and the pain in my foot that seemed to correspond to that date being the 17th Anniversary exactly of Spiritual Experience Five back in 1983, conspired together. With the fact that I was devastated that Shabs was due to return to her original hospital in London the next day, Friday 10th November - this was an awful lot to take in one week - of 'drug hell' again!

This 'drug hell' lasted about a month in total, and without the personal emotional support I could have expected from Shabs, was at times almost too much to take. The 'honeymoon' had ended on 3rd November, and this was cemented by Shabs' departure a week later.

I was into the very heart of the darkness of the 'crucifixion experience' predicted by Image Two of Spiritual Experience Twenty.

For I soon found, by checking a leaflet freely available in a rack in the Ward, that there are about 20 known side-effects possible from psycho-active drugs. Droperidol, which you will recall I was being threatened with an injection to be forced to take the three liquid doses a day, gave me nearly all the listed ones.

I had dizziness, acute dry throat and thirst, blurred vision, tiredness, and sexual dysfunction ('impossible arousal' - with dry testicles) from day one. The first couple of days I got acute palpitations and thought I was having a heart attack!

So on and so on. After enduring about ten days of this, I started refusing odd doses when I already felt saturated with the stuff, balancing the risk of refusing too many doses with having a depot injection of clopixol aqua-phase.

Luckily the haldol depot was increasingly 'cutting in'. Also I was for a while tried on olanzapine tablets at night. These sometimes seemed to do something, other times not, so I was ambivalent about taking these nightly tablets as well.

However, the upshot was that after about four weeks of starting the dreadful droperidol, I was able to talk my way out of being given it any more - with no clopixol depot. Soon after that, on 16th December, I was judged well enough to go back to Hopkins, even though as it turned out I was to be discharged direct instead.

Drug hell over!

How Shabs, my 'temporary Pakistani girlfriend', at first provided the first of 'two handfuls of exotic tropical fruit' as in Spiritual Experience Nineteen – see the sequel to this book about the other! – and how this relationship collapsed like the crown of thorns falling off my head in Image Two of Spiritual Experience Twenty

We have come across my initial encounter with Shabs in this account, and now the way she left. My brief five-week relationship with her there, which was followed by three weeks of frequently telephoning each other while she started her stay back at her original hospital in Chingford, constituted the 'secondary crucifixion' of this 'crucifixion experience' portended by the crown of thorns in Spiritual Experience Twenty.

I now describe how it blossomed, and was finally crushed and brutally ended by her just eight weeks later. To be followed by a solicitor's letter threatening legal action when I continued to write and send her odd presents; and the final insult and injury, an informal police caution by telephone after I was so upset, I wrote two or three times more after that. When the police warned me off completely by saying that if I ever wrote to or contacted her again in any way I would immediately be put in jail on harassment charges!

Although we both recognised a strong attraction for each other, both physical and mental, we immediately discussed this, and formed a mutual pact to remain Father Figure and 'Daughter Figure'. Big age difference, the fact I was a white Christian and she a Pakistani Muslim, and her fear of her family discovering any relationship was going on, in that place of confinement, were our reasons.

However, it took me some days to persuade her to telephone her father for help there, whom she was apparently very afraid of, as a very conservative Muslim who followed the traditions of that faith very closely. Indeed, after that they called nearly every day, in numbers, and she got a lot of support - but was initially often in tears, especially at furious demands she could not find it in herself to comply with, to give up the smoking she had started at her previous hospital.

Indeed, on her paltry £13.50 a week benefit, she could scarcely afford phone calls home, let alone cigarettes! Pretty soon, as in 1995 with Diamond, and 1999 with Dobbyn, guess who came gullibly to her aid! For the five weeks of our time together, I was to supply her with most of her cigarettes as well as flowers, sweets, drinks, and gifts that I could barely afford myself. A £10 walk-man and a £40 stereo CD/radio/cassette player were the main ones. After one row, and once just feeling embarrassed to have been given them, she tried to return all these, but left the ward five weeks on, with all of them.

For the first three weeks of our friendship, we circled round each other, mostly with her receiving my much older 'moral and emotional support' and in particular pleas that she should 'calm down' and not react to provocation, like hitting Ned whenever he leered at her! She was clearly terrified at this, her first ever and very youthful stay in such an awful place, and frequently 'played up' and took all her possessions to the locked door and sat down in tears. I should say that I played a major part in helping the staff to stop her showing such histrionics.

One clear schizophrenic symptom she showed, even though she turned out to have a very similar condition to my own, was hearing loud screeching noises that nobody else could hear, which made her scream out herself. Very quickly I started holding my hand over the affected ear and doing 'laying on of hands' healing, which always worked. Pretty soon she was coming to me, not the staff, for this healing, which seemed to be effective (or was it the olanzapine and lithium she was taking, starting to take effect?) Anyway, after about the first two weeks of my being there, these noises had completely stopped…

As we saw earlier, she seemed at first very unpractised at 'things physical' - throwing and catching, dancing and singing and so on. Indeed, initially while I knew her, her 'dancing' consisted of jumping up and down on the spot with both feet. Luckily she merely laughed when I called it the 'Pakistani pogo' or a ruder abbreviation of that! Soon I had, after some effort, got her despite being ambidextrous, which seemed to cause the 'pogo', to move one foot then the other. Soon she was dancing normally and quite well. As well as shooting quite a lot of balls at basketball, and outdoing her enemy, Ned, at football...

Naturally I lent her copies of this book, as it was up to chapter 29 then, and my 'Spiritual Energy'. She said this book seemed 'clearly very sad' and said she 'knew exactly what my other book was about'. Whether she actually did or not I will never know now. In particular, she was fascinated by the fact I had added, elaborately and superfluously, all of five extra middle pen names to my basic 'Simon Lee' on my 'Spiritual Energy' as it then was.

I have since, disgusted by the way she ended up ditching our friendship, reverted to just the given three names. It turned out she had all of six given names and a nickname of 'Fatima' herself, including her Muslim surname, explaining her fascination with my own adopted pen-name of eight names in all. Indeed, her two love letters written while on the ward, both made a meal of this 'coincidence of long elaborate names' we seemed to share. It may well explain some of why she accused me of 'brainwashing her' as her reason for ending our brief eight-week friendship and later courtship...

The week before Hallowe'en cemented the 'friendship' into a 'kiss and cuddle affair'. Around then I got a nurse to go out on a shopping trip and buy two pumpkins, ready for Hallowe'en itself. The two she bought were, by chance, naturals for their intended purpose in both shape and colour. Namely, to make heads of both Ned and Bonzo, still Shabs' two principal antagonists and 'enemies'.

She laughed her head off after we sat in the kitchen and I etched caricatures of Ned and Bonzo as faces into the pumpkins. Then we added plasticine shapes, bananas in the mouths (later to be replaced by, of all things, dog biscuits!) and carried them into the lounge and placed them on the radiator. It was only days later that Bonzo smashed 'his' in the yard, in his fear of these 'black magic effigies'. Our spoof had worked - although it *was* a bit psychologically cruel!

We went about with our pet joke 'Did you hear me? I Urdu!' in deference to her native tongue (although she also spoke some Gujurati, Hindi, Hindustani, Punjabi - and French - as well) in celebration for some time after that...

341

Also before Hallowe'en, Shabs and I compounded the 'black magic' atmosphere with a lengthy series of 'werewolf and wolverine howls' in the yard! Soon we had perfected these, and they were so realistically blood-curdling I put up the following graffiti on the yard wall late one night, as well as other graffiti that most people found very amusing, in wax crayon:

'Ware wolf and Walthamstow wolverine rule OK'

I must have been very ill or just plain bored stiff then - I had never put up graffiti ever in my life!

At around that time, finally, after three rows in three days that had us both in tears, we realised that the mutual physical and mental attraction was too much to remain 'Father Figure and Daughter Figure' any longer. All through her time there, a brief five weeks that seemed a lot longer, whenever she got overwrought she would come out and hold my hand while we circled the small yard - held in my coat pocket, in the cold often wet weather. Our kisses were to be very tentative, given that she was, as far as she knew, still a virgin, and had had a handful of boyfriends yet only her very competent, sensuous kisses, no sex yet. When she half-closed her incredible - to me - red-and-green eyes to kiss, it was a real turn-on!

I say 'as far as she knew' she was still a virgin. For she hinted, during our long ill chats in the yard while we walked around talking in low voices so as not to be overheard, at a seven year history of abuse at home, school - and in her previous hospital - as long as my own history of medical abuse. For she often claimed, slightly panicking, to have been injected unconscious at the other hospital, and then found large bruises on her thighs when she awoke. Probably jumping to dramatic conclusions, she specifically blamed four particular male nurses there and one lesbian nurse for this 'alleged rape'! However it really seriously worried her, particularly when she had to go back on 10th November...

We got so involved with each other for these two weeks at the start of November of 'kissing and cuddling', that we even tried to work out how we, as Christian and Muslim, could marry and have children! We immediately even decided mutually on two boys and a girl! Meanwhile, she often kept backing down from such romantic talk, saying she was bound by tradition to end up in a pre-arranged marriage...

Highlights of this romantic two weeks were two takeaway curries that I bought for us to share. We ate these alone in the kitchen, with one nurse - Clare, both times, the Jewish student nurse - acting as supervisor and attentive 'waitress'. At the first of these her table manners were appalling! My jokes at her expense, and teasing, were so rich that four times she came round the table and pretended to knee me in the groin!

After she left on 10th November, she called about twelve hours later, and soon had her mobile phone available, so I called about twice a day, or she less often called me. Then, after her first full weekend at home on leave, on December 3rd, a Sunday, I anxiously called, as there had been no contact between us since the Thursday, after three weeks of at least one phone call a day. The phone call was dramatically short (42 seconds, said my phone bill later!) and brutal. Comments on her part were as follows, effectively: "You must never call me again! If you try, the staff here will stop you! My father will return all your stuff! You BRAINWASHED me!" The final remark was devastating, and unthinkingly, instead of trying to argue back, I was so shocked I just said feebly, 'But I really helped you!' before putting the phone down, so ending contact for ever with her, little did I know at the time...

However, although she had said I could never call her again, there seemed nothing to prevent me writing, so I sent several letters in the next three weeks, as well as an inexpensive but attractive bracelet and her favourite 'Westlife' CD. The only reponse, on 20th December, was, as I have said, a letter from her solicitor threatening legal action if I contacted her ever again. How cruel and surly after all my help to her - and our kissing sessions! Following a couple of further letters from me this year of 2001, she has called in the police to give me an informal caution - so I have given her up for good, very distressed...!

Indeed my depression for three weeks after the fateful phone call, was so great it really made me well very quickly. By December 16th I was judged by the Doctors 'fully fit and ready for discharge back to Hopkin's Ward!' For I was crying, mostly inside, in frustration, and often on my face, for all those

343

three weeks. This period of healing was no doubt helped by the fact that on 1st December, the Friday before the fateful phone call, I had realised that my haldol depot had run out early by a week, and with my parents' intervention, had eventually persuaded the Nurses of that fact. I was now given a higher dose, which was to turn out to greatly speed up my return to health!

The main problem that I had on that Ward, especially after just a week, apart from the 'drug hell' period in November that I described earlier - was sheer unremitting tedium. After a while I knew every inch of the limited walls of the ward, and had a problem of communication level with many of the other patients, many of whom said either very little - or were by contrast uncouth and swore a lot! So as ever I smoked a lot, and after my benefit went down by a factor of four (yes!) after just six weeks, and most of this time spending heavily on Shabs, as well as spending on myself, there was a battle to stay solvent and 'keep in tobacco'.

My money problems, partly caused by spending on Shabs but mostly by my own smoking levels, were greatly eased by a 'TV/telephone grant' of £250 from the ever generous IEE Benevolent Fund in November. They followed this with a £100 'Christmas Gift' that enabled all my Christmas shopping to happen at all… My parents must also have very kindly given me several hundred pounds in cigarettes, sweets and drinks and fruit in the three months as well.

A highlight of my time on that Ward was the surprise arrival of twelve copies of a poetry anthology featuring ten of my own poems, which I soon gave out to those around me, especially Shabs of course. The staff deliberately did not give me the parcel until the end of a particularly bad day when it arrived…!

I had visits from my new 'Assertive Outreach' social worker and CPN, especially frequently from my new CPN, Jess. Also Paul, the leader of my local NSF drop-in club, visited several times, and my friend Mark visited once. My ever-loyal parents called in at least once or twice a week, as well as often telephoning. My illness often had my mother in tears of frustration, but she loves me so much, they kept coming back for more antagonism!

I had leave on Christmas Day and Boxing Day, New Year's Eve and Day, and five days in the New Year. Finally, on January 10th, having waited for a bed 'upstairs' for all of four weeks, I was discharged unusually, direct from Shannon House Ward. The facts that I had a Management Appeal due on January 18th, and that my mother had formally requested my Section be lifted, really helped...

Dr George had two parting remarks to my parents an I that I could not help but disagree with, in view of the rest of this book you have already read.

Firstly, although my illness was basically an affective disorder, because of what he called 'my level of acute psychotic delusions' as observed by the staff during my time, he felt my correct diagnosis, like so many before him, was 'schizo-affective disorder'. My condition and its symptoms is best described as a 'bipolar (I) affective disorder', even taking my propensity to some delusions into account.

I still felt very drugged up and sleepy, so was very surprised when both Doctors urged me to keep taking my olanzapine as well as the now fully-restored haldol depot. Virtually my first act after discharge was to stop taking olanzapine!

CHAPTER THIRTY-ONE

Friday 9th March 2001. After discharge from the 'dual crucifixion experience' of Spiritual Experience Twenty, in Harlow Hospital yet again, I was propelled 'like a torpedo from a yellow submarine' from one form of tedium to another, the isolation and boredom of enforced isolated convalescence.

A year out of the last two spent in these places, of over two and a half years in the past seven since 1993! What have I lost thanks to Whore's totally arrogant incompetence, followed by a string of further 'prima donna Doctors' acting in deliberate ignorance of the near-total success 1983-1993 in treating my condition?

The world, especially around Harlow, England, drifted into what I will always think of as the '*real* Millennium Year, 2001' having already in my view prematurely celebrated the Millennium at the end of 1999. It was obvious straightaway on my discharge on 10th January 2001 back to my flat in Ware, that the weather was continuing to be cold, wet, often snowing soon, and due to the time of year - very dark. I had been discharged at the same mid-winter time of year as my first serious hospital episode of six weeks in 1983.

However, I only had a bleak, lonely flat to go back to this time, not as well, as in 1983, the money-earning and job satisfaction potential of a secure job. However, everybody concerned was pleasantly surprised at how well I adapted back to looking after myself, with all the cooking, washing and cleaning and so on. Three months of having nearly all those things - apart from washing clothes - taken care of on Shannon House Ward, did not prove too big an obstacle to get over!

However, for the two months since discharge I have been aware that I am engulfed in a different type of solitude, boredom and loneliness than 'on the Ward'. Sure, I have my freedom to set my own hours and schedule, and in fact pretty well all the time feel exhausted from this last ordeal of many, so sleep long hours as well as needing an afternoon nap of an hour or two on top! However, what with the solitude of the flat compared to the ever-busy ward, there is some considerable adjusting to do. One of my main preoccupations is to stop the boredom and loneliness, and hence frustration, making me smoke too much...

One thing I am able to indulge in now, which makes me feel a lot calmer, is going back to having several cups of coffee (if not six or so!) first thing in the morning. I never felt human on the Ward until I had several cups of coffee at ten o'clock! However, to contrast that, I immediately became aware of the 'thump-thump-thumpity-thumpity-thump' beat from the 'music' from the flat below. This was horrifying – to return to that!

However, luckily both Jess and Mildred from my new 'Assertive Outreach team' that I mentioned in the last chapter had immediately each started calling once a week, so Jess got onto the Environmental Health Office for me. They in turn have got in touch with the Housing Officer, and I hope for a full reduction of the intolerable racket in due course...

There were the usual problems with restoring full benefits, and claiming money for my total of a week of leave from the Ward. It took all of six weeks, and a steady stream of relatively small, itsy-bitsy giro-cheques from the two benefit offices concerned, before I finally settled down to a steady weekly income. This evening my parents have specially come over and given me some money to pay the last few dribs and drabs of bills from when I was ill, as well as lend me some £30 just to get over this difficult week, which is incredibly kind. Jess from Assertive Outreach secured me £150 of a requested £950 from the Social Security Social Fund, ostensibly to buy me a three-piece suite, amongst other furniture.

However, my father and I spent an afternoon fitting new hinges, with some difficulty, that I had come across in a furniture shop, to my existing sofa-bed. Then Jess got hold of a decent easy-chair for me, free of charge from a charity. Free of the need to spend the £150 on part of a three-piece suite, I paid off some bills with it. Bills, bills, bills, from when I was ill and before! Luckily, with help from Jess and my parents, they are now as good as under control again. Now that I have them all on monthly budget payments, the problem should be over. Till the next time in hospital, if that ever happens!

Almost inevitably, that vast problem, of the 'rotating door syndrome' I had got into over the past seven years, of frequent lengthy periods in hospital, was the main problem as far as Jess and Mildred of Assertive Outreach were concerned.

Jess told me that I should definitely not try to do any paid work for 'six months to a year' after discharge from Harlow, at our very first meeting. 'Our top priority is keeping you out of the ordeal of hospital for a long while yet' he said. Pretty well he had settled down to two main objectives. Recognising my academic achievement level, he fully appreciated that I needed to get out of my own flat a lot more than last year, and encouraged me to investigate as many social activities, and voluntary work, as possible. Secondly, it had finally dawned on 'the system' that the only medication that had ever helped me rather than hinder me was haloperidol (haldol) and lithium. So he got me straightaway to draft out an 'Advance Directive' or unofficial 'living will' made while I was well, as now, as to my treatment should I ever get unwell again! I have no compunction in reproducing it overleaf: -

ADVANCE DIRECTIVE by Simon Lee

I suffer from a form of mental illness, ambiguously diagnosed in the past as either a bipolar (I) affective disorder, or more commonly by more psychiatrists, as a schizo-affective disorder.

Should I become unwell and unable to make informed choices, I should very much like the following issues to be taken into consideration by those involved in my care: -

1. Since 1993 to the present day I have had treatment with haldol depots and lithium carbonate (priadel) tablets withdrawn by various Doctors for spurious reasons, on four separate occasions. Each time I relapsed rapidly requiring me to be placed on a section of the Mental Health Act. Withdrawal of haldol and lithium treatment by Dr Whore of the Queen Elizabeth II Hospital, Welwyn Garden City, Hertfordshire, between all of October 1993 and August 1995, led directly to my divorce, loss of my home, and nearly all contact with my daughter.

2. The following drugs have all been tried in the intervening period, and I have had a very adverse reaction to all of them ('every "side" effect going'!). As such I never again wish to have these drugs administered: -

- Clozapine ('clozaril')
- Chlorpromazine
- Modecate
- Droperidol
- Thiarodazine ('melleril')

3. The following have also been used on me, with the result only being a further relapse. As for (2) above, I never wish to have these drugs administered again:

- Risperidone
- Sulpuride
- Clopixol
- Depixol

4. If I do ever relapse again, as far as possible I should like to be treated at home with haldol and lithium, possibly with the use of haloperidol 5mg or olanzapine 10mg orally as intervention drugs.

5. Should my behaviour or state of mind ever be such that I have to go into hospital, I should like to be presented with

349

this document in order that it should serve as a reminder of my wishes when well. This then may negate the need for a formal admission, giving me the opportunity to go to hospital (if necessary) as an informal patient.

The four times I was taken off haldol were: -
1. in 1993, by Whore, the worst and most arrogant culprit
2. in 1997, by the nearly as arrogant Harlot
3. in 1999, after Thatcher refused totally to 'up my dose' and so avoid my relapse
4. in 2000, by Dr Ballitch, who very unwisely changed me to clopixol after problems with my haldol depot had surfaced!

It turned out that a forte of the Assertive Outreach Team's approach was getting social life going. In both January and February they gave me a lift to the ten-pin bowling centre at nearby Bishop's Stortford. The ten of us, staff and 'clients' mixed together, played one game the first time, in two teams of five. I came fourth out of ten. However the second time, in February, we played two games this time. I amazed myself by coming a close second in the scoring in the first game, which again our team narrowly won. Then in the second game, my concentration was to go completely, and this was to last several days in fact. I came a miserable last - still with more recovery from hospital obviously to come!

I also made inquiries at Ware's indoor swimming pool, about public swimming times, and about six weeks ago, one evening, my CPN Jess and I went swimming. He plays and trains at rugby, so seemed to expect to be far fitter and stronger a swimmer than me. When I lapped him, and finished the target we had set of twenty lengths, two lengths ahead of him, he was genuinely amazed and complimentary! "You have a real talent for this - especially given all your time in Shannon House smoking room! I thought you would be totally unfit!" he said.

The most frequent mainstays of my social life, however, remained the local NSF drop-in, and Contact with my daughter Jenny, along with my immediate family. I have recently been invited to lead an extensive quality control exercise at the drop-in, essential to secure funding from social services by proving that the club is actually doing everything it claims to do in its plans - as 'quality control officer'. Since making friends with Chris there more this year, a 25 year-old Sri Lankan athletic type, who also smokes, I have played a lot more pool and table-tennis there, with him and others. I am starting to enjoy it a lot more as a result...

Apart from one occasion when Helen and her partner brought Jenny and his daughter, Fiona, to see me in hospital, the only times I had seen her in those months were my two leaves at Christmas (on Boxing Day) and New Year. Now, I was delighted when Helen agreed to fortnightly Contact resuming immediately on discharge, back at my parents' house. In addition, on Jenny's and Libby's joint 10th and 40th birthdays, on Thursday 22nd February just passed, my parents treated all of us, as well as Jem and Jane and their three kids, to a day out at Hampton Court Palace in London.   Highlights were the maze and the jester! This was followed by a genuine Spanish meal in Richmond, five miles away. A great time was had by all, and we are seeing Jenny again tomorrow (Sunday 11th March).

One of the first weeks out of hospital, having got my then still rickety finances starting to come into some kind of order following innumerable calls and visits to my local benefits office, I was at last in a fairly secure financial position.

Sufficient to afford to get some more social life, by signing up for classes at the local College in Ware. However, my old mainstay the previous whole year, the Creative Writing Class, had been cancelled for lack of interest. I was judged unsuitable to join the GCSE French class as term had already started.

However, I did manage to join the drawing and painting class starting the second lesson of the Easter term, the following Monday. I have since been to three classes and missed two. I have had a lot of laughs with two ladies in their fifties, that I sit next to, and last Monday drew two pictures, both of which attracted the comment from the professional tutor, that 'you have real talent there - which you should encourage by practising!'

As we said earlier and come to again in due course, I have needed an awful lot of sleep since my discharge. At seven o'clock on the evenings of the two classes that I missed, I simply fell asleep for the night!

As well as all these attempts at least at starting some social life in my new enforced hometown of Ware - there was always the local pub. I was on friendly terms with a bloke and his two female thirty-something friends there, who were always game for a laugh whenever they were in for a drink at the same time. Chris, my friend from the drop-in, also had this as his 'local' so I often saw him too in here, to share a round with.

Meanwhile I had not given up hope, while in hospital, of submitting 'Omega' to Cambridge for a PhD. The only obstacle to this turned out to be, on closely reading the 'Special Regulations' from Cambridge while in hospital, the £385 examination fee, which was totally beyond me, then and now. The book *had* been (electronically) published - and electronic publishing counted in the Regulations! - in 2000, by Authors Online. All the other requirements were met. I thought of whom I could ask to give me £385, on Shannon House Ward.

My father's response was very disappointing, a real put-down in fact: "I wouldn't want to throw good money down the drain like that!" I remember being very hurt by that acid remark, and have not involved him in my further, eventually successful efforts to secure this £385 - from, as ever, the ever helpful IEE Benevolent Fund! They immediately replied to my approach from hospital, saying effectively 'Yes! - once you have been discharged from hospital and stabilised for a while!'

Indeed Julian, who had had an operation for a long-term problem with his knees, himself, visited me at home in late January - and was duly impressed with the quality and volume of hard work that I had evidently put into 'Spiritual Energy'. As we see shortly, their cheque payable to Cambridge University arrived a few weeks later, to my utter delight and eternal gratitude!

I had just, never one to give up, instead to keep plugging away, just 'mail-shot' a select nine publishers of the massive 140 or so I had contacted over the previous eighteen months back in 1999-2000, as we saw earlier exhaustively (and exhaustingly to me - very frustrating!) This 'mail shot' had focussed, a little prematurely, on the fact that my 'Omega' book was now a Cambridge PhD thesis. Now that was in the bag - and fact - not a 99% confident prediction!

I have heard back from four of these nine since early February, when I sent this mail-shot. All three 'Church'- based or Christian publishers I wrote to, either wrote or e-mailed back saying 'No!' A further publisher, Element, who featured earlier, replied (or rather, their liquidator replied) saying they had ceased trading and gone into receivership.

The only new publisher I had written to was Jonathon Cape ltd., as I had read a review of one of their books, rather damning of the book, but at least it was about trying to marry up science and faith. So, they might conceivably be interested in my own 'Omega Course'? I hold out only limited hope for a positive reply, or indeed any reply at all, from them or the other four publishers yet to reply. My main hope for a 'route to being in print' remains after any, presumed successful, granting of a PhD to me by Cambridge University...

All these efforts at social life, the mail-shot and perhaps, above all, my PhD application, may sound easy, but were overshadowed by a real trauma of tears, grief, and frustration - often amounting to complete physical weakness. For the 'crown of thorns of my crucifixion experience in Shannon House crumbling' after her initial glorious 'exotic, tropical promise', with the brutal ending by her of my brief 'kiss and cuddle friendship' with Shabs had brought back vicious memories.

Of loss of relationships with other women - or worse, in the case of my neighbour in Hertford in 1999, leading to eviction! I ended up going over all these in my mind - leading to feelings of being reminded of great traumatic loss, blaming myself unfairly, and above all the pain involved.

An in-depth session with my CPN, Jess, helped reassure me that, apart perhaps from the incident of being drunkenly a bit misplacedly sexually forward with Mary last year in the middle of the night on her answer-phone, I was completely blameless in fact.

Finally, two weeks after that, this last week, ending this Saturday 10th March, two months exactly since discharge, has helped 'put behind me' – as writing about it always does – any misplaced feelings of guilt and grief. As well of course as putting down on paper, and so also behind me, a lot of other memories of my latest awful experiences in hospital.

We have already adequately covered in this book, my feelings of betrayal into the hands of a fellow medic, as she saw him, whom I only found to be a devious crook, in the form of 'Doctor' Whore, by my ex-wife. This betrayal now surfaced in my memory again.

The way in which Shabs had abruptly cut me off, I now rationalised with the help of Jess, was just as hurtful and confusing as that of Diamond two years earlier. Because I was genuinely in love with both women, and had just been greatly helping them, so the horror of a psychotic and irrational 'throwing the baby (me!) out with the bathwater' had been a result of them trying to shed a large and painful piece of their memories.

Diamond 'shed' me from her life as part of the last three years of thirty years of being an alcoholic, which she has since, by all accounts, magnificently managed to end - and so stay sane.

Likewise Shabs had been terrified to the hilt, of an arduous, long, first stay in hospital, and no doubt inspired by rebukes about any relationship, while on her first leave at home in months. So she had come up with the ludicrous excuse to dump me out of her life very brutally that 'I had BRAINWASHED her!' Aaarrgh!

I could instantly dismiss as irrelevant to these feelings, of the ludicrous and histrionic attacks, and in the latter case a totally psychotic set-up organised by Welwyn Ward staff, of my neighbour in Hertford, and of Dobbyn on Welwyn Ward in 1999. How a Valentine Card, little more, nearly got me arrested is beyond me still! Also how it was enough to make the woman neighbour concerned get so paranoid as to get me evicted, over *those* slushy sentiments!

So, ironically, I was left feeling that the only one of these women who were in any way justified in involving the police and/or a solicitor, was the only one who, to her great credit, had shown some common-sense, Mary. Despite having almost certainly the most semi-valid case for either, she had simply remained silent, obviously hurt quite a lot, yet involved neither legal recourse to attack me.

Apart from her I had suffered losing contact with, since 1995 a surfeit of instead histrionic, and in three cases, Diamond, Dobbyn and Shabs, clearly psychotic women. Plus my ex- is plain for all to see, revealed as a mad cow!

Two things occurred very dramatically to end all this grieving, before this writing it all down has since served to crystallise and finally end all these emotions.

First, the grief was so much that I ignored the letter from Shabs' solicitor from 20th December and sent her, in fact, two letters and a note inside a Valentine's card, the latter two weeks before Valentine's Day itself. The last of these provoked a furious response - she reported me for 'harassment' to Chingford Police! On 6th February, they rang up, and in a severe lecture warned that if I ever contacted her in any way at all, I would immediately be arrested and charged with harassment! Clearly, I had no choice but to back off completely now, resign myself to never ever hearing from her again - and indeed have had no further thoughts of writing to or - suicidal! - phoning her.

I had seen Julian from the IEE on 29th January, got the 'go ahead' for my vital £385 cheque, and been told to wait 'two or three weeks' for it to arrive. In eager anticipation of this event, I now put together a parcel, left ready unsealed for the cheque, with the completed surprisingly brief forms. Basically stating I was a Cambridge graduate, what the work(s) were and that they had been both published and not submitted for a higher degree anywhere else. I typed out two copies of a four-page 2000 word summary, as required, and added in two copies, as stipulated, of the vital 'Spiritual Energy' book itself. Then I waited...

On Tuesday 13th February, quite early in the process I had been led to expect by Julian, you can imagine my excitement when the vital cheque duly arrived in the post! I immediately went down with it securely placed in my parcel, to the local Post Office in Ware High Street, where they were used to seeing me appear with heavy parcels, after all my activities of the previous year! I sent the parcel expensively by 'Special Delivery' normally securing next day arrival, which was also guaranteed to get there by the Post Office...

I waited outside an adjacent optician after posting it, and reflected that I had got through the last six months, three of them in hospital, with only my prescription sunglasses. I had lost both my clear pairs while on 'jaunts' in town whilst ill in Summer 2000, leading up to the hospital trauma. As an eye-test and glasses (one pair, anyway) would be virtually free to me as I drew Income Support, I went in to book a test, fully expecting an eye-test in a week or so. It turned out they had

had a cancellation for 3.45 pm on Valentine's Day, the very next day!

As ever in the past few years, the post held no Valentine's cards for me the next day. Mind you, apart from a regular card from Helen while married, I had had no cards for many years.

On the Thursday afternoon, 15th February 2001, I thought to ring Cambridge to ensure my vital parcel with my thesis had indeed arrived safely. It had, and so I asked which of the faculties it had been forwarded to. I had thought Natural Sciences *and* Divinity might be involved, and said so in my covering letter. "Oh, Doctor Friday, the Secretary of the Board of Graduate Studies, immediately sent the package onto the Faculty of Divinity, after one look at your books."

CHAPTER THIRTY-TWO

8^{tth} August 2001. The last six months have involved Three Terribly Trying Tales, paralleled and greatly countered, by Seven Success Stories. "Good News" last!

1. Terribly Trying Tale One. I fail to get a PhD for 'Spiritual Energy' (formerly 'the Omega Course') from Cambridge Divinity then Philosophy Faculties. Attempts to find another PhD scheme like it, fail to succeed despite e-mailing virtually every Psychology and Philosophy Faculty in the country. I give up the quest for such recognition and possible aid to a new career - in dismay!

After waiting all of four months for a reply from the Divinity School at Cambridge to my application for a 'PhD under the Special Regulations', when it arrived it very tersely, in two lines, dismissed my application, with no reason given at all. I immediately did two things. I faxed Cambridge Board of Graduate Studies asking that the book now go to the Philosophy Faculty in turn, which within two weeks they had, seemingly reluctantly, agreed to. I also e-mailed every Psychology Faculty in the country, having got their addresses from a Graduates' Handbook in the local library. Within a month, Cambridge Philosophy Faculty also tersely turned me down, and so about then I nearly gave up all attempts to get a PhD for my work.

Then, two weeks later, I got an e-mail from the Psychology Department at the little-respected Luton University, one of the new Universities converted from a Technical College. Although this turned me down too, it left open the glimmer of a hope that if I badgered them enough, they did have a scheme open to non-alumni, unlike most Universities offering such a PhD by Examination of Published Work. So I badgered them for about a month - only to be completely turned down and my 'Spiritual Energy' - re-titled from 'the Omega Course' back in July – returned. I did try vainly for a while - by e-mail - to find a suitable British Philosophy Faculty offering such a PhD to people who are not graduates of that University nor members of staff. I am left concluding that British Universities are a 'closed shop' as far as PhD degrees for Published Work are concerned.

Stuff that for a lark!

2. Terribly Trying Tale Two. Recovering from hospital is hard enough, without the frustration of Jenny and myself being denied most Contact by a Vet ex-wife who is clearly Mad About Money - and not emotional concerns!

This last six months has been successful, as we see overleaf in my Seven Success Stories, but boring and frustrating a lot of that time as well! In particular, my damned selfish, lying ex- has been too concerned with 'Money Matters' to worry about Jenny and I seeing each other, so Contact has been fraught with difficulties!

At the start of the year, it turned out later, my ex- entered into a 'Professional' Partnership with her boss at her Vets' practice - whom she promptly threatened to sue for milking the Practice Accounts of tens of thousands of pounds! The upshot was he settled out of court. She got not only two of the three Practices in the Partnership, but the Practice's NAME. Not content with that, she got her new *sexual* partner, mid-fifties and a builder, to renovate a building, as a rival Practice, opposite her *Vet* ex-partner's only remaining Practice! Sheer vicious spite! Typical of the Tart of Tarts!

She has been so involved with all these dubious financial 'doings' this year, that Jenny's and my needs for Contact with each other have totally fallen by the wayside. I scarcely see her every three weeks rather than the former fully-established two weeks! I finally conceded at a 'Care Programme Approach' (CPA) meeting with my entire medical support team on 1st August, that I now needed, after six years of dismissive abuse, to take my ex- to Court to secure decent Contact! This is now about to start happening...

To compound all this, at the start of this year, for all of three months, there were endless rumours from Jenny that her mother was vacillating about important aspects of Jenny's future at school next year. *With absolutely no reference to or discussion with me as Jenny's Father!* For some time it looked like my ex- was planning to send Jenny to a local 'middle school' a year before her primary school education ended, next year in fact. We as a family, myself in particular, were very relieved when these rumours ended with 'Madam' deciding Jenny should stay at her Primary School next year. This has the advantage she will be taught by her favourite (male) teacher!

3. *Terribly Trying Tale Three. I countenance, for several months, the awful prospect of taking the various Doctors who have 'done my life in' over the past few years, to Court to get damages. Awful, because it is very complex and lengthy a history, as you have seen, and a lot of mud would fly - most of it at me! As I write I'm preparing to write to my new Litigation Solicitor, backing out of this...*

Back around May, my Mother read in the 'Times' newspaper an article about a legal firm in Newcastle that had outraged the Government by vehemently pursuing cases of litigation against Doctors and their NHS Trusts, where there had been Clinical Negligence. She got their address from the article, and first she then I spoke to a solicitor there who was very keen to take on my case. There has been a flurry of mail since, without us actually getting to meet this man. However, just some of the many problems with my litigating are as follows: -

1. I may be well, but have been advised not to work for months or years, and then only part-time, by my medical support team. I am then in a very common 'benefit trap', as I have to find a job, part-time at that, that is not stressful, yet nets me more salary than my substantial benefits - as 'self-declared disabled'. Any Court Case could last three or four years, my solicitor says, if as expected the various defendants actually defend in Court, which would only add to this 'benefit trap'. I could only work in that time if, very unlikely indeed, I got enough money to fund the case, in place of the Public Funding, formerly called 'legal aid', that I would get if I remained on benefit. The abuse I have suffered over all of eight years means that I will need to undertake a lot of re-training if I decide

to return to Information Technology as a career. Choosing any different new career will mean even more training, for obvious reasons, and losing benefit if I choose a medical career of some sort, as strongly suggested last week by the Careers Guidance Service at my local secondary college. This 'benefits trap' is indeed formidable!

2. There is a legal 'Limitation Period' of three years in which to litigate after alleged Clinical Negligence, and it was in 1993-1997 that the worst 'Abuse by Doctors' happened in my case - 4-8 years ago! Our only counter to this would be to argue a fairly tenuous case that I only had it confirmed in writing that I actually suffer from 'bipolar (I) affective disorder' this May, overturning all that 'schizo' and 'schizo-affective' nonsense from all those years ago.

3. The East Hertfordshire NHS Trust and the Essex and Hertfordshire NHS Trust have recently merged into the new 'Hertfordshire Partnership NHS Trust' which obviously I come under. Whether I choose to direct my litigation against either of the two QEII or Harlow Hospitals, the 2001% political nature of Psychiatric ""Medicine"" means I would end up medically compromised and almost certainly victimised if I took my own Trust to Court.

I have therefore reluctantly decided that the legal and above political impediments are overwhelming, and will be dropping this case shortly. Once I finish this chapter I am sending a letter to that effect, with the above reasons, to my lawyer...

361

SEVEN SUCCESS STORIES

1. Success Story One. My health, back on the right drugs, just goes on improving... The entire new team is unanimous for the first time ever, that I suffer from a 'bipolar (I) affective disorder', as I've maintained for over twenty-two years, with unbelievable opposition from the Psychiatric 'profession'...!

Since writing, signing and presenting to them, the Advance Directive reproduced in the last chapter, my medical team, Doctor, Community Psychiatric Nurse, and Social Worker, have been united in backing it, unlike last year, 2000. Last year all the problems were due to Dr Ballitch clinging ferociously to the old lie that I was in some unfathomable way, "schizophrenic" as well as having a bipolar disorder. He therefore stuck to the old lie that I had a 'schizo-affective disorder', and foolishly changed my depot to clopixol from haloperidol, even though the former has not the same euphoria-dampening effect as my usual latter depot, single-handedly overruling Viv my amazing CPN then, and Julia my social worker.

Everybody involved says I am now doing very well indeed as a result - dramatically, and extremely welcome news indeed, with little or no prospect of ever needing to re-enter the gates of one of those damned mental hospitals ever again! The fact that the diagnosis is now for the first time ever, a unanimous 'bipolar (I) affective disorder' guarantees the continuing correct treatment, and was the very prompt for temporary thoughts of litigation as in the last paragraph!

My dose of haloperidol depot ('haldol' for short) has just been lowered at my request, and I no longer sleep 12-14 hours a day as a result. Furthermore, it is now *precisely* at the level Dr Gander gave me, but now all in depot not mostly tablet form, between 1983-1993, my last 'Great Successful Period' - when as you will recall, I held down good well-paid jobs, married, and had a four-bedroom house and a big car. Never again should I 'lose the lot' due to 'dumb Psychiatrists' as I did shortly after that 'honeymoon period' with haldol, now I am back on it!

It turns out that this new 'Assertive Outreach Team' specialises in 'difficult cases' with, in my case, all the 'difficulties' nevertheless being nervous breakdowns actually caused by the medical 'profession'! I eventually find four hours a week with three members of the team too much like four hours of questioning and 'interrogation by the S.S.S. (Psychiatric Social Services)' and tell the Social Worker so quite bluntly! As a result I have only yesterday seen her for the first time in two months, for a pleasant yet fairly interrogatory coffee at the local garden centre...

The Team also organise monthly 'Outings' for us 'clients', usually to go ten-pin bowling. On a riverboat trip up the River Lee locally recently, the sight of eight or nine rough-looking blokes, smoking against a wall and not talking because they don't know each other from Adam, at the picnic at lunchtime, has put me right off such 'Outings with fellow loonies'. So I have cancelled my place for the trip to the coastal resort of Morden in Essex tomorrow...

2. Success Story Two. Despite her Mother's Money Madness – apparently to the exclusion of all other considerations, especially the feelings of others – like me! – JENNY is doing really well at school, at work, social life and now sport. I was never much good at the latter at either junior or secondary school, so this delights me very much, in particular!

We saw the problems with my ex- in Terribly Trying Tale Two. Despite all that, Jenny's school report for this year, with 'good' for maths and science, and simply a glowing 'excellent' for the other four subjects, earned her a £10 note from me. She was 'talent-spotted' playing netball in the schoolyard by the sports teacher earlier in the year, and soon earned a place in the school netball team as goal shooter or 'centre forward' in soccer terms with which I am more familiar. We all – of course, not her mother - turned up to watch her score all of eleven goals as her team came fourth of ten teams in a tournament on 18th March. On 20th June we watched her valiantly just fail to retrieve her team from finishing last in a 'sports relay' at the local pool, where the first swimmer came in first of four but dropped the bucket of balls they were handicapped to carry while swimming...

Other extra-curricular outings when we had occasional Contact were to the snowdrop gardens at nearby Hatfield House on February 18th, and Hampton Court Palace with my brother's entire family and ours on Thursday February 22nd for her joint birthday with her Aunt Libby (Jenny's 10th). On 8th April we took her to a free 'classical science fiction' concert at Hatfield's shopping centre, 'the Galleria'. She particularly liked the 'Star Wars' theme! Last month we visited a genuine French market in Ware one Saturday, where I bought her a purse and some cheese she liked, then spent the Sunday with my brother's family. For the second year running, she enjoyed singing and dancing in the chorus line in the school play, this time 'Chitty Chitty Bang Bang'. I was too depressed at the prospect of revisiting Dane End to go, but my immediate family went, and thoroughly enjoyed it...

The highlight of the school year for both Jenny and I had to be her sports day. Her team came second this time, a lot thanks to her, as opposed to her first in the previous year's team event. She also came second and third respectively in her two individual races, one with bean-bag, one involving picking up disks, putting them on a pole, then sprinting to the finish. At first I was reluctant to enter the Dad's race, despite her pleas, until I saw it was an obstacle race like hers with four disks, not a sprint like the one two years previously, where I had come in last.

We were both delighted, Jenny in particular, when I led this race up to the sprint, only to be overtaken and so come in second. My parents commented, "Well done indeed! You just made Jenny's day complete!" The winner was a lot shorter than my 6' 1½", so much better at sprinting. It was obvious that day that Jenny is also very popular with her peers. All in all, despite her mother, she is turning out to be a delightful young lady!

3. *Success Story Three. My social life starts off better than last year, and gets better (see 4. below as well). Also, unexpectedly, a written offer to Diamond, as a passing thought, to typeset her book like I have done mine, results in a typically melodramatic overnight stay here - without us*

touching, sharing the same bed - the following night. This trip results in me resuming, after a two and a half year break in communications, in supporting her through several onsets of her paranoia....

My social life, as we saw in the previous chapter or so, had been diabolical, but this year has taken a definite turn for the better, as we see in this Story and Success Story Four below. Most of it has inevitably centred round my trips most Mondays and Wednesdays in the afternoon, and Sunday afternoons if I am not busy with Jenny, to the local 'drop-in club' run by the National Schizophrenia Fellowship 'only for members who have had acute mental health problems'.

Old female acquaintances, from Harlow hospital back in 1997, both in need of losing some weight, keep me amused down there – 'Tweezers', my nickname for Teresa, now over her father's death last year so much more frequent a visitor to the 'Connect 3' club - and the jovial Irish 'Joannie baby'! Chris is a 25- year-old Sri Lankan bloke, whom I have frequently entertained here rather than the club, when it is particularly boring (according to us). He is a frequent partner in drinking and smoking in the local pubs, and has recently got a flat so I sometimes go there, even though it is still yet to be more fully furnished... He can be very off-hand, and has been with me since an initial jolly greeting when he came round, after his return from a six-week trip to Sri Lanka on Sunday. Perhaps it is because I asked him to repair the broken leg and missing tusk of his present to me before giving it to me, a bull elephant carved out of a king coconut!

The social highlight (and often deep low-light!) of the year, as well as meeting my new friend Martha as in the next Success Story below, was totally unexpected. It was the typically melodramatic re-entry into my life, on a rather tentative and often volatile basis, after two and a half years in 'outer space', of the ever-effervescent Diamond! The prompt for this was that I wrote a note to her, as I had occasionally been wont to do since not seeing her since 1998, on the Equinox, Thursday 21st March. This note made the very generous offer of typesetting her 'book', after scanning the text and numerous pictures I remembered from the previous time this happened in 1998, into my computer - at cost of ink and paper with no labour charge for my time and effort. I expected as ever, no response at all. Imagine my astonishment to have a telephone call from Diamond at eight the following evening, clearly ill, for some of her remarks were very bizarre indeed: -

"Your note was very timely! My life is seriously under threat in this town and I have to get out! Can I come and discuss your offer right now - and stay with you tonight? Don't worry about the fact that you only have one room and one bed - I'll take care of that!"

"I haven't worn any underwear for six weeks now!"

"I haven't had a drink for two whole years and spent all that time in my armchair in my lounge apart from going to the supermarket! I'm reformed as a result - you can trust me now!"

"No, I cannot possibly catch a bus over! Don't you understand, my life is seriously in danger from certain people in this town - I dare not walk anywhere, especially now it is dark! You'll just have to call me a taxi - I'll pay, luckily I've got £35! I'll just bring night-clothes and probably catch the bus back in the morning!"

I duly arranged a cab, telling her they had told me it would cost around £15 for the ten-mile or so trip over from Welwyn Garden City to Ware. She duly arrived in jumper, trousers and shoes (and it turned out with absolutely nothing else underneath!) at quarter to ten. It was as if the intervening 'wilderness' of two and a half years not on speaking terms had never happened, both saying that the other had hardly changed. While she was clearly quite ill and paranoid, so any thought at all of her being there for sexual reasons was unthinkable, she sat in my armchair and I sat on the bed, as if nothing had ever come between us in the previous few years. Mostly she talked about the charges of sexual abuse against her - unthinkably, I know her too well for them to be true... - concerning her granddaughter Isobel, whom she only sees for under an hour every Friday, now she has been taken into care. Just like Isobel's mother Rebecca before her...!

After an hour sipping tea, and discussing also her joy at kicking her predominant problem, alcohol, for two years now (she really believes), and her repeated attempts since to quit smoking as well, she suddenly announced it was bed-time. To

366

my alarm and chagrin, she stripped off her jumper to reveal that indeed, she was wearing no underwear! A much plumper torso and even plumper boobs than I remembered from 1998 emerged - then she displayed more modesty and decorum, by slipping on some elaborate and sexy black night clothes before embarrassing me in any way by removing her trousers without first doing so! She was ill, so untouchable, yet still apparently flirting with 'stranger' me!

It turned out her way of 'sorting out' the sleeping arrangements in my tiny studio flat - was for us to share my bed without touching! She kept me awake till four with her snoring, but I must have caught three hours deep sleep in the end. For when she woke me up at seven with a request for a cup of tea, much, much earlier than I am used to these days, 1 did not feel at all tired. It was raining, and she had brought only night-clothes and toothbrush in her bag, without thinking, in her distracted state, of coat, or umbrella - and certainly not underwear - so was in no way prepared to catch the bus. She spent the rest of her £35 getting home by taxi (bus fares for the two days would have cost just £2.40!) then got Muggins here to post her a postal order for £20. This took six weeks to recover from her in £5 instalments by post, after the aftermath to this weird overnight adventure...

For the following evening I got a very angry Diamond on the phone, obviously getting very paranoid indeed now, for she wildly accused me of "drugging and raping her while she was asleep"!!! There was a break in communications following several heated phone calls from and to me that followed, until she sheepishly rang up out of the blue the next week and apologised - her period had started so it was all in the realms of typical Diamond allegations!

Then in the very early morning indeed of Wednesday 28th March, at 5.33am, I was rudely awakened by the phone - with yet another 'Diamond distress delivery'! She positively assured me she had been up all night, terrified for her life, and blurted, 'You are the only person who I can trust to come and look after me in case my house is attacked!'. Warily, I agreed to catch the first available bus (as early as 6.l0am!) over to her house, and arrived there, surprisingly wide awake as I had gone to bed early the previous night, just after seven - at dawn!

I stayed just three hours, and spent £5 on breakfast for both of us, in the process bumping into her daughter, giggly and totally irresponsible as ever! Then came a second blow from Diamond in a week, when she disowned me on the telephone. She rang up a week later, starting a series of 'hot and cold, on and off' discussions about her book, with apparently all forgiven. It was not until after endless prevarication on her part, that she invited me around and handed over, in two instalments, the first part or 'year' of her autobiographical book, 1991.

It took me nearly a week to transform her badly typed, poorly spelt, grammatically error-prone first thirty pages. Lessons learned from that meant it only took just five hours to bring the total up by 40 more pages to 70 sides of writing and monochrome illustrations. Then a few weeks ago, having handed the work over to her weeks earlier, she rang up several times out of the blue, often late at night, and dramatically made yet more wild allegations: -

"You have stolen my 1992 work, I can't find it anywhere in the house! You stole it when you came to collect the stuff for 1991! You will swing for this!"

"You have been in my house and shuffled everything you gave me and put it in different cupboards! I can't find anything in it now!"

At the weekend of that same week, she rang to sort of lamely apologise, saying she had found everything, having at the start of that week bought a cheap and nasty bottle of *vodka*, despite supposedly now being a 'reformed character' concerning alcohol. That on top of her paranoia, and 'hearing voices' due to schizophrenia recently, was hard to take!

My new CPN, Jess, on hearing this sorry saga, said she was clearly a character to avoid at all costs and otherwise it would definitely 'all end in tears for you, Simon'! I just hope he is wrong. So far it has been damned hard work, and especially recently, she keeps putting off coming over to continue working with me here on her book. Not exactly a sound basis for a relationship, with me doing all the giving, but there you go. My satisfaction with it comes from the 'noble' thought, "I've just got to do my best to help others less fortunate than myself...'

Even though she is having an affair, despite being in the 'midst of the menopause', she says, with a man who is married with four kids, who seems just to appear for sex, without looking after Diamond...!

Diamond has an excuse for every piece of bad behaviour she exhibits. I mentioned that she drank a bottle of cheap vodka before one such episode above. She unashamedly tried to blame other episodes described here on giving up smoking and so feeling 'ratty'. I really feel a lot of it is due to non-admitted illness!

4. *Success Story Four. After a few years, once more, I try to make yet more friends - by advertising for blind dates in the local newspaper! - and meet the even more 'spiritual' yet moody like me, Martha.*

I was bored and frustrated one day in April this year, when 1 picked up the phone and recorded an advertisement - about myself! - once more in the local newspaper. I got about ten responses, met four, and the first I met was the only one who 'stayed the course with me as a friend' - the equally stress-prone Martha, who turned out to have a seven year old son. Her response on the recording machine to my advertisement said 'You sound fascinating. I am 43, single, and attractive - very attractive'. She arrived here at 11am on Monday 14th May, having scorned the safer option of meeting up in a pub or café first. It was all true - she is very attractive - but rather overweight for it looked like she was literally bursting out of her blouse, size 10 waistcoat (!) and jeans, which caused us both many ensuing laughs, over the next few days of intense phone calls!

We spent an hour here then I bought us both a drink and scampi and chips at a local pub. She took away a copy of this book and my 'Spiritual Energy' (then still called 'Spiritual Energy'), to read, saying they sounded fascinating! We were on the phone every day for months after that, firm friends...

Footnote. 'Success Story Four' turns to failure. Friday 10th August 2001. I have had to replace the original material here *as Martha has terminated what was just a friendship, for very valid reasons, nothing to do with me!*

After failing to contact Martha for several days this week, and assuming she was still depressed since finishing some exams, I finally left a message on her mobile this afternoon, mentioning the original description I had written of her here instead of this footnote. Within five minutes, she rang back, very angry indeed at being included, and virtually ending the friendship on the spot, saying quite rightly it had 'never been a relationship, Simon'!

I rang back and said I had not used her or her son's real names, but she still prickled. Then the real reason for the 'end' emerged. Mostly for their son's sake, she and her former partner are in the throes of reuniting.

Spiritual Experience Twenty-One. August 2001 - SHARED with my daughter Jenny. A SPHINX, or lion with the head of a woman, 5 miles south of Ware in a cloud, with its tail pointing toward Waltham Abbey and its head toward Oxford...

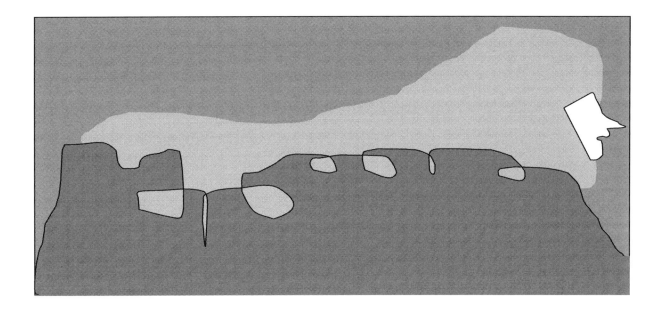

Jenny, as I said, was the first to spot this apparition. We had just finished playing in the Park opposite my bed-sit flat. "Look, Daddy, over those trees, there is a huge cloud in the shape of a lion!" There, 15 miles away, was Spiritual Experience Twenty-One - which I was astonished to be sharing with my daughter! - as above, trees in front. It was only many months on from August, in May, that Martha came along to fit the Spiritual Experience! Only more recently, that that fact dawned on me, as well as the close resemblance in its prediction - about a woman - to Spiritual Experience Eleven!

5. Success Story Five. All Hail the Incorporated Benevolent Fund of the Institution of Electrical Engineers (IEE)! I continue to be amazed at their generosity and support! Thank God that I thought to keep up my membership for all the requisite five years, in the days I couldn't afford to!

The IEE Benevolent Fund continues to be a second major benefactor after the government, with the big difference that they have only ever helped me, and are not paying for the crass incompetence of the government's own ""Doctors""... Since February they have done all the following for me: -

- Continued to pay my £20 a week 'pension', and what is more pledged to continue it until at least this time next year
- Paid off my £100 overdraft and a £34 electricity bill
- To my absolute delight, for it was a noose round my neck, written off my only debt of all, to them, of £850, dating back to hospital 'bad times' in 1999!
- Provided not just one but two holidays this year. One tranche, of £500, paid for all my spending money, and a lot of necessary preparations like replacing my trainers, for my week-long holiday in an expensive 'respite centre' for people like me damaged by mental health problems. The actual accommodation was paid for in full by Social Services, as I am still on a Mental Health Act 'Section 17' (after-care after a long stay - or stays - in hospital). The second tranche was even bigger, at £600, and will fund a 'singles holiday' for me in October in Turkey, which I eagerly await. I'll have £175 of that as spending money, on top of my benefit for the week, as they will pay £425 for the holiday itself.
- Finally, they have at my prompt paid some months early, an annual £250 'TV/telephone' grant given out to all their beneficiaries. However, until Martha gathers her strength to actually take me to a Car Boot Sale to 'sell odd stuff', as offered these last two weekends, to reimburse this money in my bank account, I have to spend it at once on other things. (I am diverting it to the vital need to pay for the successful outcome in what follows below in Success Story Six).

6. *Success Story Six. After months of 'chasing' various publishers here and abroad, last week the first copy of my 'Spiritual Energy' arrived – in print!*

I unsuccessfully sent a summary of my book, on four pages, to a selection of my 'top 10' likely publishers from the last 2 years in the UK mail-shots I had sent.

Back in April I added a final 'Appendix' to my book, then still called 'Spiritual Energy', on the subject of DNA - and its 'spiritual nature', in that it *must* in my view 'carry spiritual intelligence' as the only way to explain the complexity of humans, and other living creatures. Around then I also e-mailed about ten USA, and one Australian, publishers that I found on the Internet. The Australian one came up trumps, or so it seemed - then asked AUS$2,500 - about £1,200 - just to get the book in print and produce an initial 25 copies for me, not them, to send to USA 'spiritual book' distributors.

I went along with this offer until it occurred to me to approach my existing Web publisher, Authors Online, based not 12,000 miles but 2 miles away in next- door town Hertford! When they said they could do the same job for £250 + 17.5% VAT, it was inevitable I would 'change horses'! That was six weeks ago. I re-titled the book from 'the Omega Course' to the present 'Spiritual Energy', and everybody I have shown it to agrees this title has much more immediate impact - especially in 'marketing' the contents! Ten days ago, on 3rd August 2001, I received the first copy of the printed book! However, sadly, there were various errors, some due to me working from a size of the original A4 down to a custom size somewhat bigger than A5, all on my computer screen without being able to print out, which I normally much prefer. The errors are being corrected as I write, and my editor, Richard, assures me this will only cost £30 or so. I can meet this out of revenue from my benefits, if not the long-overdue car boot sale, and we saw where the basic £250 has come from - the IEE - in the last Success Story.

The remaining £43.25, topped up to £100 to enable me to purchase 10 copies of my own book from my publisher at half list price, to send to distributors and sell on as well, is being provided by yet another charitable body! Paul, the Project Manager of the NSF drop-in I mentioned in Success Story Three, has pledged to pay this on production of invoices. Initially, when I dared to ask for help, he had no funds, then an unexpected £1200 turned up, he said, and he can spare £100 for my 'worthy cause'. My luck is in again!

My only point of grievance in all this is that I cannot show my 'pride and joy' - 'Spiritual Energy' in print - to my own parents. They are so very much against all such efforts of mine, being quite vehemently anti-Christian, that my mother wept over my last mention of my 'writings', as they dismissively call these two books!

7. Success Story Seven. I interested two US distributors of such spiritual books just last week, following the inspiration of receiving my first copy

Immediately after receiving my book's first ever copy (one went to my editor Richard for reference) and specifying the necessary corrections, soon to result in a fresh and hopefully finalised draft, I got busy on the Internet! I set about looking for US 'spiritual distributors', most of whom seem to be Christian among the literally thousands of results from the 'Yahoo!' search engine! I was a bit overwhelmed by this, so have only so far e-mailed 10 or so with my 'Review of Spiritual Energy by Simon Lee - by Simon Lee'!

At least that is the final form it took, as later sent to just one of two of the ten who actually asked to see the book. The first of them has asked for a printed copy to be mailed to their address in the USA, which I will do in due course once the order mentioned above for ten copies has arrived.

However, Pamela, the Founder and Principal of my main e-mailing 'success' initially said she thought my book sounded suspiciously 'New Age', what with a female Holy Spirit portrayed as 'both Wife and Mother of God'. It was only after some persuasion, with a second e-mail correcting this to what the new Review below finally now says, that she said 'Wow. You can have another chance (now you have confirmed your book is basically Christian, despite involving various faiths)...'

So I have since sent all of, extracts (the first few papers), the whole book, a finalised Review, and a tiny summary of the book you are reading to boot.

CHAPTER THIRTY-THREE

New Year's Eve 2001. After a lot has happened in the last five months, my fate seems to hang in the balance, with Success Story Three going completely pear shaped, with a distinct possibility of Diamond trying to have me IMPRISONED for absurdly alleged 'harassment' dating way back, apparently. On the other horn of what amounts to a terrible dilemma for me as January approaches, in that month I may hear the outcome of Success Story Six. That is when the finalised version of my other book 'Spiritual Energy' may well be well received and taken on by the largest distributor in North America of 'Mind Body Spirit' books. Will I indeed at last see such literary success - or will I be rotting in prison when I do? What a suspenseful end to this first real year of the New Millennium!

Before relating the mixed threads of the two main themes of this new chapter, hopefully really and truly now approaching the end of the book, ideally by next month January 2002, I will relate what happened to the Terribly Trying Tales and the outstanding Success Stories of the last chapter. I will be brief!

Terribly Trying Tale One. Attempt to get a PhD for my book 'Spiritual Energy'. As Universities are a total closed shop for granting PhD's, following my lack of any success at my own University of Cambridge I took sound advice from several people along the way, and drew a line under getting a PhD for 'Spiritual Energy'. I put my efforts into getting recognition by following up Success Story Six, as described below in the rest of this chapter, by trying to make the book available commercially in bookshops to a wide audience.

Terribly Trying Tale Two. My ex-wife's intransigence over contact. Normally her response to any request by my family for any Contact, on any specific date, has been a terribly infuriatingly vague "I will have to think about it!" On September 20ᵗʰ my assistant social worker, supposedly an expert on divorce and contact, and I, saw my solicitor in St. Albans. He avoided any question of using legal means to secure a formal arrangement, and asked my own full social worker via her assistant Linda who was with me, to write to my ex- in the first instance.

Very rudely and typically arrogantly, there has been no reply to this letter from my ex-, and I am due to telephone my solicitor today or in the New Year. To respond to his written request received on Friday 28th December for information about the letter and contact in general, and for us to decide what to do next. Still totally one-sided and with my ex- treating me as sub-human!

Terribly Trying Tale Three. Litigation.
Having backed out of this just as described in the last chapter, I thought about it long and hard after that. I realised that if I threw away this, my only chance to sue the Health Service for all it did to me in the 1990's, I would never get another. After some persuasion my solicitor, based in Newcastle upon Tyne, has reopened the case, with the legal aid turning out to he still valid due to technicalities with the Legal Aid Board's regulations over payment of fees to my solicitor for work done to date of originally closing the case.

If I wait patiently for two or three years, without having to go to Court at all, my solicitor says, I should get some kind of outcome either way. That is, unless the case is judged to be outside a legal three-year limit, despite me only receiving the correct diagnosis last year for the first time. Will this end up as a success story in fact, in due course? I am warned it will be very stressful...

Success Story One. My health is maintained - a year out of hospital, a major target achieved for my Male Community Psychiatric Nurse (CPN) and myself!
A year out of hospital has as good as passed (the Anniversary is actually 10th January 2002). Hurray! I remain fully well throughout the year, despite after much anguished discussion with Jess, my CPN, and the new locum Psychiatrist, having changed regime of drugs totally in October. For much of the year, just like last year, I had painful hot lesions ('bumps') in my posterior after each fortnightly injection, so after a lot of

soul-searching they accepted my request to change to the equivalent dose of tablets of the same drug haloperidol. This so far has not presented any problems at all, even though I have to remember to take a pink pill three times a day instead of the depot injection, and the same three white pills of lithium only at night. Long may I remain off painful depots! Besides, they are very humiliating...

Success Story Two. My wonderful daughter Jenny continues her progress triumphantly into her final year at junior school!

I did not see Jenny much during the summer holidays, only once at my flat, and a couple of times with my family, despite this being a time for any ex-wife with any compassion to maximise Contact. This was the final insult, the final spur for the letter from my social worker after I saw my solicitor with Linda, which has achieved nothing so far. We did take her to Whipsnade Zoo in August, however. I say nothing has been achieved, yet although I cannot intervene as I am supposedly subhuman according to my ex-, this winter term we have all seen quite a lot of Jenny. This has been down to a lot of frustrated negotiation by my parents, notably my Mother, with my ex-, for which obviously I am very grateful.

Jenny continues to be in the 'top stream' in her Year 6 class, and preparing for her 'SAT' tests later this academic year. She now gets homework, and I helped her with her maths and science the other week. It took me two hours going quite fast! Quite a task for a ten-year old! Her netball continues in the school team, which has won both of its matches, which we all went to watch, by 3-1 and then 12-6 against supposedly the best team in the area. Now Jenny, the outstanding player in the team, now as 'goal attack', and scoring a lot of goals, is starting to dare to talk about even winning the Netball Tournament that we saw last year's team come fourth in, last year! She has taken up piano and joined the choir, as well as continuing her recorder, and the choir were very good in a ten-choir carol concert at the huge All Saints Church in Hertford the week before Christmas. I teased her by calling her 'Ebenezer' after she boldly played Scrooge in a reading from 'the Christmas Carol' to all the 400 people there! She thoroughly enjoyed it when my parents treated my sister, Jenny and I to a viewing of some films. Our preview of 'Harry Potter' in November delighted her, but was surpassed by the 'Lord of the Rings' last week, which Jenny described as 'the best film I have ever seen'. I was inclined to agree with my pride and joy of a daughter!

Success Story Three turns into Terribly Trying Tales Four, Five and Six - in the end of nightmare proportions.

I have continued to 'drop in' and so get patchy social life at the 'Connect 3 Club' as it is now called, even though my only friend there close enough to borrow money from or lend to when either of us is in need, is the young Chris. He has ended the year coming round here quite a lot, very depressed over what he regards as a year of steady decline fur him, shedding both supposed 'friends' due to too ready a willingness to discuss his problems, enough to put most people off, and interests. Now he has his own flat he is finding it impossible to manage his money.

As I have hinted, Diamond had been a distant phone-pal, to coin a phrase, until the atrocities in the USA on 11th September 2001, caused her paranoia to flare up. Talk in the media of World War, computerised ID cards for all, global terrorism, jihads and 'Holy' Wars caused her to glue herself to the screen, buy the paper regularly and generally panic - and start to ask me round to stay the night quite often 'in case of terrorists'. She even admitted wanting to bed 'Orgasma Bed Linen' as I jokingly called him in a letter to her, even though he is the world's most wanted man still as I write. Staying the night in October soon led to several naked full body massages between us, and inevitably, without us going all the way, the closest to sexual intercourse we could get without it! However, as soon as media attention fell away from its initial massive coverage of the war in Afghanistan, following the New York outrage, she fell away from me too.

We fell out several times after that, once when she got very ill, and one day begged me several times that I stay the night, when I just had to get home as my medication had changed to tablets just that week, so it was vital to take them. The following afternoon she phoned up and casually told me it was all over. That was 3rd November, and I could not talk to her as her phone stayed off the hook till the 15th when we chatted for half an hour and mostly made up the friendship - strictly on the grounds, now the media flap was over, of a 'hands off basis'.

Shortly after we started talking again in this way, she revealed that she had got THE POL1CE to open a couple of exasperated letters I had written during her 'radio silence'. In these I had sworn at her for winding me up - when actually it was because she was very ill - which I had no way to know due to her silence. Catch-22! The police, she claimed, were due to call to see her to discuss me on 26th November, but I had to wait till 20th December when she told me she had seen them that day with her CPN. We obviously finally fell out for good after that, and apart from the briefest three phone calls possible due to her animosity and threats of 'harassment' charges by her if I rang again, over Christmas, she actually sent a letter that arrived last Saturday. For someone claiming I had been very abusive, she was very abusive back, saying as I could not handle her I could not handle any woman - and ending that I ought to see a prostitute rather than bother stripper Diamond - the next step away, surely. I thought long and hard and replied, saying mainly she was very different to most 'normal' women - and that I was very glad to part company from her own very tiresome and stressful companionship.

I perhaps exaggerated the situation at the start of this chapter. The police have not been in touch with either myself or social services about Diamond's complaints since the 20th when she saw them, so I can expect a caution first, having already given myself the New Year's Resolution never to contact her again. I had ummed and ahhed and then did give her the Christmas present of two Simon Drew cartoon mugs - with a female VIBRATOR thrown in! As what I told her was a 'therapeutic device for your main problem - of lack of orgasms', SO the feeling is likely to remain mutual forever now.

End of 'Diamond diversion', after 7 years with a 3 year gap in the middle!

Success Story Four appears to end sadly as a Sorry Saga. By September Martha was back with her partner and father of her child, and we hardly ever spoke again. So the image of the Sphinx predicting 'a woman from Waltham Abbey – and Oxford' was totally accurate - the relationship with Martha had been 'mystical' - temporary, tenuous and lacking substance.

Success Story Five. The IEE - and the Connect 3 Club - help fund my book.
I have yet to confess to the IEE, but their £250 TV/telephone grant, as well as the balance of the money left after penalties after I cancelled a planned holiday to Turkey in the wake of September 11th for fear of Muslim terrorism, got diverted - to 'Spiritual Energy'! I had no other way to fund the printing of the first couple of copies, necessary revision, and the 45 copies I have had produced since. It has cost around £1,000 in these costs and postage to market as below so far, with the NSF Connect 3 Club providing about £190 and myself only about £150 of that, the IEE the rest!

Success Stories Six and Seven completed? Is a deal with the biggest 'Mind Body Spirit' distributor in the USA imminent in the New Year of 2002?
We jumped the gun somewhat when on the previous few pages I quoted the Stop Press of September to my finished book. I forgot to mention that from receiving the first copy in the last chapter, I went through immense anguish as the book had to be revised all of three more times, two of which revisions I paid a total of about £90 only for... At the point of the penultimate edition, when every single inverted comma on every page was misplaced and 'looked peculiar', incidentally distorting the right hand margin so it was all ragged, I actually gave up all hope. At that point my editor interrupted his 'holiday at home' and assured me that if I waited till he returned on the Monday following, it would all be 'all right'.

Indeed he soon sorted out that the problem was with the printers, and in the end I only paid the £90 I mentioned to add first the review, then the Stop Press given above. This also covered corrections that were my fault, to the very first draft - the printers paid for their own mistakes, as originally promised by my editor Richard. So it was that the first 10 copies of the book, that arrived on the Thursday here immediately after

Tuesday 11th September, lack the Stop Press that went into the next 35 and any more copies I have made up. These cost £2.88 plus about £1.30 postage each, so I have to go easy on orders. I still have to pay Richard £70 towards a previous order, for instance, out of my limited benefit.

Two of the first batch of ten immediately went to the two distributors of Success Story Seven, but by December it was clear neither would take it on - Victory House saying it was in fact 'too intelligent for me to easily read' which naturally dismayed me as a reaction. Then I committed my outstanding holiday money from the IEE to ordering 20 of the finalised version, which arrived on 17th October. I got on the Internet and looked up 'spiritual book distributors' on the Yahoo search engine - which found thousands of matches, hardly any in fact relevant. Luckily, I saved myself searching through dozens of pages of entries after I came across one particular web-page commenting on all main USA book distributors classed as 'independent' - www.bookmarket.com/distributors.html .

However, after waiting an agonising two months till now, the New Year, there have been no positive results to sending ten of these copies of the book out of my batch of 20. Further exasperation came after sending the rest to selected friends - and three to National newspapers - the Times, the Guardian and the Evening Standard. When I rang these three papers they had not received their copies, nor had the local paper the Welwyn Times based in my birth town of Welwyn Garden City. I eventually got the books and postage for them, that I had refunded by the Post Office, and in fact a total of all of five books went astray. The money was invaluable, but did not of course fully compensate me for all the hassle and inconvenience of books being lost in the post, and so many.

On Friday 9th November I had my first small success - the only one to date - out of all this arduous hard work and frustration. A small 'piece' appeared in the local East Hertfordshire newspaper the 'Mercury' that was neither pro- or anti-my book, rather concentrating on 'spiritual paths through mental illness issues' than on what it said. Despite quoting Authors OnLine's telephone number, this article was far too short at about 120 words to get any results in sales.

That same week I had taken a copy of the book in person to the Herald at Welwyn Garden City to make sure they got it after the earlier copy I had sent got mislaid. They are the sister paper of the Welwyn Times. They say they have the same problems in understanding the book as Pamela of Victory House said in her e-mail from the USA, so any review they print will appear in the New Year and is likely to be critical of the book as hard to read, not praise it!

Midway through the rejection process I am now so used to, receiving one half of the total of 12 'noes' from the 12 US Distributors, I sent seven copies of my book that I had got from AonL to six national newspapers and 'New Scientist' magazine. AonL supported me in a limited way by supplying 10 copies at cost price. This was more papers than the three I had originally written to weeks before, that had all got lost in the post, but endless expensive phone calls and wasted time later they had all declined to review the book, for various reasons. The Daily Mail and the Daily Express seemed to be the closest to actually doing any feature on the book, but the Mail 'did not have enough space' and the 'Mind Body Spirit' section of the Express ended up concluding the book was 'too complicated - and intelligent - to review'!

I now realised that 'Mind/Body/Spirit' was the real marketplace for 'Spiritual Energy'. I've only one rejection from Christian and more mainstream US distributors yet to receive. All my expensive postal and telephone chasing up of the Press had only resulted in a small entry buried deep in the local paper, no news of the other local paper even as I write, and that will be detrimental when it happens, they have said! 21st November was decisive, as I sent a copy of the book to 'Cygnus', a 'mind body spirit' book club I had heard of, based in Carmarthen in Wales. By three weeks later I had got my final rejection from the National Press, from the Express, but it had been a close decision, apparently, for their 'Mind Body and Spirit' section. That reinforced the fact that the manager of the Connect 3 Club, who had avidly supported my efforts financially, at his 'hand out' to me had said the book was really 'New Age' rather than 'Christian'. It did not emphasise Jesus enough, and was too modern-day not traditionalist to be 'Christian', I realised. So I spent three days from Sunday 16th

December - just weeks ago - researching 'religious and spiritual books' on my Yahoo search engine on my Internet connection. I must have dug around on 100 different Christian, 'science and religion' and of course 'mind body and spirit' web-sites to get their e-mail addresses, then sent them all the same broadcast, a brief appeal to reply if they found my own web-site http://f16-tomcat.com interesting enough.

Only two - of course, both 'mind body and spirit'! - outlets asked to receive copies in the post. One is a chain of such bookstores and the other the biggest Mind/Body/Spirit distributor in North America, so I sent them both copies just before Christmas, and crossed my fingers till I hear back in January.

CHAPTER THIRTY-FOUR

New Year's Eve 2001 still. A time to reflect on my life, particularly the last ten years, and look forward a little to 2002. This set of books, I now realise, will only finally with a big sigh of relief from myself, be completed, once I succeed with getting some kind of 'success' with 'Spiritual Energy'. I can't wait to finish this painful autobiography - obviously ideally on a REALLY high note!

1. *Unemployment and disability.* I am painfully aware that 1st September 2002 is the TENTH anniversary of ten years more or less entirely out of work, messed about totally by the Health Service and so being divorced and 'losing it all'. Having to swallow my pride and draw disability benefits for the last four years. My career in computers is definitely over after one year out of it, not just ten! I should have been on £60,000 a year as a manager by now but that is impossible now! I am just so grateful I had the foresight, or whatever it was, to join first the Institute of Measurement and Control, then the IEE of course, all those ten years ago! The IEE have saved me from bankruptcy. Yet I reflect that although my B1AD condition together with my heavy smoking make me unsuited to nine-to-five office work, I DO work still - on my books, at home!

2. *Relationships.* We have seen Chris decline this year, losing most of his interests and friends, and being unable to cope with his finances - or, incidentally, looking after, even cooking for, himself. I have unwisely sought girlfriends FAR too soon out of the HELL of Shannon House last year, and Martha and much more briefly, Sally, have just been false hopes. The two main relationships, one so up and down and on and off it has been pure stress, with Diamond, now at last forever ended, under threat of Court action of all things, and with unbelievably ever-loving, ever-loyal Jenny, are pure opposites.

3. *Interests.* I am making up for backing out of French and English Literature AS Level courses at the local college due to 'Diamond problems' last Autumn, by taking up the much less demanding pottery, painting and drawing and object-

oriented programming of computers in the New Year. Hopefully I can make some - resolvedly platonic in the first instance! - friendships with both sexes on those three courses, and hopefully they will help my acute boredom!

4. *Health.* I have stood the test, and despite a change of medication regime midway, have achieved my Nurse's objective and remained clear of hospital all year. I am overcoming demoralisation at being out of formal work by pursuing publication of 'Spiritual Energy' as a potentially lucrative hobby, that the same nurse calls a 'passion'. I am aware I smoke far too much and drink too much quite often, and still deliberating New Year Resolutions for those.

5. *Spiritual Experiences.* I am absolutely delighted and flabbergasted to have at long, long last, been able to put all my Spiritual Experiences firmly behind me as 'fulfilled' as of the week of Ground Zero in the USA – 11th September 2001. I have nearly entirely managed to completely forget what this book, mostly written to put them behind me as dreadful 'premonitions and omens', even says about their very intricate futuristic predictions.

6. *The main outstanding theme of this book - potential lucrative success for 'Spiritual Energy'?* My book has been written in a huge battle with my health - prompted of course, as we have seen throughout, by wild all-powerful Doctors, in the 1990's. FIVE TIMES I have been put back on the current regime - THREE of these times only after being placed in a Psychiatric Secure Unit! This year, especially in September, has seen my Spiritual Experiences coming to an abrupt end in bothering me - never again do I possibly wish to see another one of the damnable things! This has coincided with a major hurdle in the 23 year long writing of 'Spiritual Energy' - publication, albeit resorting to just a vanity publisher where all else failed - and getting it into print and on sale. As a friend commented at the Connect 3 Club, 'Tweezers', it has come on by leaps and bounds this year! Having naively thought it might appeal to the Church, Spiritual Experience Fourteen has been backed up by the evidence and comments by friends. No, it is definitely to succeed if it does, in the 'Mind Body and Spirit' field, and outlets of that sort will comment on it shortly into the New Year! If they all say 'no!', a search on

the Web in the New Year after tomorrow - New Year's Day - under 'mind body spirit book distributors' should yield lots more to write to having e-mailed first. I have a small problem in having absolutely no copies of the book left to send out but my editor has had three returned to him, which should be in the post.

My Father is giving me a lift to their house for the duration of New Year festivities in 10 minutes, at 6pm, so I leave the latest ending of this book, only hoping that 'an End of All My "Spiritual Experiences" ' could well spell success with 'Spiritual Energy'. I plan to get hold of an ink cartridge next week, when I can again afford it, and print out the last chapter and this one of this present book, and have them bound.

Which Witch Doctor?

Simon Richard Lee *BA, MA (Cantab.) CEng MIEE MInstMC*

The author is a Chartered Instrument Engineer as well as a graduate of Cambridge University, who also writes poetry. In addition, he has been known to have 'Spiritual Experiences' – that all 'come true'!

The book describes how he himself, just like Jeanne d'Arc, and George Fox, founder of the Quakers, saw symbolic 'Spiritual Experiences', or twenty-one 'Powerful Petrifying Premonitions', between 1977–2000, a 23-year period – over half his lifetime until then. These Experiences were paralleled by his being treated for a 'schizophrenic or schizo-affective illness' 1978 onwards. Simon maintained with great difficulty in the face of such fierce labels, throughout all this, that his illness was instead an 'affective disorder' – 'moody' rather than 'mental' – and that the Psychiatric staff made a huge mistake by calling him 'schizo'.

In 1999 he was evicted because of a relapse of his illness, exacerbated by the wrong diagnosis and hence incorrect treatment. Now in 2000-2001 AD, rehoused in a different area of the County, and hence different National Health Service 'Trust', fresh Psychiatric staff, *from abroad,* have at long last been totally objective and unaffected by the dreadful mistakes of their predecessors. They have independently come to share the view of Simon and his family that he had been falsely diagnosed 'schizo' for **22+ years – half his lifetime.** He really has *'hypo mania' – a relatively TRIVIAL 'mood disorder'!*

Simon has suffered terribly from the myth about him, that this ability to see and interpret Spiritual Experiences made him 'a schizophrenic'. To try to dispel this myth once and for all, Simon very carefully and painstakingly *proves* in this set of books that his own 21 Spiritual Experiences over 23 years were in fact symbolic premonitions from God – and have now all 'come prophetically true' – always in hindsight... The conclusion of this is that genuine religious experiences like his are always misunderstood, and condemned in complete ignorance of their spiritual reality, as 'schizophrenic', by the psychiatric 'profession'. This is almost entirely Atheist and its theories are very materialistic and based entirely on 'bio-chemicals and drugs'.

Simon passionately argues that 'they' should at least *allow for* 'the Spiritual Patient' like himself**...**

Zen Buddha

40703086R00222

Printed in Poland
by Amazon Fulfillment
Poland Sp. z o.o., Wrocław